Oxford Studies in Metaphysics

OXFORD STUDIES IN METAPHYSICS

Oxford Studies in Metaphysics

Volume 13

Edited by
KAREN BENNETT
and
DEAN W. ZIMMERMAN

OXFORD
UNIVERSITY PRESS

OXFORD
UNIVERSITY PRESS

Great Clarendon Street, Oxford, OX2 6DP,
United Kingdom

Oxford University Press is a department of the University of Oxford.
It furthers the University's objective of excellence in research, scholarship,
and education by publishing worldwide. Oxford is a registered trade mark of
Oxford University Press in the UK and in certain other countries

© the several contributors 2023

The moral rights of the authors have been asserted

First Edition published in 2023

Impression: 1

Published in the United States of America by Oxford University Press
198 Madison Avenue, New York, NY 10016, United States of America

British Library Cataloguing in Publication Data

Data available

Library of Congress Control Number: 2022945432

ISBN 978-0-19-288603-3

DOI: 10.1093/oso/9780192886033.001.0001

Printed and bound in the UK by
TJ Books Limited

Preface

Oxford Studies in Metaphysics is dedicated to the timely publication of new work in metaphysics, broadly construed. The subject is taken to include not only perennially central topics (e.g. modality, ontology, and mereology) but also metaphysical questions that emerge within other subfields (e.g. philosophy of mind, philosophy of science, and philosophy of religion). Each volume also contains an essay by the winner of the Sanders Prize in Metaphysics, a biennial award described within.

K. B. & D. W. Z.

New Brunswick, NJ

Contents

Contents

The Sanders Prize in Metaphysics

Sponsored by the Marc Sanders Foundation* and administered by the editorial board of *Oxford Studies in Metaphysics*, this essay competition is open to scholars who are within fifteen years of receiving a PhD or students who are currently enrolled in a graduate program. (Independent scholars should inquire of the editors to determine eligibility.) The award is $5,000, and the competition is biennial. Winning essays will appear in *Oxford Studies in Metaphysics*, so submissions must not be under review elsewhere.

Essays should generally be no longer than 10,000 words; longer essays may be considered, but authors must seek prior approval by providing the editor with an abstract and word count by November 1. To be eligible for next year's prize, submissions must be electronically submitted by January 31, 2024. Refereeing will be blind; authors should omit remarks and references that might disclose their identities. Receipt of submissions will be acknowledged by email. The winner is determined by a committee of members of the editorial board of *Oxford Studies in Metaphysics* and will be announced in early March. At the author's request, the board will simultaneously consider entries in the prize competition as submissions for *Oxford Studies in Metaphysics*, independently of the prize.

Previous winners of the Sanders Prize are:

Thomas Hofweber, "Inexpressible Properties and Propositions," Vol. 2

Matthew McGrath, "Four-Dimensionalism and the Puzzles of Coincidence," Vol. 3

Cody Gilmore, "Time Travel, Coinciding Objects, and Persistence," Vol. 3

Stephan Leuenberger, "*Ceteris Absentibus* Physicalism," Vol. 4

Jeffrey Sanford Russell, "The Structure of Gunk: Adventures in the Ontology of Space," Vol. 4

Bradford Skow, "Extrinsic Temporal Metrics," Vol. 5

Jason Turner, "Ontological Nihilism," Vol. 6

---

* The Marc Sanders Foundation is a nonprofit organization dedicated to the revival of systematic philosophy and traditional metaphysics. Information about the Foundation's other initiatives may be found at www.marcsandersfoundation.org/.

Rachael Briggs and Graeme A. Forbes, "The Real Truth about the Unreal Future," Vol. 7

Shamik Dasgupta, "Absolutism vs Comparativism about Quantities," Vol. 8

Louis deRosset, "Analyticity and Ontology," Vol 9

Nicholas K. Jones, "Multiple Constitution," Vol. 9

Nick Kroll, "Teleological Dispositions," Vol. 10

Jon Litland, "Grounding Grounding," Vol. 10

Andrew Bacon, "Relative Locations," Vol. 11

T. Scott Dixon, "Plural Slot Theory," Vol. 11

Harjit Singh Bhogal, "Nomothetic Explanation and Humeanism about Laws of Nature," Vol. 12

Martin Pickup, "The Situationalist Account of Change," Vol. 13

Inquiries should be addressed to Dean Zimmerman at: dwzimmer@philosophy.rutgers.edu.

PART I
PARTS AND PLURALITIES

1

Paraphrase Techniques for Nihilists

Peter van Inwagen

1. 1

Nihilists hold that there are no composite objects—that everything lacks proper parts, that everything is a mereological simple. Cian Dorr and Gideon Rosen (Rosen and Dorr) and Ted Sider (Sider) have defended nihilism.[1] *Semi-nihilists* hold that there are some composite objects, but many fewer of them than most people would suppose. Trenton Merricks, Eric Olson, and I are semi-nihilists.[2]

Both nihilists and semi-nihilists deny that there are composite inanimate objects, and it is only that denial that we shall be concerned with. I will therefore—simply for convenience' sake—ignore the distinction between nihilism and semi-nihilism, and refer to both nihilists and semi-nihilists as nihilists. But what will nihilists say about such pairs of sentences as these:

(1)   Some chairs are heavier than some tables

(2)   Some bricks are heavier than some houses?

If there are no chairs or bricks, then both sentences are false (or express false propositions)—at least if they have the quantificational structure they appear to have. (If chairs, tables, bricks, and houses exist, it is at least apparently true that they are material objects composed of smaller material parts. We may therefore say that (1) and (2)—in virtue of their apparent quantificational structure and the meanings of the count-nouns they contain—*apparently imply the existence of composite material objects*.) And yet those who say that both sentences are false must somehow account for the fact that most people (even most philosophers, and certainly most of "the

---

[1] Rosen and Dorr 2002; Sider 2013.   [2] Merricks 2001; Olson 2007; Van Inwagen 1990.

Peter van Inwagen, *Paraphrase Techniques for Nihilists* In: *Oxford Studies in Metaphysics Volume 13*.
Edited by: Karen Bennett and Dean W. Zimmerman, Oxford University Press. © Peter van Inwagen 2023.
DOI: 10.1093/oso/9780192886033.003.0001

folk") would say—and with great confidence—that although (2) was false, (1) was true. (Suppose a large number of people, chosen at random from the populace, were given a true-false test that included these two sentences. They would all mark (1) 'true' and (2) 'false'—and without any pause for reflection.)

Nihilists typically respond to the challenge presented by such pairs of sentences by the familiar philosophical device of paraphrase. I, for example, have offered the following paraphrase of (1) (Van Inwagen, p. 109):

(1′)   There are xs that are arranged chairwise and there are ys that are arranged tablewise and the xs are [collectively] heavier than the ys.

(Here 'there are xs' and 'there are ys' are "plural quantifiers" that bind "plural variables"—'the xs', 'the ys'.) Sentence (1′) is what might be called a mereologically neutral paraphrase of (1)—a paraphrase of (1) in that it agrees with (1) about how simples (objects without proper parts) are spatially, temporally, and causally related to one another, neutral in that it is consistent with both the truth and the falsity of nihilism.[3] Sentence (1′) is, moreover, a *transparently* neutral paraphrase of (1)—for it is obvious and uncontroversial that it is consistent with both the truth and the falsity of nihilism.

In the sequel, an unqualified occurrence of 'paraphrase' will mean 'transparently neutral paraphrase'.

The corresponding paraphrase of (2) is, of course,

(2′)   There are xs that are arranged brickwise and there are ys that are arranged housewise and the xs are heavier than the ys.

One important difference between (1) and (2) is this: If simples are spatially, temporally, and causally related to one another as they actually are, and nihilism is true, then (1) is false but has a true paraphrase, whereas not only is (2) false, but *even its paraphrase* is false.

---

[3] In *Material Beings* the plural variables in paraphrases were not used with any "understood" restriction—that is, 'there are xs that are arranged chairwise' meant 'there are objects of some description that are arranged chairwise'. I will here assume that, e.g., chairs are necessarily fusions of things that are arranged chairwise, and I will assume that there are things (things of any sort) that are arranged chairwise (tablewise, computerwise,...) if and only if there are simples that are arranged chairwise (tablewise, computerwise,...). (These assumptions entail, among other things, that chairs, tables, and computers have no "gunky" parts.) In the present chapter, plural variables in paraphrases range only over simples.

The topic of sections 1.1–1.3 of this chapter is a purely technical question—the question whether certain sentences that apparently imply the existence of composite material objects can be provided with transparently neutral paraphrases. (The answer to this question is Yes, and the paraphrases are provided in section 1.3. Section 1.4 concerns difficulties that attend the project of applying the "paraphrase techniques for nihilists" employed in section 1.3 to sentences other than those "certain sentences.") But that question, as befits a purely technical question, must be framed very carefully.

I begin with definitions. Let us call a sentence a *target sentence* if it satisfies the following three conditions:

- Its vocabulary, like the vocabulary of (1) and (2), is that of everyday, non-technical English (or some other natural language).
- Like (1) and (2), it apparently implies the existence of composite material objects.
- Ordinary speakers ("the folk"), if polled, would be in agreement as to its truth-value (as is the case with (1) and (2)).[4]

And let us say that a sentence that is offered as a paraphrase of a certain target sentence (call that sentence the *target of* the paraphrase) is an *adequate* paraphrase of its target just in the case that it satisfies both these conditions:

- Like (1′) and (2′), it is true if and only if "the folk" would mark its target 'true' and it is false if and only if the folk would mark its target 'false'.
- Like (1′) and (2′), it is transparently neutral; that is, it is evident that it does not imply the existence (or the non-existence) of composite material objects.

Gabriel Uzquiano has contended (Uzquiano) that certain target sentences cannot be given adequate paraphrases that satisfy the following two conditions:

---

[4] Perhaps it would be prudent for me to work with a slightly idealized version of the folk: the folk have an excellent grasp of logic and they do not hold false beliefs that might influence their judgments about potential target sentences—beliefs, that is, that are false for reasons that have nothing to do with mereology or metaphysics. (For example: 'All tables weigh more than 30 kilos and all chairs weigh less than 25 kilos'.)

- the quantificational apparatus they employ is first-order singular or plural quantification (as opposed, for example, to second-order quantification and to so-called perplural or plurally plural quantification).
- the domain of their quantifiers includes only physical or material simples (as opposed to, for example, sets of material simples, or regions of space that contain material simples).

I will call an adequate paraphrase of a target sentence that satisfies these two conditions an *Uzquiano paraphrase* of that sentence.

Uzquiano considers four such sentences—that is, four sentences that supposedly cannot be provided with adequate paraphrases that satisfy his conditions:

(3) The chairs outnumber the tables

(4) Some computers communicate only with one another

(6) Some bricks are touching each other[5]

(8) Some brick houses are mixed together with some cobblestone houses.

(I have numbered the sentences as they are numbered in Uzquiano.) These sentences are certainly "target sentences" as I have defined the term. The "purely technical question" I will address is: Is it possible to find Uzquiano paraphrases of these four sentences?[6] (Or, it will transpire, of (3), (4), (8) and a target sentence I shall consider in place of (6); when we have got to that point, I will explain why I offer a paraphrase of that other sentence and not of (6).)[7]

Uzquiano raises no objection to the employment by nihilists of '-wise' plural predicates like 'the xs are arranged chairwise', and "collective" plural predicates like 'the xs are heavier than the ys' in the construction of their

---

[5] Nothing is implied by the use of different reciprocal pronouns (as 'one another' and 'each other' are called) in (4) and (6).

[6] Since the folk would (or so I am prepared to stipulate) mark each of these four sentences 'true', the paraphrase of each must be true.

[7] Why would nihilists *want* to have Uzquiano paraphrases of the target sentences—as opposed to adequate paraphrases of some other kind? *I* want Uzquiano paraphrases because (a) I believe that the only variables are singular and plural nominal variables—the familiar 'x', 'y', and 'z' of the logic textbooks, and 'the xs', 'the ys', 'the zs', their plural analogues. I therefore eschew perplural and second-order paraphrases for reasons that have to do with logic rather than metaphysics, and (b) I know from experience that if I were—for example—to propose to replace talk of tables with talk of sets whose members are arranged tablewise, nine philosophers out of ten would say, "Van Inwagen thinks that tables are sets of simples arranged tablewise." Well, at any rate, seven out of ten. Cf. Uzquiano 2004, pp. 439–440, 441–443, and 443–449.

paraphrases.[8] I therefore regard myself as free to employ such predicates in my paraphrases of these sentences.

I will present no general recipe for constructing Uzquiano paraphrases of target sentences. But the paraphrases I shall offer will require very little new vocabulary,[9] and none of the new vocabulary I introduce will be primitive: it will comprise only defined predicates whose definitions involve nothing beside the apparatus of first-order quantification (singular and plural) and predicates like 'the xs are arranged chairwise' and 'the xs are arranged computerwise'—"kind-arrangement plural predicates," I'll call them. (And I'll abbreviate that unwieldy phrase to 'arrangement predicates'). That is to say: An arrangement predicate consists of a plural variable followed by 'are arranged' followed by an adverb formed by suffixing '-wise' to a composite-object count-noun.

Once we have introduced the new predicates, the paraphrases of Uzquiano's target sentences will more or less write themselves. It is because these predicates render the task of paraphrase so easy that I have given this chapter the title "Paraphrase Techniques for Nihilists." Nevertheless, I must concede that there are target sentences for which it is almost certainly impossible to provide Uzquiano paraphrases even with their aid (a point to which I will return in section 1.4). Indeed, for all I know, there may be target sentences for which it is impossible to provide an Uzquiano paraphrase in any terms whatever.

1. 2

Our new predicates are of two kinds: *fusional arrangement predicates* and *arrangement-indexing predicates*. To each arrangement predicate, there corresponds a fusional arrangement predicate and an arrangement-indexing predicate.

The fusional arrangement predicates that correspond to 'the xs are arranged chairwise' and to 'the xs are arranged computerwise' are:

---

[8] In the present chapter, I am not going to bother to distinguish open sentences from predicates (important though that distinction is in some contexts).

[9] Other than vocabulary required by content specific to individual target sentences. For example, if we are to paraphrase 'The chairs outnumber the tables', we shall have to have some vocabulary item that has something to do with numbering. In the remainder of this chapter, generalizations about "new vocabulary" are about new vocabulary other than such words and phrases as may be needed to express content peculiar to particular target sentences.

the xs are arranged fusion-of-chairs-wise

and

the xs are arranged fusion-of-computers-wise.

The following definition of the former can serve as a template for the definition of any fusional arrangement predicate.

The xs are arranged fusion-of-chairs-wise $=_{df}$

$\forall y$ (y is one of the xs → for some zs (the zs are among the xs & the zs are arranged chairwise & y is one of the zs)).

Note that a fusional arrangement predicate is, as the term suggests, an arrangement predicate. (After all, chairs, if they exist, are composite objects, and fusions of two or more chairs, if they exist, are likewise composite objects. If simples can be arranged chairwise whether or not there are chairs, why can simples not be arranged fusion-of-my-dining-room-chairs-wise whether or not there is such a thing as the fusion of my dining-room chairs?) The arrangement-indexing predicate that corresponds to 'the xs are arranged chairwise' is

The xs chair-index the ys $=_{df}$

the ys are arranged fusion-of-chairs-wise, and the xs are among the ys, and for any zs (the zs are among the ys and the zs are arranged chairwise. → ∃!w (w is one of the xs and w is one of the zs)).

(If any simples arranged chairwise have a unique fusion and if something is a chair if and only if it is a fusion of simples that are arranged chairwise, then the xs chair-index the ys just in the case that the ys are the simple parts of some fusion of chairs z, the xs are among the ys, and every chair that is a part of z has exactly one of the xs as a part. Consider, for example, three chairs, Alfa, Bravo, and Charlie. The xs chair index the simple parts of Alfa, Bravo, and Charlie just in the case that the xs are three simples, and one of the xs is a part of Alfa and not a part of Bravo or Charlie, one of the xs is a part of Bravo and not a part of Alfa or Charlie, and one of the xs is a part of Charlie and not a part of Alfa or Bravo.)

1. 3

We now have the vocabulary we need (other than the vocabulary required by the content peculiar to individual target sentences—see note 9) to offer Uzquiano paraphrases of four target sentences—Uzquiano's sentences (3), (4), and (8), and the sentence I shall consider in the place of his sentence (6).

All but one of our paraphrases will involve arrangement-indexing predicates. (The exception is the paraphrase of 'Some computers communicate only with one another'.) I will concede at the outset that these paraphrases are "adequate" (in our technical sense) only given the truth of certain assumptions about composite objects (or about the ways in which simples are arranged). Those who affirm the existence of composites can state the needed assumptions schematically this way:

> For any x and for any y, if x is an F and y is an F and x is not identical with y, there is no z such that z is a part of x and z is a part of y.

And nihilists can state them this way:

> For any xs and for any ys, if the xs are arranged F-wise and the ys are arranged F-wise and the xs are not identical with the ys, there is no z such that z is one of the xs and z is one of the ys.

(The needed assumptions are the instances of this schema that can be obtained by substituting count-nouns for 'F'—these at least: 'chair', 'table', 'brick', 'house', 'cobblestone'.)

These assumptions and various problems and questions they raise will be the topic of section 1.4.

And now the paraphrases.

Target sentence (3): The chairs outnumber the tables.

This is Uzquiano's description of the general problem target-sentence (3) is meant to illustrate: "cardinality comparisons."

In addition to two predicates of the kinds we have already discussed (an arrangement predicate and an indexing predicate), we shall need the content-specific predicate

the xs outnumber the ys.

We can simplify our paraphrase if we define a one-place indexing predicate that is a special case of our two-place 'the xs chair-index the ys', namely, 'the xs chair-index'.

Say that a simple is "enchaired" just in the case that it is one of some simples arranged chairwise. Then we may say that the xs chair-index (period, full stop) just in the case that they chair-index the enchaired simples.[10] (If any simples arranged chairwise have a unique fusion and if something is a chair if and only if it is a fusion of simples that are arranged chairwise, the xs chair-index just in the case that the xs are all parts of chairs, and every chair has exactly one of the xs as a part.)

The paraphrase of (3) is:

(3′)   For some xs, those xs are arranged chairwise,[11] and...

for any ys and any zs, if the ys chair-index and the zs table-index, the ys outnumber the zs.

Target sentence (4): Some computers communicate only with one another.

(That is to say: For some xs, those xs are computers, and for all y and all z, if y is one of the xs, and y communicates with z, then z is one of the xs.[12]) This is Uzquiano's description of the general problem target sentence (4) is meant to illustrate: "plural quantification over composites."

We shall need the content-specific predicate

the xs communicate (collectively) with the ys.

---

[10] A full, formal definiens for 'the xs chair-index' is

Some ys are such that $\forall z$ (z is one of those ys ↔ for some ws, those ws are arranged chairwise and z is one the ws), and the xs are among the ys, and for any vs (the vs are among the ys & the vs are arranged chairwise. → $\exists!w$ (w is one of the xs & w is one of the vs)).

[11] Why this clause? Suppose it were omitted. And suppose no simples were arranged chairwise. Then there would be no simples that chair-indexed, and the second clause of (3′) would be vacuously true. But if no simples were arranged chairwise, 'The chairs outnumber the tables' would be judged false by the folk—and false even if no simples were arranged tablewise: those who believe that there are no dragons and no unicorns will say that 'The dragons outnumber the unicorns' is false.

[12] Cf. Uzquiano (2004), p. 434. This reading implies that if some computers communicate with nothing, then some computers communicate only with one another. And it implies that if, for any computers, some among them communicate with something that is not a computer, then it is false that some computers communicate only with one another. Uzquiano says (p. 434) that (4) is modeled on the famous Geach-Kaplan sentence 'Some critics admire only one another'. I expect that most people would not regard it as false that some critics admire only one another simply because, for any critics, there were some among them who admired certain politicians or certain athletes (who were not also critics).

The paraphrase of (4) is:

(4′)   For some xs, those xs are arranged fusion-of-computers-wise, and . . .
for any ys and any zs, if the ys are arranged computerwise and the ys
are among the xs and the ys communicate with the zs, then the zs
are arranged computerwise and the zs are among the xs.

Target sentence (6): Some bricks are touching each other.

This is Uzquiano's description of the general problem target sentence (6) is
meant to illustrate: "plural predicate collectively satisfied by composites."
But here I confess myself somewhat puzzled by the example. Why must
the target sentence (6) be regarded as containing a plural predicate?
Uzquiano says that (6) should be read this way:

(7)   For some xs
$\forall y$ (y is one of the xs → y is a brick) and the xs are touching each
other.[13]

But why not instead read (6) this way:

(7a) $\exists x \exists y$ (x is a brick and y is a brick and x and y are touching each other[14])?

Whether one prefers to read (6) as (7) or (7a), those two sentences certainly
seem to be logically equivalent. Obviously, (7a) follows from (7). (If the zs are
bricks that touching each other, then there is a brick x and a brick y such
that x and y are touching each other.) Suppose then that (7a) is true. Then there
are two bricks (I assume that nothing "is touching" itself)—call them X and Y—
that are touching each other. And then there are xs—X and Y—such that
$\forall y$ (y is one of the xs → y is a brick) & the xs are touching each other.[15]

---

[13] I use the notation and vocabulary I favor. Uzquiano's actual sentence (7) was 'Some
composites, the xxs, are such that (i) for every x, if x is one of the xxs, then x is a brick, and (ii)
the xxs are touching each other'. My version of (7) in the text assumes that bricks are composite
objects. One could always append 'those xs are composite objects, and' to my 'For some xs'.

[14] Or 'x is touching y & y is touching x', or even 'x is touching y'.

[15] If 'Some bricks are touching *only* one another', had been proposed as a target sentence, it
would have had to be read as containing a plural predicate—in some such way as this:

For some xs, those xs are bricks, and for all y and all z, if y is one of the xs, and if y is touching z,
then z is one of the xs

—which is our "computers" sentence with 'bricks' for 'computers' and 'is touching' for 'communicates with'. There is no difference in logical structure between 'Some bricks are touching only

Since (6) need not be read as containing a plural predicate, let us replace it with a target sentence that can only be read as containing a plural predicate:

Target sentence (6a): Some bricks are arranged in a circle.

(I am going to make things easy for myself by assuming that all bricks are of at least approximately the same size and that we do not have a case of "bricks arranged in a circle" unless the diameter of the circle—the greatest distance between any two of the bricks—is large in comparison with the dimensions of a brick.)

We shall need the content-specific predicate

the *x*s are arranged in a circle.

The paraphrase of (6a) is:

(6a′)   For some *x*s, those *x*s are arranged fusion-of-bricks-wise, and, for some *y*s, those *y*s brick-index the *x*s and the *y*s are arranged in a circle.

But can (6a′) serve as a template that will show us how to construct an Uzquiano paraphrase of just any target sentence that contains a "plural predicate collectively satisfied by composites"? We may imagine an Interlocutor who protests,

> That's all very well, but that kind of paraphrase won't work for just any plural predicate collectively satisfied by composites. Granted, if you have twenty standard bricks, each of them at least two meters from its nearest neighbor, and if twenty simples (or twenty silicon atoms or twenty tiny things of any sort), each of them a part of one of the bricks, are arranged in a circle, then the twenty bricks must be arranged in a circle. But suppose the target sentence had been 'Some bricks are arranged in a circle and were all manufactured on the same day'. Simples are never manufactured—and even if they were, it wouldn't follow from the twenty simples being manufactured on the same day that the twenty bricks were manufactured on the same day!

The Interlocutor's observation is valid, but it has no important philosophical implications beyond, perhaps, underscoring the point that I have not presented, and do not claim to be able to present, a systematic method for

one another' and 'Some computers communicate only with one another'. The presence of the word 'only' in (4) is the, well, is the *only* essential difference between (4) and (6).

generating Uzquiano paraphrases of target sentences. In any case, finding an Uzquiano paraphrase of the Interlocutor's target sentence is not difficult. One need only introduce a "plural analog" of 'x and y are bricks that were manufactured on the same day'—say, 'the xs are arranged brickwise and the ys are arranged brickwise and the day when the xs were caused to become arranged brickwise is the day when the ys were caused to become arranged brickwise'. (For short: 'the xs and the ys were sameday-brickwised'.) Then:

For some xs, those xs are arranged fusion-of-bricks-wise, and...

> for some ys, those ys brick-index the xs and the ys are arranged in a circle, and...

> > for any zs and any ws, if the zs are arranged brickwise and the ws are arranged brickwise and the zs are among the xs and the ws are among the xs, then the zs and the ws were sameday-brickwised.

Target sentence (8): Some brick houses are mixed
together with some cobblestone houses

This is Uzquiano's description of the general problem target sentence (8) is meant to illustrate: "plural predicate collectively satisfied by composites of composites."

I will make my task easier by assuming that brick houses are fusions of bricks and cobblestone houses are fusions of cobblestones—although, of course, items such as layers of mortar and bathtubs and ceiling fixtures will be parts of real houses of either sort.

We shall need the content-specific predicate

The xs are mixed together with the ys.

And we can greatly simplify our paraphrase of (8) if we make use of two defined predicates, namely,

the xs are arranged fusion-of-brick-houses-wise

the xs are arranged fusion-of-cobblestone-houses-wise.

We first define

the xs are arranged brickhousewise $=_{df}$

> the xs are arranged housewise and the xs are arranged fusion-of-bricks-wise

and

the *x*s are arranged cobblestonehousewise.

We may now obtain definitions of 'the *x*s are arranged fusion-of-brick-houses-wise' and 'the *x*s are arranged fusion-of-cobblestone-houses-wise' by substituting 'the *x*s are arranged brickhousewise' and 'the *x*s are arranged cobblestonehousewise' for 'the *x*s are arranged chairwise' in our definition of 'the *x*s are arranged fusion-of-chairs-wise'.

The paraphrase of (8) is:

(8′)   For some *x*s and some *y*s, those *x*s are arranged fusion-of-brick-houses-wise and those *y*s are arranged fusion-of-cobblestone-houses-wise and...

> for any *z*s and any *w*s, if the *z*s house-index the *x*s and the *w*s house-index the *y*s, the *z*s are mixed together with the *w*s.

I conclude that it is possible to provide Uzquiano paraphrases of Uzquiano's target sentences (3), (4), and (8), and of the sentence (6a) (our "replacement" for his (6)). It is true that the paraphrases are different in logical form from their targets, and that they are complex and involuted. But these are features they share with many famous philosophical paraphrases. (One might cite "token reflexive" paraphrases of tensed statements and "adverbial" para-phrases of statements that apparently imply that items like sense data and qualia can be the objects of direct or immediate awareness.) The reader is particularly invited to compare the paraphrases offered in this chapter with the Quine-Goodman paraphrase of 'There are more cats than dogs' (Goodman and Quine, pp. 109–110) and the Lewis-Lewis paraphrase of 'There are as many holes in this piece of cheese as there are crackers on that plate' (Lewis and Lewis, p. 210).

1. 4

I have said that our paraphrases were adequate only if chairs did not overlap one another (tables did not overlap one another, bricks did not overlap one another,...). Or, to speak in terms acceptable to the nihilist, only if:

For any xs and for any ys, if the xs are arranged chairwise and the ys are arranged chairwise and the xs are not identical with the ys, there is no z such that z is one of the xs and z is one of the ys.

It is not hard to see why this is so. Suppose that there are five simples, a, b, c, d, and e, that a and b are arranged chairwise, that b and c are arranged chairwise, and that, for any xs, if those xs are arranged chairwise, either those xs are a and b or those xs are b and c. Suppose, further, that d and e are arranged tablewise and that, for any ys, if those ys are arranged tablewise, those ys are d and e. (Our present topic is logic and semantics, and not metaphysics or joinery, so there's no need to be realistic about numbers.) Or, to speak in terms *not* acceptable to the nihilist, suppose there are exactly two chairs, one a fusion of a and b and the other a fusion of b and c, and that there is exactly one table, a fusion of d and e. The reader will find it easy to verify both that a and c chair-index a, b, and c and that, more surprisingly, the simples identical with b—that is, the xs such that $\forall y.\ y$ is one of the xs ↔ $y = b$—chair-index a, b, and c. And, therefore, in the situation imagined, (3′) is false. Then the simples identical with d table-index the simples arranged tablewise—but it is false that the simples identical with b outnumber the simples identical with d.

It is not difficult to revise our definitions in such a way that the revised definitions provide the materials for adequate paraphrases of our target sentences in situations in which, e.g., there are chairs that overlap chairs—*provided* "overlap" does not go so far as to become a case of proper parthood. (Our paraphrase of (3) will be adequate only if there are xs that chair-index and those xs and the chairs are equinumerous, and every chair has exactly one of the xs as a part. This condition can be satisfied if chairs "merely overlap"—if they overlap without any chair being a part of another—but it cannot be satisfied if one chair is a part of another.[16])

I therefore confess: if I lived in a world that had the following three features:

---

[16] Well, as a first approximation. The pedantically correct statement is that it cannot be satisfied if there is a chair each of whose simple parts is also a part of *some* other chair. If chairs are fusions of simples, 'Some chair is a part of another chair' is equivalent to '$\exists x \exists y$ (x is a chair & y is a chair & $y \neq x$ & $\forall z$ (z is a simple & z is a part of x. → z is a part of y))'. This statement entails, but is not entailed by, the weaker statement, '$\exists x$ (x is a chair & $\forall z$ (z is a simple & z is a part of x. → $\exists y$ (y is a chair & $y \neq x$ & z is a part of y)'.

- It contained one table and two chairs
- One of the chairs was a proper part of the other
- The folk, knowing everything about the tables and chairs one could learn by examining them and talking about them with the people who made them, would agree that sentence (3) (that is, 'The chairs outnumber the tables') was true,

I should be unable to find a sentence that satisfied these four conditions:

- It would have the same implications as (3) in all matters pertaining to the ways in which simples were spatially, temporally, and causally related to one another
- It would be evident that it did not imply the existence of chairs or the existence of tables (or the existence of any other composite material objects)
- It would be true
- The domain of its quantifiers would comprise only simples (as opposed to, for example, sets of simples, or regions of space that contained simples).

It is easy enough to find sentences that satisfy the first three of these conditions:

The chairwise sets outnumber the tablewise sets,

for example, or

The chairwise regions outnumber the tablewise regions.

(A "chairwise/tablewise set" is a set of simples whose members are arranged chairwise/tablewise. A "chairwise/tablewise region" is a region of space whose simple occupants are arranged chairwise/tablewise.) But these paraphrases, although adequate (to my mind, at least) are not Uzquiano paraphrases.

This difficulty arises only if our target sentences are indeed target sentences. It seems to me to be evident that in the actual world, the folk will agree about the truth-values of our sentences (3), (4), (6a), and (8)—or at least they will if they have visited my friend Tilly, who lives in a brick house mixed in with some cobblestone houses and whose hobby is the production of circles of bricks. But would this be case if objects of the sorts to which those sentences refer had proper parts that were of their own kind? Is it evident that the folk would agree about the truth-value of 'The chairs outnumber the tables' if they lived in a world in which it was true both that

…there are xs arranged tablewise and, for any ys, if the ys are arranged tablewise, the ys are the xs'

and that

…there are xs arranged chairwise and there are ys arranged chairwise and the ys are properly among the xs, and, for any zs, if the zs are arranged chairwise, the zs are the xs or the zs are the ys?

Perhaps not. Perhaps there is a real possibility that if—in that simple world—a representative sample of the folk were given a true-false exam which included the question, '"There are more chairs than tables"—true or false?', some would answer 'true', some 'false' and some 'I can't say' or 'I suppose it depends on how you define "chair"' or 'The question is unclear'. And, if that was indeed the response, 'The chairs outnumber the tables' would not be a target sentence.

Is there a clear case of an object that the folk *would* say was a chair that had chairs as proper parts—or a bicycle that had bicycles as proper parts, or a trash bin that had trash bins as proper parts? Dean Zimmerman has suggested (in correspondence) that the folk might regard the Palatine Tiara—the most famous of the papal triple crowns—as a crown that had three crowns as proper parts.[17] The Tiara is a sort of beehive-shaped helmet on whose outer surface three crowns seem to be resting—in just the way an ordinary crown rests on the (presumably uneasy) head of a monarch. I say "three crowns seem to be resting" because it is not clear to me whether the "crowns" are actual crowns or mere representations of crowns—mere complications in the surface of the beehive-shaped helmet. I suppose that few of the folk would judge that a bronze bas-relief of a crowned king has a part that is a crown, and I am inclined to doubt whether, if they had been allowed to examine the Palatine Tiara carefully, many of the folk would judge that it had crowns as proper parts.

We could, of course, alter the Tiara in our imaginations. We could *imagine* that there were once three crowns (all of them worn as crowns for

---

[17] The triple crown or triregnum that was placed on the head of a new pope in the days when the ceremony that the Holy See now calls an inauguration was called a coronation. The Palatine Tiara is actually only the best known of more than twenty papal crowns.

many years by various kings and electors and sovereign grand dukes) that were eventually brought together and "arranged crownwise" with the intention of producing a crown symbolizing the three principal aspects of the pope's authority. And we could *imagine* that if we ask the folk—who are witnessing the coronation of a newly elected pope (and who are well-informed about the physical structure of the tiara being placed on his head)—"How many crowns did the protodeacon just place on the head of the new pope?", they will all give essentially the same answer: some variant on, "Four—three small ones and one large one made up of the small ones." If we imagine these things, we are imagining an assertion about the number of crowns that satisfy a certain condition, and this assertion resists Uzquiano paraphrase. Or, at any rate, the indexing technique employed in most of the paraphrases presented in this chapter fails to provide an Uzquiano paraphrase of 'Four crowns were placed on the new pope's head'. (Suppose the six simples *a*, *b*, *c*, *d*, *e*, and *f* are arranged crownwise; suppose that *a* and *b* are arranged crownwise, that *c* and *d* are arranged crownwise, and that *e* and *f* are arranged crownwise; suppose that, for any *x*s, if those *x*s are among *a*, *b*, *c*, *d*, *e*, and *f* and are arranged crownwise, those *x*s are *a*, *b*, *c*, *d*, *e*, and *f* or those *x*s are *a* and *b* or those *x*s are *c* and *d* or those *x*s are *e* and *f*. Then for no *x*s among *a*, *b*, *c*, *d*, *e*, and *f* is it the case that exactly one of the *x*s is one of *a*, *b*, *c*, *d*, *e*, and *f*, exactly one of the *x*s is one of *a* and *b*, exactly one of the *x*s is among *c* and *d*, and exactly one of the *x*s is among *e* and *f*.)

And imagine we must, for imagination is all we have. Our modifications of the Tiara are fictional—even if, like many other things one encounters in works of historical fiction, they have a certain tenuous connection with reality. It would be better to have a non-fictional example of a chair that has chairs as proper parts or a crown that has crowns as proper parts or... And I think that there in fact is such a thing—a statue that has statues as proper parts.

Achille Varzi has called my attention to a statue that is a fusion of statues. Manolo Valdés's *La Dama Ibérica* is a large statue in Valencia that is of the same shape as, and is composed of 22,400 small copies of, *La Dama de Elche*, an Iberian sculpture of the 5th or 4th century BC.[18] (Varzi learned of *La Dama Ibérica* from Jordi Valor Abad of the University of Valencia.)

I am reasonably confident that the folk will, uniformly and without hesitation or qualification, echo the words I used to describe it—confident,

---

[18] *La Dama Ibérica* can be seen at http://emedobletaller.blogspot.com/2007/09/dama-iberica-de-manolo-valdes.html.

that is, that they will say that the photograph to which there is a link in note 18 shows a large statue that is composed of many thousands of small statues.

The technique of "indexing," which figured in all but one of our paraphrases, cannot be applied to statues in any case in which each of the simple parts of some statue is also a part of some other statue. And it seems that *La Dama Ibérica* presents just such a case: each constituent simple of the large statue is also a part of one of the small statues, and every simple that is a part of any of the small statues is a part of the large statue. There are no xs such that (i) those xs number 22,401, and (ii) for any y, if y is either *La Dama Ibérica* or one of the 22,400 small copies of *La Dama de Elche* of which *La Dama Ibérica* is composed, exactly one of the xs is a part of y.

It seems, therefore, that "indexing" does not provide Uzquiano paraphrases of all target sentences. Whether the "residual" target sentences can be given Uzquiano paraphrases by some other method is a question for further investigation.[19]

References

Goodman, N. and Quine, W. V. (1947). Steps toward a constructive nominalism, *The Journal of Symbolic Logic*, *12*, 105–122. doi: 10.2307/2268144

Lewis, D. and Lewis, S. (1970). Holes, *Australasian Journal of Philosophy*, *48*, 206–212. doi: 10.1080/00048407012341181

Merricks, T. (2001). *Objects and Persons*. Oxford: Oxford University Press.

Olson, E. (2007). *What are We?: A Study in Personal Ontology*. Oxford: Oxford University Press.

Rosen, G. and Dorr, C. (2002). Composition as a fiction. In Gale, R. (ed.) *The Blackwell Guide to Metaphysics* (pp. 151–174). Oxford: Blackwell.

Sider, T. (2013). Against parthood. In Bennett, K. and Zimmerman, D. (eds.), *Oxford Studies in Metaphysics*, 8 (pp. 237–293). Oxford: Oxford University Press.

Uzquiano, G. (2004). Plurals and simples, *The Monist*, *87*, 429–451. doi: 10.5840/monist200487324

Van Inwagen, P. (1990). *Material Beings*. Ithaca, NY: Cornell University Press

[19] I am grateful to John Hawthorne, Trenton Merricks, Gabriel Uzquiano, Achille Varzi, and Dean Zimmerman for valuable comments on various versions of this paper, comments that have led to extensive revisions. They are, of course, responsible neither for the content of this, the final version, nor for any errors it may contain.

2

Composite Objects are Mere Manys

Simon Thunder

2.1 Introduction

I will defend the claim that composite objects are *mere manys*. To be a mere many is to be many in number without also being one in number.[1] In particular, I'll argue that composite objects are merely many *parts*. For example, before me on my desk is a mug. It is composed of some simples. Thus my mug is merely many simples.

An immediate consequence of this is that my mug is *identical* to some simples (taken together). For a mere many is not a single set-like entity that somehow has other entities as members. If it were, then, although it would be intimately related to a mere many (namely its members, taken together), it itself would be one in number, and thus not a mere many. So to say that my mug is merely many simples is simply to say that the mug just is those many simples.

The view I'm introducing here is a novel view about the nature of material reality. It rejects an assumption that is otherwise more or less completely ubiquitous in metaphysics: the assumption that material objects, if they exist at all (and regardless of what else may be true of them), must each be one in number. More specifically, it rejects the assumption that in order for a composite object to exist, it must be some single thing that is made out of its parts, rather than simply being those many parts themselves. I call the view that results from dropping this assumption *manyism*. The purpose of this chapter is to argue for manyism.

Before that, though, we must first get some more details of the view on the table.

---

[1] The caveat 'without also being one in number' is important because it distinguishes the view I'm defending from *composition as identity*—see the fifth clarification of manyism later in this section. The terminology of 'mere many' is due to Cameron (2012: 533).

Simon Thunder, *Composite Objects are Mere Manys* In: *Oxford Studies in Metaphysics Volume 13*.
Edited by: Karen Bennett and Dean W. Zimmerman, Oxford University Press. © Simon Thunder 2023.
DOI: 10.1093/oso/9780192886033.003.0002

First, manyists do not think that all material objects are mere manys. Whilst each composite object is merely many parts, non-composite, simple objects have no parts (or rather, they each have just one part, namely themselves), and are thus each one in number.

Second, manyists claim that all material objects are composed of simples.[2] Thus all composite material objects are merely many simples.

Third, manyists nevertheless accept the obvious fact that most composite objects admit of multiple decompositions. True enough, my mug is composed of simples. But it is also composed of molecules, and of a handle and a cylindrical body, and so on. Since manyists claim that my mug is merely many parts, it can be described not only as merely many simples, but also as merely many molecules, and as merely a handle and a cylindrical body, and so on. In other words, my mug is identical not only to a certain plurality of simples, but also to a certain plurality of molecules, and to the plurality of the handle and the cylindrical body. There is no contradiction here, and manyists accept the entailment, via the Euclideanness of identity, that e.g. the handle and the cylindrical body are together identical to the plurality of simples. After all, on manyism, the handle is (on one description) just many simples, and the cylindrical body is also (on one description) just many simples, and the many simples that the handle is and the many simples that the cylindrical body is are together the many simples that the mug is. The descriptions of my mug as merely many *simples*, and merely many *molecules*, and merely a handle and a cylindrical body, and indeed (merely) a *mug*, are all just equivalent ways of conceptually carving up a certain bit of reality.

Fourth, different ways of carving up a certain bit of reality yield different counts of that bit of reality. Consider again my mug. My mug is one mug, but it is also a certain number of molecules (say, 100), and a different number of simples (say, 1000), etc. These different counts are analogous to conceiving of the number 1000 as amounting to ten 100s, and two 500s, and one 1000, and one thousand 1s, and so on. Nevertheless, and importantly, there is a way of counting that doesn't depend on the way in which we choose to conceive of reality, and that instead offers a more metaphysically perspicuous way to count that tracks reality's true, mind-independent cardinality. If other ways to count are relative to a certain way of conceptually dividing up reality into chunks, this is a way of counting *simpliciter*. And it is

[2] That is, manyists reject that material reality is gunky, i.e. infinitely divisible into non-simple parts (see e.g. Simons 1987: 42). See §2.3.3.2 for further discussion.

because my mug is many in number according to *this* way of counting—i.e. many in number *simpliciter*—that my mug is a mere many.

I'll have more to say about manyist counting in §2.3.2. For now, the last thing that needs to be noted is that the manyist holds that counting *simpliciter* corresponds to counting simples. For I have just said that simples are each one in number, meaning one in number *simpliciter*. Thus if my mug is 1000 simples then it is 1000 in number *simpliciter*.

Fifth, manyism is importantly different from the view known as composition as identity (CAI). On CAI, composition is the many–one identity that many parts bear to one whole, and so composite objects turn out to be both many *and* one in number.[3] Though manyism joins CAI in equating composition with identity, it departs from it in rejecting that composite objects are each one in number in addition to being many in number. On manyism, the result of composition—*what gets composed*—is a mere many. Composition is not many–one but many–many (aka plural) identity:

PLURAL IDENTITY: $xx = yy =_{df}$ for all z, z is one of xx iff z is one of yy[4]

Indeed, this is suggestive of a helpful way of understanding manyism: start with CAI, complete with its commitment to each composite object being both one and many in number, and simply subtract the claim that composite objects are each one in number. What remains is the claim that each composite object is many in number. That is manyism.[5]

Sixth, manyism is importantly different from mereological nihilism. Nihilists deny the existence of composite objects, positing only simples (see e.g. Rosen and Dorr 2002). Whilst you might think that to say that composite objects are each merely many simples (and are in no important sense single things made out of the simples) is really just a roundabout way of saying that they don't exist at all, manyists explicitly insist that composite objects do exist and are just as real as simples. They repudiate the nihilist

---

[3] On CAI see e.g. Baxter (1988a,b), Wallace (2011a,b), and the essays collected in Baxter and Cotnoir (2014). For the explicit characterisation of CAI as claiming that composites are both many and one in number, see Cameron (2012), McDaniel (2013: 217–218), Merricks (1999: fn3), Turner (2013: 316), and Wallace (2011b: 820–821).

[4] I note that manyists take plural identity to obey Leibniz's Law.

[5] I don't think it's unreasonable to take the terminological stance that manyism is really just a non-standard form of CAI. Nonetheless, it seems to me that CAI is essentially committed to composite objects being one (as well as many) in number, so I'll take manyism to be a distinct view. At any rate, manyism remains importantly different from standard versions of CAI, for the reasons given. See §2.3 for an extended discussion of the relative pros and cons of manyism and CAI.

idea that there are only really individual simples. What's more, they think that composition is a ubiquitous feature of material reality, as common as some xx being identical to some yy. Manyists are not nihilists.[6]

Seventh, and relatedly, manyists further claim that other mereological notions besides composition similarly correspond to genuinely real aspects of the world. Indeed, to our exegesis of manyism we can add some further principles to arrive at a rudimentary manyist mereology. First, parthood:

PARTHOOD: xx are a part of yy =$_{df}$ xx are among yy.

Thus manyists take parthood to amount to amonghood:

AMONGHOOD: xx are among yy =$_{df}$ for all z, z is one of xx only if z is one of yy

Note that, given PARTHOOD, the relata of the parthood relation can be mere manys. That's because plural variables like 'xx' and 'yy' can take as assignments proper pluralities, i.e. pluralities with more than one member, i.e. mere manys. This is of course a feature, not a bug, of the manyist's analysis: composites are often parts of other composites, and on manyism composites are mere manys, so the manyist parthood relation must be capable of relating mere manys to one another. I also note that, as is conventional, singular variables such as 'z' may take as values only things that are one in number (*simpliciter*). For this reason we can check whether a given object is a part of another by considering both objects as pluralities of things that are one in number *simpliciter*, i.e. as pluralities of simples. For example, consider a mug and its handle; in particular consider the mug under the description *plurality of simples, aa*, and the handle under the description *plurality of simples, bb*. Since any simple that is one of bb is also one of aa, bb are among aa, and thus the handle is a part of the mug.

PARTHOOD can furthermore be supplemented with:

PROPER PARTHOOD: xx is/are a proper part of yy =$_{df}$ xx are among yy and yy are not among xx.

We can then define the notion of a simple in the usual way:

SIMPLEHOOD: xx is/are a simple =$_{df}$ xx has no proper parts.

---

[6] See §2.3.3.3 for further discussion of the distinction between manyism and nihilism.

SIMPLEHOOD has the desired consequence that to be simple is to be one in number. Suppose a given quark is simple. By SIMPLEHOOD it has no proper parts. It follows from our definitions that any xx that are n in number have $2^n - 2$ proper parts, so if the quark were n in number for some n greater than 1 then it would have at least two proper parts. So our quark must be one in number. Similarly, suppose a given lepton is one in number. Then it has no proper parts, and so, by SIMPLEHOOD, is simple.

That concludes our enumeration of the central claims of manyism.

2.2 Objects, individuals, and a quasi-Quinean metaontology

I think we should be manyists. Later, I'm going to suggest that a case for this emerges from a comparison between manyism and CAI. But first I need to establish that the view makes sense in the first place. For I concede that a natural reaction to manyism is to think that, insofar as it is (as I've insisted) a form neither of mereological nihilism nor of CAI, it is simply incoherent. In this section I'll consider two (related) ways of trying to articulate the thought that manyism is incoherent, and respond to them.

2.2.1 The alleged singularity of objects

Here's one reason to think that manyism might be incoherent: perhaps it's built into the *meaning* of terms such as 'object', 'mug', and so on, that what they denote must be one in number. Van Inwagen appears to be sympathetic to this sort of thought:

> Many philosophers, in conversation and correspondence, have insisted, despite repeated protestations on my part, on describing my position in words like these: "Van Inwagen says that tables are...nothing more than collections of particles." These are words that darken counsel. They are, in fact, perfectly meaningless.... There are certain properties that a thing would have to have to be properly called a 'table' on anyone's understanding of the word...If anything did have [these properties], it would be a true object, actually a *thing*..., and something more than a collection of particles. (1990: 99–100, emphasis original)

For van Inwagen, then, a table is by definition not a mere many: it is by definition a single thing, as opposed to a mere collection or plurality of particles. In general, you might think that being an object (or a thing) analytically entails being one in number (*simpliciter*). This thought can also be found elsewhere in the literature: Yi, for example, tells us that "nothing (no one object) whatsoever can be many.... This is a logical truth" (2014: 169); Whitehead and Russell worry that "if we admit classes as objects, we must suppose that the same object can be both one and many, which seems impossible" (1962: 72), a worry which only makes sense if they suppose that being an object trivially implies being one in number. And if being an object analytically entails being one in number, then the claim that some objects fail to be one in number is self-contradictory.

Let's introduce a new bit of terminology. Let's reserve 'genuine individual' as a general term for something that is one in number in the metaphysically perspicuous, objective sense—that is, one in number *simpliciter*. The worry that we're considering is that, by virtue of the meaning of 'object', every object is a genuine individual.

But I simply don't see the pressure to accept that there's an analytic entailment from being an object to being a genuine individual. Perhaps there is an understanding of the term 'object' according to which an object is by definition one in number *simpliciter* (and perhaps this is the sense of 'object' that Yi and Whitehead and Russell are employing), but I am not using 'object' in that way. Rather, I'm using 'object' in what I take to be the ordinary, everyday way according to which objects are just things like mugs and tables.[7] Thus if e.g. a mug can be many in number, then an object can be too. And although you might think that it's false that my mug is many in number (or at least, false that my mug fails to be one in number), it doesn't seem at all plausible that the falsity of this follows from the meaning of 'mug'. For one thing, if the world plays any significant role in determining the meanings and denotations of our terms, as semantic externalists maintain,[8] then it looks question-begging against the manyist to deny on analytic grounds that 'mug' might pick out a mere many. It was after all, according to manyism, a mere many that was ostended during the introduction of the

---

[7] I don't mean to *define* 'object' as the disjunction of 'table', 'mug', 'planet', etc. That would be to adopt what Thomasson (2009: 459–460) calls the *covering sense* of 'object', and would preclude the existing objects that don't fall under any extant sortal (Korman 2019: 241–242). My understanding of 'object' is closer to Thomasson's sortal sense (2009: 458–459). This can been seen in the list of plausible hallmarks of objecthood I offer on the next page.

[8] Putnam (1975) and Kripke (1980) are the loci classici on semantic externalism.

term 'mug'. And as regards theories that place a greater emphasis on the descriptive content speakers associate with their terms in determining their meaning, I think it'd be hard to make plausible the claim that ordinary speakers associate the idea of being *one* in the metaphysically perspicuous, mind-independent sense with terms such as 'mug'. To suggest that ordinary speakers require the reference of 'mug' to be one in number *simpliciter*—one *genuine individual*—as opposed to just being one *object* or one *mug*, seems to ascribe too much metaphysical theorising to the folk, who, when deciding whether to apply or withhold 'mug', presumably care much more about the suitability of certain portions of reality for holding coffee than they do about whether those portions are each ultimately one or many.[9]

So I don't think that there's any analytic reason to think that 'object', on the usual meaning of that term at least, can't be a general term or predicate that pluralities, including proper pluralities, can satisfy.

Further, manyists can supplement this negative claim about what 'object' doesn't mean with at least a partial characterisation of what she thinks it does mean. The manyist offers the following as some plausible hallmarks of objecthood, i.e., some conditions that are typically satisfied by some *xx* that satisfy 'is an object':

- *xx* are well-bonded together.[10]
- *xx* display a unifying causal relation.[11]
- *xx* are adjacent to one another,[12] or display spatiotemporal continuity.[13]
- *xx* contrast with their surroundings more than they do with each other.[14]
- *xx* act jointly[15] or have a joint function.[16]
- The activities of *xx* constitute an event that imposes sufficient unity on the *xx*.[17]

These need not be taken to be necessary or (in any combination) jointly sufficient conditions on *xx* satisfying 'object', nor should we necessarily expect there to *be* any such necessary and jointly sufficient conditions. Certainly, philosophers have done a good job of finding counterexamples to proposed necessary and sufficient conditions on when some plurality

---

[9] I intend 'portion of reality' to refer to some thing or things in a way that is neutral with regard to its/their cardinality. See Lewis (1991: 81).

[10] Cf. Thomasson (2009: 458; 2015: 110); Carey (2009: ch. 3); see also Lewis (1986: 211).

[11] Cf. Hoffman and Rosenkrantz (1997: 4).   [12] Cf. Lewis (1986: 211).

[13] Cf. Carey (2009: ch. 3).   [14] Cf. Lewis (1986: 211).   [15] Cf. Lewis (1986: 211).

[16] Cf. Rose and Schaffer (2017).   [17] Cf. Carmichael (2015: 479).

might form a *composite* object (see e.g. van Inwagen 1990: 56–71). Rather, 'object' might well be a cluster concept, and/or its application conditions might be vague.

Indeed, there is some independent plausibility to the thought that it is to some extent vague exactly when 'object' applies, and this amounts to further evidence that 'is an object' does not analytically entail 'is a genuine individual', i.e., 'is one in number *simpliciter*'. For sentences that assert that there are exactly *n* genuine individuals cannot be vague,[18] and so unless the meaning of 'object' is divorced from that of 'genuine individual' we can't accommodate the datum that it's sometimes vague whether some portion of reality is an object or not. The manyist's claim that being an object is a matter of satisfying a predicate, on the other hand, can accommodate this datum, since predicates can of course be sources of vagueness.

At any rate, I see no reason for the manyist claim that composite objects are mere manys to be ruled out on the basis of the meaning of 'object'.[19]

2.2.2 Quantifiers and Quine

A different (though related) concern about the coherence of manyism may persist: contra the manyist, isn't it the case that to *be* is to be a *genuine individual*? This sort of thought posits a tight link between existence and being one in number *simpliciter*, and will appeal especially to those sympathetic to a broadly Quinean background metaontology. Thus van Inwagen lists the following as the fourth of five theses that he takes to constitute a Quinean metaontology (to which he himself subscribes):

Thesis 4. The single sense of being or existence is adequately captured by the existential quantifier of formal logic.   (1998: 237)

---

[18] Sider (2001: 126–128) and Lewis (1986: 212); see also Fine (1975: 267).

[19] An objection that I can't consider here, given space constraints, is the deflationary one that there simply is no available sense of 'genuine individual' or 'one in number *simpliciter*' that is distinct from 'object' or 'being one object' as I've characterised them (see e.g. Thomasson [2009: 457–466; 2015: 108–111], see also Hirsch's denial of a metaphysically privileged quantifier [e.g. 2002]). Here I simply say that I think we can make sense of 'genuine individual' and 'being one in number *simpliciter*' as I've characterised them, and that I think this is the standard view, but concede that manyism (like many other metaphysical views) remains hostage to the fortunes of ontological realism.

He goes on to write the existential quantifier to which he refers here as '∃x' (240ff.). This is the singular existential quantifier; the plural existential quantifier would be written '∃xx'. What's distinctive about the singular existential quantifier is that it binds only singular variables, such as 'x'; what's distinctive about singular variables is that they can by definition take as a value only a genuine individual. Thus van Inwagen's Thesis 4 is more or less equivalent to the famous slogan with which Quine is associated: to be is to be the value of a bound variable (where 'bound *singular* variable' is apparently what is meant) (see Quine 1953: 13–14). According to Quineanism, so characterised, there cannot *be* anything that is incapable of being the value of a bound singular variable. Since mere manys are not genuine individuals—that is, since they are not each one in number *simpliciter*—they cannot be the value of a bound singular variable, and so they cannot *be*; they cannot exist. The manyist claim that, for example, my mug exists and is a mere many turns out to be self-contradictory.[20]

If the previous objection located manyism's alleged incoherence in the meaning of 'object', then this one locates it in the meaning of 'exists'. In response, I think the manyist should deny that 'exists' means what the Quinean says it does. That is, she should reject the idea that the singular existential quantifier adequately captures the single sense of being or existence (i.e., she should reject van Inwagen's Thesis 4). Instead, she should say instead that it's the *plural* existential quantifier that performs this role. The plural existential quantifier binds *plural* variables, such as 'xx', which are variables that can take both proper and improper pluralities as values. A claim of the form

(1)   F exists

is then analysed as

---

[20] Note that the Quinean position here is not the plainly implausible one that it is self-contradictory to say of a plurality of individuals that they exist. For example, Quineans can accept as consistent and true the sentence 'there are two desks'. The point is that the Quinean says that this sentence only tells us about what exists insofar as it implies a sentence using only the singular existential quantifier, such as 'there is a desk, and there is another desk' (this example assumes that desks are genuine individuals rather than mere manys). In other words, when the Quinean says of a plurality that it exists, she means only that each individual member of that plurality exists, which is consistent with her thought that the singular existential quantifier is what captures what we mean by 'existence'. When the manyist says of a composite object *qua* mere many that it exists, on the other hand, she takes herself to be saying more than just that each individual within the plurality to which the composite object is identical exists (if that was all she meant then she'd be a nihilist): for the manyist, the plurality itself, i.e. the composite object, exists too. That the manyist says this whilst denying that the plurality/composite object is a genuine individual is what the Quinean finds incoherent or self-contradictory about manyism.

(2) $\exists xx\ Fxx$

where 'F' should be understood as a plural predicate that can be satisfied by either a proper plurality or an improper plurality. Thus to commit to the existence of an F leaves open the question of whether that F is one in number *simpliciter* or not, i.e., whether it's a genuine individual or a mere many. Note that this does not prevent us from expressing the idea that something exists and is one in number *simpliciter*. Let '1' mean 'is one in number *simpliciter*'. Then

(3) $\exists xx\ (Fxx \wedge 1xx)$

expresses that there is an F that is one in number *simpliciter*. The claim that F is many in number *simpliciter* can be expressed as

(4) $\exists xx\ (Fxx \wedge \neg 1xx)$.

Notice also that (3) is equivalent to

(5) $\exists x\ Fx$.

So by combining '$\exists xx$' with '1' we can recover the singular existential quantifier.

On this metaontological view, the distinction between existence and being many in number is not, as the Quinean would have it, the distinction between existence and non-existence, but rather simply between satisfying and failing to satisfy a predicate. Nonetheless, I don't think that this metaontology is very far away from what Quine and his followers have in mind. I've simply tweaked the Quinean slogan of *to be is to be the value of a bound variable* so that it reads (paraphrasing Boolos [1984]) *to be is to be the value(s) of a bound variable*. All of the other Quinean doctrines remain untouched: for example, we can maintain that existence, as expressed by '$\exists xx$', is univocal, that there are no non-existent objects, and so on. So the resulting view is Quinean in spirit if not in letter, and so worthy, I think, of the descriptor 'quasi-Quinean'. And on this quasi-Quinean view, manyism is not incoherent, because the claim that, e.g., my mug is a mere many is not analysed as the self-contradictory

(6) $\exists x \ (x$ is my mug $\land \ \neg 1x),$

but rather as the perfectly consistent

(7) $\exists xx \ (xx$ are my mug $\land \ \neg 1xx).$

Manyism's coherence thus depends on our acceptance of this quasi-Quinean metaontology over the traditional Quinean one (or at least, it depends on our acceptance of a metaontology similarly tolerant of the existence of mere manys). But why should we accept this alternative metaontology?

Well, why *shouldn't* we? As far as I can see, nothing Quine et al. say addresses why we should think that the singular quantifier, rather than the plural one, best captures what we mean by 'exists'. Quine himself, for example, was mainly concerned with rejecting Meinongianism and providing an account of ontological commitment that could help to adjudicate thorny metaphysical disputes about universals, both of which goals are equally well served by the proposed alternative quasi-Quinean metaontology. Nor does there seem to be any obvious argument for traditional Quineanism over its quasi-counterpart. For example, there's no straightforward argument from grammar for Quineanism: true, '*F* exists' is a grammatically singular construction, but to generate any sort of argument from this observation to the claim that '$\exists x$', rather than '$\exists xx$', features in the correct analysis of this sort of sentence, we'd need the auxiliary assumption that grammatical singularity tracks one-in-number-*simpliciter*-hood, a claim that quasi-Quineans do not accept (they can instead claim that grammatical singularity in ordinary English tracks single *object*hood). And without an argument for why the traditional Quinean view is better, it simply begs the question against the manyist to rule her view out as incoherent on the basis of the traditional view.

I think we can also say something positive in favour of the quasi-Quinean metaontology I've sketched here. It has to do with methodology. As a very general characterisation, when we're doing metaphysics what is going on is that we're being confronted with reality and are trying to make sense of it. Suppose we're confronted with a bit of reality that, in non-philosophical contexts, we call a mug. As metaphysicians our task is to work out what is really going on in that bit of reality. Now, one thing we might conclude is that really there is no mug in that bit of reality. But suppose we think that the mug exists (after all, we can apparently apprehend it with the senses, drink tea from it, etc.). Next question: What is the mug *like*? What is its nature? Crucially, traditional Quineans place an *a priori* limitation on what our answer to this question can be: we're not allowed to claim that the mug is many in number without also being one in number. Such a view is ruled out from the get-go. This seems like an aberration with respect to an open-minded investigation into the nature of reality.

Indeed, it is particularly aberrant because there is some evidence that various capable and serious analytic philosophers have even *held* views according to which various putative bits of reality are many in number without being one in number, and which are apparently rendered incoherent by traditional Quineanism (though none have defended manyism). In his early work, for example, Russell apparently countenanced the existence of *classes as many*, i.e., classes that are each many in number whilst not also being one in number (1903: 76ff.); Black (1971) argued for a similar view about sets, on the one hand analysing set-talk as merely plural reference to the members of the set in question (631ff.), whilst on the other insisting that 'a set is a thing in its own right' and affirming the existence of sets (635).[21] With regard to material objects, Barker and Jago, in the course of introducing their bundle theoretic view, note that an 'alternative (broadly Kantian) approach is to take a material object to be its [many] properties, insofar as they are thought about "in a certain combining manner"' (2018: 2970), citing Bennett (1987: 201), who suggests this view on behalf of Locke. But perhaps the clearest example is Eddington's well-known musings on the distinction between, first, the table as common sense understands it, and second, the table as modern science would describe it:

> My scientific table is mostly emptiness. Sparsely scattered in that emptiness are numerous electric charges rushing about with great speed; ... it turns out to be an entirely efficient table.... If I lean upon this table I shall not go through.... I need not tell you that modern physics has by delicate test and remorseless logic assured me that *my second scientific table is the only one which is really there*.   (1929: x–xii, emphasis mine).

---

[21] Arguably, Black's view has distinguished precedent in Georg Cantor, who writes, "Unter einer 'Mannigfaltigkeit' oder 'Menge' verstehe ich nämlich allegemein jedes Viele, welches sich als Eines denken läßt" (1883/1932: 204); "by a 'manifold' or 'set' I understand in general any many that can be thought of as one" (my translation). Now, it should also be conceded that, as Black notes (1971: 618), other things Cantor said suggest that he regarded a set as some single entity formed out of its members. Kreisel suggests a possible explanation of this, which is that the notion of a set in Cantor's time "looked more like a mixture of [distinct] notions" (1969: 93). Nevertheless, in light of Cantor's words, it seems that the idea of a set-as-mere-many was one of those notions. Hewitt (2015: 327) apparently agrees, suggesting that one reason why the naïve comprehension axiom was a feature of early set theory was because of the then-common conception of a set as a plurality (since plurality formation obeys naïve comprehension).

Thus Eddington claims tables to exist (to be *really there*) but to amount to nothing more than (emptiness and) many electric charges.[22]

Of course, it's almost always possible to interpret philosophers who apparently have posited the existence of mere manys either as really disavowing ontological commitment to the phenomenon in question (thus Hewitt [2015: §1.1] labels Black a set-theoretic nihilist) or else as regarding the phenomenon as being an individual entity that is somehow made up of further entities. But if these readings are motivated solely by an unthinking background assumption of Quineanism then in this context they beg the question against the quasi-Quinean. And without that illicit background assumption, the above examples strike me as respectable precedents for the thought that certain elements of reality that really exist (sets, classes, material objects) may nonetheless be many in number without also being one in number.

To the extent, then, that we want metaphysical inquiry to be open-minded and unprejudiced—and in particular, open to views that capable philosophers have apparently even *held*—we should prefer the metaontology that does not rule out any otherwise coherent hypothesis before the inquiring has even begun. Heil's words are instructive here:

> A technical vocabulary can be liberating, but it can be constraining as well, channelling thoughts along familiar paths. Occasionally this can lead to the dismissal out of hand of alternatives that could otherwise appear attractive. Philosophers, of all people, should be open-minded, especially in domains where there is little or no settled agreement. If over-reliance on a technical framework produces philosophical blind spots, we should be willing to forgo, or at least re-examine, the framework once we hit an impasse.
>
> (2003: 2)

I agree. Quasi-Quineanism rules out fewer potentially attractive hypotheses in comparison to Quineanism, and so is to be preferred. We should avoid ruling manyism to be incoherent on the basis of a traditional metaontology that may be blinding us to attractive alternatives to extant views.

I'll proceed, then, on the basis that manyism is coherent.

---

[22] See also Simons (2003), who argues that the universe is a multiplicity.

2.3 Why we should be manyists

We shouldn't just think that manyism is coherent: we should also think that it is true. I think the most effective way to argue for this is to consider manyism in comparison with a rival view with which it has much in common: CAI. In §2.1 I said that manyism and CAI agree both that composite objects exist and that they are identical to their parts, but are separated by their differing views on the nature of composite objects and, relatedly, the nature of composition: CAI holds that composition is many–*one* identity, and that composite objects are each both many and one in number; manyism instead holds that composition is many–*many* identity, and that each composite object is merely many in number. My argument in the remainder of this chapter is going to be as follows. CAI is in many respects an extremely attractive view, but is ultimately unacceptable because there can be no many–one identities. We should all feel that we *want* to endorse CAI, because it seems to get so much about composition and parthood right, but also that we *can't* endorse it, because many cannot be identical to one. Manyism, on the other hand, gets right the same things that CAI gets right about composition and parthood, without similarly positing many–one identities in order to do so. So we can and should endorse manyism.

I'll start by making my positive case, before turning to objections.

2.3.1 Manyism as an improvement on CAI

The most important benefit of CAI is its ability to capture a set of powerful and deeply held intuitions that together concern what has come to be known as the *intimacy of parthood*. As has been observed many times before,[23] the relationship between parts and whole seems to be remarkably intimate in a number of respects (e.g., wholes are located wherever their parts are, wholes are nothing over and above their parts, etc.), to the extent that the composition relation between parts and whole seems to be more similar to the most intimate relation of them all, i.e. identity, than it is to any other relation (Sider 2007: 54–55). By claiming that composition *just is* identity, CAI goes a long way toward capturing and explaining the intimacy of parthood. Indeed,

---

[23] See Wallace (2011a: 804–805), Lewis (1991: 85), Sider (2007: §2 and §4), and Cameron (2014: 90–91).

CAI purports to be unique among candidate theories of composition in its ability to account for and explain the intimacy of parthood. Other views typically claim that composition is *analogous* to identity, precisely in that it is an extraordinarily intimate relation that licenses claims of "nothing over and above," that renders the co-location of its relata unproblematic, etc. (e.g. Lewis 1991: 81–87). But to say that composition is analogous to identity in certain respects is just to stipulate that composition has certain features that identity also has, and fails to explain or ground the fact that composition has these features (Wallace 2011a: 809; Cameron 2014: 93). Only by claiming that composition really *is* identity, as opposed to just being analogous to it, can we secure the benefit of explaining the intimate nature of composition and parthood. This is the main selling point of CAI.

Manyism co-opts this benefit of CAI. In fact, I think manyism does a *better* job of capturing and explaining the intimacy of parthood than CAI does (so really it's manyism, not CAI, that is uniquely able to account for the intimacy of parthood). The reason that manyism does at least as good a job as CAI in explaining the intimate nature of parthood is because CAI's ability to explain the intimacy of parthood is entirely down to its identification of the relations of composition and identity, and manyism also identifies composition with identity. Manyism does a *better* job than CAI at capturing the intimacy of parthood because, unlike CAI, it can capture the *automaticity* of composition. This is the idea that no extra metaphysical ingredient is required beyond the existence of some objects for those objects to compose (Lewis 1991: 85). The automaticity of composition is one facet of the intimacy of parthood: the relation between parts and whole seems to be so intimate that once you've got some parts you can't fail to have a whole composed out of those parts too. It sometimes used to be thought that CAI could capture the automaticity of composition, in that it sometimes used to be thought that CAI's claim that composition is identity entails universalism, the thesis that all pluralities of (disjoint) objects compose.[24] After all, if a composite whole just is its parts, then doesn't the existence of the composite whole follow (automatically) from the existence of the parts, in every case? But when the claim that composition is identity is understood as the claim that composition is *many-one* identity, the entailment to universalism is blocked. For it could be that there is a plurality of objects that are (jointly) many in number without also being one in number, in which case those

---

[24] See Merricks (2005: 629), Harte (2002: 114); see also Sider (2007: 61–62).

objects do not bear the relation of many–one identity to anything, and so don't compose (this is essentially Cameron's [2012] proof that CAI doesn't entail universalism). That is, CAI does not capture the automaticity of composition because it does require there to be an extra metaphysical ingredient beyond the mere existence of some objects for those objects to compose: those objects must be (jointly) one in number. Manyism, on the other hand, makes no such requirement. Manyism says that composition is many-*many* identity. So, on manyism, all some *xx* have to do to compose is to bear the relation of many–many identity to some *yy*.[25] Since all *xx* trivially bear the relation of many–many identity to themselves, all *xx* trivially compose. So unlike CAI, manyism entails universalism, and thereby captures the automaticity of composition.

There's another, related benefit of CAI that manyism co-opts and that's worth drawing out here, which is CAI's extreme parsimony. That CAI is extremely *ontologically* parsimonious is essentially just a consequence of one of the ways in which it captures the intimacy of parthood. On CAI, composite wholes are nothing over and above their parts, simply because they are identical to their parts. That suggests that composite objects should be regarded as ontologically innocent with respect to their parts, in that we should not count composite objects as an extra ontological commitment once we've already ontologically committed ourselves to the parts. After all, if composite wholes are identical to their parts then an ontological commitment to a composite whole seems to be nothing more than an ontological commitment to some parts (see Lewis 1991: 81–85, Varzi 2014: 47–48, Sider 2007).[26] So CAI seems to be just as ontologically parsimonious as a nihilistic view that only posits simples—i.e. very parsimonious. Since manyism also identifies composite wholes with their parts, it is likewise very ontologically parsimonious. What's more, CAI and manyism are both also very

---

[25] Note that I don't say here that, on manyism, all some *xx* have to do to compose *an object* is to bear the relation of many–many identity to some *yy*. Since the manyist takes objecthood to typically require things like being well-bonded, having a joint function, etc., it's possible for some *xx* to compose some *yy* without *yy* being an object.

[26] An interesting question here is whether the putative ontological innocence of composite objects on CAI is threatened by the non-automaticity of composition, given CAI. As we've just seen, to say that a composite object exists in addition to its parts does incur some extra commitment over and above just commitment to the existence of the parts, on CAI: it requires commitment to those parts being jointly one in number. The question is whether that extra commitment (which after all immediately implies the existence of something that wouldn't exist otherwise) is rightly regarded as an extra *ontological* commitment or not. I won't try to settle this question here, but note that manyism's claim that composite objects are ontologically innocent is not subject to the same threat.

ideologically parsimonious. For unlike other views that employ mereological concepts in their theories of reality, neither CAI nor manyism (need) regard mereological concepts as primitive, and can rather define them in terms of non-mereological primitives that everyone else already countenances. For example, we've already seen (§2.1) that manyism reduces composition to many–many identity, and parthood to amonghood, and so on (in CAI's case the reductions are a little different—see Bohn [2014: 143-4]). So CAI and manyism both seem to be more ideologically parsimonious than most rival views.[27]

So, in sum: What's good about CAI is that it allows us to respect and account for (most of) the ways in which composite objects are intimately related to their parts, and offers a way of accepting both the existence of composite objects and that reality has a genuine mereological structure without offending against either ontological or ideological parsimony; manyism co-opts these good-making features of CAI, and can even claim to do a better job of capturing the intimacy of parthood. The reason that manyism is superior to CAI, then, is simply that manyism secures all of these significant benefits without having to postulate many–one identities. There's a reason why almost no-one accepts CAI, understood as the claim that composition just is identity (rather than the weaker claim that composition is analogous to identity): it just seems absurd for many things to be identical to one thing. Sometimes this thought is presented as an argument from Leibniz's Law against CAI, the idea being that the many have a property that the one doesn't have, namely *being many in number*, and the one has a property that the many doesn't have, namely *being one in number* (Lewis 1991: 87; McKay 2006: 38). Now, presumably most supporters of CAI will retort that this rests on the illicit assumption that cardinal properties exclude each other, and insist that parts and whole are each both many and one in number (Wallace 2011b: 820–821, McDaniel 2013: 217–218). The trouble is that this is just implausible, or at the very least, radically revisionary with regard to our usual conception of number.[28] Whilst it might be worth it to revise our concept of number if doing so is the

---

[27] My argument here relies on the claim that non-primitive bits of ideology do not count against ideological parsimony. That claim is plausible, and standard—see e.g. Cowling (2013: 3893) and Schaffer (2015: 649–651).

[28] An alternative response on behalf of CAI is to allow that the parts are many and not one, and that the whole is one and not many, and to hold on to the identity of parts and whole by allowing that the identicals can be discernible (Baxter 2014). But this response is surely just as objectionably revisionary, this time with regard to our conception of identity, a central component of which is that identity obeys the indiscernibility of identicals.

only way to secure important theoretical benefits (cf. Sider 2007: 63), equally if we can have the theoretical benefits without making the revisions then it's better not to make them. Since manyism does secure the same theoretical benefits concerning the intimacy of parthood that CAI purports to, the fact that manyism *doesn't* require doing any violence to our intuitions about cardinality surely puts it at a significant advantage. For manyism takes composition to be many–many identity, and can join everyone else in repudiating many–one identities and the objectionable consequences they bring.

That, then, is my positive argument for manyism: it captures everything that CAI was designed to capture, so co-opts CAI's considerable strengths, without sharing the commitment to many–one identities that makes CAI unacceptable to almost everyone. I turn now to considering two important objections to this conception of manyism as a significant improvement on CAI.

2.3.2 Objection 1: Manyism is really no different from CAI

Is the distinction I've drawn between manyism and CAI a distinction without a difference? I've said that manyism differs from CAI in taking composition to be many–many identity, as opposed to many–one identity, and relatedly in taking composite objects to each be mere manys, rather than both many and one in number. But I also said (in §2.1) that the manyist thinks that there is a sense in which each composite object can (rightly, truly) be counted as 'one', and that my mug, for example, is not only (identical to) many simples but is also (identical to) one mug. So on manyism my mug is one mug that is identical to many simples. Isn't that just what CAI says? And isn't manyism thereby committed to objectionable many–one identities after all, in just the same way that CAI is?

The short answer is no. The longer answer requires some more discussion about what manyism says about cardinality and counting.[29] To that end, the manyist can appeal to a model of counting that Cotnoir (2013: 301ff.) has offered on behalf of CAI, albeit with an important twist. That model works as follows. Consider a certain portion of reality, and suppose that it contains

---

[29] Thanks to an anonymous referee for pressing me to say more about the manyist account of counting.

some simples. Let A be the set containing those simples. Now consider the notion of a *partition* of A. Informally, a partition of A is the result of carving A up into non-overlapping subsets without remainder. The partition is just the set of those subsets. Since there are multiple ways to carve A up into non-overlapping subsets without remainder, there are multiple partitions of A. For example, we could carve A up into ten non-overlapping subsets, with one tenth of the simples in A belonging to each subset (though there is no requirement that the subsets be equally sized). Thus one partition of A is the set of those ten subsets. Alternatively, we could carve A up into subsets that each contain just one simple, resulting in a different partition of A. Trivially, another partition of A is simply A itself—we can think of this as the partition that doesn't carve A up at all. As Cotnoir says, we can treat each partition of A as a different *way of counting* the portion of reality to which A corresponds. To do so, we simply count the number of subsets that the partition carves A up into. Thus the partition of ten subsets of A represents a way of counting what is in the portion of reality to which A corresponds as ten in number; the partition of A that is simply A itself represents a way of counting what is the portion of reality to which A corresponds as one in number; and so on.

Where the manyist's 'twist' comes in is in the attitude she takes toward the different ways of counting this partition-based model affords. For the manyist regards one way of counting as uniquely privileged, in that it is the way to count that tracks the objective cardinality of reality. Reality, says the manyist, comes pre-carved up into genuine individuals. There is an objective, mind-independent fact of the matter about whether any given portion of reality is a genuine individual or instead many individuals. The genuine individuals are the simples. Thus the way to count that tracks the objective cardinality of reality corresponds to the partition that carves reality up into simples. Other partitions are imposed on reality by us in the way we conceptualise it. For example, consider again the mug. Objectively speaking, the mug is not a genuine individual—rather, its cardinality is equivalent to the number of simples to which it is identical. But for us it's usually useful and appropriate to conceptually group together all of those simples and to count them as 'one'. At the very least, this is the case when we're counting how many *mugs* there are. In general, when we're interested in how many Fs there are, it makes sense to count relative to the partition that groups together and counts as 'one' any plurality of simples that jointly satisfy F. Hence manyists say that my mug is one mug, and (say) 100 molecules, and so on.[30] Nevertheless, says the manyist, these ways of counting do not accurately reflect reality's objective cardinality. When we say that the mug (or the molecule, etc.) is one in number, the manyist insists that what we're doing here is conceptually grouping together and treating as 'one' what is really, objectively speaking a proper plurality. As we might put it, though my mug is one in number relative to the partition that groups the simples to which it is identical into one subset, it is many in number *simpliciter*.[31]

That is why manyism really is distinct from CAI, and why manyism isn't really committed to many–one identities. CAI rejects the idea that any one partition of reality is privileged over the others, instead holding that it's just as correct and 'objective' to count each composite object as one as it is to count it as many.[32] In any sense in which my mug is *really* many, it is *really* one as well. Hence CAI's (objectionable) commitment to many–one identities. In saying instead that composite objects are each really many in number without being one in number, the manyist avoids postulating any many–one identities. On her metaphysic there are only one–one and

---

[30] What about in situations in which we don't explicitly invoke a sortal like 'mug' or 'molecule'? Manyists should say that in these situations we typically count how many *maximal objects* there are. We've already seen that by 'object' the manyist means any plurality of simples that are sufficiently well-bonded to each other, or that have a joint function, etc. (see §2.2.1). A maximal object is an object that is not a proper part of another object. For example, one of the molecules that is a part of my mug is an object but not a maximal object, because it is a proper part of my mug. My mug, however, is a maximal object, as there's no object of which it is a proper part. Thus if we were to ask how many things are left to wash up, then in a situation in which only my mug remained unwashed, the appropriate answer would be 'one'.

[31] This represents a superficial similarity between manyism and Donald Baxter's version of CAI, which accepts the claim that 'the whole, then, is just the parts counted loosely. It is strictly a multitude and loosely a single thing' (1988a: 580–581). But Baxter's view is not manyism. Among other things, Baxter's view, unlike manyism, implies that the whole is ('loosely') identical not just to the parts taken together, but also to each *individual part* (this is explicit in his [2014: 246]). See Turner (2014) for further discussion of Baxter's view. Incidentally, Baxter also later disavowed his 1988 claim that counting the parts as 'many' is stricter or more accurate than counting them as 'one' (2014: 245).

[32] Cotnoir disagrees with this, claiming that "the composition as identity theorist is free to endorse a single way of counting as the correct one" (2013: 317). But such a "composition as identity theorist" is plausibly just a manyist (as least, as long as she says that the single correct way of counting corresponds to counting the number of simples). I've already conceded (footnote 5) that it's possible to regard manyism as a non-standard form of CAI. Insofar as I'm claiming manyism to be distinct from CAI, I'm talking about *standard* versions of CAI, which do indeed take it to be the case that there are multiple 'correct' ways of counting. That's the only explanation of why CAI is near-universally regarded as being drastically revisionary with regard to our concepts of number and identity, in virtue of positing instances of many–one identity (e.g. Sider 2007: 63): CAI *wouldn't* be particularly revisionary with regard to those concepts if the only sense in which it were committed to many–one identities were via the claim that what are really many things can nevertheless be treated or conceptualised as one thing.

many–many identities, despite the fact that what are many can be treated or conceptualised as one for certain purposes.

2.3.3 Objection 2: We need composite objects to be one in number

The other objection that I'll consider here is that there are very good *reasons* for saying that composite objects are each one in number, and correspondingly very serious problems with saying instead that composite objects are mere manys. That is, although CAI incurs theoretical costs by taking composite objects to be one in number, perhaps those costs are worth paying in order to avoid even greater problems that come with denying this. I'll consider three ways of trying to press this point.

2.3.3.1 Superplural semantics

The first concerns semantics. If we hold that composite objects are mere manys, we must understand ordinary quantification over composite objects as *plural* quantification, i.e., quantification over pluralities of individuals. Plural quantification is relatively well-understood and is generally regarded as legitimate, so this in itself isn't especially problematic.[33] The difficulty comes when we consider what purports to be irreducibly plural quantification over composite objects, i.e., quantification over pluralities of composite objects.[34] If each composite object is itself a plurality, then quantification over pluralities of composite objects turns out to be quantification over pluralities of pluralities of (genuine) individuals. Such quantification is not merely plural but *super*plural quantification.[35] The trouble is that the legitimacy and intelligibility of superplural quantification is far more controversial than that of plural quantification, and as such, the threat to manyism is

---

[33] On plural quantification and related matters, see e.g. McKay (2006), Oliver and Smiley (2016), and Linnebo (2017).

[34] An instance of plural quantification is irreducible iff it cannot be adequately reformulated using only singular resources (for example, 'there are two chairs' can be reformulated as 'there is a chair, and there is another chair, and the second chair is distinct from the first', but 'the chairs are arranged in a circle' cannot be reformulated as a claim or conjunction of claims about individual chairs).

[35] See Hazen (1997: 247) for an early mention of superplural (or in his terminology, 'perplural') quantification. See Bennett (2009: 59–60) for the claim that *nihilism* is committed to superplural quantification in much the same way that manyism is.

that its denial of the 'oneness' of composite objects commits it to an unintelligible semantics.

The manyist can say two things in response. The first is that we hardly escape semantic difficulties concerning ostensibly plural quantification over composites if we join CAI in saying that composite objects are each not only many in number but also one in number (see Sider 2007: §3.1, §3.3; 2013). But second, and more to the point, the manyist is entitled to ask why we should think that the intelligibility of superplural quantification is in doubt. Is it that no adequate formal system of superplural logic has been developed? That is surely an unfounded complaint—see Rayo (2006) and Oliver and Smiley (2016: ch. 15) for such formal work. Is it that what look like genuine instances of superplural quantification can in every case be adequately analysed using merely plural resources, leaving us without illustrative examples of superplural quantification (Ben-Yami 2013: 89ff.)? Then one of two things is true: either the superplural quantification that the manyist thinks she needs to employ can similarly be adequately analysed using merely plural resources, in which case the manyist doesn't need superplural quantification after all, or the superplural quantification she relies on doesn't reduce to merely plural quantification, in which case we have a genuine illustrative example of superplural quantification. Or, relatedly, do doubts about the intelligibility of superplural quantification stem from the idea that natural language contains no instances of it (Uzquiano 2004: 439, Ben-Yami 2013: 82, 85)? But this begs the question against the manyist, who after all thinks that we employ superplural quantification in natural language each time we utter something that looks on the surface like an instance of merely plural quantification over composite objects. Or, finally, is the problem that the usual characterisation of superplural quantification as the result of iterating the step from singular quantification to plural quantification is objectionable (Rayo 2006: 227, Ben-Yami 2013: 82–84)? But the manyist isn't wedded to this conception of superplural quantification. All she needs to say is that she takes superplural quantification simply to be whatever kind of quantification we would use if we were to quantify over composite objects *qua* mere manys (and, as already noted, if this turns out to be merely plural quantification of some sort, then so be it).

So I don't think that concerns about the legitimacy of superplural quantification provide good motivation for saying that composite objects are each one in number as well as many in number, rather than mere manys.

2.3.3.2 The gunk objection

Here's a different reason for thinking that CAI is right to insist that composite objects are each one in number. It concerns so-called gunk.[36] Consider:

GUNK: An object o is gunky $=_{df}$ all of o's parts themselves have proper parts.

An instance of gunk is thus an instance of infinite descent, a never-ending chain of objects such that each link is a proper part of the previous one. As others have observed, gunk seems to be conceivable, and therefore possible (Sider 1993, Schaffer 2003: 501). But the possibility of gunk seems incompatible with the conception of composite objects as mere manys, at least given the manyist's reduction of parthood to amonghood. For given that reduction, GUNK is equivalent to:

M-GUNK: An object oo is gunky $=_{df}$ oo is a mere many such that all of its subpluralities themselves have proper subpluralities.

Given M-GUNK, a gunky object would be a non-well-founded plurality. That is, it would be a plurality that isn't ultimately made up of genuine individuals. That seems impossible. To say that the only answer to the question of 'what is oo a plurality of' is 'more pluralities' simply looks like a conceptual mistake. What it is to be a plurality is ultimately to be many genuine individuals. If there are no genuine individuals, then there can't be a plurality.

On the other hand, if we allow that each composite object is one in number, as CAI does, then we can accept the possibility of gunk. On CAI, though a gunky object is (identical to) the plurality of its gunky parts, each of those gunky parts is not only a proper plurality of further parts, but is also a genuine individual. So CAI's gunky objects are (identical to) pluralities of genuine individuals, which is unproblematic.[37]

Difficulty accommodating the possibility of gunk does seem like a genuine downside to manyism's denial of the oneness of composite objects. But I doubt it's a very significant downside. For one thing, manyists *can* accept the possibility of gunk if they back away from the claim that manyism is

---

[36] The term 'gunk' is due to Lewis (1991: 20).

[37] Here's a reason for thinking, on the contrary, that CAI is inconsistent with the possibility of gunk: Calosi (2016) and Loss (2018) have argued that CAI entails nihilism, and nihilism is inconsistent with the possibility of gunk (Sider 1993). For the purposes of this discussion, though, I'll grant CAI the benefit of the doubt and assume that it can avoid necessitating nihilism.

necessarily true, and claim only that it is actually true (cf. Cameron 2007: 101–102). Then they can allow that at other worlds composite objects are genuine individuals, and in some cases, gunky genuine individuals. This may not be particularly palatable to manyists, but it is an option open to them. Alternatively, manyists can (to some extent at least) alleviate the cost of denying the possibility of gunk by copying a strategy suggested by Williams (2006) on behalf of the nihilist in response to the gunk objection, which is to say that there is some non-gunky possible world that generates the non-veridical illusion that gunk is possible. In particular, a world containing an infinite descent of smaller and smaller simples, each one occupying a subregion of the region of space occupied by the previous one, would be perfectly consistent with manyism and would look just like a gunky world. There's probably some cost to saying that the apparent possibility of gunk is illusory in this way, but it doesn't seem prohibitive. In general, I doubt that a desire to avoid having to say something a bit awkward about gunk gives us good enough motivation for taking on the problems associated with saying that composite objects are each one in number as well as many in number.

2.3.3.3 A collapse to nihilism?

So neither the semantics to which we would be committed nor the problem of gunk seems to represent serious enough problems with the idea that composite objects are mere manys to motivate saying instead that composite objects are manys that are also ones. All well and good. But I suspect the main reason why supporters of CAI feel the need to maintain that composite objects are each one in number is simply the assumption that saying as much is an automatic consequence of accepting the *existence* of those objects. Now, as we've seen, manyists reject this assumption, and hold that the claims that composite objects fail to be one in number and that composite objects exist are perfectly compatible. But given the centrality of this point to the comparison between manyism and CAI, it's worth dwelling on it a little more.

In particular, it's worth saying something more on behalf of the manyist in response to the thought that manyism fails to be anything more than a form of mereological nihilism with a fancy semantics bolted on. Mereological nihilism is standardly characterised as the view that composite objects do not exist and that simples are the only material objects that there are. Nevertheless, the sparse ontology of nihilism can be combined with a semantics according to which terms that purport to refer to composite *F*s instead refer plurally to simples arranged *F*-wise, and predicates that purport to ascribe properties to single composite objects instead ascribe plural properties to pluralities of simples, and so on (Liggins 2008, Contessa 2014). Given such a semantics, nihilists can agree with the manyist that, for example, my mug exists and that it is identical to a certain plurality of simples arranged mug-wise (for the nihilist the latter follows immediately from the claim that 'my mug' refers to that plurality of simples arranged mug-wise). Indeed, as long as her semantics are sophisticated enough, it looks as though the nihilist can say *everything* that the manyist says. All she has to do is to stipulate that 'composition' expresses the relation of many–many identity, that 'parthood' expresses the relation of amonghood, and so on, and she'll be able to copy the manyist's description of reality word for word.

Where, then, is the daylight between manyism and this sort of nihilism? The question is especially worrisome for manyists in light of the fact that Cameron has suggested that the only way in which the supporter of *CAI* distinguishes herself from a 'fancy talking nihilist' is via her commitment to the oneness of composite objects, i.e. to her claim that when many simples jointly compose (and thus are identical to) a composite object they are identical to something that is one in number (2012: 547). Perhaps that, then, is why *CAI*'s claim that composite objects are each one in number is so vital: if we join the manyist in denying it, then we end up as nihilists.

The manyist response to this grows out of the answer to the question of why it would be so *bad* for manyists for their view to end up being a form of nihilism. The answer to that question, surely, is that for all her fancy semantics there remains an important, ontologically heavyweight sense in which the nihilist denies the existence of composite objects. We can leave open here how exactly the fancy talking nihilist should characterise this 'ontologically heavyweight' sense. Perhaps she'll want to maintain that *really* (Cameron 2008: 6–7), or *strictly speaking*, there are no composite objects; perhaps she'll clarify that *when in the context of the ontology room* it's true that there are no composite objects (van Inwagen 1990: 101–103); perhaps she'll say that composite objects are not among the *truthmakers*, and as such that she is not *ontologically committed* to them (Cameron 2008, 2010); perhaps she'll insist that composite objects are not in the domain of the most *fundamental, perfectly joint-carving* quantifier (Sider 2013: §3; see also Sider 2011). The point is that if nihilists say none of these things, nor anything like them, then they aren't nihilists any more. And indeed, this is why nihilism remains unacceptable to most. Here's how Markosian puts the point:

Speaking for myself, at least, the relevant intuition is not merely that sentences like (2) [i.e. 'There is a chair in the corner'] are sometimes, loosely speaking, true; rather, the relevant intuition is that there *really* are such composite objects as stars and chairs…That is, according to my intuitions, there simply are far more composite objects *in the world* than Nihilism allows.   (1998: 220–221, emphasis mine)

Plausibly, the effect of locutions like 'there really are' and 'in the world' is to make salient the most ontologically heavyweight reading of the phrases in which they feature. Interpreted thus, I think Markosian's intuition here is widespread. Most of us think that there really are composite objects out there in the world. No nihilist can agree with that.

But manyists can. Composite objects, says the manyist, really, strictly speaking, exist; it's true that they exist even when we're in the context of the ontology room; they are among the truthmakers, and are in the domain of the most fundamental, perfectly joint-carving quantifier. On manyism, there is *no* ontologically significant sense on which composite objects do not exist.[38] Of course, that's not to say that there is no sense at all on which the manyist thinks that composite objects do not exist. The manyist is as capable as everyone else of using the ordinary singular existential quantifier, and given her claim that composite objects are mere manys, she must say that when 'exists' is stipulated to express the ordinary singular quantifier it's false that composite objects exist. But the point is that the manyist denies that the sense of 'exists' that corresponds to the singular existential quantifier is the ontologically important or heavyweight sense. In line with her quasi-Quineanism (see §2.2.2), the manyist thinks that what we mean by 'exist-ence' is really captured by the plural existential quantifier, and as such that this meaning of 'existence' is the one that is ontologically significant. On this sense of 'existence', it's true that composite objects *qua* mere manys exist.[39]

So manyism is distinct from nihilism in precisely the way that it needs to be to avoid the counterintuitive consequences of that view. The manyist, but not the nihilist, accepts the existence of composite objects even when we

---

[38] Cf. Turner's way of distinguishing *CAI* from nihilism: "[given CAI], *even when speaking with all metaphysical seriousness*, we can truly say that there's a glass" (2013: 315, emphasis original).

[39] An analogy may be helpful here: the singular existential quantifier is to the manyist a bit like what a quantifier that is restricted to range only over *fundamenta* is to ordinary metaphys-icians who posit both fundamenta and non-fundamenta. Ordinary metaphysicians can pre-sumably *use* the restricted quantifier if they like, but they'll insist that it is only a restricted version of the quantifier that corresponds to what we really mean by 'existence'.

stipulate that we are speaking in the most ontologically heavyweight way possible, and nothing about the manyist's conception of composite objects as mere manys prevents her from doing so.[40] The upshot is that we do not need to say that composite objects are each one in number in order to secure their existence.

2.4 Conclusion

Manyism rejects an assumption that is otherwise more or less ubiquitous in metaphysics, namely the assumption that composite objects are each one in number. Good things follow from dropping this assumption: manyism is not only coherent, but also well-motivated. Most notably, it joins CAI in being able to account for the intimacy of parthood in a way that no other view can (and plausibly it can even claim to do so *better* than CAI). More generally, I've argued that by accepting CAI's claim that the relation of composition is just the relation of identity, manyism co-opts all of the formidable benefits that CAI secures. But I've also argued that by taking composite objects to be mere manys, manyism avoids CAI's fatal flaw, namely its commitment to many–one identities. I think we should all be impressed by what CAI gets right about composition, and disappointed in equal measure by what it gets wrong about identity and number. Manyism is what happens when we fix what CAI gets wrong. McDaniel once wrote that CAI is 'an intuition in search of a formulation' (2008: 128). Manyism is not accurately categorised as a species of CAI. But nonetheless, perhaps in it we have found the formulation we were looking for.

Acknowledgements

Special thanks to Jonathan Tallant, Nikk Effingham, and Dave Ingram for comments and discussion of earlier drafts of this chapter, and to Karen Bennett and the referees for *Oxford Studies in Metaphysics* for their many helpful

---

[40] I've focused here on the manyist's ability to accept the genuine existence of composite objects, but note also that the manyist likewise accepts that some composite objects really bear mereological relations to other objects, and really admit of multiple decompositions into parts, and so on. Thus manyism is not vulnerable to the concern, floated by an anonymous referee, that it fails to capture reality's putative complex compositional structure (cf. Bennett 2009: 59–60).

suggestions. I'm also very grateful to the Mind Association for funding my research whilst I wrote this chapter.

References

Barker, S. and Jago, M. (2018) 'Material Objects and Essential Bundle Theory' in *Philosophical Studies* 175: 2969–2986.

Baxter, D. (1998a) 'Identity in the Loose and Popular Sense' in *Mind* 97(388): 575–582.

Baxter, D. (1988b) 'Many-One Identity' in *Philosophical Papers*, 17: 193–216.

Baxter, D. (2014) 'Identity, Discernibility, and Composition' in A. Cotnoir and D. Baxter (eds) *Composition as Identity*. Oxford: Oxford University Press, pp. 244–254.

Baxter, D. and Cotnoir, A. (eds) (2014) *Composition As Identity*. Oxford: Oxford University Press.

Bennett, J. (1987) 'Substratum' in *History of Philosophy Quarterly* 4(2): 197–215.

Bennett, K. (2009) 'Composition, Colocation, and Metaontology' in D. Chalmers, M. Manley, and R. Wasserman (eds) *Metametaphysics*. Oxford: Oxford University Press, pp. 38–76.

Ben-Yami, H. (2013) 'Higher-Level Plurals versus Articulated Reference, and an Elaboration of *Salva Veritate*' in *Dialectica* 67(1): 81–102.

Black, M. (1971) 'The Elusiveness of Sets' in *The Review of Metaphysics* 24(4): 614–636.

Bohn, E. (2014) 'Unrestricted Composition as Identity' in A. Cotnoir and D. Baxter (eds) *Composition as Identity*. Oxford: Oxford University Press, pp. 143–168.

Boolos, G. (1984) 'To Be Is To Be A Value Of A Variable (Or To Be Some Values Of Some Variables)' in *The Journal of Philosophy* 81(8): 430–449.

Calosi, C. (2016) 'Composition is Identity and Mereological Nihilism' in *The Philosophical Quarterly* 66: 219–235.

Cameron, R. (2007) 'The Contingency of Composition' in *Philosophical Studies* 136(1): 99–121.

Cameron, R. (2008) 'Truthmakers and Ontological Commitment' in *Philosophical Studies* 140(1): 1–18.

Cameron, R. (2010) 'How to Have a Radically Minimal Ontology' in *Philosophical Studies* 151(2): 249–264.

Cameron, R. (2012) 'Composition as Identity Doesn't Settle the Special Composition Question' in *Philosophy and Phenomenological Research* 84(3): 532–554.

Cameron, R. (2014) 'Parts Generate the Whole But They Are Not Identical to It' in A. Cotnoir and D. Baxter (eds), *Composition as Identity*. Oxford: Oxford University Press, pp. 91–110.

Cantor, G. (1883/1932) 'Abhandlungen zur Mengenlehre' in G. Cantor, *Gesammelte Abhandlungen*, ed. E. Zermelo. Berlin: Springer-Verlag, pp. 115–356.

Carey, S. (2009) *The Origin of Concepts*. Oxford: Oxford University Press.

Carmichael, C. (2015) 'Toward a Commonsense Answer to the Special Composition Question' in *Australasian Journal of Philosophy* 93(3): 475–490.

Contessa, G. (2014) 'One's a Crowd: Mereological Nihilism without Ordinary-Object Eliminativism' in *Analytic Philosophy* 55(2): 199–221.

Cotnoir, A. (2013) 'Composition as general identity' in D. Zimmerman and K. Bennett (eds) *Oxford Studies in Metaphysics vol. 8*. Oxford: Oxford University Press, pp. 294–322,

Cowling, S. (2013) 'Ideological Parsimony' in *Synthese* 190: 3889–3908,

Eddington, A. (1929) *The Nature of the Physical World*. Cambridge: Cambridge University Press.

Fine, K. (1975) 'Vagueness, Truth, and Logic' in *Synthese* 30(3/4): 265–300.

Harte, V. (2002) *Plato on Parts and Wholes: The Metaphysics of Structure*. Oxford: Oxford University Press.

Hazen, A. (1997) 'Relations in Lewis's Framework Without Atoms' in *Analysis* 57(4): 243–248.

Heil, J. (2003) *From an Ontological Point of View*. Oxford: Oxford University Press.

Hewitt, S. (2015) 'When Do Some Things Form a Set?' in *Philosophia Mathematica* 23(3): 311–337.

Hirsch, E. (2002) 'Quantifier Variance and Realism' in *Philosophical Issues* 12: 51–73.

Hoffman, J. and Rosenkrantz, G. (1997) *Substance: Its Nature and Existence*. London: Routledge.

Korman, D. (2019) 'Easy Ontology Without Deflationary Metaontology' in *Philosophy and Phenomenological Research* 99(1): 236–243.

Kreisel, G. (1969) 'Two Notes on the Foundations of Set-Theory' in *Dialectica* 23(2): 93–114.

Kripke, S. (1980) *Naming and Necessity*. Oxford: Blackwell.

Lewis, D. (1986) *On the Plurality of Worlds*. Oxford: Blackwell.

Lewis, D. (1991) *Parts of Classes*. Oxford: Blackwell.

Liggins, D. (2008) 'Nihilism Without Self-Contradiction' in *Royal Institute of Philosophy Supplement* 62: 177–196.

Linnebo, O. (2017) 'Plural Quantification' in E. Zalta (ed.) *The Stanford Encyclopedia of Philosophy*. Available at: https://plato.stanford.edu/archives/sum2017/entries/plural-quant/, accessed on 31.1.2020.

Loss, R. (2018) 'A Sudden Collapse to Nihilism' in *The Philosophical Quarterly* 68(271): 370–375.

McDaniel, K. (2008) 'Against Composition as Identity' in *Analysis* 68(2): 128–133.

McDaniel, K. (2013) 'Existence and Number' in *Analytic Philosophy* 54(2): 209–228.

McKay, T. (2006) *Plural Predication*. Oxford: Oxford University Press.

Markosian, N. (1998) 'Brutal Composition' in *Philosophical Studies* 92(3): 211–249.

Merricks, T. (1999) 'Composition as Identity, Mereological Essentialism, and Counterpart Theory' in *Australasian Journal of Philosophy* 77(2): 192–195.

Merricks, T. (2005) 'Composition and Vagueness' in *Mind* 114(455): 615–637.

Oliver, A. and Smiley, T. (2016) *Plural Logic*. Oxford: Oxford University Press.

Putnam, H. (1975) 'The Meaning of "Meaning"' in *Minnesota Studies in the Philosophy of Science* 7: 131–193.

Quine, W. (1953) *From a Logical Point of View*, 2nd edition. London: Harvard University Press.

Rayo, A. (2006) 'Beyond Plurals' in A. Rayo and G. Uzquiano (eds) *Absolute Generality*. Oxford: Oxford University Press, pp. 220–254.

Rose, D. and Schaffer, J. (2017) 'Folk Mereology is Teleological' in *Noûs* 51(2): 238–270.

Rosen, G. and Dorr, C. (2002) 'Composition as a Fiction' in R. Gale (ed.) *The Blackwell Guide to Metaphysics*. Oxford: Blackwell, pp. 151–174.

Russell, B. (1903) *The Principles of Mathematics*. Cambridge: Cambridge University Press.

Schaffer, J. (2003) 'Is There a Fundamental Level?' in *Noûs* 37(3): 498–517.

Schaffer, J. (2015) 'What Not to Multiply Without Necessity' in *Australasian Journal of Philosophy* 94(4): 644–664.

Sider, T. (1993) 'Van Inwagen and the Possibility of Gunk' in *Analysis* 53: 286–289.

Sider, T. (2001) *Four Dimensionalism*. Oxford: Oxford University Press.

Sider, T. (2007) 'Parthood' in *The Philosophical Review* 116(1): 51–91.

Sider, T. (2011) *Writing the Book of the World*. Oxford: Oxford University Press.

Sider, T. (2013) 'Against Parthood' in D. Zimmerman and K. Bennett (eds) *Oxford Studies in Metaphysics vol. 8*. Oxford: Oxford University Press, pp. 237–293.

Simons, P. (1987) *Parts: A Study in Ontology*. Oxford: Oxford University Press.

Simons, P. (2003) 'The Universe' in *Ratio* 16(3): 236–250.

Thomasson, A. (2009) 'Answerable and Unanswerable Questions' in D. Chalmers, D. Manley, and R. Wasserman (eds) *Metametaphysics*. Oxford: Oxford University Press, pp. 444–471.

Thomasson, A. (2015) *Ontology Made Easy*. Oxford: Oxford University Press.

Turner, J. (2013) 'Existence and Many-One Identity' in *The Philosophical Quarterly* 63(251): 313–329.

Turner, J. (2014) 'Donald Baxter's Composition as Identity' in A. Cotnoir and D. Baxter (eds) *Composition as Identity*. Oxford: Oxford University Press, pp. 225–243.

Uzquiano, G. (2004) 'Plurals and Simples' in *The Monist* 87(3): 429–451.

Van Inwagen, P. (1990) *Material Beings*. Ithaca, NY: Cornell University Press.

Van Inwagen, P. (1998) 'Meta-Ontology' in *Erkenntnis* 48: 233–250.

Varzi, A. (2014) 'Counting and Countenancing' in A. Cotnoir and D. Baxter (eds) *Composition as Identity*. Oxford: Oxford University Press, pp. 47–69.

Wallace, M. (2011a) 'Composition as Identity: Part 1' in *Philosophy Compass* 6(11): 804–816.

Wallace, M. (2011b) 'Composition as Identity: Part 2' in *Philosophy Compass* 6(11): 817–827.

Whitehead, A. and Russell, B. (1962) *Principia Mathematica*. Cambridge: Cambridge University Press.

Williams, R. (2006) 'Illusions of Gunk' in *Philosophical Perspectives* 20: 493–513.

Yi, B-U. (2014) 'Is There A Plural Object?' in A. Cotnoir and D. Baxter (eds) *Composition as Identity*. Oxford: Oxford University Press, pp. 169–191.

3

A Special Composition Puzzle

Joshua Spencer

3.1 Introduction

The Special Composition Question may be formulated as follows:

For any *x*s whatsoever, what are the individually necessary and jointly sufficient conditions those *x*s must satisfy in order for it to be true that there is a *y* such that those *x*s compose *y*?[1]

This question has generated quite a bit of discussion over the past couple of decades and several answers have been skillfully defended in the literature. Unfortunately, I believe that there is a puzzle for which, given many of the most ably defended answers, there is no obvious solution. In this chapter, I present the puzzle in the abstract and then demonstrate the strength of the puzzle by considering two instances involving prominent answers to The Special Composition Question. Finally, I show how defenders of a less prominent answer to The Special Composition Question might plausibly respond to the puzzle and I conclude with a general lesson about what a correct answer to The Special Composition Question might look like. The lesson I take away from this discussion is that we should take more seriously The General Composition Question:

For any *x*s whatsoever and *for any y*, what are the individually necessary and jointly sufficient conditions those *x*s must satisfy in order for it to be true that those *x*s compose *that y*?

---

[1] See van Inwagen (1990) for an initial formulation of the question. My formulation follows Markosian (2008, 2014) and is a mere notational variant of van Inwagen's.

Joshua Spencer, *A Special Composition Puzzle* In: *Oxford Studies in Metaphysics Volume 13*. Edited by: Karen Bennett and Dean W. Zimmerman, Oxford University Press. © Joshua Spencer 2023.
DOI: 10.1093/oso/9780192886033.003.0003

For I believe that those who endorse answers to the General Composition Question and corresponding answers to the Special Composition Question are often better-positioned to answer this puzzle than those who don't.

3.2 The Puzzle

The puzzle is generated with an assumption about how the conditions of composition relate to composition itself. Specifically, I assume that an answer to The Special Composition Question provides conditions that are not meant merely to be necessarily co-extensive with the occurrence of composition, but rather that are meant to *explain* why composition occurs. I will say that an answer to The Special Composition Question purports to provide the conditions that *fully ground* or, henceforth, *ground* composition.[2,3] But I do not take a stand on whether or not *grounding* is a unique relation of metaphysical explanation; nor do I take a stand on whether or not *grounding* is primitive.[4] I assume, just for simplicity of exposition, that *grounding* relates facts or true propositions. I assume, as a substantive thesis, that *grounding* connections imply necessary connections. Specifically, I assume every instance of the schema: if [φ] grounds [ψ], then it is necessary that if [φ], then [ψ].[5] Finally, I assume the substantive thesis that existential facts are grounded in

---

[2] Van Inwagen (1990) says that an answer to The Special Composition Question must be informative. If an informative answer is an answer that explains why composition occurs, then anyone who accepts van Inwagen's informativeness constraint might be subject to the puzzle I present. Markosian (2014) explicitly claims that when we answer The Special Composition Question, we are attempting to give the conditions in virtue of which composition occurs. Anyone who agrees with Markosian will be subject to the puzzle I present.

[3] Some might claim that answers to The Special Composition Question merely purport to provide *partial grounds* for composition. If those partial grounds are part of some full grounds for composition, then the puzzle I present will still apply. Admittedly, the puzzle will not be a puzzle specifically about The Special Composition Question; it will be a puzzle about what we might call "The Strong Special Composition Question," a question that explicitly asks about the *full* grounds for composition. One might claim, in response to the puzzle, that those partial grounds are not part of *any* full grounds for composition, perhaps because there are no full grounds for composition at all. In that case, we will have learned something interesting about the nature of composition. Specifically, we will have learned that there are no full grounds for composition and that lesson may open the door to a variety of hitherto unconsidered answers to The Special Composition Question. Thanks to Kris McDaniel for discussing this with me.

[4] Hence, everything I say in this chapter is compatible with Wilson's (2014) conclusion that there are several distinct grounding relations, some of which are analyzable. That does not mean, however, that anyone who agrees with Wilson and accepts some several distinct grounding relations will be subject to the following puzzle.

[5] The claim that grounding connections imply necessary connections is defended by, among others, Audi (2012a, 2012b), Correia and Schnieder (2012), deRosset (2010, 2013), Rosen

their instances. Specifically, I assume every instance of the schema: if [φa] is a true instance of [∃xφx], then [φa] grounds [∃xφx].⁶

Now let's generate the puzzle. An answer to The Special Composition Question should provide conditions, C, such that for any *x*s, if those *x*s satisfy C, then the fact that those *x*s are C grounds the fact that there is a *y* such that those *x*s compose *y*. So, let's consider some particular particles that compose a large complex object, like an organism, and let's call them "Bits."⁷ The following, then, will be true:

(1)   [Bits are C] grounds [there is a *y* such that the Bits compose *y*].

But if there is a *y* such that Bits compose *y*, then there is a particular *y*, call it "Whole," such that Bits compose it. Moreover, since the claim that there is a *y* such that Bits compose *y* is an existential proposition, it must be grounded in its instances. Hence, the following seems to be true:

(2)   [Bits compose Whole] grounds [there is a *y* such that Bits compose *y*].

It seems to follow, then, that the existential claim that there is a *y* such that Bits compose *y* is grounded *both* in the claim that Bits are C and in the claim that Bits compose Whole. But I will argue below that (1) and (2) would constitute an unacceptable overdetermination of grounding explanation. If they constitute an unacceptable overdetermination of grounding explanation, then the following is true:

(3)   It is not the case that both [Bits are C] grounds [there is a *y* such that the Bits compose *y*] and [Bits compose Whole] grounds [there is a *y* such that Bits compose *y*].

This piece of the puzzle is difficult to motivate. After all, I am not categorically opposed to overdetermination of grounding explanation. If Magpie and Possum are cats, then the fact that there is a cat is grounded both in the

(2010), and Trogdon (2013). Fine (2012) endorses similar principles according to which grounding connections imply some sort of necessary connections. For the opposing view, see Skiles (2015).
  ⁶ This principle is endorsed by Correia and Schnieder (2012), Fine (2012), and Rosen (2012). For an interesting argument against this principle see Melamedoff (2018).
  ⁷ Please note that Bits need not be arbitrarily chosen. We just need one example to generate the puzzle and an example involving particles that compose a complex organism seems to work quite well.

fact that Magpie is a cat and in the fact that Possum is a cat. But that's an acceptable instance of overdetermination. Why should we believe, then, that the composition case is an *unacceptable* case of explanatory overdetermination? In other words, why should we believe that (3) is true?

Let's pause for a moment to think about causal overdetermination. Suppose we find someone dead in the forest and find that there seem to be two sufficient causes of his death. Those two sufficient causes might be *explanatorily dependent* on one another; that is, they might have a common cause or ground or one of them might have been a cause or ground of the other. If the causes were explanatorily dependent on one another, then there would be an explanation for the overdetermination and, consequently, the overdetermination would be acceptable. For example, if we were to discover that the person died from two gunshot wounds and that the wounds were inflicted by two different soldiers in a firing squad, then the fact that there are two sufficient causes for his death could be explained by the further fact that those causes were explanatorily linked to one another by being part of the same firing squad.

On the other hand, although unlikely, it's certainly possible that the two causes of death are *explanatorily independent* of one another; that is, it's possible that they have no common cause or ground and that neither of them caused or grounded the other. In that case, although we might seek an explanation of the unlikely coincidence, there *might* be nothing unacceptable about the overdetermination itself.

However, if we were to discover *a counterfactual* dependence between the two causes, then it would be harder to maintain that they really were *explanatorily* independent of one another. Why? Because there is some sort of intimate connection between counterfactuals dependency and explanatory dependency. I am inclined to believe that explanatory dependencies partly ground counterfactual dependencies, but there are others who think the partial grounding goes the other way around.[8] Either way, it seems prima facie unacceptable for there to be two explanatorily independent overdetermining causes that are nevertheless counterfactually dependent on one another.

Causal connections and grounding connections are in the same family; they are both explanatory connections. Given that fact, there are similarities

---

[8] David Lewis (1973), for example, holds a counterfactual account of causation according to which causal connections are understood partly in terms of counterfactual connections. Lewis, however, might not be happy with the "grounding" talk.

between causation and grounding. So, if it is prima facie unacceptable for there to be two explanatorily independent overdetermining causes that are nevertheless counterfactually dependent on one another, then it seems like it would also be prima facie unacceptable for there to be two explanatorily independent overdetermining grounds that are nevertheless counterfactually dependent on one another. But we don't necessarily need to see causation and grounding as members of the same family to see that the principle about overdetermining grounds is true. The fact that the two overdetermining factors are *causes* doesn't seem to be playing an essential role in this discussion. *Generally* speaking it seems prima facie unacceptable for there to be two explanatorily independent factors that are nevertheless counterfactually dependent. If the general claim is true, then it follows that it is prima facie unacceptable for there to be two explanatorily independent overdetermining grounds that are nevertheless counterfactually dependent. Or, to put it the other way around, if two grounds are counterfactually dependent on one another, then, prima facie, we should think that there is a common cause or ground of those two grounds or that one of those grounds causes or grounds the other one.

Before moving on, I would like to introduce a caveat to the discussion so far. Causes are typically contingent, but some grounds might be necessary. Suppose that there are two facts, F_1 and F_2, each of which is necessary. Given the standard theory of counterfactuals, then, those two facts will be counterfactually dependent on one another. After all, if F_1 is necessarily true, then if F_1 had *not* been the case, then F_2 would not have been the case turns out to be a counterfactual with a necessarily false antecedent. But supposedly a counterfactual with a necessarily false antecedent is vacuously true. Similarly, if F_2 had not been the case, then F_1 would not have been the case is also vacuously true. Hence, F_1 and F_2 are counterfactually dependent on one another. But arguably there is nothing even prima facie unacceptable about explanatorily independent facts that are *vacuously* counterfactually dependent on one another. Now, I am inclined to reject the claim that counterfactuals with necessarily false antecedents are vacuously true. But I don't think I need to reject the standard view of counterfactuals in order to generate the puzzle of this chapter. So, instead, I will just introduce a caveat to our principle: it is prima facie unacceptable for there to be two explanatorily independent *and contingent* grounds that are counterfactually dependent on one another.

Typically, then, if a fact has two explanatorily independent grounds each one of which is contingently true, then those grounds should be counterfactually independent of one another as well. So, for example, even though the fact that there is a cat is grounded in the fact that Magpie is a cat and also in the fact that Possum is a cat, that overdetermination is acceptable. Why? Because, assuming that neither Magpie nor Possum is a parent of the other, that is, assuming that the facts in question are explanatorily independent, the facts would also be counterfactually independent. If the claim that Magpie is a cat had been false, perhaps in a circumstance in which Magpie is never born, the claim that Possum is a cat would still have been true; moreover, if the claim that Possum is a cat had been false, if Possum had never been born, then the claim that Magpie is a cat would still have been true. These independent grounds are counterfactually independent of one another. The overdetermination does not seem to be prima facie unacceptable.

But now consider the two grounds of [there is a y such that Bits compose y]; i.e., consider [Bits are C] and [Bits compose Whole]. Plausibly, those two grounds are counterfactually dependent on one another. After all, Bits can't compose anything if they don't satisfy the conditions of composition. So, if Bits had not been C, if they had not satisfied the conditions of composition, then they wouldn't have composed anything. Hence, they would not have composed Whole. That's the easy direction of counterfactual dependence. The other direction of counterfactual dependence is harder to establish, but it's very plausible given certain moderate views of composition. Recall that Bits are some particles that compose a complex organism, Whole. Let's suppose that just a few hours before Bits composed Whole, some of Bits were parts of an apple while others were parts of Whole. If Bits had not composed Whole, then that would have been because Whole did not eat an apple or Whole did not eat the particular parts of an apple that Whole in fact ate. In any case, if Bits had not composed Whole, then some of Bits would have remained scattered from others, perhaps because some of them would have remained parts of an apple whereas others would have been parts of Whole. So, given certain moderate views of composition, if Bits had not composed Whole, then they would have been scattered and hence would not have composed anything else. So, at least on some views of composition, if Bits had not composed Whole, then Bits would not have been C.

One might respond to the foregoing motivation by claiming that the two grounds in question are not really explanatorily independent of one another. It might be that one of these two grounding facts is grounded in the other. That is, it might be either that [Bits are C] grounds [Bits compose Whole] or that [Bits compose Whole] grounds [Bits are C]. Consider the first case. If [Bits are C] grounds [Bits compose Whole], then it is necessary that if

[Bits are C], then [Bits compose Whole]. But, typically, some things can satisfy the conditions of composition without composing the particular thing that they in fact compose. For example, some particles that in fact compose a particular organism might have composed something completely different, perhaps an organism of a completely different species or maybe even a non-organic unity.[9] So, it is not necessary that if [Bits are C], then [Bits compose Whole]. Hence it is not the case that [Bits are C] grounds [Bits compose Whole]. On the other hand, it seems as though the claim that [Bits compose Whole] grounds [Bits are C] gets things backwards in an important respect. Mereological facts generally, and composition facts in particular, are not fundamental facts. To claim that [Bits compose Whole] grounds [Bits are C] leaves the particular compositional fact, [Bits compose Whole], unexplained and hence (relatively) fundamental. So, it seems that neither of these two grounding facts grounds the other.[10]

Finally, one might claim that the two grounding facts are not independent of one another because they have a common ground. Although I will ultimately defend a solution to the puzzle that involves this kind of response, it's not obvious how this kind of response might be accommodated given the most ably defended answers to The Special Composition Question. So, let's turn to a few instances of the puzzle before I present my preferred solution.

3.3 Instances of the Puzzle

Above, I presented the puzzle in the abstract. But the details of the puzzle might vary a bit when we consider particular theories of composition. So,

[9] Skiles (2015: 722) has some nice examples that motivate the claim that some *xs* that compose *y* might have composed something other than y. We might suppose that Bits are slowly swapped out of Whole in a Ship of Theseus style transition that preserves Whole through the process and that Bits are rearranged to form a duplicate of Whole at the end of the process. Since, at the end of the process, Bits compose a duplicate of Whole and Whole is composed of some things other than Bits, it seems that Bits satisfy the conditions of composition without composing Whole. Although I like Skiles' examples, I think it is independently intuitively plausible that some *xs* that compose *y* might have composed something other than *y*. Thanks to Kris McDaniel for pointing me toward Skiles' examples.
[10] I find it intuitively plausible that compositional facts are not fundamental. An anonymous reviewer, though, has suggested to me that this premise follows from the claim that composite objects are always less fundamental than their parts in conjunction with the claim that a fundamental fact can only involve fundamental entities. If Whole is less fundamental than Bits, then [Bits compose Whole] will be a fact that involves a non-fundamental entity, namely Whole. Hence [Bits compose Whole] cannot be a fundamental fact. The claim that fundamental facts can only involve fundamental entities is akin to Sider's (2011) Purity Thesis. Although the Purity Thesis is plausible, some people who believe in grounding will want to reject it.

let's look at a couple of plausible answers to The Special Composition Question and see how they fare with respect to this puzzle. First, let's look at The Life View:

Necessarily, for any xs, there is a y such that those xs compose y iff the activities of those xs constitute a life or those xs are one in number.[11]

Now let's consider a particular case of composition. Let's call the mereological simples that compose Magpie right now 'Simples'. If an answer to The Special Composition Question should provide conditions, C, such that for any xs, if those xs satisfy C, then the fact that those xs are C grounds the fact that there is a y such that those xs compose y, then given The Life View it follows that:

(1L)   [The activities of Simples constitute a life] grounds [there is a y such that Simples compose y].

But since existential facts are grounded in their instances, it also seems to be true that:

(2L)   [Simples compose Magpie] grounds [there is a y such that Simples compose y].

Finally, if these were both true, then [there is a y such that Simples compose y] would seem to have two explanatorily independent grounds. But this over-determination is prima facie unacceptable. We can use our counterfactual test, in this case, to see that the overdetermination would be prima facie unacceptable. The fact that Simples compose Magpie and the fact that the activities of Simples constitute a life are counterfactually dependent on one another. If the claim that Simples compose Magpie had been false, then those very simples wouldn't have composed anything else; they would have just remained a somewhat loosely scattered bunch of simples, some of them parts of Magpie while others were parts of an uneaten bit of kibble. Moreover, if the claim that the activities of Simples constitute a life had been false, then (given the view in question) those simples would not have composed any-thing, much less Magpie. It looks, then, as if we have a case of unacceptable overdetermination of grounding. Hence, the following seems true:

---

[11] Famously defended by van Inwagen (1990).

(3L)   It is not the case that both [The activities of Simples constitute a life] grounds [there is a y such that Simples compose y] and [Simples compose Magpie] grounds [there is a y such that Simples compose y].

So, The Life View fits into our puzzle.

Again, one might try to respond by claiming either that [the activities of Simples constitute a life] grounds [Simples compose Magpie] or that [Simples compose Magpie] grounds [the activities of Simples constitute a life]. The former option cannot be correct, since it's possible for the activities of Simples to constitute a life without composing Magpie. After all, their activities might have constituted a life while they composed a completely different organism. The latter option cannot be correct since it leaves the particular compositional fact, the fact that Simples compose Magpie, as a (relatively) fundamental fact. Finally, one might claim that some third fact grounds both [the activities of Simples constitute a life] and [Simples compose Magpie]. But no such fact has been advanced by defenders of The Life View and it's hard to see what that fact might be.[12]

Now let's look at a different answer to The Special Composition Question, Universalism.

Necessarily, for any xs, there is a y such that those xs compose y iff each of those xs exists.[13]

Some people who endorse Universalism also endorse Mereological Essentialism, the thesis that, necessarily, every composite object has its parts essentially. Mereological Essentialism seems naturally combined with what we might call "Mereological Sufficialism," the thesis that, necessarily, if some things compose an object, o, then necessarily, if those objects compose anything at all, they compose o. But for the purposes of this chapter, I would like to focus on a version of Universalism that is *not* combined with either Mereological Essentialism or Mereological Sufficialism.[14]

---

[12] However, in footnote 18 I sketch a third-fact-involving view that might be advocated by someone who defends a slight variant of The Life View.

[13] Universalism has been defended by, among many others, Heller (1990), Hudson (2001), Lewis (1986), Sider (2001), and Van Cleve (1986; 2008).

[14] Rea (1998; 2002; 2010) explicitly defends a version of Universalism while rejecting Mereological Essentialism. Chisholm (1973) and van Cleve (1986) both endorse versions of Universalism that are combined with Mereological Essentialism. For the record, the combination of Universalism and Mereological Sufficialism, along with certain theses about what

Now consider a particular case of composition. Let's call the wrought iron beams that compose The Eiffel Tower 'Beams'. If an answer to The Special Composition Question should provide conditions, C, such that for any *xs*, if those *xs* satisfy C, then the fact that those *xs* are C grounds the fact that there is a *y* such that those *xs* compose *y*, then given Universalism it seem to follow that:

(1U)   [Beams exist] grounds [there is a *y* such that beams compose *y*]

But since existential facts are grounded in their instances, it also seems to be true that:

(2U)   [Beams compose The Eiffel Tower] grounds [there is a *y* such that Beams compose *y*].

But if [Beams compose The Eiffel Tower] and [Beams exist] were both grounds for [there is a *y* such that Beams compose *y*], then [there is a *y* such that Beams compose *y*] would have two explanatorily independent grounds. In this case, however, there is no mutual counterfactual dependence. If Beams had not existed, then Beams would not have composed anything and hence would not have composed The Eiffel Tower. So, there is a one-way counterfactual dependence. But the counterfactual dependence doesn't obviously go in the other direction. After all, even if Beams had not composed The Eiffel Tower, they might still have existed, perhaps as a pile of unused wrought-iron beams. But in this case, the one-way counterfactual dependence still seems problematic and, intuitively, the overdetermination is still unacceptable.

What's weird about Universalism is that the conditions of composition, mere existence, are necessarily had by any things whatsoever. That's what undermines one direction of the counterfactual dependence. But set aside

grounds what, has the resources to respond to the puzzle of this chapter. For, arguably, given that combination of theses, one would be able to formulate an answer to the General Composition Question. Let *f* be a function that takes a plurality of things, the *xs*, to the unique object that they compose if they compose anything at all. Given Mereological Sufficialism, we might claim that, necessarily, for any *xs* and any *y*, the *xs* compose *y* iff the *xs* exist and $y=f(xs)$. Moreover, one might claim that the existence of the *xs* grounds the existence of $f(xs)$ and thereby also grounds that there is a *y* such that the *xs* compose *y*. Hence, even though there is overdetermination of grounds, there is a common ground that explains that overdetermination. This is an instance of a strategy, which I endorse in section 3.4, for responding to the Special Composition Puzzle. Thanks to Dean Zimmerman for suggesting that one version of Universalism might have the resources to respond to the puzzle.

Universalism for a second and consider the following case. Let's suppose that the conditions of composition, C, are not necessarily had by any things whatsoever. Let's suppose that some things don't compose anything at all. And let's suppose that some things that do compose something could have, in a very distant possible scenario, failed to compose anything at all. Perhaps the conditions are that the activities of the xs constitute a life or something like that. But additionally let's suppose that, by pure coincidence, for any composing things whatsoever, if they had not composed the thing that they in fact compose, then they would have composed something else. That is, by coincidence, for any composing things whatsoever, if they had not composed the thing that they in fact compose, then they still would have satisfied condition C. Given this set-up, although it's possible for some things to fail to satisfy C, whenever they do satisfy C, they also do so in all nearby possible scenarios. In that case, even though the two-way counterfactual dependence would be undermined, the overdetermination would not thereby be acceptable. It seems to me that this coincidence case is a lot like the Universalism case. There is an accidental quirk that prevents the two-way counterfactual dependence, but this accident is not a feature and cannot be plausibly used to *explain* the overdetermination. This bolsters my intuition that the overdetermination in the universalism case is unacceptable. So, the following still seems plausible to me:

(3U)   It is not the case that both [Beams exist] grounds [there is a y such that Beams compose y] and [Beams compose The Eiffel Tower] grounds [there is a y such that Beams compose y].

So, Universalism fits into our puzzle too.

One might try to respond by claiming either that [Beam exists] grounds [Beams compose The Eiffel Tower] or that [Beams compose The Eiffel Tower] grounds [Beams exist]. The former option cannot be correct since it's possible for Beams to exist without composing The Eiffel Tower. After all, those very beams might have been used in a completely different construction project. The latter option cannot be correct since it leaves the particular compositional fact, the fact that Beams compose The Eiffel Tower, as a fundamental ungrounded fact. Moreover, it just seems plainly obvious that [Beams exist] is not grounded in [Beams compose The Eiffel Tower]. Finally, one might try to claim that there is a common ground of [Beams exist] and [Beams compose The Eiffel Tower]. But it's hard to see what could possibly ground both the existence of Beams and the fact that Beams compose The Eiffel Tower.

3.4 A Spatial Approach to Mereology and General Composition

I want to point out one strategy for responding to the puzzle. Generally, I think it's a good idea to try to find a common ground for the problematic counterfactually dependent grounds I have noted. There may be several strategies for developing such a response to the puzzle. But I want to highlight just one such strategy. Recall that Peter van Inwagen introduced another question about composition, one that has received far less attention than the Special Composition Question. That other question is the General Composition Question:

For any *x*s and any *y*, what are the individually necessary and jointly sufficient conditions those *x*s must satisfy in order for it to be true that those *x*s compose *y*?

Some people think that there is a correct and explanatory answer to The General Composition Question and that a correct and explanatory answer to The Special Composition Question will just follow from our answer to The General Composition Question.[15,16] One answer to the General Composition Question is General Regionalism:

Necessarily, for any *x*s and any *y*, those *x*s compose that *y* iff the union of the regions occupied by those *x*s is occupied by *y*.

Moreover, an answer to The Special Composition Question, let's call it "Special Regionalism," seems to follow:

Necessarily, for any *x*s, there is a *y* such that those *x*s compose *y* iff there is a *y* such that the union of the regions occupied by those *x*s is occupied by *y*.[17]

---

[15] Van Inwagen (1990) notes that any answer to the General Composition Question will logically entail an answer to the Special Composition Question. However, he does not think that any such answer to The Special Composition Question will necessarily be the best or most informative or most interesting answer. His discussion of this point involves the General Regionalist view discussed in the rest of this section.

[16] I (Spencer, 2017) argue that an answer to The Special Composition Question follows from Strong Composition as Identity, which might be taken as an answer to The General Composition Question.

[17] A slight variant of this view was introduced and briefly discussed by van Inwagen (1990) and it has recently been defended by Markosian (2014).

Just as with the views I have discussed, this view is subject to The Special Composition Puzzle. Using The Eiffel Tower example, we get the following three inconsistent statements:

(1R)   [there is a *y* such that the union of the regions occupied by Beams is occupied by *y*] grounds [there is a *y* such that Beams compose *y*]

(2R)   [Beams compose The Eiffel Tower] grounds [there is a *y* such that Beams compose *y*].

(3R)   It is not the case that both [there is a *y* such that the union of the regions occupied by Beams is occupied by *y*] grounds [there is a *y* such that Beams compose *y*] and [Beams compose The Eiffel Tower] grounds [there is a *y* such that Beams compose *y*].

But, unlike the views I have discussed, the defender of General Regionalism can plausibly claim that there is a common ground to [there is a *y* such that the union of the regions occupied by Beams is occupied by *y*] and [Beams compose The Eiffel Tower]. In other words, the defender of General Regionalism can claim that the two overdetermining grounds are not explanatorily independent of one another. First, the defender can claim that [the union of the regions occupied by Beams is occupied by The Eiffel Tower] grounds [Beams compose The Eiffel Tower]. Why? Because answers to the General Composition Question provide the conditions that ground when the composition relation obtains between some things and the particular thing they compose. Second, since [the union of the regions occupied by Beams is occupied by The Eiffel Tower] is a true instance of [there is a *y* such that the union of the regions occupied by Beams is occupied by *y*], it follows that the former grounds the latter. Hence, [Beams compose The Eiffel Tower] and [there is a *y* such that the union of the regions occupied by Beams is occupied by *y*] have a common ground. If there is a common ground, then the facts in question are *not* explanatorily independent of one another. Moreover, their counterfactual dependence on one another can be explained by their mutual ground and their overdetermination of [there is a *y* such that Beams compose *y*] would be acceptable. Hence, the defender of General Regionalism could legitimately reject (3R) in this puzzle.[18]

---

[18] An anonymous reviewer has suggested that The Life View might be combined with the following answer to The General Composition Question: Necessarily, for any *x*s and any *y*, those

This sort of solution can be generalized. Suppose that there is an answer to the General Composition Question and that the conditions specified are the conditions that ground when some things stand in the composition relation to a whole:

Necessarily, for any xs and any y, those xs compose that y iff those xs R y.

Suppose we accept the corresponding answer to The Special Composition Question and accept that the conditions specified are the conditions that ground when composition of something or other occurs:

Necessarily, for any xs, there is a y such that those xs compose that y iff there is a y such that those xs R y.

Then, focusing on The Eiffel Tower case, we can say that [there is a y such that Beams R y] and [beams compose The Eiffel Tower] both ground [there is a y such that Beams compose y]. But the overdetermination is acceptable because [Beams R The Eiffel Tower] grounds both [there is a y such that Beams R y] and [beams compose The Eiffel Tower].

I want to emphasize that for this strategy to be successful, at least two conditions must be met. First, there must be an answer to the General Composition Question which, for any xs and any y, provides *grounds* for the xs composing y. Second, there must be an answer to the Special Composition Question, entailed by our answer to the General Composition Question, and which, for any xs, provides *grounds* for the xs composing something or other. So, for example, someone who thinks that General Regionalism is a correct and explanatory answer to the General Composition

---

xs compose y iff the activities of those xs constitute the life of y. The defender of The Life View would then be able to give the same sort of common-ground response as the defender of General Regionalism. I am not opposed to this kind of response. The main point I wish to argue for in this chapter is that someone who advocates for an answer to The Special Composition Question that follows from an answer to The General Composition Question is better-positioned to respond to the puzzle of this chapter than one who advocates only for an answer to The Special Composition Question. I will note, however, that this response works only if The Life View is modified to read "Necessarily, for any xs, there is a y such that those xs compose y iff there is a y such that the activities of those xs constitute the life of y" and that this modification is *not* equivalent to the standard formulation of The Life View. In particular, the standard formulation of The Life View is not compatible with the claim that there are things the activities of which constitute an irreducibly plural life whereas the revised formulation is. An irreducibly plural life is one that is not a life of a single thing but is rather the life of several things taken together. For more details, see my (2021).

Question and that Special Regionalism is a correct and explanatory answer will be well-positioned to respond to the Special Composition Puzzle using my proposed strategy. But suppose someone thinks that although General Regionalism is a correct and explanatory answer to the General Composition Question, Special Regionalism is *not* an explanatory answer to the Special Composition Question. Instead, perhaps the person thinks that The Life View is the correct and explanatory answer to the Special Composition Question. This is a strange, but consistent combination of views. The defender of this combination of views is *not* in a position to employ the strategy that I have suggested. The defender of this combination of views does not have, ready to hand, a common ground to explain our problematic counterfactual correlations. In this case, the defender has failed to meet the second condition required for successfully employing my suggested strategy.

Moreover, one cannot simply create a monster answer to the General Composition Question by combining an answer to the General Composition Question and a disparate answer to the Special Composition Question and thereby be in a position to employ my strategy. For example, suppose someone combined General Regionalism and the Life View into the following Monster View:

Necessarily, for any *x*s and any *y*, those *x*s compose that *y* iff the union of the regions occupied by those *x*s is occupied by *y* and the activities of the *x*s constitute a life.

If General Regionalism is a correct and explanatory answer to the General Composition Question and the Life view is a correct and explanatory answer to the Special Composition Question, then the Monster View would be a correct answer to the General Composition Question as well. But the Monster View would not be an *explanatory* answer to the General Composition Question. That is, it would not provide the *grounds* for the *x*s composing *y* in any particular case of composition. Why? Well, suppose that Simples compose Magpie. Then according to the Monster view, the Simples compose Magpie iff the union of the regions occupied by simples is occupied by Magpie *and* the activities of Simples constitute a life. But the conjunction on the right-hand side of that biconditional does not *ground* that Simples compose Magpie. Rather just the first conjunct of the right-hand side of the biconditional does so. Moreover, the conjunction does not ground that Simples compose something or other. Rather just the second conjunct does so. So, even if you can create a correct monster view by combining disparate answers to the General Composition Question and the Special Composition Question, doing so does not put you in a position to employ my suggested strategy. The defender of a monster view has failed to meet the first condition required for employing my strategy.[19]

3.5 Conclusion

Answers to The Special Composition Question that can also answer this new Special Composition Puzzle will have an advantage over answers that cannot. Moreover, explanatory answers to The Special Composition Question that follow from explanatory answers to The General Composition Question can plausibly answer this Special Composition Puzzle by identifying a common ground for the overdetermining facts. Traditional answers to the Special Composition Question, putatively explanatory answers that do *not* follow from an explanatory answer to The General Composition Question, do not have such a readily available reply to the puzzle. It seems to me, then, that the former sorts of answers have a prima facie advantage over the latter sorts of answers.[20]

Bibliography

Audi, Paul (2012a) "A Clarification and Defense of the Notion of Grounding," in F. Correia and B. Schneider (eds.), *Metaphysical Grounding: Understanding the Structure of Reality*. Cambridge: Cambridge University Press, pp 101–121.

Audi, Paul (2012b) "Grounding: Toward a Theory of the In-Virtue-of Relation," *The Journal of Philosophy* 112: 685–711.

Chisholm, Roderick (1973) "Parts as Essential to their Wholes," *Review of Metaphysics* 26: 581–603.

Correia, Fabrice and Benjamin Schneider (2012) "Grounding: an opinionated Introduction," in F. Correia and B. Schneider (eds.) *Metaphysical Grounding: Understanding the Structure of Reality*. Cambridge: Cambridge University Press, pp 1–36.

[19] Thanks to Dean Zimmerman for helpfully pushing me to clarify how my suggested strategy works.
[20] Thanks to Kris McDaniel, Dean Zimmerman, and anonymous reviewers for helpful comments on earlier drafts of this chapter. Thanks to Chad Carmichael, Sam Cowling, Shieva Kleinschmidt, Matt McGrath, David Sanson, Alan Sidelle, and Chris Tillman for helpful discussions when I was first developing this puzzle.

deRosset, Louis (2010) "Getting Priority Straight," *Philosophical Studies* 149: 73–97.

deRosset, Louis (2013) "Grounding Explanations," *Philosophers' Imprint* 13: 1–26.

Fine, Kit (2012) "Guide to Ground," in Fabrice Correia and Benjamin Schneider (eds.), *Metaphysical Grounding: Understanding the Structure of Reality*. Cambridge: Cambridge University Press, pp 37–80.

Heller, Mark (1990) *The Ontology of Physical Objects: Four-Dimensional Hunks of Matter*. Cambridge: Cambridge University Press.

Hudson, Hud (2001) *A Materialist Metaphysics of the Human Person*. Ithaca, NY: Cornell University Press.

Lewis, David (1973) "Causation," *Journal of Philosophy* 70: 556–567.

Lewis, David (1986) *On The Plurality of Worlds*. Oxford: Blackwell.

Markosian, Ned (2008) "Restricted Composition," in John Hawthorne, Theodore Sider, and Dean Zimmerman (eds.), *Contemporary Debates in Metaphysics*. Basil: Blackwell, pp 341–363.

Markosian, Ned (2014) "A Spatial Approach to Mereology," in Shieva Kleinschmidt (ed.), *Mereology and Location*. Oxford: Oxford University Press, pp 69–90.

Melamedoff, Damian (2018) "Against Existential Grounding," *Thought: A Journal of Philosophy* 7: 3–11.

Rea, Michael C. (1998) "In Defense of Mereological Universalism," *Philosophy and Phenomenological Research* 58: 347–360.

Rea, Michael C. (2002) *World Without Design: The Ontological Consequences of Naturalism*. Oxford: Oxford University Press.

Rea, Michael C. (2010) "Universalism and Extensionalism: A Reply to Varzi," *Analysis* 70: 490–496.

Rosen, Gideon (2010) "Metaphysical Dependence: Grounding and Reduction," in B. Hale and A. Hoffman (eds.), *Modality: Metaphysics, Logic, and Epistemology*. Oxford: Oxford University Press, pp 109–136.

Sider, Theodore (2001) *Four-Dimensionalism. An Ontology of Persistence and Time*. New York: Oxford University Press.

Sider, Theodore (2011) *Writing the Book of the World*. Oxford: Oxford University Press.

Skiles, Alexander (2015) "Against Grounding Necessitarianism," *Erkenntnis* 80: 717–751.

Spencer, Joshua (2017) "Counting on Strong Composition as Identity to Settle the Special Composition Question," *Erkenntnis* 82: 857–872.

Spencer, Joshua (2021) "On the Explanatory Demands of the Special Composition Question," *Synthese* 198: 4375–4388.

Trogdon, Kelly (2013) "Grounding: Necessary or Contingent?" *Pacific Philosophical Quarterly* 94: 465–485.

Van Cleve, James (1986) "Mereological Essentialism, Mereological Conjunctivism, and Identity Through Time," *Midwest Studies in Philosophy* 11: 141–156.

Van Cleve, James (2008) "The Moon and Sixpence: A Defense of Mereological Universalism," in Ted Sider et al. (eds.), *Contemporary Debates in Metaphysics*. Oxford: Blackwell, pp 321–340.

Van Inwagen, Peter (1990) *Material Beings*. Ithaca, NY: Cornell University Press.

Wilson, Jessica (2014) "No Work for a Theory of Grounding," *Inquiry: An Interdisciplinary Journal of Philosophy* 57: 535–579.

PART II
CAUSATION, COUNTERFACTUALS, AND ESSENCES

4

The Varieties of Relevance

Bradford Skow

4.1 The great misclassification

Non-causes are often misclassified as causes, and everyone knows it. In one
famous example, economists observed the strong (negative) correlation
between inflation and unemployment, and advised governments that
increasing the inflation rate could cause unemployment to go down. This
mistake produced the high-inflation high-unemployment 1970s (see
Landsburg 2012: 272). But correlations are not the only kind of non-cause
mistaken for a cause. Also mistaken for causes are things that are close to
being causes; things that are, in some way, causally relevant to the outcome.
My aim is to describe and categorize the varieties of causal relevance,
compare them to the varieties of relevance in some other domains, and
explain why recognizing them is important. The benefits will include a
defense of the transitivity of causation, and a diagnosis of when double
prevention is, and is not, causation. My view might be called pluralism about
causal relevance, and this name brings to mind pluralism about causation:
the thesis that causation itself comes in many varieties. I'll say something
about the relation between these in section 4.12.

Exhibit A in my case for causal relevance without causation is the
presence of oxygen in a room, when a match is lit. Many philosophers
classify this, if only implicitly, as a cause of the match's lighting, but it is
not. Causes have to be events, and the presence of oxygen is not an event. An
event happens only when, and in virtue of the fact that, something does
something. When I strike a match I thereby do something (what I do is
strike a match), so in virtue of my doing it there is an event, the striking. But
when I am human I do not thereby do anything (it is not true that what I do
is "be human"), so even though I am human no event is happening in virtue
of this fact. Applying this criterion to our case, no event happens in virtue of
the oxygen's being present in the room, since *being present in the room* is not

Bradford Skow, *The Varieties of Relevance* In: *Oxford Studies in Metaphysics Volume 13*. Edited by:
Karen Bennett and Dean W. Zimmerman, Oxford University Press. © Bradford Skow 2023.
DOI: 10.1093/oso/9780192886033.003.0004

something the oxygen is doing. So the presence of oxygen isn't even the right sort of thing to be a cause.[1]

This argument relies on heavyweight premises about what can be causes, and about the conditions under which events happen, which I have defended elsewhere, and which I will say more about.[2] Another argument leverages the distinction between being directly and being merely indirectly relevant to why something happened. Causes, and only causes, are directly relevant. The striking of the match is directly relevant to why the match lit. The oxygen, or the presence of oxygen, on the other hand, is only indirectly relevant. It is only relevant to why the match lit because it is a condition in which the striking of the match can cause the lighting. Without the oxygen, the striking could not have that effect. So the oxygen bears on why the match lit by bearing on the relation between the lighting and one of its causes; and that is an indirect way of bearing on why the match lit. Since it is only indirectly relevant, the presence of oxygen is not a cause. The presence of oxygen exhibits a variety, or mode, of relevance to the match's lighting, and to why the match lit, different from the one exhibited by causes of the lighting.

4.2 More on direct vs indirect relevance

My second argument that the presence of oxygen is not a cause distinguished direct from indirect causal relevance. One might object that this distinction is not real. But a distinction between direct and indirect relevance is all over topics outside of causation, and if it exists outside causation surely it also exists inside.

One place where it exists is in inquiry into normative reasons. The canonical articulation of such a reason takes the form "that P is a reason

---

[1] Philosophers who implicitly misclassify the presence of oxygen as a cause include David Lewis, whose theory of events in (Lewis 1986b) entails that the presence of oxygen is an event, and whose theory of causation in (Lewis 1986a) entails that it is a cause of the lighting. Ned Hall never articulates a theory of events, but he frequently treats things like a forest's being present, or a bit of train track's being present, as events and as causes (2004: 231; 2000: 207). The structural equations approach to the metaphysics of causation, which has many advocates, but see (Woodward 2003) for one canonical statement, says that (token) causes are cases of a variable taking on a value, and allows a model to contain a variable that takes value 1 when oxygen is in the room and 0 when it is not.
[2] See chapter 2 of (Skow 2018), where I also defend a version of the argument to follow. The theory of events is not original with me. It has its roots in Davidson's use of events in the semantics of action verbs (1967), and a similar theory receives a thorough defense in (Steward 1997).

for X to Z": that Jones is in need is a reason for me to help her; that the store down the street sells chocolate is a reason for me to go there. Now a normative reason answers a certain kind of why-question. A reason for someone to do something is part of the answer to why they should do it. If that P is a reason for X to Z, then that P is part of why X should Z. Part of why I should go to the store is that it sells chocolate. The reasons there are for me to go to the store, then, are directly relevant to why I should go.

By contrast, other facts, in particular facts about what I want, like the fact that I want to eat some chocolate, are (in the usual case) only indirectly relevant. My wanting to eat chocolate is relevant to why I should go only because it makes it the case that the fact that the store sells chocolate is a reason for me to go. More generally, someone's desires are (weird cases aside) indirectly relevant to why they should do this or that; they are relevant only by helping determine whether some fact is a reason for them to do this or that, and so whether that fact is directly relevant to why they should.[3]

The appearance here of the distinction between direct and indirect relevance is plausible on its face. The distinction is also built in to one popular theory of reasons to act. The theory says, roughly speaking, that the fact that P is a reason for X to Z if and only if a belief that P could be a premise in good practical reasoning that moved X to Z.[4] Maybe X does not in fact believe that P—maybe I've been told the store doesn't sell chocolate. Still, if I have some mental states M (including, say, a desire for chocolate), and if it would be good practical reasoning for me to be moved to go to the store by M-together-with-the-belief-that-the-store-sells-chocolate, then that the store sells chocolate is a reason for me to go. On this theory good

[3] Note that I am not making the strong claim that whenever something is a reason for someone to act, some desire they have makes this the case. This claim or something like it is sometimes called "the Humean theory of reasons"—see for example (Schroeder 2007).

Schroeder also argues strenuously for something like the distinction between direct and indirect relevance: he holds that the best version of the Humean theory says that, if X's having a desire D makes it the case that R is a reason for X to Z, it does not automatically follow that X's having D is also a reason for X to Z.

Jonathan Dancy, as part of his defense of particularism about reasons, also argues for a distinction between reasons to act, and factors that determine whether something is a reason, or determine the strength or valence of a reason (Dancy 2004). For him, facts about what the agent desires are not the only such factors.

The weird cases I have set aside are ones like this: a philosophy department promises a high salary to applicants who want to teach large introductory classes. In this case, the fact that I want to teach large introductory classes is a reason for me to apply for the job. It is directly relevant to why I should apply. (That I want a higher salary is, though, only indirectly relevant: it makes the fact that I want to teach large classes directly relevant.)

[4] Among many others, (Setiya 2014) defends a theory like this.

practical reasoning may and often does involve desires helping (as parts of M) to move one to act. But in good practical reasoning beliefs about one's desires need not help move one to act, and in fact this is the normal case.[5] So, again, the fact that I want some chocolate is not itself a reason for me to go to the store. But still—that I want some chocolate is relevant to why I should go! It is indirectly relevant.

Indirect relevance is also there in epistemology, in the distinction between rebutting and undercutting defeaters. I might get some evidence E, which supports an hypothesis H, and then get some more evidence D that defeats my support for H. Defeat comes in direct and indirect varieties. The new evidence D might directly support an alternative to H, and support it strongly enough that overall my evidence is against H: then D is a rebutting defeater. Jones tells me that there is a rabbit in the next room; that's evidence that there is. I then go in and see for myself, and don't see a rabbit, or any of the paraphernalia that usually accompany them. This new evidence supports the no rabbit hypothesis more strongly than Jones's testimony supported the rabbit hypothesis, and in virtue of this the new evidence defeats the evidential support Jones's testimony gave to the hypothesis that there was a rabbit.

Undercutting defeaters, by contrast, do not directly support an alternative to H. What they do, in the first instance, is undermine my original evidence E's support for H. If, when facing a wall with my eyes open and inquiring into its color, all I have to go on is how the wall looks, then that the wall looks red to me is evidence that it is red. But if I learn that the wall is illuminated by a red light, this new fact defeats my original evidence's support for the red hypothesis. But it does not do this by directly supporting some other hypothesis about the color of the wall. It does it by directly destroying the support my first evidence was giving the red hypothesis.

These differences in what the kinds of defeater bear on most directly translates into a difference in their mode of relevance. Rebutting defeaters are directly relevant to whether I should believe H. Undercutting defeaters are (only) indirectly relevant. What I see when I enter the allegedly rabbit-inhabited room is directly relevant to whether I should believe that there is a rabbit, because it directly supports the "no" answer. But the fact that the wall is illuminated by red light is only indirectly relevant to whether I should

---

[5] This is a thesis about good practical reasoning; what about the practical reasoning we actually engage in, which may not be good? Pettit and Smith (1990) argue that here also beliefs about one's desire rarely help move one to act.

believe the wall is red: it is relevant only by making the fact that the wall looks red irrelevant.[6]

In these other manifestations of the direct/indirect relevance distinction there is a special role reserved for things that are directly relevant. The things directly relevant to why I should Z are the reasons for me to Z; the indirectly relevant things, like my desires, are not reasons. The things directly relevant to whether I should believe H constitute my evidence for and against H. The indirectly relevant things, like undercutting defeaters, are not evidence for or against H. What they are is evidence that something I earlier took to be evidence for H in fact is not. It is the same with causation: the things directly relevant to why E happened are the causes of E; the indirectly relevant things are not causes, though they are, as we might say, "relevant to the causing."

Before going on, a note: *being directly relevant to E*, the notion I've been explaining, is distinct from *being a direct cause of E*, and indeed indirect causes, being causes, are directly relevant to their effects. Indirect causes act by way of intermediate causes, as when the lighting of the fuse causes an explosion by way of causing the gunpowder to ignite. This is quite different from indirect relevance.

4.3 Background conditions as indirect mode

The presence of oxygen is a non-cause of the lighting of the match that is still, indirectly, relevant to why the match lit. But, I will argue, there are many kinds of indirect causal relevance. A good name for the kind that the presence of oxygen exhibits is *background condition*.

The standard view about background conditions is that the notion is, in Hall's words, "greatly infected with pragmatics":

> When delineating the causes of some given event, we typically make what are, from the present perspective, invidious distinctions, ignoring perfectly good causes because they are not sufficiently salient. We say that the *lightning bolt* caused the forest fire, failing to mention the contribution of the oxygen in the air, or the presence of a sufficient quantity of flammable

---

[6] A canonical source for the distinction between rebutting and undercutting defeaters is (Pollock and Cruz 1999). Undercutting defeat is not just a kind of indirect relevance, it is also a kind of negative relevance: it prevents some evidence from supporting an hypothesis that it otherwise would. I will have more to say about negative relevance later, when I discuss prevention.

material. But in the egalitarian sense of "cause," a complete inventory of the fire's causes must include the presence of oxygen and of dry wood.

(2004: 228)

I think the opposite is true: there are good metaphysical (and so non-pragmatic) reasons for excluding the oxygen from the list of causes. Summarizing the differences that drove my two arguments, a background condition to C's causing E is (i) a state (rather than an event), that is (ii) a reason why C caused E. Clause (ii) captures the sense in which background conditions are indirectly relevant.[7] But more should be said about the difference between states and events.

4.4 Event/state and activity/stative

Here again is my existence condition for events:

Events: if something did something, then in virtue of that fact an event occurred, and if an event occurred, that's so in virtue of the fact that something did something.[8]

If a verb V can be put into "What he/she/it did was V" to produce something grammatical, then that verb denotes[9] something that can be done—acts, we might call them. I will call these verbs activity verbs, and verbs that are not activity verbs, stative verbs.[10] States go with stative verbs in the way events go

---

[7] I defend this theory, and argue against alternatives, in (Skow 2018). A useful table summarizing alternative ways of drawing the cause/background condition contrast is in (Goldvarg and Johnson-Laird 2001). (Their table is described as summarizing ways to draw the "cause/enabling" condition contrast, and while I will later distinguish background conditions from enabling events, they are not distinguished by these authors.)

[8] The quantifiers take wide scope: for any X and Y, if X did Y, then in virtue of the fact that X did Y, an event occurred. The case where X is plural is also allowed. I am using "event" broadly; it also includes processes. While standing is something that may be done, some linguists say that "Jones stood" (and sentences with other, similar "doing" verbs) entails the existence, not of an event, but of a state, just a special kind of state: a "dynamic state" (Bach 1986: 6) or a "Davidsonian state" (Maienborn 2008: 109). Verbs that do not report doings, like "be tall," they say entail a different kind of state, a "static" or "Kimian" state. But I use "event" to include dynamic/Davidsonian states; the only states are "static/Kimian" states.

[9] In the sense of "has as its semantic value"—verbs of course are not referring expressions like "Barack Obama" or "him."

[10] Some linguists use "activity verb" in a more restricted sense, so that only some non-stative verbs are activity verbs. To keep things simple, I am using "activity verb" and "non-stative verb"

with activity verbs. The existence condition for states is harder to frame than the one for events; one way is this:

States: if something Vs, where "V" is a stative verb, then in virtue of that fact a state obtains, and if a state obtains, that is so in virtue of the fact that something Vs.[11]

A problem with this statement is that English does not have a stative verb for every possible stative verb meaning, so it is insufficiently general. If we had a variable V that could occupy verb position, and moreover ranged only over things that can be denoted by stative verbs, then we could write the condition like this:

States: if $\exists V \exists x(xV)$, then in virtue of that fact a state obtains, and if a state obtains, then $\exists V \exists x$(it obtains in virtue of the fact that xV).[12]

Now: the verb in "Oxygen is present in the room" is stative, so the state corresponding to it meets the first condition on being a background condition. As for the second: that that state obtained is indeed a reason why the striking of the match caused it to light. Without the oxygen, the striking would not have caused the lighting.

The distinction between activity verbs and stative verbs runs deep in natural languages. This distinction, and the notion of doing something that it relies on, are real and metaphysically important. If the distinction is less familiar to philosophers than to linguists, it is because philosophers learn too early to formalize their arguments in artificial languages where the distinction is invisible. In those languages a predicate has some number of argument places, but other than that all predicates are grammatically indiscernible. They are not divided into activity predicates and stative predicates.

---

interchangeably. Important early papers distinguishing stative from (a variety of) non-stative verbs are (Vendler 1959) and (Kenny 1963). (Dowdy 1979) contains a then-comprehensive list of tests for the distinction.

[11] Again the quantifier takes wide scope and the plural case is allowed. Should we recognize states even for the narrow-scope reading—a state that goes with [someone is tall], separate from the one that goes with [Jones is tall]? Maybe. Nothing in this chapter will turn on this question. A referee asked whether a vacuum is a state, on this view. If a vacuum is a region of space that is empty, the answer is yes; "is empty" is stative.

[12] I suspect that I don't actually need to "reify" states; the arguments and conclusions I want to reach could probably be reached by always talking about stative verbs. But it is easier this way. (Maienborn 2008 argues that the semantics of stative verbs requires reifying states.)

These artificial languages are not eliminating an irrelevant distinction; they are blinding themselves to a relevant one.

Some philosophers accept something close to the thesis that an event happens whenever something satisfies a predicate, any predicate, and so in effect treat the distinction between activity and stative verbs (and predicates) as superficial and of no metaphysical significance, akin, maybe, to the distinction between predicates of English and predicates of Japanese, or the distinction between verbs that begin with "s" and those that do not.[13] The latter two distinctions are obviously metaphysically (and grammatically) irrelevant, but the first is not.

I've given one reason already: if V is an activity verb phrase, then "X Ved" is a possible answer to "What did X do?," and so denotes something that can be done. If V is a stative verb phrase, "X Ved" makes no sense as an answer to this question, and does not denote something that can be done. And the notion of doing something is metaphysically important.

Another thing that makes the activity/stative distinction metaphysically important is its connection to locations in space. Activity verbs accept locative modifiers with spatial interpretations, while stative verbs do not. For example, "The bomb exploded in the courtyard" is interpretable when the modifier has a spatial reading, but "Jones was 6 feet tall in the courtyard" is not. The immediate metaphysical consequence is that events, which go with activity verbs, have locations—every event happens somewhere—while states, which go with stative verbs, do not. I earlier asserted that only events can be causes, and you might have wanted me to say more about why. There are many reasons, but here is one: states cannot be causes because causes and effects are things in space and time, and states are at best only in time.[14]

---

[13] Kim (1993: 33) is relatively explicit about this. Lewis's theory (Lewis 1986b) also has this consequence. Neither really says that the happening of an event goes with the satisfaction of just any predicate: Lewis for example restricts the thesis to "relatively natural" predicates, in the sense of natural articulated in (Lewis 1983), but naturalness is orthogonal to the activity/stative distinction.

[14] The inference that states lack spatial locations is strongest if it is assumed that stative verbs have hidden argument places for states, in the way that (neo-)Davidsonians assume that activity verbs have hidden argument places for events. For then at the level of semantic interpretation there is a state variable available for the location predicate to attach to, and so the ungrammaticality of adding locative modifiers must be due to states' inability to have locations (see Maienborn 2005, 2008). But I think that the argument has force even without these semantic assumptions, on which I take no stand.

Another argument that only events can be causes is that in the form "X caused Y to Z by Ving"—"Jones caused the window to break by kicking it" is an example of an instance—only activity verbs (and so only verbs that go with events) may go in for "Z" and "Ving"; see (Skow 2018) for more on this argument.

The second, stative, example in this argument ("Jones was 6 feet tall in the courtyard") is admittedly tricky, because the sentence is interpretable—but only when "in the courtyard" is read, not as a locative modifier, but as a temporal modifier that restricts the past tense, making it equivalent to "When Jones was in the courtyard, he was 6 feet tall."[15] So when does a locative modifier "in W" have a spatial interpretation in a sentence "S in W," and when does it have some other function, like restricting a quantifier? One useful criterion: when the occurrence of "in W" can be questioned with "where." You can question "The bomb exploded in the courtyard" with "Where did the bomb explode?"; but you cannot question "Jones was 6 feet tall in the courtyard" with "Where was Jones 6 feet tall?"[16]

Related to this is a third metaphysically relevant difference between activity and stative verbs: only activity verbs can appear in complements to perception verbs (Maienborn 2005). "Smith saw the bomb explode" is grammatical but "Smith saw Jones be 6 feet tall" is not. This is to be expected if only events have spatial locations: you can only perceive what happens in space.

4.5 Ennoblers

States, and the event/state contrast, came up when I said that background conditions are states, and so are never causes, even though they are often misclassified as such. The air's being still is not a cause, but is instead a background condition, when I draw a bow and release the arrow at a certain angle, and thereby cause the arrow to hit the bullseye. The valve on my radiator's being open is not a cause, but is instead a background condition, when I turn up my thermostat and thereby cause my radiator to get hot. The existence of background conditions shows that being a cause of E is not the only way to be causally relevant to the occurrence of E. What's more, *cause* and *background condition* are just two of a whole menagerie of kinds of causal relevance. If you want to cultivate a sensitivity to the varieties of

---

[15] If this still sounds funny, it is because we know that people move around much faster than their heights change. But this shows only that the sentence is odd to assert (since it may carry the false implication that Jones was some other height before he was in the courtyard), not that it is uninterpretable.

[16] See (Maienborn 2001: 6). It is, of course, intelligible to ask, "Where was Jones when he was 6 feet tall?"; but this questions, not the target sentence, but "Jones was 6 feet tall when he was in the courtyard," where the modifier restricts a quantifier (a tense).

causal relevance, a good place to start is Stephen Yablo's paper "Advertisement for a Sketch of an Outline of a Prototheory of Causation" (2010). Yablo begins with Plato, or maybe it was Socrates, who distinguished between *the cause* and *that without which the cause would not be a cause*, when he said to Cebes, in the *Phaedo*, "Imagine not being able to distinguish the real cause from that without which the cause would not be able to act as a cause" (99b). Yablo himself distinguishes between two distinctions this sentence could be used to draw. The first is "the distinction between causes and enabling conditions," where enabling conditions are "conditions that don't produce the effect themselves but create a context in which something else can do so; conditions in whose absence the something else would not have been effective" (98). Enabling conditions typically have the feature that "if you imagine them away, the cause...ceases to be *enough* for the effect" (98) Enabling conditions thus defined sound a little bit like background conditions; more on their relation in a minute. If enabling conditions make the cause "enough" for the effect, could there also be, Yablo asks, "conditions such that the cause ceases to be *required* for the effect, if you imagine them away" (98)? He answers yes, and calls them *ennoblers*. Yablo repurposes an example of Hartry Field's to illustrate ennobling:

> Billy puts a bomb under Suzy's chair; later, Suzy notices the bomb and flees the room; later still, Suzy has a medical checkup (it was already arranged) and receives from her doctor a glowing report.   (Yablo 2010: 98)

The bomb's presence is an ennobler, because "The bomb does not help Suzy's leaving to suffice for the glowing report [as an enabler would]; rather it makes Suzy's action important, required, indispensable" (99). He goes on: "What an ennobler contributes is just a raising of status. Suzy's removing herself from the room is elevated from something that just happens to something that *had* to happen, if Suzy was later going to be healthy" (99). In general, "An ennobler contributes by closing off potential routes to *e* [the effect], that is, all the routes not running through *c* [the cause]" (99). By raising the status of Suzy's leaving from something that merely preceded the glowing report to something that had to happen for the glowing report to happen, the bomb's presence ennobled the leaving into a cause of the report.

Interestingly, while Yablo first characterizes ennoblers in terms of what would happen in their absence (the effect wouldn't have required C, where C is an actual cause of E), he almost immediately switches to, and then for the rest of the paper works with, a definition in terms of what would happen in their continued presence: he says that G ennobles C into a cause of E iff had C not happened and G still obtained, E would not have happened (this is later made more complicated). The bomb example fits both definitions: without the bomb, Suzy's leaving would not have been required for the glowing report (that's the definition in terms of absence); and if Suzy hadn't left, but the bomb had still been there, she wouldn't have received a glowing report (presence). It's an interesting question whether these two characterizations of ennobling are equivalent; but that question is a rabbit hole that I will gladly side-step. The two characterizations certainly agree on the examples I will discuss.

What matters right now is that ennoblers are not causes. We know enough about them that this is obvious. "An ennobler," again, "contributes by closing off potential routes to e, that is, all the routes not running through c. This is anything that *hurts* e's chances" (99). It's hard to see how something that works against E's happening could be a cause of E. Ennoblers play for the other team.[17]

I admit to finding *ennobler* a trickier concept than *enabling condition*. Maybe helpful is looking at more examples. If I set up ten sling-shots to sling rocks at a window in quick succession at the push of a single button, and the first nine mechanisms jam (coincidentally) when I push it, then the jamming of those mechanisms ennobles the slinging of the tenth rock into a cause of the breaking of the window. Without the jammings, the slinging of the tenth rock was not causally necessary for the breaking; holding fixed the nine jammings, had the tenth sling not happened, the window would not have broken. The jammings are certainly not causes of the breaking—there's no pull to say that at all. But they are relevant to the causing of the breaking, because they help make something else into a cause. Examples with essentially this structure are easy to produce. We have won free pizza for the evening, and it is on its way. I don't know this, so seeing nothing in the fridge I order pizza from a different restaurant. The first delivery guy is pulled over for speeding and the pizza he's carrying spoils in the back seat, never making it to my house. His detention ennobles my order into a cause of my family's eating; without the detention, my order would not have caused the eating,

---

[17] This phrase comes up a lot in discussions about ennoblers I've participated in, and I was sure that Yablo himself used this metaphor, but it turns out it does not appear in his writings. My research suggests that Daniel Muñoz came up with the phrase and misattributed it to Yablo. Still: it is something Yablo should have said, in the way that Rick in *Casablanca* should have said "Play it again, Sam," or Sally Field in her Oscar acceptance speech should have said "You like me, you really like me!"

since we would have eaten the free pizza. Holding fixed the detention, had I not ordered, my family would have gone hungry.

So Yablo gives us *enabling condition* and *ennobler* to set alongside *cause* and *background condition*: four kinds of causal relevance. But do we really have four? As the list grows so does the danger that it is redundant. In fact it is: enabling conditions are background conditions under a different name. Enabling conditions, we are told, "don't produce the effect themselves but create a context in which something else can do so," and that's the defining feature of background conditions. The oxygen didn't produce the flame, the striking of the match produced the flame; but it was only in a context where oxygen was present that the striking could do that. So really we have a three-item list. And this shorter list is not redundant. We have already seen arguments that neither background conditions nor ennoblers are causes; and background conditions are distinct from ennoblers, since (in Yablo's terminology) background conditions make the cause enough, while ennoblers make the cause required.

4.6 Enablers

This shorter list is not redundant, but neither is it complete. Suppose I fill a previously evacuated room with oxygen, just before you, standing in the room and holding your breath, strike a match, thereby lighting it. Your striking of the match caused it to light. The oxygen in the room was a background condition to the lighting: in virtue of its presence, your striking sufficed for the lighting. What about my filling of the room with oxygen? In doing that, I caused the onset of a background condition.[18] No doubt that is something causally relevant to the lighting; this kind of thing belongs on our list, a true fourth entry. But "cause of the onset of a background condition" is unwieldy; can we come up with a shorter, punchier name? We can, by retrofitting the term we just crossed off. Yablo's "enabling condition," a term for a kind of condition, suggests "enabling," a term for a kind of act. Enabling is what enablers do. In the ordinary sense, people who are enablers clear the way for someone else to indulge in their bad habits. An enabler will pay off your gambling debts so you can keep going to the track.

---

[18] I didn't cause the background condition itself—the presence of oxygen—since this is a state and cannot be caused. But the onset of a state, or a state's beginning to obtain, is an event, and so can be caused.

An enabler will cover for you at work so you can keep hitting the bar at night without getting fired. If we generalize this idea, abstracting away from the requirement that enablers be people and enable other people, we get the idea of something that affects the conditions that determine the course of a causal process. By paying someone's debts the enabler ensures that the gambling does not lead to their being fired; it's the same with covering for a heavy drinker at work. But manipulating the conditions that determine what effects C has just is putting into place conditions that are background conditions to C's having its actual effects (where other conditions would have made C produce different effects). If that is what an enabler does, then enabling is the doing of it. Enabling is causing the onset of a back-ground condition. In more detail, if something caused the onset of a background condition to C's causing E, then that thing enabled C to cause E, and so is an enabler (and conversely).[19]

I've gotten the term "enabler" from thinking about something Yablo wrote, but really Lawrence Brian Lombard had the term, and the concept, much earlier (Lombard 1990). He distinguished between "the causes of events" and "those conditions or states the obtaining of which merely makes it possible for one event to cause another" (201); those conditions or states are, in my terms, background conditions. And he then defined an enabler, more or less as I do, as "an event that causes a thing to be in a state that makes it possible for an event to cause e [the effect in question]" (202).

Lombard cited no precedents, but in fact use of the concept of an enabler goes back much farther. Philippa Foot, in a 1967 paper, identified enabling with "the removal of some obstacle which is, as it were, holding back a train of events" (1978: 26). If a stretch of track is blocked by some rubble and I remove the rubble, I on this definition enable the train's departure to cause its arrival at the station further on. But Foot's definition is narrower than mine, and I think the wider definition is better. Removing an obstacle to C's causing E is one way to enable C to cause E, but not the only way; creating a path to C's causing E is also a way to enable, and is a different way. If a ball is rolling down a mountain and I build a little ramp so that it jumps over the stream at the bottom and lands safely on the other side, then I say that I enabled the initial rolling to cause the landing, but I haven't removed some

<hr/>

[19] Yablo actually uses the term "enabler" in his paper, and identifies enablers both with enabling conditions and with causes: "Enablers make a dynamic contribution. They help to bring the effect about" (99). That's not what background conditions do at all, nor is it what enablers, as I've defined them, do (my arguments for this second claim are yet to come). Yablo is another philosopher who mistakenly identifies some non-causes as causes.

obstacle to the rolling's having that result. What would the obstacle be? The absence of a ramp? Did I, in building the ramp, remove the absence of a ramp? Is the sky full of obstacles to my death, full of "absences of meteors heading toward me," that thankfully no one has removed? No. Yet there is a kind of relevance to one thing's causing another that building the ramp and removing the rubble have in common.

So enabling belongs on the list of kinds of causal relevance. But are we sure that adding it doesn't make the list redundant? Well it is clearly different from ennobling. And certainly *causing the onset of a background condition* is distinct from *being a background condition*. For one thing, the first is something only events can do, while the second is something only states can be.

What about causation itself? Is enabling just a kind of causing? Well of course in a sense it is: by definition, if you enable C to cause E then you cause something (the onset of a background condition to C's causing E). But that's not what I mean. We are compiling a list of ways of being causally relevant *to* E, so the question that needs answering is whether enabling C to cause E is really a way to be a (another) cause of E. I am convinced that it is not. This claim might raise eyebrows. Background conditions aren't causes, I said, because they aren't events. But enablers are events, have to be events, since they cause background conditions to begin obtaining. So if an enabler of E isn't a cause of E, it isn't for the reason that background conditions aren't. What's more, enablers of E pass a standard counterfactual test for being causes of E. If you hadn't struck the match, it wouldn't have lit, and the striking is a cause of the lighting. Well, similarly, if I hadn't filled the room with oxygen, the match wouldn't have lit; so shouldn't my filling of the room also be a cause?

But look closer and the similarities between enablers of E and causes of E are swamped by deep differences. For one thing, enablers fail to be directly relevant to the effect, the way causes are supposed to be. An enabler inherits its mode of relevance from the mode of the background condition it puts into place. And background conditions, again, are only indirectly relevant. So my turning of the knob is relevant to the lighting of the match only by helping put in a place a background condition (the presence of oxygen) that makes it possible for the striking cause the lighting. That's not the kind of direct relevance to the lighting that makes for causation.

Of course in special circumstances something that enables C to cause E might also be a cause of E. If I turn a knob to open a valve that lets oxygen fill the room, and my turning of the knob also creates a spark that lights a fuse connected to the match, and the fuse burns to the end, lighting the match, then my turning of the knob enables the spark to cause the match to light, and is also a cause of the lighting of the match, in virtue of being a cause of the spark. But here my turning of the knob, the enabler of the lighting, is not a cause in virtue of being an enabler. That's the thesis I assert: something that enables C to cause E is not, just by virtue of this fact alone, a cause of E.

Some evidence in the psychological literature supports the idea that enablers are indirectly relevant. In some experiments when subjects are told that something identified as an enabler happened, they don't expect the effect to have happened unless something identified as a cause also happened (see for example Golvarg and Johnson-Laird 2001, and Sloman et al. 2009). One explanation of these results—the correct one, I think—is that people believe that an enabler is relevant to an effect's occurring only indirectly, by being relevant to a cause's power to produce it. (Of course as I use them here I intend "enable" and "enabler" to be quasi-technical terms, and the subjects in these experiments were not instructed to interpret them in my technical sense. But my technical meanings are not too far from these words' ordinary English meanings, so these experiments are still relevant.)

4.7 Depicting indirect relevance

Neuron diagrams are a popular device among certain metaphysicians for representing and thinking about causal relationships. They also perfectly exemplify the fact that background conditions and enablers are overlooked, ignored, and even suppressed in philosophical discussions of causation. In the simplest two-neuron neuron diagrams, as shown in figure 4.1, neuron A is connected to neuron B by a stimulatory connection, meaning that if A fires, that will cause B to fire. That's what happens in the top diagram:

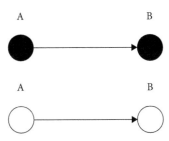

Figure 4.1

neurons A and B both fire and this is represented by the blackening of the circle representing each neuron. In the bottom diagram neither neuron fires, so neither circle is blackened.

So the color of a neuron is used to represent the occurrence, or non-occurrence, of an event (a firing). How do the diagrams represent states, including background conditions? They don't. There is no standard way to represent the obtaining, or not, of a state. The metaphysician's standard tool for representing causal structures literally makes background conditions invisible. If we want a neuron diagram that illustrates a background condition to one thing's causing another, we're going to have to invent a scheme for representing that ourselves.[20]

Here's kind of a silly example. Suppose that neuron A's axon passes through a room on its way to neuron B. Whether the signal from A can make it through the room depends on what state obtains in the room: if it is filled with oxygen, the signal can pass through, otherwise it cannot. (So now we're departing even farther than usual from the way actual neurons work.) Figure 4.2 shows the setup: I'll use grayscale to indicate whether the room is filled with oxygen.

Now look at figure 4.3: neuron A has fired, oxygen was present, so the firing caused neuron B to fire. While clear enough, the figure is misleading, since it uses the same thing—color (or black/white/gray shading)—to represent two different kinds of things: which events happen, and also what states obtain.

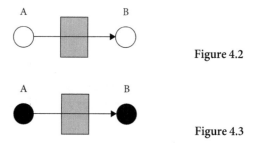

Figure 4.2

Figure 4.3

---

[20] A referee pointed out that the arrows between neurons represent states. For example, the arrow in the top diagram of figure 4.1 represents the state that goes with "A and B are connected by a stimulatory connection." So some states are represented in these diagrams. But there is no standard way to represent these states changing, or to represent other causally relevant states. Since metaphysicians use neuron diagrams to represent the causal structures of a variety of situations (not just actual neurons), this puts serious limits on what features of such situations the diagrams can represent, without resorting to ad hoc devices. Any event can be represented by a neuron firing, but not just any state can be represented by an arrow.

One way to separate these things out is to represent time as well as space. States typically persist through longish stretches of time, while events, or at least neuron-firings, happen very quickly. So each figure should contain a sequence of diagrams, read from top to bottom, that shows how things unfold over time. Momentary colorings represent events—firings—while persisting colors represent states. That's what we've got in figure 4.4: it shows that the state that is the presence of oxygen in the room obtained for a while, then neuron A fired, and that event took just a moment, and then the signal traveled down the axon leaving A and, because there was oxygen in the room, got all the way through the room, and caused neuron B to fire. (If persisting colors represent states, then the persisting whiteness of, for example, neuron B for the first part of the sequence should represent a state, right? Yes, indeed: it represents the state of the neuron's being dormant.)

Now let's put an enabler into the scenario. Neuron C in figure 4.5 represents an oxygen pump, connected to the room by a hose, that can fill the room with oxygen. When neuron C is blackened, that represents

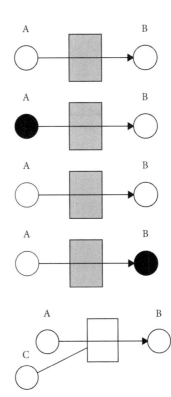

Figure 4.4

Figure 4.5

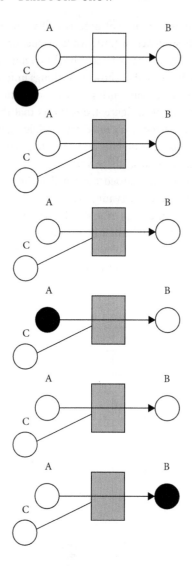

Figure 4.6

that pumping is occurring. In figure 4.6 this happens: first C pumps oxygen down the hose, thereby causing the onset of a state (the presence of oxygen) in the room. After the pump shuts off and the room is full nothing happens for a moment. Then A fires, and because oxygen is present, it causes B to fire.

‌

4.8 Enabling, causing, and locality

The scenario in figure 4.6 is the basis for another argument that enablers are not causes. The main premise is a locality requirement: a cause of E must be connected to E by a continuous sequence of intermediate causes (at least, this is so when we can ignore the kind of non-local causation that, some say, quantum mechanics permits). An enabler of E need not be; so enablers are not causes.

The locality requirement has a spatial and a temporal part. The spatial part: if a cause C happens here, and its effect E happens way over there, then there is an intermediate event that is an effect of C, happens right next to C, and is itself a cause of E. This principle iterates, until we get an intermediate event that is an effect of C, is a cause of E, and happens right next to E.[21] But important for us is the temporal part: if C finishes happening at one time, and E begins happening some non-zero amount of time later, then there is an intermediate event that is an effect of C, happens right after C, and is itself a cause of E. (This principle also iterates.)

Now consider again the scenario in figure 4.6. The enabler, the pumping of the oxygen, causes the movement of the oxygen (an event), and the movement of the oxygen causes the onset of the state of oxygen's being present, and then, for a while, *nothing happens*. No events occur. Eventually A fires, and a spatially and temporally continuous sequence of intermediate causes connects that firing to B's firing (these causes are events involving changes in the state of the axon connecting A to B and are not represented in the diagram), a sequence that passes through the room. But the onset of the state of oxygen's being present cannot cause any of these events, not even the ones that happen where it is, the ones that happen in the room, because there is a temporal gap between those events and the onset of the state, a gap that is not filled by any intermediate events.[22]

---

[21] This could be made more precise, but more precision isn't needed here. In iterating the principle I assume that causation is transitive; I discuss transitivity more in section 4.14.

[22] Lombard (1990: 201) also argues that enablers fail a temporal locality requirement on causation.

If you think the motions of the oxygen molecules constitute intermediate events, suppose that part of the scenario (especially the third diagram) happens at such a low temperature that the molecules are at rest. Being at rest is not something molecules can do, so being at rest generates no events.

4.9 Indirect relevance and structural equations

Drawing neuron diagrams is, by now, an old way to conduct disputes about the metaphysics of causation. The new way is to present causal models using structural equations. Like neuron diagrams, these causal models also erase the distinction between causation and other modes of causal relevance.

A structural equation causal model of a situation consists of a set of variables and a set of equations relating those variables. In the simplest case, a variable represents an event: a variable X, for example, might take the value 1 if an explosion happens, and the value 0 when it does not. But variables need not be limited to two possible values: a variable might take the value e when an explosion releases e joules of energy, where e is any non-negative real number; and, as we will see, variables need not be limited to representing events.

The variables in a model come in two kinds, endogenous and exogenous. An exogenous variable's equation just sets that variable to a specific value: if V is exogenous, the equation says $V := v$ for a certain value v. An exogenous variable gets its value from "outside the system." An endogenous variable gets its value from inside: the equation for an endogenous variable Y determines its value from the values of other variables $X1, \ldots, Xn$. The equation $Y := f(X1, \ldots, Xn)$ is to be understood to mean that the Xi are all the direct causes of Y; this itself is taken to mean that the value of each Xi at least sometimes makes a difference to the value of f.[23] There are other constraints that a set of variables and equations must satisfy to constitute a possible causal model of a possible situation, but we will not need them.

To model a situation where I strike a match, causing it to light, let S be a variable with value 1 if I strike, 0 if I don't, and L be a variable with value 1 if the match lights, 0 if it doesn't. The equations of the model are

$S := 1,$

$L := S.$

Given a causal model, one wants to know what it takes for one variable X's taking on a value x to be a cause of another variable Y's taking on a value y. One popular answer says that $X = x$ is a cause of $Y = y$ in a given model M iff

[23] $X1$ makes no difference to the value of f iff for all values $x2, \ldots, xn$ of $X2, \ldots, Xn$, $f(a, x2, \ldots, xn) = f(b, x2, \ldots, xn)$ for any possible values a, b of $X1$.

there is a sequence, or path, of variables $(X, V1, \ldots, Vn, Y)$ where X appears on the right-hand side of the equation for $V1$, $V1$ appears on the right-hand side of the equation for $V2$, and so on, and, intuitively, there is a possible value for X with the property that, had X taken that value, while the variables off the given path from X to Y had been held fixed at their given values, then Y would have taken some other value.[24] In our simple example there are no off-path variables, so all it takes for $S = 1$ to be a cause of $L = 1$ is for it to be true that if S had been 0, L would have been 0.

There are many philosophical questions about how these causal models are to be understood.[25] Here only one question is important: what sort of things can a variable in a causal model be used to represent? The standard answer, I take it, is there are almost no restrictions on what a variable can represent—a variable can correspond to any indirect question, from *whether event E happened* and *how much energy the explosion released* to *whether the room contained oxygen* and beyond.[26] Variables are given so much representational power because they have a big job to do. If you have something causally relevant that you want to represent in a causal model then the only way to represent it is to use a variable.

This makes it impossible to distinguish causes from background conditions, and from things with other modes of causal relevance, in these models. The oxygen in the room, when I strike a match, is, again, a background condition to the lighting, not a cause. But if you want to explicitly represent the presence of oxygen and its relation to the lighting in our causal model,

---

[24] This claim about what value Y would have taken if X had had value $x1$ is understood as a claim about what value Y does take in a specific alternative to M. First define a model $M1$ related to M like this: if the equation for X is not $X := x$, replace it with this equation. If W is a variable not in the given sequence, and $W = w$ in M, then the equation for W in $M1$ is to be $W := w$. So all variables not on the given path from X to Y are, in $M1$, held fixed at the values they have in M. Note that in $M1$, $Y = y$, just as in M. Finally, it is true in M that Y would have had a value other than y had X had a value other than x, and so true that $X = x$ is a cause of $Y = y$, when there is some alternative value $x1$ for X such that in the model $M2$ that differs from $M1$ only in that the equation for X is $X := x1$, Y takes on a value other than y. This theory of causation is given in (Hitchcock 2001a) and (Woodward 2003), among many others.

[25] One thorough treatment of such questions is in (Woodward 2003). Hall (2007) thinks these questions are harder than those who like to state their theories of causation using these models take them to be.

[26] "Beyond" might include variables like *what species this individual belongs to* and *how many people are in the room*. Some authors, like (Woodward 2003), formally allow all these variables, but deny that just any of them can be a cause of something; a variable can be a cause only if it is possible to "intervene" on it—by which they mean, in part, to cause it to take another value. One might doubt that it is possible to cause the raccoon in my neighborhood to become a member of a different species.

you would have to do it by expanding the model to include a new binary variable *O*, with value 1 iff oxygen is present; the full list of equations would be

$O := 1$,

$S := 1$,

$L := SO$.

The variables *O* and *S*, for whether there is oxygen and whether the match is struck, enter these equations symmetrically. There is nothing in the model to tell you whether one is a cause or a background condition. And in fact *O*'s having value 1 satisfies the condition stated earlier for being a cause of *L*'s having value 1—even though it is not a cause.

A causal model is often accompanied by a directed graph, where the nodes are the model's variables and an arrow is drawn from (the node for) *V* to *W* iff *V* appears on the right-hand side of the equation for *W*. I'll draw these graphs with dotted lines so they won't be confused with neuron diagrams. The graph for our model is in figure 4.7.

The roles of *O* and *S* in this graph, like their roles in the model itself, are symmetric. But, as I have argued, the presence of oxygen, and so *O*, is only indirectly relevant to the lighting, and so to *L*. To depict indirect relevance, we should draw an arrow, not from *O* to *L*, but from *O* to the arrow from *S* to *L*, as in figure 4.8, because what *O* does is modulate whether and in what way *L* depends on *S*.

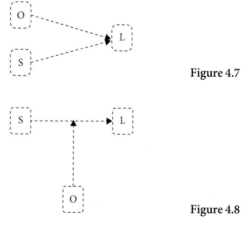

Figure 4.7

Figure 4.8

If we could depict causal models this way, direct and indirect modes of causal relevance would look different, and that would be an improvement.[27] But limitations would remain—there would still be no way to distinguish variables that represent background conditions from those which represent enablers. For all that figure 4.8 shows, O could be either.

What about the causal models themselves, the sets of variables and equations? Incorporating into them a distinction between direct and indirect relevance is not so easy. One could complicate the models by designating some variables as modulator variables, and then determining the value of an endogenous variable using a function from modulator variables to a function from (directly relevant) variables to values. For example, the match-oxygen system would need a function from the modulator variable O to equations showing how S depends on L:

$$O = 1 \rightarrow L := S,$$
$$O = 0 \rightarrow L := 0.$$

This system is mathematically equivalent to the earlier equation, $L := SO$. But we are doing metaphysics, and the systems are not metaphysically equivalent. Only the second makes explicit that O is indirectly relevant to L.

4.10 Direct vs indirect relevance in scientific contexts

James Woodward, who favors a structural equations approach to causation, takes as his entry into thinking about causation the idea that causes are things "potentially exploitable for purposes of manipulation and control" (2003: v). Manipulating whether the match is struck and manipulating whether oxygen is in the room are both ways to control whether the match lights. If you think that the key to causation is manipulability then the striking and the presence of oxygen look to be on a par. If you think that the key to causation is manipulability then you may doubt that there is a metaphysically interesting distinction between causes and background

---

[27] I mean: an improvement if you want a metaphysically clear representation of a situation's causal structure. A referee pointed out that, in another way, this change is not an improvement: it would make causal models useless for the causal discovery algorithms scientists have produced. But it's the first perspective that I care about here.

conditions (and other indirect modes of relevance). You may welcome a formalism that makes that distinction invisible.

I think you should not welcome it, because the distinction between being a cause and being indirectly relevant to the causing is mirrored by a distinction between direct and indirect ways to manipulate or control something. Manipulating whether a match is struck is a direct way to control whether the match lights. Manipulating whether oxygen is present is an indirect way: what it controls is the way in which whether the match lights depends on whether it is struck.

Woodward might reply that this direct/indirect distinction, even if real, is one only metaphysicians care about, and so insofar as one wants a theory of causation that incorporates only distinctions that are important in science, one will ignore it. But the direct/indirect relevance distinction is important in science, as a few examples can establish.

In *The Selfish Gene* Richard Dawkins briefly takes up the question of why we die of old age, and (citing Peter Medawar) observes that natural selection will weed out genes that tend to harm or kill us when we are young, while leaving in place genes that tend to harm or kill us after we have reproduced. He observes further that if this is the case

> we could try to 'fool' genes into thinking that the body they are sitting in is younger than it really is. In practice this would mean identifying changes in the internal chemical environment of a body that take place during aging. Any of these could be the 'cues' that 'turn on' late-acting lethal genes. By simulating the superficial chemical properties of a young body it might be possible to prevent the turning on of late-acting deleterious genes. The interesting point is that chemical signals of old age need not in any normal sense be deleterious in themselves. For instance, suppose that it incidentally happens to be a fact that a substance S is more concentrated in the bodies of old individuals than of young individuals. S in itself might be quite harmless, perhaps some substance in food which accumulates in the body over time. But automatically, any gene that just happened to exert a deleterious effect in the presence of S, but which otherwise had a good effect, would be positively selected in the gene pool, and would in effect be a gene 'for' dying of old age. The cure would simply be to remove S from the body.
>
> What is revolutionary about this idea is that S itself is only a 'label' for old age. Any doctor who noticed that high concentrations of S tended to

lead to death, would probably think of S as a kind of poison, and would rack his brains to find a direct causal link between S and bodily malfunctioning. But in the case of our hypothetical example, he might be wasting his time!

(1976: 41–42)

Dawkins thinks it is important and interesting, both to pure science and to medicine, that the presence of S might be, not a cause of bodily malfunction, but instead a context in which something else, lethal genes, have a "deleterious" effect.

Switching from popular to more esoteric science, endocrinologists say that some hormones in some contexts have what they call a "permissive effect." It turns out that to have a permissive effect is really to be an enabler. One textbook gives this definition:

> hormones may regulate receptors for other hormones. Estrogens increase the number of uterine receptors for progestins. Such an effect, in which one hormone induces production of receptors for a second hormone, or otherwise brings about the conditions necessary for the second hormone to be effective, is called a permissive effect.   (Nelson 1995: 76)

Brings about the conditions necessary for the second hormone to be effective. That's almost exactly my definition of enabling. Deciding whether a hormone has a permissive effect is important in endocrinology, and permissive effects are common. Thyroid hormone is "essential for growth but is not itself directly responsible for promoting growth. It plays a permissive role"—note that this passage labels permissive effects as indirect (Sherwood 2015: 658). And in milk production the main cause is prolactin, which "acts on the alveolar epithelium to promote secretion of milk to replace the ejected milk," but "at least four other hormones are essential for their permissive role in ongoing milk production: cortisol, insulin, parathyroid hormone, and growth hormone." (Sherwood 2015: 769).

So scientists care about direct vs indirect relevance in their thinking about particular cases. Scientists also care in the abstract. Discussions of statistical methods emphasize the importance of the notion of a "moderator variable," which is defined as a variable that "affects the direction and/or strength of the relation between an independent or predictor variable and a dependent or criterion variable" (Baron and Kenny 1986: 1174). Moderator variables are indirectly relevant. One textbook's "conceptual diagram" for moderation is, in fact, exactly my figure 4.8, showing one variable influencing the relation between two others (Hayes 2013: 209). How important is the notion of a moderator variable? That textbook's author writes that "moderation analysis" is one of "the more widely used statistical methods in the social, behavioral, and health sciences" (Hayes 2013: viii).[28]

4.11 Counterfactual dependence

I have distinguished between background conditions and enablers—an enabler causes the onset of a background condition. When I turn a knob to release oxygen from a tank, and fill the room where you're about to strike a match with oxygen, my turning of the knob is an enabler relative to the striking and the lighting. Enablers are events. Now if I hadn't turned the knob to release the oxygen, the match wouldn't have lit. If neuron C hadn't fired, in my neuron diagram of enabling, neuron B wouldn't have fired. These counterfactuals are still true. And isn't counterfactual dependence (between distinct events) sufficient for causation? Its sufficiency is after all enshrined in David Lewis's original counterfactual theory of causation (Lewis 1986a) and many of its descendants; the major problem its descendants face is the existence of cases where counterfactual dependence is not necessary.

The answer is no, counterfactual dependence is not sufficient for causation. The "Dependence Thesis" is false. Ned Hall has done more than anyone to blunt its appeal. Dependence, he argues, is inconsistent with the claim that causation is transitive, with the claim that causation is local in space and time, and with the claim that causation is intrinsic (roughly: a duplicate of a causal process connecting C to E is also a causal process). So you can't accept any of those and also Dependence; Hall argues that it is better to give up Dependence than the other three (Hall 2000, 2004). Hall's arguments aside (well not entirely, since locality has come up in my argument too), I think that the appeal of Dependence fades as you explore the distinction between enabling and causing.[29] If C is a cause of E and N enables C to cause E, it may be (if we set aside redundant causation) that E counterfactually depends on both C and N. But the reasons why the

---

[28] To be fair to Hayes, he also thinks (in my terms) that the direct/indirect relevance distinction is in how we think, not out in the world; conceptualizing X as a cause and M as a moderator, and conceptualizing M as a cause and X as a moderator, are both correct (Hayes 2013: 217). Needless to say, I disagree.

[29] Lombard (1990) also thinks enabling falsifies Dependence.

counterfactuals are true are so different in the two cases! With the case of N (the enabler) there are all the complications about the state whose onset N causes, and that state's being a reason why C is cause; all these factor in to why the counterfactual is true. Not so in the case of the counterfactual about C. These differences more than justify jettisoning the idea that counterfactual dependence is sufficient for causation.

4.12 Two kinds of causation?; and, who cares?

I said that Hall argues against Dependence, but that's not quite right. His considered view is (or was) a version of causal pluralism: there are two concepts of causation, and Dependence is true only of the less central one. The central concept is the one that is transitive, local, and intrinsic. My view is that what Hall calls the central concept is the only concept, and that the one he says is characterized by Dependence is not a concept of causation at all. But I think that the list I have been compiling, of the varieties of causal relevance, can help someone with Hall's view. What is this second concept of causation, the one characterized by Dependence? What makes it tick? Can we get inside the way it works? What exactly is its relation to the central concept? They should answer that (what they call) the less central concept is a gerrymandered disjunction: to fall under that concept is to be either a cause or a background condition or an enabler.

But enough aid and comfort for the enemy. I've argued that indirect varieties of relevance are not causation. I reject Hall's causal pluralism; I deny that there is any kind of causation of which Dependence is true. But it may be that some version of causal pluralism can be defended without confusing causation with other varieties of relevance. An example might[30] be Hitchcock's version: he holds that one way to be a cause is to be a

---

[30] Why "might"? Hitchcock motivates his distinction with cases where something is a "positive" cause in one way and a "negative" cause in another, as in the philosophically famous example of birth control pills, which are a negative net cause of thrombosis, but a positive component cause, along a path that excludes its effects on pregnancy. But (I say) there is no negative causation, only prevention (see section 4.15), which is a different variety of relevance. Also, my focus is the causation of particular events by particular events (so-called "token causation"), and so the question here is whether pluralism about token causation is correct; but the birth control pill example most directly supports pluralism about "type" causation ("birth control pills are a component cause of thrombosis" is a type-causal claim). It's doubtful this example supports token causation pluralism, since, as Hitchcock admits (2001b: 375), no particular pill-taking event can both cause someone to get a blood clot, and also prevent them from getting a blood clot.

"component cause" (roughly, cause along a particular causal path) and another is to be a "net cause" (cause when all paths are considered) (Hitchcock 2001b, 2003; a similar distinction appears in Woodward 2003; Pearl 2000 is the common cause). I insist that causal relevance comes in many kinds, not that causation itself does not.

Some people are okay with the idea that there is more than one variety of causal relevance, but not with my claim that only one of them is true causation—not because they disagree, but because they can't see why it matters. What real mistake is someone making who agrees that there are important differences between the presence of oxygen and the striking of the match, but insists that both are causes? I find this question frustrating, though my answer will surely frustrate those who ask it. The mistake is that their answer to *which things are causes?* is wrong, and that a wrong answer to this will inevitably lead to a wrong answer to *what is causation?*. And *what is causation?* is an important question. It's on the list of questions that are mandatory for a complete metaphysics. So it's bad to get the answer wrong.

I know people who won't accept that *what is causation?* is important until I tell them how answering it will help answer other important questions. While I think their demand can be satisfied (the examples are as usual: causation is connected to explanation and responsibility among other notions), I also think they demand too much, in this case and in general. *No question is important unless answering it helps answer some (distinct) important question* is obviously a vicious regress, entailing that no question is important. Some questions must be important for their own sake. *What is causation?* is one of them.

4.13 Basic vs derived varieties

So far I have identified three varieties of causal relevance:

Name	Relation to Causation
Cause	—
Background Condition	Explains why C caused E rather than something else
Ennobler	Explains why C rather than something else caused E
Enabler	Cause of the onset of a background condition

In this list there is a pleasing symmetry between background conditions and ennoblers. Each explains why C caused E, but the explanations target different contrasts. Background conditions target why C had one effect rather than another—wiggle the background conditions, and you change what effects C has. Ennoblers target why E had one cause rather than another—wiggle the ennoblers, and you change which of the events preceding E earns the status of cause. The category of an enabler, however, is a dangler. It doesn't really belong with the other three. *Cause, background condition,* and *ennobler* are what we might call basic mode of causal relevance. But *enabler* is a derived mode, got by applying *cause* to *background condition.*

Now if applying *cause* to *background condition* generates a derived mode, then presumably combining any two (basic or derived) modes generates a derived mode. Something might be a cause of an ennobler, or a background condition to something's causing an enabler. Once we contemplate this ever-expanding hierarchy of derived modes, we might wonder whether the expansion always goes on forever, or whether instead some combinations of modes "collapse" into lower modes. If $M1, \ldots, Mn$ are modes of causal relevance, and so are $R1, \ldots, Rm$, does it ever happen that $Mn \ldots M1$ (the result of applying $M2$ to $M1$, and then $M3$ to the result, and so on) is identical to $Rm \ldots R1$? Enablers of E are not (thereby) causes of E, but are causes of facts that ennoble C into a cause of E thereby causes of E? While I doubt that collapse happens very often, these questions are hard, and I will mostly avoid them, except for one that has drawn a lot of attention: the question of whether preventers of preventers are causes. But I can't discuss double prevention until I discuss single prevention. Prevention is a kind of negative causation, and so a kind of causal relevance. But where does it fit on the list?

4.14 Transitivity

Having raised questions about prevention, I want to postpone them. First I want to use the distinctions made so far to resolve part of the debate over whether causation is transitive: whether, necessarily, if C is a cause of E and E is a cause of F, C is a cause of F.

Transitivity is threatened by switching examples. A train track starts at station A and divides into two parallel tracks which reconverge just before station B (figure 4.9). Back at station A a train departs. Before it reaches the division point I pull the lever that sets the junction to send the train down the lower track. It does so, and later arrives at station B. The argument goes:

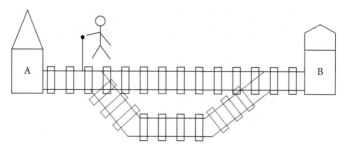

Figure 4.9

my pulling the lever causes the train's being on, or moving along, the lower track; its moving along the lower track causes its arrival at B; but my pulling the lever does not cause its arrival, since it would have arrived at B anyway (indeed, the case can be set up so that it would have arrived at the same time). If all that is right, then this is a counterexample to transitivity.

I shall argue that switches are not counterexamples to transitivity. Now Hall (2000) claims that all problem cases for transitivity involve either short circuits, or switching, or both. He also argues that short circuits are only counterexamples to transitivity if there is causation by double prevention.[31] Since I deny that the double prevention in short circuits is causation (section 4.20), showing that switches are not counterexamples makes for a full defense of transitivity. Hall argues for this too, but, as I will explain, my argument that switches are not counterexamples differs from his.

If causation is transitive, then either (i) my pulling of the lever is, after all, a cause of the train's arrival; or (ii) my pulling of the lever is not, after all, a cause of the train's moving on the lower track; or (iii) the train's moving on the lower track is not, after all, a cause of the train's arrival at B. Claim (iii) is clearly false.[32] Hall argues at length that option (i) is the way to go (2000). But that's the wrong solution. Really it is (ii) that is correct, and the concept of an enabler puts us in a position to see this. My pulling of the lever is an enabler: it enables the train's departure to cause the train's motion along the

---

[31] A canonical short circuit: "Billy sees Suzy about to throw a water balloon at her neighbor's dog. He runs to try to stop her, but trips over a tree root and so fails. Suzy, totally oblivious to him, throws the water balloon at the dog. It yelps" (Hall 2000: 201). Billy's beginning to run is a cause of his tripping, and if double-preventers are causes, his tripping is a cause of the yelping, but the running is not a cause of the yelping.

[32] On a view like Paul's (2000), (iii) is true: it is the train's moving toward B, an event that could have happened on either track, that is a cause of the arrival. Hall (2000) argues that this response does not generalize to all switching cases.

lower track. It puts in place a state—one consisting in the tracks at the junction pointing toward the lower track—that is a background condition to the departure's causing the motion on the lower track. But something that enables the departure to cause the motion is not itself a cause of the motion. If you lack the concept of an enabler it is easy to think that, since the pulling of the lever is obviously causally relevant to the train's motion on the lower track, it must be a cause of the train's motion. But the existence of other varieties of causal relevance shows this to be bad reasoning.

Hall's arguments that my pulling of the lever is, after all, a cause of the train's arrival are faulty for similar reasons. Here is one of them:

> Notice, first, that among the (highly nonsalient) causes of the train's arrival is the presence of a certain section S of the track down which the train travels, during the time that the train is, in fact, on S. And among the causes of the presence of S at this time is the presence of S a day earlier. So we should say: among the causes of the arrival is the presence of S a day earlier. That is certainly odd, but it is odd in the familiar way to which writers on causation have grown accustomed: whatever the exact nature of the causal concept we are trying to analyze, it surely picks out a very permissive relation, one which does not distinguish between events that we would normally single out as causes and events we would normally ignore because their causal relationship to the effect in question is too boring or obvious to be worth mentioning, or is easily hidden from view as part of the "background conditions." The presence of S a day earlier is like that.
>
> But the relationship that the switching event bears to the arrival is just like the relationship that the earlier presence of S bears to the arrival: for the relationship that the switching event bears to the setting of the switch as the train passes over it is just like the relationship that the earlier presence of S bears to the later presence of S, and the relationship the setting of the switch as the train passes over it bears to the arrival is just like the relationship the later presence of S bears to the arrival. . . . the switching event causes the setting of the switch, which interacts with the passing train in the same way as the mere presence of a piece of track interacts with the passing train, and so on.   (2000: 207–208)

Yes, absolutely, this is almost exactly fifty percent right. Hall draws an analogy between the role the switching (the pulling of the lever) plays in causing the train's arrival, and the role the presence of section S of the track plays (figure 4.10). It is a good analogy, but it works against the truth of (i),

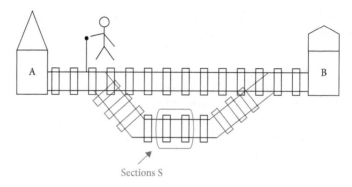

Sections S

Figure 4.10

not in its favor. The switching and the presence of S are similar, not because both are causes, but because neither is. The presence of S is a state that has obtained ever since S was installed. It obtained when the train passed over S, and it obtained a day earlier. And that state was a background condition to the train's departure's causing the train's arrival. It is part of why the departure caused the arrival. But that does not make the presence of S a cause of the arrival; a background condition to C's causing E is not a cause of E. So if we are to look at the role the presence of S plays when figuring out the role that the junction's pointing toward the lower track plays, we will want to say that it too is a background condition (to the train's departure's causing the train's motion on the lower track). The same goes if we are to look at the role that the presence of S a day earlier plays when figuring out the role that the pulling of the lever plays. Here the analogy is not perfect: the pulling of the lever causes the junction to begin to point toward the lower track, while the presence of S a day earlier does not cause the presence of S today. Still, neither is a cause. (The earlier presence of S is the same state as the presence of S today, while the pulling of the lever is an enabler.)

Hall is willing to call the presence of S a background condition, but he doesn't think that shows it is not a cause; he thinks that background conditions are non-salient causes. And he thinks they are causes because he accepts a very liberal theory of events, one that counts the presence of S as an event. If that were an event, then yes, it would be hard to see how it differed from the train's departure. But that liberal theory is false; the presence of S is not an event. Events, again, go with doings, but in being present S is not doing anything.

Hall also uses a "subtraction test" to argue that the pulling of the lever is a cause of the train's arrival (2000: 206). Imagine that a portion of the upper track, the track the train never passes over, had not been there. In that scenario the pulling of the lever would have been a cause of the train's arrival (right?). But whether the pulling is a cause shouldn't depend on what is going on with a bit of track that the train never gets near. So even when the upper track is intact, the pulling is a cause. Right: whether the pulling is a cause shouldn't depend on something far away from where the train ever was. But the right conclusion is not that the pulling is a cause even when the track is present, but that the pulling is not a cause even when the track is absent. In a scenario where part of the upper track is missing, the pulling of the lever to set the junction to send the train to the lower track is (still) not a cause; it is still (just) an enabler. Pulling the lever puts into place a state that is a background condition to the train's departure causing its arrival. Pulling the lever, or leaving it in place, is a way of manipulating what states obtain, and so manipulating the background conditions. The difference is, with the upper track in place, either way, pull the lever or do nothing, a state will be in place that will determine that the train's departure from A causes its arrival at B. Not the same state: pull and one state will obtain, do nothing and another will. But either state determines the departure to have the same (ultimate) effect, the arrival at B. When a piece of the upper track is missing, on the other hand, manipulating the background conditions matters to the departure's ultimate effect: pull the lever, and the departure causes the train to arrive at B; leave the lever where it is, and the departure causes the train to derail when it hits the broken track. But, again, neither enabling the departure to cause the arrival, nor enabling it to cause a derailment, is the same as causing the arrival, or a derailment.[33]

The way neuron diagrams for switches are sometimes drawn makes it hard to appreciate that they are enablers rather than causes, for reasons I've already mentioned: the invisibility of background conditions in those diagrams. Paul and Hall's canonical neuron diagram for switching is drawn as in figure 4.11 (2013: 232). The relation the firing of C bears to the firing of B does not appear to differ in any way from the relation the firing of A bears to it. But of course it does: the firing of C puts in place a state that determines which axon is excited when B fires. The firing of A does something different: it just causes B to fire. A more perspicuous diagram is in figure 4.12. We may

---

[33] Similar remarks apply to Hall's "variation test" argument that pulling the lever is a cause of the arrival (2000: 207).

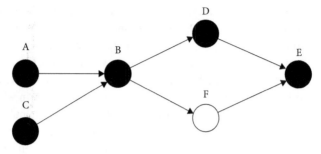

Figure 4.11

imagine, fancifully, that which axon is excited when B fires depends on whether oxygen is present around B. This diagram makes clear the different roles that A and C play; it makes clear that C is an enabler.[34]

4.15 Prevention

A fourth basic way to be causally relevant is to prevent something. If I douse your match with water and then you strike it and it fizzles but does not light, I have prevented your match from lighting. Similarly if I suck the oxygen out of the room before you strike. Preventing is, in a way, a kind of negative of causing, though we will need to get clearer on the way in which this is so.

Preventing is different from the varieties we have already seen. If something exhibits any of the earlier kinds of causal relevance, then it is relevant to a causing. But prevention is not. If I prevent the match from lighting, what I do is not relevant to the causing of the lighting, because, obviously, there was no lighting and no causing of a lighting. But if I prevent the match from lighting, what I do is relevant to something; it is relevant to your failure to cause the match to light. You failed because, although you did something that normally causes matches to light, namely strike the match; although

---

[34] A referee asked whether switches are essentially enablers. Suppose Jupiter shakes an asteroid loose and it heads toward the earth, but Superman punches it away; but then, since he miscalculated, it bounces off the moon and hits the earth anyway. Superman's punch didn't enable Jupiter's pull to cause the asteroid to hit the moon. It was itself a cause of the asteroid's hitting the moon. But wasn't it also a switch with respect to the asteroid's path? Since the moon bounce is a cause of the asteroid's hitting the earth, transitivity is true only if Superman's punch is a cause of the asteroid's hitting the earth—but isn't this the sort of claim I've been trying to deny? I admit to being troubled by this question and unsure what to say. My current view is that Superman's punch is a cause of the earth impact, and also that the reasons for denying this are much weaker than the reasons for denying that switching the train track is a cause of the train's ultimate arrival.

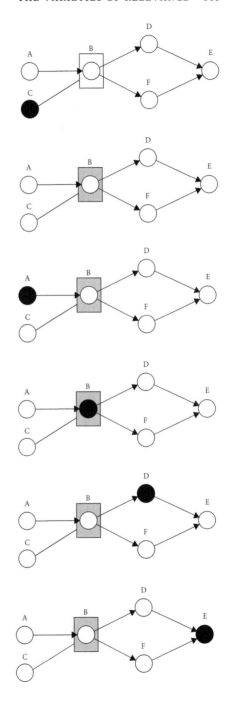

Figure 4.12

you did something that started a process that was heading toward a lighting of a match, as a result of my dousing it that process fizzled out before it could get there. One way in which preventing is a kind of negative of causing is that it is relevant to a failure to cause, rather than a success.

4.16   Against causing a negative: the analogy to undercutting defeat

One might object that preventing is after all a kind of causal relevance that we have already seen: it is a kind of causing, namely "causing a negative." Preventing the match from lighting is just causing the match not to light. This view says that preventing is bearing a "positive" relation (causation) to something negative ("not lighting"), while my view says that preventing is what it looks like on the surface: bearing a negative relation (prevention) to a positive thing (lighting).

One argument that preventing is not causing a negative goes by analogy. Preventing as a kind of causal relevance is analogous to undercutting defeat as a kind of evidential relevance. Here again is a canonical example of undercutting defeat: when facing a wall with my eyes open and inquiring into its color, if all I have to go on is how the wall looks, then that the wall looks red to me is evidence that it is red. But if I learn that the wall is illuminated by a red light, this new fact defeats my original evidence's support for the red hypothesis. It, as it were, prevents my first evidence from supporting the red hypothesis. Undercutting defeaters are certainly evidentially relevant. But undercutting defeaters are not evidence for a negative. That the wall is illuminated by a red light is not evidence that the wall is not red, or that it is some color other than red. So, given the analogy, preventing something from happening is not causing a negative.

4.17   Against causing a negative: there are no negative acts

I also have a direct argument that preventing is not causing a negative. Preventing is not causing a negative because it is not possible to cause a negative. It is not possible, for example, to cause a match not to light.[35]

---

[35] This is a metaphysical argument that preventing is not causing a negative. There is also psychological evidence that people do not equate preventing with causing a negative; see (Walsh and Sloman 2011).

I have been switching back and forth, since the beginning, between two ways to use "cause." On one use, the dominant one so far, it is events that cause and get caused. "The striking caused the lighting"—that's the first use. On the second use, it is things (that are not events) that cause and get caused. "*I* caused *the match* to light by striking it"—that's the second use. The cause is me, and I'm not an event, and the direct object of "cause" is "the match," and the match is not an event. If we label causation described the first way "event causation" then we can label causation described the second way "agent causation." Agent-causal claims are more complicated, because there are (or can be) two prepositional phrases following the direct object: I caused the match *(i) to light (ii) by striking it*. The two kinds of causal talk occupy different metaphysical levels, with (on my view) agent causation more basic, and event causation derived from it.[36]

Now notice that if I cause something to V, I cause it to do something; only when an activity verb goes in for "V" is the result something that can be true. Similarly, if I cause something to V by Zing, I cause it to V by doing something; only when an activity verb goes in for "Zing" is the result something that can be true. These observations provide the material for showing how event causation arises from agent causation: if X causes Y to V by Zing, then X and Y both did something, and so in virtue of their doing those things, two events happened, a Ving and a Zing; and the Ving is a cause (an event-cause) of the Zing. If I caused the match to light by striking it (that's agent causation), then my striking caused the lighting (event causation).

Let's operate at the level of agent causation. The argument that it is impossible to cause a negative is this. As I just claimed, causing is always causing something to do something. So causing a negative would be causing something to do a negative act. But there are no negative acts.

Why are there no negative acts? If there are any, there are lots of them. If there are any negative acts, then the operation that generates the negative of an act is defined everywhere; every act has a negative. But the act of waving my hand does not have a negative. If it did, "not waving my hand" would denote or express it, so it would make sense to say that one thing I am doing right now is not waving my hand. But this does not make sense (and not on some philosophically sophisticated meaning of "not make sense"—it is literally ungrammatical).

---

[36] For arguments that agent causation is more basic see (Lowe 2008), (Skow 2018), and (Baron-Schmitt Ms).

Of course it does make sense to say that one thing I am not doing right now is waving my hand. But that is to mention a positive act (waving) that I am not performing, not to mention a negative act that I am performing.

Here are some more arguments against negative acts. Whenever something does something, it makes sense to ask how and where it did that thing. So if "not waving my hand" denotes or expresses a (negative) act, then whenever I am not waving my hand it makes sense to ask how and where. But these do not make sense. If I say I did not wave my hand just now you cannot meaningfully ask "How did you do it?" or "Did you do it quickly?"; you cannot meaningfully ask "Where did you do it?" or "Did you do it outside?" And while it is meaningful to say "I did not wave my hand quickly," this does not entail that I did something quickly. The meaningful interpretation here groups the words as "I did not [wave my hand quickly]"; if there were negative acts, there would be another meaningful interpretation corresponding to "I [[did not wave my hand] quickly]." But there is no such interpretation.[37] Finally, if X is something that can be done, then it always makes sense to ask how often I did it during some time period. So if there were negative acts, and so if "not wave my hand" denoted an act, then it would make sense to ask how often I did it. But neither "How often did you not wave your hand yesterday?" nor "I didn't wave my hand yesterday six times" (grouped as "I [[didn't wave my hand] six times yesterday]") make sense.[38]

Since there are no negative acts, it is impossible to cause something to perform one of them; it is impossible to cause a negative.

4.18 Against causing a negative: there are no negative events

When I say that you can't cause a negative I mean you can't cause something to perform a negative act. But most discussions of whether you can cause a negative ask whether you can cause a negative event. I have not yet said anything about whether there are negative events or, if there are, whether they can be caused. But my theory of the relation between events, acts, and doings implies answers to these questions. It implies that there are no

---

[37] A similar argument is in (Maienborn 2005: 310), but she is arguing that "I did not wave my hand quickly" does not entail that any event happened. For that argument, see section 4.18 and footnote 39.

[38] See (Herweg 1991: 974); like (Maienborn 2005), he is arguing against negative events, not negative acts.

negative events, and so no negative events around to get caused. For, again, events go with doings: if an event happens, that's because something did something. If that's what it takes for an event to happen, when does it take specifically for a negative event to happen? It has to be that the occurrence of a negative event requires that something perform a negative act. So if there is such a negative act as not-waving-one's-hand, and I perform it, then in virtue of this fact a negative event, a "not-waving of my hand," would happen. But, again, there aren't any negative acts to be done.

The ideas in the argument against negative acts can be used to construct a direct argument against negative events, one that does not depend on my theory of events.[39] Pronouns can refer to events that have not been explicitly introduced into the discourse, if a fact in virtue of which an event happened has been asserted. The sentence "A bomb exploded yesterday" does not itself mention any events, but since in virtue of its truth an event (an explosion) occurred, we can go on to say "…It was loud," where "it" refers to the explosion. So if there are negative events, then if a bomb (say, the biggest one in the local bomb shop) did not explode yesterday, in virtue of this fact a negative event occurred. So it should be okay to say "The bomb did not explode yesterday. It was quiet," where "it" refers to an event. But this is not okay. Similarly, "The bomb exploded yesterday. It happened in the remote desert" is fine, while "The bomb did not explode yesterday. It happened in the remote desert" can only evoke bewilderment. The conclusion, again: there are no negative events.

Now some philosophers, Woodward (2006) being a good example, resist denying that there are any negative events, on the ground that events can seem negative when conceptualized one way and positive when conceptualized another, when neither way of conceptualizing them is better than the other. Moreover, he says, some events that seem negative certainly exist and cause others. "[A]s an illustration of these points," he writes (note that Woodward uses "presence/absence" where I use "positive/negative event"— but he's clearly discussing the same distinction):

consider death. Is it a presence or an absence? Looked at one way, it is about as clear a case of an absence (of life, of brain activity) as one could imagine. Nonetheless, we often treat death as a "positive" occurrence, and it is certainly not a mere "nothing" in the sense in which we might describe,

---

[39] In fact, as I mentioned in note 37, I got the materials for the argument against negative acts from Maienborn's arguments against negative events (Maienborn 2005).

say, an empty box as containing nothing. (Typically a body is present that is in a certain condition.) No one doubts that deaths can be effects (inquests investigate the causes of death), and it seems arbitrary to deny that deaths can be causes (of physiological changes to the body, of grief on the part of others, of the collapse of the empire) as well.   (22)

Woodward doesn't come right out and say it, but his view seems to be that the question of whether death is a positive or a negative event is a defective question: "looked at one way" death is negative, looked at another it is positive, and neither way of looking is objectively correct, so all that can be said about whether death is negative is that it depends on how you look at it. And if this is right then a theory of causation should not care about which answer is correct. A theory of causation should not give positive events and negative events different statuses, or causal powers.

I don't think the question of whether death is a negative event is a bad question. I don't think it depends on how you look at it. And I know the (objectively correct) answer: death is a positive event. That's because something's death is an event that happens in virtue of the fact that it died. Dying is an act, it is something that something can do. And dying is a not a negative act. It is not a negative act because, as I have argued, there are no negative acts.

Now my argument against negative acts assumed that if there are negative acts then some of them can be denoted or expressed by phrases of the form "not Ving" (not lighting a match, not waving my hand). Someone might reject this premise, and say that while there are negative acts, and every act has a negative, none of them can be denoted or expressed by phrases of this form, and few can be denoted or expressed in English in any way. Dying is one of these rare few. This seems like a wild position to me. If negative acts are as abundant as positive ones, it would be important to be able to talk about them, and so a terrible defect in English that it does not provide a simple way to take an activity verb phrase V and generate a verb phrase denoting the negative of the act V denotes.

But the merits of this position in general don't matter. There are independent reasons to deny that dying is a negative act. If dying is a negative act, it is the negative of living. There doesn't seem to be any better candidate positive act for dying to be the negative of. But if dying is the negative of living, then if something is dying, it is doing so in virtue of not living. That's just what it means to call the act of dying the negative of the act of living. But it is false that if something is dying, it is doing so in virtue of not living.

A person suffering through the end stages of a deadly illness is dying, and is also living. They are doing both. And if they are doing both, it cannot be that they are dying in virtue of the fact that they are not living.[40]

I am not saying, note, that there is no relation between the process of dying and the process of living. Maybe something is dying if something is happening to it that will bring its life to an end. Defining death and dying in terms of life faces obstacles, but even if this definition is right, it would not make dying the negative of living.[41]

Of course whether one should recognize the existence of negative events is and should be a complicated affair. I've presented what one might call "language-y" arguments against them, but one might maintain that there are still quite important ways in which a metaphysical theory that postulates negative events is better than one that does not. Here is one way you might argue. If I douse your match with water just before you strike it, surely there's something causally relevant going on; it is very different from a situation in which the match just sits in a cool room, unmoved, even if, in both cases, the match does not light. If we postulate negative events, the idea goes, we can capture the difference by saying that in the first case, I caused a negative event (the match's failure to light), while in the second case, nothing caused anything (relevant).

If there were no other good way to capture this difference than by postulating negative events (and maybe also the negative acts needed to generate them), that would constitute at least some reason to believe in them. But there is another way to capture this difference. Instead of complicating our theory of acts and events, we can—as I am suggesting—complicate our catalog of kinds of causal relevance. We can reject the thesis that preventing is causing a negative, and say that in the first but not in the second case something prevented the match from lighting.[42]

[40] Paul and Hall (2013: 179–180) reply to a similar argument by saying that both life and death are positive events, but do not have the connection between negative events and negative acts to appeal to in support.

[41] Feldman (1994) discusses the obstacles.

[42] What I say here about postulating negative events applies also to saying that the basic kind of causation relates facts, so that "negative facts" like the fact that the match did not light could be effects (see Mellor 1998). Better to understand prevention as a species of causal relevance distinct from causation. (I think there are other problems with fact causation; see chapter 5 of Skow 2018.) A philosopher might agree that there are no negative events, but maintain that preventing is causing, just causing a positive event "negatively described"; see (Schaffer 2005) for one approach. For reasons of space I cannot discuss this view; see (Paul and Hall 2013: chapter 4) for criticism.

4.19 Preventing is indirectly relevant

There are other problems with taking preventing to be causing a negative. Preventing is more like enabling than causing: it is a kind of indirect causal relevance. So taking preventing to be causing a negative gives it, wrongly, a kind of direct causal relevance. When I enable the match to light by filling the room with oxygen, I manipulate the conditions in the room so that they become conditions favorable to your striking having its usual effect. I make the conditions into background conditions to your striking's causing the lighting. That's a case of enabling; what is its opposite? A case of preventing.[43] When I douse your match with water, I manipulate the condition of the match so that it becomes a condition unfavorable to your striking's having its usual effect. In one central kind of case at least, when X prevents Y from Zing, something has done something that would other-wise cause Y to Z; and what X has done is interfere with the process before it can achieve this, by manipulating the conditions that determine the course that process will follow.[44]

It becomes clearer that preventing is, like enabling, an indirect kind of causal relevance, when you look at standard neuron diagrams containing prevention. The simplest neuron diagram depicting prevention is in figure 4.13. There are three neurons—that's important. Neuron A is hooked up so that it can send neuron C a stimulatory signal. Neuron B is hooked up so that it can send C an inhibitory signal. The "neuron laws" say that if C is receiving an inhibitory signal, then it will not fire, even if it receives a

---

[43] Lombard (1990) also notices that preventing is an opposite of enabling: he calls preventing "disenabling" (202).

[44] Other philosophers who deny that preventing is causing a negative include Dowe (2000, 2001) and Moore (2009: 453): Dowe, because he thinks that a physical process must connect cause to effect, and such processes cannot include negative events; Moore, because he thinks that there are no negative events to be caused. Hitchcock (2007) is agnostic about whether preventing is causing, because the relation between a preventer and what it prevents is not, in his terms, "self-contained." While this phrase has a quite technical meaning in his theory, it is not far from the idea that preventing is an indirect kind of causal relevance. Dowe's counterfactual theory of prevention also in effect treats prevention as a kind of indirect relevance.

The psychological literature contains support for the idea that prevention is a kind of indirect relevance. Cheng (1997) presents evidence that subjects infer the existence of what she calls a "preventive" cause only when a (potential) "generative" cause is also present. Woodward (2006) cites her paper and asserts that "the operation of a preventing cause requires the presence of a generative cause but not vice-versa. Preventive causes prevent by interfering with or blocking generative causes" (29). (These authors assert not just that prevention is indirect but also that it is a kind of causation, while I am arguing that prevention's indirectness precludes it from being causation.) The psychological experiments on prevention in (Walsh and Sloman 2011) also suggest that subjects think of prevention as indirect.

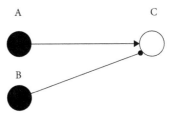

Figure 4.13

stimulatory signal.[45] In the scenario this diagram depicts, A and B both fire, and C does not, and it does not fire because it is being inhibited by B's signal. That is: B prevents C from firing, by preventing A's signal from causing C to fire. Clearly, then, preventing is indirectly relevant: B's signal is relevant to whether A's signal can cause C to fire.

I spoke of one kind of preventing being, like enabling, a matter of manipulating the conditions: in the one case, to make them unfavorable to the effect, in the other, to make them favorable. That's what's going on here. The relevant condition is that of neuron C. If B does not fire, C is "receptive": it will fire if stimulated. But if B does fire, it makes C unreceptive: it will not fire if stimulated.

Since what is being manipulated here are conditions, that is states, figure 4.13 is misleading, since it is not drawn in a way that makes visible what states obtain when. We should redraw it using our conventions for representing states. First we need to specify what the neuron looks like when receptive, and when unreceptive. So let its wall be of normal thickness when it is receptive, and be extra thick when unreceptive. Then the sequence of events in figure 4.13 unfolds as in figure 4.14. This figure makes it even more clear that preventing is like enabling; it makes it even more clear that preventing is changing what states obtain that determine the effects of a given cause, in this case the firing of A. (I have B fire right before A, to make clear that the inhibitory signal gets to C before the stimulatory one.)

If preventing were a kind of direct causal relevance, as causation itself is, then we ought to be able to draw a two-neuron diagram containing prevention. But we cannot. Of course nothing stops us from writing down the diagram in figure 4.15. It has just neuron B and its inhibiting connection to neuron C. B fires, and sends an inhibitory signal to C. But that's all: it is not true in this scenario that B prevents C from firing. A neuron that sends an

---

[45] This is the standard way of understanding inhibitory signals, enshrined in the canon by David Lewis's presentation of the neuron laws (1986a: 200–201).

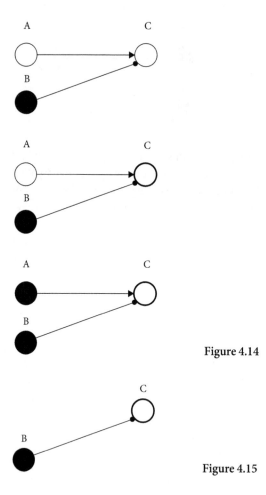

Figure 4.14

Figure 4.15

inhibitory signal does not prevent anything, does not prevent the signaled neuron from firing, unless that neuron is also being sent a stimulatory signal.

Of course you could imagine neurons that behave differently from these. What if neuron C, in figure 4.15, fires spontaneously, every five seconds, but B sends an inhibitory to C just before the five seconds are up, so that it doesn't fire? Then, yes, B prevented C from firing, even though there are only two neurons in the diagram. But this does not undermine my point. The prevention in this scenario is still indirect: B's signal prevents whatever mechanism in the neuron it is that recognizes that five seconds have passed from causing the neuron to fire. There is still a potential cause of the firing that is blocked, it is just not another neuron (and so is not represented in the diagram).

My thesis is really that in some cases preventing is the opposite of enabling. There is another variety of prevention. Enabling as I have defined it always involves manipulating the conditions that determine the course of a causal process: enabling steers the process toward an effect. In the examples so far preventing also involves manipulating the conditions, to steer the process away. But there are other ways to prevent one thing from causing another, besides manipulating the conditions. If you throw a baseball at a window, and I blast the baseball with my laser gun before it gets to the window, I prevent you (and the baseball) from breaking the window, but not by manipulating which states obtain. The same goes if I throw another baseball at yours, knocking it aside. That's not changing the states that determine the baseball's path; it is, in a more direct way, causing the baseball to take a different path.

4.20 Double prevention

Enabling, I said in section 4.13, is not a basic mode of causal relevance; instead it is causing the onset of a background condition. This observation raised the question of when one combination of varieties of relevance reduces to another; and I set the question aside. Now I want to bring it back. Does the combination *preventing a prevention* reduce to causation? Is double prevention causation?

Examples of double prevention became prominent in debates about causation largely through the efforts of Hall (2000; 2002; 2004) and Schaffer (2000). One of Hall's canonical examples is *Newt's Failed Mission*:

> It's a typical day during World War III, and the Good Guys have sent Bomber Billy on a mission to destroy an enemy target. Earlier in the day, one of the Bad Guys' fighter pilots—let it be Nasty Newt—takes off in his fighter plane on a routine patrolling mission. The Bad Guy ground-based radar defense system has just spotted Billy, and orders are about to be sent to Newt to go shoot him down, when a malfunction occurs in Newt's plane, and, sensitive thing that it is, it explodes. Billy's mission goes through completely undisturbed, and he destroys his target. But if the malfunction *hadn't* occurred, Newt would have shot down Billy, and the target would *not* have been destroyed. So the malfunction prevents something (Newt shooting down Billy) which would have prevented something else (Billy destroying the target).... (Hall 2002: 277–278)

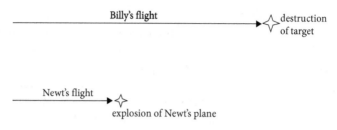

Figure 4.16 shows the events of the story.

Hall's conclusion is complicated. There are two kinds of causation, he says, "production" and "dependence"; and the malfunction is not a productive-cause of the destruction of the target. Double prevention is not (productive) causation. I think there is just one kind of causation, though many varieties of causal relevance. But the relevant changes being made, I agree with Hall: the malfunction is not a cause of the destruction.

For more evidence that Newt-style double prevention is not causation, consider psychological theories of personal identity. They say, with a lot of qualifications and clarifications, that a person P at a time t is identical to a person O at some earlier time iff P's psychological states are caused by O's psychological states. A common motive for these theories is the possibility of teletransportation. The person who appears on the planet after the transporter machine has read off Mr Spock's mental state and beamed that information down—that person is Mr Spock. But if double prevention is always causation, then these theories are not worth taking seriously. If I step into the transporter, which beams information about my mental state toward the planet, and that beam hits an asteroid, knocking it off course before it could block another beam of information, a beam that by coincidence was a duplicate of the beam the transporter sent but which was there by some freak statistical-mechanical fluctuation, and this second beam arrives on the planet and creates a duplicate of me, then, if double prevention is causation, the person on the planet's psychological states are caused by mine. My mental states prevent the asteroid from preventing the second beam from reaching the planet and creating my duplicate. But in this case the person on the planet is certainly not me.

Case closed? Definitely not. The clear verdict that these cases of double prevention are not causation is matched by opposite but equally clear verdicts about other cases: some cases of double prevention are quite obviously cases of causation. Canonical here is Schaffer's description of how guns fire and the accompanying blueprint for a gun (figure 4.17):

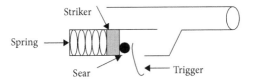

Figure 4.17

pulling the trigger causes the removal of the sear from the path of the spring, which causes the spring to uncoil, thereby compressing the gunpowder and causing an explosion, which causes the bullet to fire.   (2004: 199)

Pulling the trigger prevents the sear from preventing the spring from uncoiling. And pulling the trigger causes the firing of the gun.

Most treatments I am aware of treat all double prevention as of a piece: either it is always, or it is never, causation. But the cautious conclusion to draw from these examples is that double prevention sometimes is, and sometimes is not, causation.

This, of course, is unsatisfying if nothing can be said about when it is and when it isn't. And in fact there is an argument that nothing can be said. Newt's Mission and Schaffer's gun are, the idea goes, indistinguishable, suitably described. After all, both are represented by the same neuron diagram, and therefore there can be no causal difference between them. Well, are the neuron diagrams really the same? The standard diagrams for the two are in figure 4.18 (adapted from Hall 2004: 242) and figure 4.19 (adapted from Schaffer 2000: 287). And these are the same, differing only in how they are labeled.[46]

But the examples are not indistinguishable. Double preventions can be divided into the causal and the non-causal. Here is how.

In Newt's Failed Mission, the malfunction on Newt's plane prevents Newt from intercepting Billy. Newt is a would-be preventer, stopped by the malfunction before he can interfere with Billy. That makes it a case of what I will call blocking double prevention. In blocking double prevention, one process produces the final event, in this case the destruction of the target; and a second process that would have prevented it from doing that is blocked before it can even begin preventing it. At no time is Newt preventing

---

[46] The diagram in (Hall 2004) is not labeled with names for events in the story, but the intended labeling is clear. (The story is also slightly different from the one in Hall 2002, in irrelevant ways.) The diagram in (Schaffer 2000) has its neurons in different places, but my moving them does not change the meaning of the diagram. I've also added a neuron and two labels for clarity: "spring cocked" (in its second occurrence) and "spring uncoiling." If you are wondering about how to interpret the unlabeled white neuron in the diagram, stay tuned.

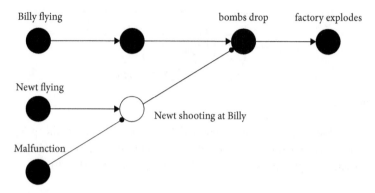

Figure 4.18

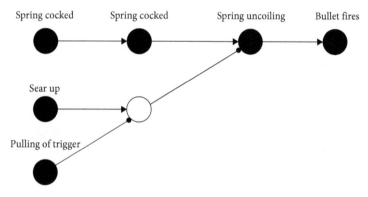

Figure 4.19

Billy from doing anything. Newt's preventing is purely hypothetical: something he might have done, had the malfunction not happened.

Schaffer's gun, by contrast, exhibits what I will call interrupting double prevention. Pulling the trigger prevents the sear from preventing the spring from uncoiling, yes. But when the trigger does that, the sear has been preventing the spring from uncoiling for a long time. If the gun has been cocked for an hour before it is fired, then the sear has been preventing the spring from uncoiling for an hour. In interrupting double prevention, the process that produces the final event, in this case the spring uncoiling and smashing the striker into the back of the bullet casing, has been interfered with, held back, by something else, for some stretch of time, before something, here the pulling of the trigger, interrupts this interference; it prevents that preventer from continuing to hold it back.

Interrupting double prevention is when one thing stops another from continuing to prevent something; blocking double prevention is when one thing prevents something from even beginning to prevent something. My thesis is that interrupting double prevention is causation and blocking double prevention is not.

I've extracted this thesis from two examples; let's look at more. First, Paul and Hall's two pillars (2013: 191). Two pillars are leaning against each other, holding each other up. You push one of the pillars away, and the other falls. This is double prevention: you prevent the first pillar from preventing the second pillar from falling. And it is causation: your shoving the first pillar is a cause of the falling of the second. My thesis agrees, since this is interrupting double prevention. The first pillar was already preventing the second from falling before you acted. When you shoved it, you stopped it from continuing to prevent this.

Next, Bennett's heavy rain example:

> There was heavy rain in April and electrical storms in the following two months; and in June the lightning took hold and started a forest fire.
>
> (1987: 373)

The rain is a double-preventer: it prevents the May lightning from preventing the June lightning from burning the forest. But the rain is not a cause of the fire— it takes a lot of philosophy to shake people's conviction in this. My thesis agrees. When the rain falls, the May lightning has not yet started preventing anything (it has not even happened yet!). The rain prevents the lightning from even beginning to prevent anything. This is a case of blocking double prevention.

Also a case of blocking is this example from Michael Moore:

> DP sees his old enemy V drowning in the ocean, which makes DP happy. Then DP spies a lifeguard, L, getting ready to save V. So DP ties up the lifeguard, and V drowns. DP has prevented ... L from preventing V's death. But DP has not caused V's death.   (2009: 62)

Right: because when DP acted, L had not yet begin to prevent V's death.

So my thesis sorts these cases of double prevention in the same way as our intuitive judgments do. If you're worried that the diet of examples is too small, here are a few more. A bullet prevents someone's heart from preventing their brain from dying from oxygen starvation. Some calcium prevents some tropomyosin from preventing a muscle fiber from contracting. Both, Schaffer (2000) says, are cases of causation; and both are interrupting double prevention. In *E. coli*, lactose inactivates a protein that represses the genes that produce the enzymes needed to metabolize lactose. Woodward says that this is causation and that genetics texts agree (2006: 35); it is also interrupting double prevention.

Woodward (2006) offers an hypothesis (that competes with mine) about when we judge double prevention to be causation: double prevention seems causal to us when it is "stable," which means, roughly, that the counterfactual dependence between the final effect and the double preventer would still hold, under a wide range of changes in circumstance. Woodward's hypothesis entails that unstable interrupting double prevention will not look like causation. I submit that it does. For example: Suzy shoves pillar A, so that it stops supporting pillar B, which falls. The shove is a cause of the falling, even if many other shovers were ready to shove it instead if the room's temperature had been the least bit different. "Had Suzy not shoved, the pillar would not have fallen," while true, is not sensitive; even tiny changes to the background temperature would make it false.

Paul and Hall think that there is a strong case that double prevention is (always) causation, but look closely at their abstract description of double prevention:

> whenever two systems X and Y are stably interacting in such a way that the continued presence of X is inhibiting Y from behaving in a certain manner, then an event that "removes" X will thereby cause a change in Y, but do so by double prevention.   (Paul and Hall 2013: 191)

This doesn't describe double prevention in general, only interrupting double prevention. Their generalization is right: that's always causation. Their mistake is thinking their description covers all cases of double prevention.

What about arguments that double prevention is never causation that are driven by abstract principles about causation, rather than reflection on examples? When you look closely, those arguments actually target blocking double prevention, and not interrupting double prevention, and so support my thesis.

Hall offers two principled arguments (2000, 2002). First, causation is local in space and time, as long as we can ignore quantum-mechanical weirdness. The spatial part of locality says that if C is a cause of E, then either C and E happen right next to each other, or there is a sequence of intermediaries $C=X1,X2,\ldots, Xn=E$, each event a cause of the next, where X_i and X_{i+1} happen right next to each other. But if double prevention is causation, it is non-local causation: the malfunction of Newt's plane does not happen right next to the explosion of the target, or any event involving Billy's bombs, or any event involving Billy's plane.[47]

Newt's mission is a case of blocking double prevention. And certainly the argument is right that, if blocking double prevention is causation, it is non-local causation. For in cases of blocking, the prevention of the would-be preventer can be far away in space from the process leading to the final effect (Billy's flight, leading to the explosion of the factory). But blocking double prevention is not causation. What about interrupting double prevention: does it threaten locality? No. Now the would-be preventer cannot be far away from the processes leading to the final effect. In the case of Schaffer's gun, the preventing event, the trigger's pulling on the sear, happens where the sear is. And the sear is right next to the spring, and so right next to the uncoiling of the spring. And there is a clearly a sequence satisfying locality's demands from the uncoiling to the firing of the bullet. It is the same with the two pillars: the pillar holding up the other pillar is right next to it, in physical contact with it. The preventing event, someone's pushing of the first pillar, happens where that pillar is; which happens right next to the fall of the second pillar. Locality is satisfied.

Now Hall's second argument: causation is transitive, but if double prevention is causation, there are counterexamples to transitivity. Suzy drops a tree branch above a bottle, and Billy, wanting to protect the bottle, starts running to intercept the branch, but trips, and falls, and fails; the bottle breaks. The tripping prevents Billy from preventing the branch from breaking the bottle. If double prevention is causation, the tripping is a cause of the breaking. But the running is a cause of the tripping and not also—as transitivity requires—a cause of the breaking. This is an example of a short circuit, and in general short circuits contain double prevention, and, if double prevention is causation, are counterexamples to transitivity.

But Billy's running and tripping is (another) case of blocking double prevention. The argument at most shows that, if blocking double prevention is causation, there are counterexamples to transitivity. But blocking double prevention is not causation. What about interrupting double prevention: does it threaten transitivity? No. Double preventers threaten transitivity when they appear in short circuits, but only blocking double preventers appear in short circuits. When a process X is on its way to causing an event E, a short circuit both launches a process P that threatens to prevent X from causing E, and also interferes with P so that it never succeeds. But only blocking double preventers never succeed.

Try turning Billy's attempt to stop Suzy's branch into a case of interrupting double prevention, while keeping it a counterexample to transitivity. It can't be done. Suppose Billy doesn't trip, but instead kicks a basketball, which caroms off a tree back toward him. He catches the branch for a moment, but then is hit by the ball and drops the branch, which continues on its way down and breaks the bottle. Billy's running is a cause of the ball's hitting him, which is a cause of the branch's falling (this is the interrupting double prevention), and the branch's falling is a cause of the bottle's breaking. For transitivity to fail, it would have to be that Billy's running is not a cause of the branch's falling (or the bottle's breaking). But it is. Interrupting double prevention does not threaten transitivity.

A third theoretical argument that double prevention is not causation is that if it is, then there can be causation by and of omissions; but there cannot (e.g., Dowe 2000; Moore 2009). Look again at the standard neuron diagram for double prevention (figure 4.20). Neuron C prevents Neuron D from firing; if D had fired, it would have prevented E from firing. So if double prevention is causation, and so the firing of C is a cause of the firing of E, then it runs through the omission "neuron D's not firing."

I accept the premise that there cannot be causation of or by omissions, that causation involves only "positive" events. But even with that premise the argument shows only that blocking double prevention is not causation. Only blocking double prevention runs through an omission. Interrupting double prevention does not. For example, the firing of a gun does not run

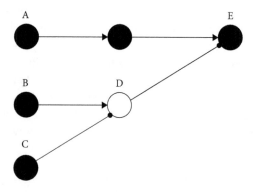

Figure 4.20

through an omission. Before you pull the trigger, the sear is pushing against the spring, and a pushing is a positive event. When you pull the trigger, the sear stops pushing on the spring. This stopping pushing is then a cause of the spring's uncoiling. And a stopping pushing is a positive event; it is not an omission. I think this is intuitive—stopping pushing is a change from pushing to not pushing, and changes are positive events. It also follows from my theory of events, since "stop pushing" names something that can be done.

The argument that all double preventions are the same, causally speaking, was that all are aptly represented by the same neuron diagram. But this discussion of omissions shows that to be false. The diagram in figure 4.20 is only apt for blocking double prevention. In interrupting double prevention, the would-be preventer has already done some preventing, before the double-preventer stops it. But, as neuron diagrams are standardly read, neuron D in the diagram never sent any inhibitory signal to neuron E; it was never preventing E from firing.

Look back at how Schaffer labels his neuron diagram for the gun (figure 4.19). The neuron labeled "sear up" sends no inhibitory signal to any neuron representing the spring. That makes the diagram wrong: when the sear is up, it is preventing the spring from uncoiling.

So we can have our cake and eat it too. If A prevents B from preventing C from doing something, it might be that B had already started preventing C from doing something, when A stopped it; that is interrupting double prevention. Or it might be that B had not started; that is blocking double prevention. When an example of double prevention looks like causation, that's because it is; it is a case of interrupting double prevention, and such cases are cases of causation. And when an example of double prevention doesn't look like causation, that's because it isn't; it is a case of blocking double prevention, and such cases are not cases of causation. Theoretical arguments about double prevention and causation—that double prevention cannot be causation, because causation is transitive, and local, and relates only positive events—even if sound, are consistent with all of this, because those arguments are sound only if they concern blocking double prevention.

4.21 Enabling vs double prevention

One thread is left hanging. I have argued the enabling is not causing. Something that enables C to cause E is not (by virtue of that fact alone) a cause of E. And I said that to enable C to cause E is to put in place a state that is a background condition to C's causing E. These claims can appear to conflict with the fact that double prevention is sometimes causation.

If a bomb explodes next to a dam, destroying it, and the water then rushes down the river and floods the village, then the explosion was a cause of the flood. This is causation by double prevention: the explosion prevents the dam from continuing to prevent the water from rushing down the river.[48] The dam was doing this by preventing gravity from accelerating the water downhill. But isn't this also a case of enabling? The explosion puts in place a state—an open space where the dam used to be—that is a background condition to gravity's pull causing the water to run down. If it is enabling, then enabling is causing, at least sometimes.

What all this shows, I think, is that enabling needs a more precise definition. True enabling, as a distinct variety of relevance, should be sliced off from causal double prevention. Enabling C to cause E is putting in place conditions in which C can cause E, where these conditions have not yet "become active" in the process C initiated. Removing an obstacle that is already holding back, or redirecting, this process, on the other hand, is not true enabling; it is causation by (interrupting) double prevention.

4.22 Conclusion

James Woodward wrote this about "what the notion [of a cause] is intended to contrast with":

> I believe that when 'cause' and cognate notions are used in the special sciences and in common sense contexts, the relevant contrast is very often with 'mere' correlations or associations. In particular, the underlying problematic is something like this: an investigator has observed some relationship of correlation or association among two or more variables, X and Y. What the investigator wants to know is whether this relationship is of such a character that it might be exploited for purposes of manipulation and control: if the investigator were to manipulate X (in the right way), would the correlation between X and Y continue to hold... or is it instead the case that under manipulation of X there would be no

---

[48] Rickless (2011) and McGrath (2003) discuss cases like this.

corresponding changes in Y...? In the former case, we think of X as causing Y, in the latter the connection between X and Y is non-causal, a mere correlation.... (2007: 71–72)

My thesis has been that this is wrong. If C is merely correlated with E, as for example the number of pool-drownings is correlated with the number of films Nicholas Cage stars in, then C is not in any way causally relevant to E.[49] But there are other alternatives to causation, and they are causally relevant: being a background condition, enabling, ennobling, and prevention. Recognizing these categories is important for its own sake, and has important benefits, including defusing threats to the transitivity of causation, and providing a clear view of when double prevention is and is not causation.[50]

References

Bach, Emmon 1986. "The Algebra of Events." *Linguistics and Philosophy* 9: 5–16.

Baron, Reuben M. and David A. Kenny 1986. "The Moderator-Mediator Variable Distinction in Social Psychological Research: Conceptual, Strategic, and Statistical Considerations." *Journal of Personality and Social Psychology* 51: 1173–1182.

Baron-Schmitt, Nathaniel (Ms.) "Thing Causation."

Bennett, Jonathan 1987. "Event Causation: the Counterfactual Analysis." *Philosophical Perspectives* 1: 367–386.

Cheng, Patricia W. 1997. "From Covariation to Causation: A Causal Power Theory." *Psychological Review* 104: 367–405.

Dancy, Jonathan 2004. *Ethics Without Principles*. Oxford University Press.

Davidson, Donald 1967. "The Logical Form of Action Sentences." In Nicholas Rescher, ed., *The Logic of Decision and Action*. University of Pittsburgh Press, 81–95.

Dawkins, Richard 1976. *The Selfish Gene*. Oxford University Press.

Dowdy, David 1979. *Word Meaning and Montague Grammar*. Kluwer.

Dowe, Phil 2000. *Physical Causation*. Cambridge University Press.

[49] See https://tylervigen.com/spurious-correlations.
[50] Thanks to audiences at MIT, Harvard, NC State-Raleigh, and to Selim Berker, Ned Hall, Gideon Rosen, Jim Van Cleve, and an anonymous referee.

Dowe, Phil 2001. "A Counterfactual Theory of Prevention and 'Causation' by Omission." *Australasian Journal of Philosophy* 79: 216–226.

Feldman, Fred 1994. *Confrontations with the Reaper*. Oxford University Press.

Foot, Philippa 1978. "The Problem of Abortion and the Doctrine of Double Effect." In P. Foot, *Virtues and Vices*. University of California, pp 19–32.

Goldvarg, E. and P. N. Johnson-Laird 2001. "Naive causality: a mental model theory of causal meaning and reasoning." *Cognitive Science* 25: 565–610.

Hall, Ned 2000. "Causation and the Price of Transitivity." *The Journal of Philosophy* 97: 198–222.

Hall, Ned 2002. "Non-Locality on the Cheap? A New Problem for Counterfactual Analyses of Causation." *Nous* 36: 276–294.

Hall, Ned 2004. "Two Concepts of Causation." In John Collins, Ned Hall, and L. A. Paul (eds.), *Causation and Counterfactuals*. Oxford University Press, 225–276.

Hall, Ned 2007. "Structural equations and causation." *Philosophical Studies* 132: 109–136.

Hayes, Andrew F. 2013. *Introduction to Mediation, Moderation, and Conditional Process Analysis*. The Guilford Press.

Herweg, Michael 1991. "Perfective and imperfective aspect and the theory of events and states." *Linguistics* 29: 969–1010.

Hitchcock, Christopher 2001a. "The Intransitivity of Causation Revealed in Equations and Graphs." *The Journal of Philosophy* 98: 273–299.

Hitchcock, Christopher 2001b. "A Tale of Two Effects." *Philosophical Review* 110: 361–396.

Hitchcock, Christopher 2003. "Of Humean Bondage." *British Journal for the Philosophy of Science* 54: 1–25.

Hitchcock, Christopher 2007. "Prevention, Preemption, and the Principle of Sufficient Reason." *The Philosophical Review* 116: 495–532.

Kenny, Antony 1963. *Action, Emotion and Will*. Routledge & Kegan Paul.

Kim, Jaegwon 1993. "Events as Property Exemplifications." In J. Kim, *Supervenience and Mind*. Cambridge University Press, 33–52.

Landsburg, Steven 2012. *The Armchair Economist*. Revised edition. The Free Press.

Lewis, David 1983. "New Work for a Theory of Universals." *Australasian Journal of Philosophy* 61: 343–377.

Lewis, David 1986a. "Causation." In D. Lewis, *Philosophical Papers Volume II*. Oxford University Press, pp 159–213.

Lewis, David 1986b. "Events." In D. Lewis, *Philosophical Papers Volume II.* Oxford University Press, pp 241–270.

Lombard, Lawrence Brian 1990. "Causes, Enablers, and the Counterfactual Analysis." *Philosophical Studies* 59: 195–211.

Lowe, E. J. 2008. *Personal Agency: The Metaphysics of Mind and Action.* Oxford University Press.

Maienborn, Claudia 2001. "On the position and interpretation of locative modifiers." *Natural Language Semantics* 9: 191–240.

Maienborn, Claudia 2005. "On the limits of the Davidsonian approach: The case of copula sentences." *Theoretical Linguistics* 31: 275–316.

Maienborn, Claudia 2008. "On Davidsonian and Kimian States." In Ileana Comorovski and Klaus Von Heusinger, (eds.), *Existence: Semantics and Syntax.* Springer: 107–132.

McGrath, Sarah 2003. "Causation and the Making/Allowing Distinction." *Philosophical Studies* 114: 81–106.

Mellor, D. H. 1998. *The Facts of Causation.* Routledge.

Moore, Michael S. 2009. *Causation and Responsibility: An Essay in Law, Morals, and Metaphysics.* Oxford University Press.

Nelson, Randy J. 1995. *An Introduction to Behavioral Endocrinology.* Sinauer Associates.

Paul, L. A. 2000. "Aspect Causation." *Journal of Philosophy* 97: 235–256.

Paul, L. A. and Ned Hall 2013. *Causation: A Users Guide.* Oxford University Press.

Pearl, Judea 2000. *Causality.* Cambridge University Press.

Pettit, Philip and Michael Smith 1990. "Backgrounding Desire." *Philosophical Review* 99: 565–592.

Plato 2002. *Five Dialogues.* G. M. A. Grube, translator, John M. Cooper, editor. Hackett.

Pollock, John and Joseph Cruz 1999. *Contemporary Theories of Knowledge.* Rowman & Littlefield.

Rickless, Samuel 2011. "The Moral Status of Enabling Harm." *Pacific Philosophical Quarterly* 92: 66–86.

Schaffer, Jonathan 2000. "Causation by Disconnection." *Philosophy of Science* 67: 285–300.

Schaffer, Jonathan 2004. "Causes need not be Physically Connected to their Effects: The Case for Negative Causation." In Christopher Hitchcock (ed.), *Contemporary Debates in the Philosophy of Science.* Blackwell, 197–216.

Schaffer, Jonathan 2005. "Contrastive Causation." *The Philosophical Review* 114: 327–58.

Schroeder, Mark 2007. *Slaves of the Passions.* Oxford University Press.

Setiya, Kieran 2014. "What is a Reason to Act?" *Philosophical Studies* 167: 221–235.

Sherwood, Lauralee 2015. *Human Physiology from Cells to Systems.* 9th edition. Cengage Learning.

Skow, Bradford 2018. *Causation, Explanation, and the Metaphysics of Aspect.* Oxford University Press.

Sloman, Steven, Aron K. Barbey, and Jared M. Hotaling 2009. "A Causal Model Theory of the Meaning of *Cause, Enable,* and *Prevent. Cognitive Science* 33: 21–50.

Steward, Helen 1997. *The Ontology of Mind: Events, Processes, and States.* Oxford University Press.

Vendler, Zeno 1959. "Verbs and Times." *Philosophical Review* 66: 143–60.

Walsh, Claire R. and Steven A. Sloman 2011. "The Meaning of Cause and Prevent: The Role of Causal Mechanism." *Mind & Language* 26: 21–52.

Woodward, James 2003. *Making Things Happen.* Oxford University Press.

Woodward, James 2006. "Sensitive and Insensitive Causation." *Philosophical Review* 115: 1–50.

Woodward, James 2007. "Causation with a Human Face." In Huw Price and Richard Corry (eds.), *Causation, Physics, and the Constitution of Reality: Russell's Republic Revisited.* Oxford University Press, 66–107.

Yablo, Stephen 2010. "Advertisement for a Sketch of an Outline of a Prototheory of Causation." In S. Yablo, *Things.* Oxford University Press, pp 119–138.

5

Counterpart Theory and Counterfactuals

John Hawthorne and Juhani Yli-Vakkuri

In 1968, David Lewis famously provided a translation scheme from the language of quantified modal logic (QML) into the language of counterpart theory (CT), one that he thought would make manifest the truth conditions of absolute—or, as we would now say, metaphysical—modal claims.[1,2] Lewis's other main contribution to the logic and semantics of modality is his celebrated 1973 semantics for counterfactual conditionals, which is put forward as a general model theory that subsumes the logic of metaphysical modality, with the metaphysical necessity of φ (□φ) defined as the negation of φ counterfactually implying a contradiction (¬φ > ⊥). It is natural for the advocate of counterpart theory to wish to extend Lewis's 1968 translation scheme for quantified modal logic to a language that includes the counterfactual conditional connective. Surprisingly, there has been hardly any discussion of such extensions in the literature. The only proposal we know of was briefly articulated by Lewis himself in his 1973 masterpiece. But, as far as we know, no one thus far has noticed that this proposal fails to validate

---

[1] We would like to thank Cian Dorr and Ted Sider for extensive written comments on a draft of this chapter as well as Andrew Bacon, Karen Bennett, Jeff Sanford Russell, Ted Shear, Jonathan Weisberg, Dean Zimmerman, and an anonymous referee for *Oxford Studies in Metaphysics* for helpful discussions and comments.

[2] An anonymous referee observes that in in 1968 the notion of metaphysical necessity had not yet been clearly distinguished from other necessity-like notions in the vicinity, and suggests that the term 'metaphysical necessity' may not be appropriate here. Lewis, however, does make it clear that he is looking for an analysis of modality *simpliciter*, contrasted with 'relative modalities' (p. 124), for which he provides a separate translation in §V, one that makes use of a Kripke-style accessibility relation on worlds. Since in the rest of the paper Lewis is giving a counterpart-theoretic translation of the most general necessity and possibility claims we can make, it is natural to think that the target claims are metaphysical necessity and possibility claims, even though he would not have used the term 'metaphysical' to describe them. Any readers who nevertheless think the term 'metaphysical' is inappropriate here should read our chapter with 'absolute' substituted by 'metaphysical'.

John Hawthorne and Juhani Yli-Vakkuri, *Counterpart Theory and Counterfactuals* In: *Oxford Studies in Metaphysics Volume 13*. Edited by: Karen Bennett and Dean W. Zimmerman, Oxford University Press.

the now standard counterfactual logic introduced in that same book. In this chapter, we will first examine the translation of counterfactual logic to counterpart theory proposed by Lewis in 1973, thereby making vivid various challenges that are faced by anyone wishing to marry counterpart theory with Lewis's logic of counterfactuals. Then we will propose a superior translation scheme within the framework of Lewis's own counterpart theory.

5.1 Principles of counterfactual logic

The now-standard semantics for counterfactuals introduced by David Lewis's *Counterfactuals* (1973) yields a combined logic of counterfactuals and metaphysical modality that has been the springboard for much of the discussion of those topics ever since. In this section we introduce some of the more important principles it validates, each of which is also validated by Stalnaker's (1968) semantics, the other *locus classicus* for the logic of counterfactuals and their interaction with metaphysical modality.

We begin with three principles from Lewis's system **VC**, which is a complete axiomatization of the logic of counterfactuals characterized by his celebrated semantics.[3]

Deduction within Conditionals (Lewis's rule (2))

If $\vdash (\chi_1 \wedge \ldots \wedge \chi_n) \supset \psi$, then $\vdash ((\varphi > \chi_1) \wedge \ldots \wedge (\varphi > \chi_n)) \supset (\varphi > \psi)$

Counterfactual Modus Ponens (Lewis's axiom (6))

$(\varphi > \psi) \supset (\varphi \supset \psi)$

And-to-If (Lewis's axiom (7))

$(\varphi \wedge \psi) \supset (\varphi > \psi)$

Here are some notable theorems of **VC**:

Substitution of Tautological Equivalents in the Antecedent[4]

$(\chi_1 > \chi_2) \supset (\chi_1[\psi/\varphi] > \chi_2)$,

whenever $\varphi \equiv \psi$ is a tautology.

---

[3] See Lewis (1973: §6.1) for completeness results for this and related systems.

[4] We write 'X[Y/Z]' for the expression that results from replacing each free occurrence of Z in X with a free occurrence of Y.

Substitution of Tautological Equivalents in the Consequent

$(\chi_1 > \chi_2) \supset (\chi_1 > \chi_2[\psi/\varphi])$,

whenever $\varphi \equiv \psi$ is a tautology.

Agglomeration

$((\varphi > \psi) \wedge (\varphi > \chi)) \supset (\varphi > (\psi \wedge \chi))$

Restricted Transitivity

$((\varphi > \psi) \wedge ((\varphi \wedge \psi) > \chi)) \supset (\varphi > \chi)$

CSO[5]

$((\varphi > \psi) \wedge (\psi > \varphi) \wedge (\varphi > \chi)) \supset (\psi > \chi)$

Here are some further notable **VC**-theorems that concern the interaction of counterfactuals with metaphysical modality, with $\Box\varphi$ defined, following Lewis (1973: 22), as $\neg\varphi > \bot$.

Substitution of Intensional Equivalents in the Antecedent

$\Box(\varphi \equiv \psi) \supset ((\chi_1 > \chi_2) \supset (\chi_1 [\psi/\varphi] > \chi_2))$

Substitution of Intensional Equivalents in the Consequent

$\Box(\varphi \equiv \psi) \supset ((\chi_1 > \chi_2) \supset (\chi_1 > \chi_2[\psi/\varphi]))$

◊-Closure

$(\varphi > \psi) \supset (\Diamond \varphi \supset \Diamond \psi)$

We also get the following theorem immediately from the definition.

□-Reducibility

$\Box\varphi \equiv (\neg\varphi > \chi)$,

where χ is any contradiction.

Also immediately, by the duality of $\Box$ and $\Diamond$ and double negation elimination, we get:

---

[5] Ted Sider suggested we 'tell [the reader] what this stands for'. This simple suggestion turned out to be surprisingly difficult to implement. 'CS' clearly stands for 'Conditional Substitution' or 'Counterfactual Substitution', but the 'O' continues to confound us. Our current favorite hypothesis is that the label is the result of a typographic mistake: someone—perhaps a typesetter—mistook a '0' in the original label for an 'O'. Other hypotheses that have been suggested (in pers. comm., quoted here with the correspondents' permission) include that 'CSO' stands for 'Conditional Substitution O-because-A-thru-N-were-already-taken' (Jonathan Weisberg) and that it stands for 'Conditional Substitution Oh-no-you-didn't!' or 'Conditional Swap-that-shit Out' (Ted Shear).

◇-**Reducibility**

$$\Diamond\varphi \equiv \neg(\varphi > \chi),$$

where χ is any contradiction.

5.2 Counterpart theory and *Counterfactuals*

'Counterpart Theory and Quantified Modal Logic' (1968) was Lewis's manifesto for what was then a revolutionary new approach to modal logics, for which the use of possible worlds semantics was just becoming widespread: *counterpart-theoretic translation*. Lewis's idea was to forgo giving semantics for the language of quantified modal logic (QML) and to instead provide a meaning-preserving translation of that language into *counterpart theory* (CT)—a first-order theory that *eliminates* modal operators from formalized discourse by providing paraphrases of our ordinary modal claims using purely non-modal, extensional notions.[6,7]

Being a kind of model theory, possible worlds semantics is entirely noncommittal about the nature of the entities its practitioners like to call 'possible worlds'. For all the semantics says, they might be numbers, apples, ants, or... and for the usual applications of possible worlds semantics— namely, proving that a logic-*cum*-theory that has been given a syntactic characterization is sound and complete on a given class of possible-worlds model structures—there is no need to consider models other than those whose 'possible worlds' are natural numbers or their set-theoretic representatives. If

---

[6] The ambition of a meaning-preserving translation is explicit in Lewis (1968: 177), but it is not important for our purposes what exactly counts as meaning-preservation. The natural test— necessary equivalence—is tricky to apply here since it's unclear how and in what language we should articulate the idea that the proposition expressed by a sentence of QML is necessarily equivalent to the proposition expressed by a sentence of CT. The idea that propositions are sets of worlds (which Lewis liked) offers little guidance here, and Lewis never explained how to cash it out in counterpart-theoretic terms: see Dorr (2005) for a discussion of the difficulties.

[7] An anonymous referee thinks we should not attribute to Lewis (1968) any Quinean aversion to nonextensionality, but one of Lewis's 1983 postscripts to that paper is titled 'Nonextensionality Tolerated', and it says:

> Whatever else may fairly be said against the language of quantified modal logic, *I withdraw my complaint against its nonextensionality*. See "Tensions" (in this volume), in which I argue that such violations of extensionality as it commits are of no deep significance. If we want to restore extensionality, we need only reanalyze the language in an otherwise pointless, but harmless, way (Lewis 1983: 46, emphasis added).

If Lewis had no aversion to nonextensionality in 1968, then there would have been no complaint to withdraw.

the sets of 'possible worlds' contained in some model structures contain genuine possible worlds—whatever that may mean—that is entirely orthogonal to the purpose for which those model structures were introduced. As Kripke explains:

> When I did my own work on the semantics of modal logic, I posited a set **K** of worlds with an accessibility relation **R**, a distinguished actual world, and a domain function. My main point was to find a definition, set theoretically meaningful, of validity, satisfiability, and other model-theoretic notions, and to be able to raise completeness problems, and so on. But the set **K** was arbitrary and, in a definition of validity, was allowed to vary. There was no concern with the unique set (or class) of possible worlds.
>
> Thus, I was not particularly concerned with questions of truth in all possible worlds simpliciter. (The distinction might be analogous to that of "truth" and "truth in a model" in standard quantificational logic.) Much less was I concerned, as David Lewis certainly was, with giving a reductive analysis of modal notions (Kripke 2011: 377–8).

By contrast, the first-order theory of worlds—not of *possible* worlds, but simply of *worlds*—that is CT is unambiguous in its vision: The counterpart theorist's worlds contain things—as Lewis (1973: 85–6, 1986: §§1.6–1.9) later made clear—in the way our physical universe contains us.[8] Nothing is contained in (or simply is *in*) more than one world, and so, for example, none of us is in any world other than the actual one. Nevertheless we are related to certain denizens of other worlds by a *counterpart* relation. Lewis accepted these claims literally, and his translation of QML to CT was not meant to be simply a technique for determining what is and isn't a theorem of some modal logic that has already been characterized in syntactic terms, but a translation that preserves meaning and helps us choose the right

---

[8] An anonymous referee says that Lewis's 'in' is a 'primitive' and suggests that it's 'best to keep it that way'. It's true that the predicate *I* is one of the non-logical primitives of Lewis's formal language, but treating something as a primitive in this sense—i.e., expressing it by a constant—does not commit one to not saying anything about what it means or even defining it outside of the formal language. For example, various combinations of '¬', '∨', '∧', '⊃', and '≡' can be defined in terms of each other, and one can informally avail oneself of any of these definitions while working with a formal language with only the constants '¬' and '∧' or '¬' and '⊃'. In fact, Lewis's later work (especially 1986) together with his 1968 axiom (P1) suggests a straightforward definition: for *x* to be *in y* in the technical sense is for *x* to be contained in *y* (in the sense in which our physical universe contains us) and for *y* to be a world.

axioms. In particular, it was supposed to help us settle 'disputed questions in quantified modal logic' (Lewis 1968: 123).

More precisely, the language of CT has four non-logical predicates:

Wx : x is a world

Ixy : x is in y

Ax : x is actual

Cxy : x is a counterpart of y

For ease of reading, we will adopt faux-variables, $w, v, u, \ldots$, for worlds, with $\forall w\varphi$ defined as $\forall x(Wx \supset \varphi[x/w])$ and $\exists x\varphi$ as $\exists x(Wx \wedge \varphi[x/w])$. CT comprises the following seven axioms.

(P1) $\forall x\forall y(Ixy \supset Wy)$[9]

('Nothing is in anything except a world.')

(P2) $\forall x\forall w\forall v\,((Ixw \wedge Ixv) \supset w = v)$

('Nothing is in two worlds.')

(P3) $\forall x\forall y(Cxy \supset \exists wIxw)$

('Anything that is a counterpart is in a world.')

(P4) $\forall x\forall y(Cxy \supset \exists wIyw)$

('Anything that has a counterpart is in a world.')

(P5) $\forall x\forall y\forall w\,((Ixw \wedge Iyw \wedge Cxy) \supset x = y)$

('Nothing has more than one counterpart in its world.')

(P6) $\forall x\forall w(Ixw \supset Cxx)$

('Anything in a world is a counterpart of itself.')

(P7) $\exists w\forall x(Ixw \equiv Ax)$

('Some world contains all and only actual things.')

By (P2) and (P7) there is a unique world that contains all of the actual things. Following Lewis, we adopt @, defined as $\iota w\,\forall x(Ixw \equiv Ax)$ ('the world that contains all and only the actual things'), as a faux singular term for that world.

---

[9] We state (P1) in primitive notation because its statement using faux world-variables $(\forall x\forall y(Ixy \supset \exists w = y))$ is more complex.

According to the counterpart-theoretic translation approach (on Lewis's 1968 translation), (i) when we say 'Adam could have been F', this is tantamount to the claim that some counterpart of Adam in some world is F. And, roughly speaking, what makes an otherworldly object a counterpart of Adam is a matter of sufficient qualitative similarity to Adam.[10] Two more features of the translation approach that will matter later: (ii) atomic sentences translate into themselves, and (iii) ordinary sentences of the form 'There is an F' that occur outside of the scopes of any modal operators translate into sentences of the form 'Something is in the actual world and is F'. 'Actual' here is not a modal operator but a first-order predicate: a world is actual if and only if it contains all and only the actual things, and a thing is actual if and only if it is spatiotemporally connected to us.[11]

For a more precise statement of Lewis's translation, let us adopt the abbreviation

$$Ct_1 \ldots t_n t'_1 \ldots t'_n w := Ct_1 t'_1 \wedge \ldots \wedge Ct_n t'_n \wedge It_1 w \wedge \ldots \wedge It_n w$$

('$t_1, \ldots$, and t_n are in w and are, respectively, counterparts of $t'_1 \ldots$, and t'_n').

Lewis's translation is as follows.

(T1) φ translates to $\varphi^@$

(Recall that $\varphi^@$ abbreviates $\varphi^{\imath w(\forall x(Ixw \equiv Ax))}$, which in turn abbreviates $\exists w(\forall x(Ixw \equiv Ax) \wedge \varphi^w)$.)

(T2a) $\varphi^w := \varphi$, if φ is atomic

(T2b) $(\neg\varphi)^w := \neg(\varphi^w)$

(T2c) $(\varphi \wedge \psi)^w := \varphi^w \wedge \psi^w$

(T2d) $(\varphi \vee \psi)^w := \varphi^w \vee \psi^w$

(T2e) $(\varphi \supset \psi)^w := \varphi^w \supset \psi^w$

---

[10] The standard of similarity will depend on the context of speech. Since this won't matter to our main discussion, we will ignore this dimension of indexicality, just as Lewis does in his 1968 paper.

[11] Here we go beyond what Lewis had to say about actuality in 1968, but the idea of actuality as spatiotemporal connectedness to us (and so of 'actual' as an indexical) is established Lewisian doctrine: see Lewis (1973: 85–6, 1986: §§1.6–1.9).

(T2f) $(\varphi \equiv \psi)^w := \varphi^w \equiv \psi^w$

(T2g) $(\forall x\varphi)^w := \forall x(Ixw \supset \varphi^w)$

(T2h) $(\exists x\, \varphi)^w := \exists x(Ixw \wedge \varphi^w)$

(T2i) $(\Box\varphi)^w := \forall\, v\, \forall x_1 \ldots \forall x_n\, (Cx_1 \ldots x_n t_1 \ldots t_n v \to \varphi^v\, [x_1 \ldots x_n/t_1 \ldots t_n])$

(T2j) $(\Diamond\varphi)^w := \exists\, v\, \exists x_1 \ldots \exists x_n\, (Cx_1 \ldots x_n t_1 \ldots t_n v \wedge \varphi^v\, [x_1 \ldots x_n/t_1 \ldots t_n])$[12]

where $t_1, \ldots, t_n$ are all the singular terms with free occurrences in φ.

It is convenient to read φ^w as 'φ is true in w', and we will often do so, but the reader should bear in mind that 'φ^w' is always an abbreviation for an expression in which 'w' occurs either only as an argument of an ordinary first-order predicate or not at all, and that there is no expression that means *true in*, in the customary sense of 'true in' (the sense in which a proposition can be true in a world) in CT.

Lewis's semantics for counterfactual logic is put forward as a more general theory that subsumes the semantics of modal logic as a special case: necessary propositions are ones whose negations counterfactually imply contradictions, and possible propositions are those that do not counterfactually imply a contradiction (see $\Box$-Reducibility and $\Diamond$-Reducibility). However, Lewis gives only a semantics for *propositional* counterfactual logic, and—not to belabor the obvious, but this point seems easy to miss—that semantics is a *semantics*, not a translation of the language of counterfactual logic into CT or an extension of it. Lewis's object language includes the nonextensional connective >,[13] which is interpreted (as the semantics is usually presented[14]) using models that come equipped with a set of 'possible worlds' and a comparative similarity relation

$w \leq_v u$ ('w is at least as similar to v as u is')

on that set. The Lewisian conditions for truth at a world w in such a model for $\varphi > \psi$ are given by:

[12] We use the standard notation for substitution: $\varphi[x_1 \ldots x_n/t_1 \ldots t_n]$ is the formula that results from replacing all free occurrences of $x_1 \ldots x_n$ in φ with free occurrences of, respectively, $t_1 \ldots t_n$, where $t_1 \ldots t_n$ are chosen according to some method (it doesn't matter which) that ensures that the replacing occurrences are free.

[13] Which Lewis spells as the concatenation of a box with an arrow.

[14] Lewis's main discussion is in terms of systems of spheres. We have adopted the alterative ideology of comparative similarity (which is also from Lewis 1973: §2.3), since it is more familiar to most readers.

$\varphi > \psi$ is true at w iff either

(1) φ is true at no world, or

(2) there is a world v such that, for any world u, if $u \leq_w v$, then $\varphi \supset \psi$ is true at u.[15]

What Lewis gives us in 1973, then, is a possible-worlds semantics for a language with intensional operators—the very kind of thing his method of counterpart-theoretic translation was meant to replace. We emphasize that the two projects need not be in conflict with each other: A counterpart theorist could treat possible-worlds semantics, as Kripke did, as pure model theory and only use it for characterizing validity. Although there is abundant evidence that this is not how Lewis thought of his 1973 project,[16] a counterpart theorist could think of it that way. But whatever else Lewis may have had in mind in 1973, it was clear which logic of counterfactuals he favored, and there is a clear open question about how to complete his 1968 project of counterpart-theoretic translation so that we translate theorems of Lewis's 1973 counterfactual logic into theorems of counterpart theory.

To complete the counterpart-theoretic translation project for which Lewis's 1968 paper is the manifesto, we must add a clause for the counterfactual conditional connective to his 1968 translation, and we must

---

[15] Lewis (1973: 49). We have simplified Lewis's semantics by omitting his restriction of the world quantifiers in (1) and (2) to S_w, the set worlds accessible from w in the model. That restriction makes no difference to the logic, except when it comes to the interaction of $>$ with certain operators but we don't.

[16] An anonymous referee conjectures that Lewis may have been far more interested in pure model theory and validity than in truth conditions in 1973. But the first sentence of *Counterfactuals* reads:

> 'If kangaroos had no tails they would topple over' seems to *mean* something like this: 'in any possible state of affairs in which kangaroos have no tails and that resembles our actual state of affairs as much as kangaroos having no tails permits it to, kangaroos topple over' (Lewis 1973: 1, second emphasis added).

The next sentence is: 'I shall give a general analysis of counterfactual conditionals along these lines' (Lewis 1973: 1). What's more, §1 of Ch. 4 is dedicated to the defense of modal realism. Lewis begins the chapter by telling the reader that if 'the common suspicion of possible worlds and of similarity were justified, then my analysis could have little interest: only the interest in connecting mysteries to other mysteries' (p. 84). Most tellingly, Lewis argues against that worlds are not 'maximal consistent sets of sentences of some language' (p. 85), but that is precisely what we usually take possible worlds to be in pure model theory when we use possible worlds semantics for completeness proofs. Indeed, Lewis himself does this in his completeness proofs (p. 125).

supplement CT with axioms governing the comparative similarity relation
on worlds:

(P9) $\leq_w$ is transitive: $\forall w \forall v \forall u \forall w'((w \leq_w u \wedge u \leq_w w') \supset w \leq_w w')$

(P10) $\leq_w$ is strongly connected: $\forall w \forall v \forall u (w \leq_w u \vee u \leq_w w)$

(P11) w is strictly $\leq_w$-minimal: $\forall w \forall v (v \leq_w w \supset v = w)$

(P9) and (P10) are standard axioms for any comparative similarity relation,
and (P11) states the natural principle that each world is the unique world
most similar to itself, an assumption that we need not try to defend, since
Lewis himself makes it.[17] We will call the theory that results from adding
these axioms to CT 'CT$_\leq$'.

Strangely enough, as far as we can tell, the issue of how to complete the
translation by adding a clause for > has been entirely ignored in the vast
secondary literature on counterfactuals, despite both the continuing popu-
larity of the counterpart-theoretic metaphysical vision and the continuing
interest in the logic and semantics of counterfactuals.

What about *Counterfactuals* itself? There Lewis touches on the subject in
a very cursory way. He only discusses the case of $\varphi(t) > \psi(t)$, where the singular
term t may have any number of free occurrences in either $\varphi(t)$ or $\psi(t)$; in 'the
degenerate case' it has free occurrences in neither (p. 38). But, as he says,
the proposal is meant to be completely general: once we know what to
do with one singular term, we know what to do with any number of
them—he calls the generalization to any number of singular terms 'rou-
tine' (*ibid.*). (However, only one of our examples in our discussion of
Lewis's proposal involves more than one singular term with a free occurrence in a counterfactual—this is the counterexample to Agglomeration
on one construal of the proposal, which is inessential to our case against
that proposal.)

According to the proposal for the one-singular-term case, $\varphi(t) > \varphi(t)$ is
true at a world w iff either (*i*) there is no counterpart of the referent of t that
satisfies $\varphi(x)$ at any world or (*ii*) there is a world v in which some counterpart of the referent of t satisfies $\varphi(x)$ which is such that every counterpart of
the referent of t that satisfies $\varphi(x)$ at a world that is at least as similar to w as v

[17] See Lewis (1973: 48). Again, we depart from Lewis's presentation in not positing a sphere
of accessibility around each world outside of which any two worlds are equally dissimilar to any
world within it.

also satisfies $\psi(x)$ at that world (p. 49).[18] On the face if it this, of course, is a semantic proposal, but it is easy enough to read a translation of $\varphi(t) > \psi(t)$ into $CT_{\leq}$ into it.

As noted, the proposal is meant to cover cases where there are zero occurrence of t in one or both of the antecedent and consequent. The tricky case here is where there are zero occurrences in the antecedent. Consider:

(1)   It is sunny > John is happy.

For us the most natural treatment in the spirit of the original proposal is one according to which (1) is true at a world w iff either (i) there is no world where it is sunny or (ii) there is a world v where it is sunny such that every counterpart of John in any world where it is sunny that is at least as similar to w as v i s happy.

However, a few people in conversation have suggested a different treatment. We might instead read Lewis as advancing a proposal according to which (1) is true at w iff either (i) there is no world where a counterpart of John is such that it is sunny or (ii) there is a world where a counterpart of John is such that it is sunny and that is such that every counterpart of John in any world where it is sunny that is at least as similar to w as v is happy.

Call the first construal of Lewis's proposal 'L1' and the second 'L2'. In what follows we focus on L1, and we will inquire briefly into how L2 impacts the points we make. (Short story: L2 makes matters even worse.)

According to L1,

$$(\varphi > \psi)^w := \quad \neg \exists v \exists x_1 \ldots \exists x_n \, (Cx_1 \ldots x_n t_1 \ldots t_n v \wedge \varphi^v \, [x_1 \ldots x_n / t_1 \ldots t_n]) \, \vee$$
$$\exists v \exists x_1 \ldots \exists x_n (Cx_1 \ldots x_n t_1 \ldots t_n v \wedge \varphi^v \, [x_1 \ldots x_n / t_1 \ldots t_n]) \, \wedge$$
$$\forall u \, \forall y_1 \ldots \forall y_n ((u \leq_w v \wedge Cy_1 \ldots y_n t'_1 \ldots t'_n u) \supset$$
$$(\varphi \supset \psi)^u [y_1 \ldots y_n / t'_1 \ldots t'_n]),$$

where $t_1 \ldots t_n$ are all of the singular terms with free occurrences in φ and $t'_1 \ldots t'_n$ are all the singular terms with free occurrences in $\varphi > \psi$, if there

---

[18] Note that Lewis does not presume that if there is a world in which a counterpart of x is F then, for any world w, there is a most similar world to w in which a counterpart of x is F. This would be to impose the limit assumption, which Lewis rejects (see Lewis 1973: §1.4).

are any. When there are no singular terms with free occurrences in φ, $t_1 \ldots t_n$ is the empty string and $\exists v \exists x_1 \ldots \exists x_n\ (Cx_1 \ldots x_n t_1 \ldots t_n v \land$ is also the empty string, with the parentheses adjusted accordingly, so that $(\varphi > \psi)^w$ is

$$\neg \exists\, v\, \varphi^v \lor \exists v(\varphi^v \land \forall u \forall y_1 \ldots \forall y_n\ ((u \leq_w v \land Cy_1 \ldots y_n t'_1 \ldots t'_n u) \supset$$
$$(\varphi \supset \psi)^u\ [y_1 \ldots y_n/t'_1 \ldots t'_n])).$$

Similarly, when there are no free occurrences of singular terms in $\varphi > \psi$, both $t_1 \ldots t_n$ and $t'_1 \ldots t'_n$ are empty, and so are the strings $\exists v \exists x_1 \ldots \exists x_n\ (Cx_1 \ldots x_n t_1 \ldots t_n v \land$, $\forall y_1 \ldots \forall y_n$, and $\land\ Cy_1 \ldots y_n t'_1 \ldots t'_n u$, and $(\varphi > \psi)^w$ is

$$\neg \exists\, v\varphi^v \lor \exists v(\varphi^v \land \forall u\ (u \leq_w v \supset (\varphi \supset \psi)^u)).$$

L1 fails to validate any of the principles from §5.1 apart from Agglomeration. To see why, it will suffice to construct a model of $CT_\leq$ that fails to model some instance of each of those principles. The domain of the model is $\{w_@, w^*, \text{Jones, Rex}\}$, and the model interprets the singular constants j and r as referring, respectively, to Jones, who is in the actual world $w_@$ and has no counterparts in w^*, and to Rex, who is in w^* and has no counterparts in $w_@$. The predicates H ('is human') and D ('is a dragon') are interpreted, respectively, by $\{\text{Jones}\}$ and $\{\text{Rex}\}$. Extending this to a model of $CT_\leq$ is straightforward.

Let's now consider how L1 applies to some simple counterfactuals. On the one hand, $\neg \exists xHx > \bot$ translates into a $CT_\leq$-sentence that is true in the model just described iff there are no humans in any worlds, and so is false. On the other hand, $\neg \exists xHx > (Hj \land \neg Hj)$ translates into a $CT_\leq$-sentence that says that either there are no humans in any world—which is false—or some world w in which there are no humans is such that all of Jones's counterparts in all worlds that are at least as close as w and contain no humans are such that those counterparts are both human and not human—which is vacuously true because Jones only has counterparts in worlds in which there are humans. $\neg \exists xHx > (Hj \land \neg Hj)$, then, is true.

Having surveyed these two examples, we are already in a position to show that the translation does not validate Substitution of Tautological Equivalents in the Consequent. Here is an instance of that schema, whose translation, we just saw, is false in the model, so is not a $CT_\leq$-theorem:

(1) $(\neg \exists\, xHx > (Hj \land \neg Hj)) \supset (\neg \exists\, xHx > \bot)$

Next consider the L1-translation of the following instance of Substitution of Tautological Equivalents in the Antecedent.

(2) $((Dr \vee \neg Dr) > \exists x Dx) \supset (\top > \exists x Dx)$

L1 takes the antecedent of (2) to a $CT_\le$-sentence that is true if every world in which Rex has a counterpart is a world in which there are dragons—which is true in the model—and L1 takes the consequent of (2) to a $CT_\le$-sentence that is true only if there are dragons in every world—which is false in the model. The reader can check that the following instances of principles from §5.1 are also false in the model.

$\Box((Dr \vee \neg Dr) \equiv \top) \supset (((Dr \vee \neg Dr) > \exists\, x Dx) \supset (\top > \exists x Dx))$
(Substitution of Intensional Equivalents in the Antecedent)
$\Box((Hj \wedge \neg Hj) \equiv \bot) \supset ((\neg\exists\, x Hx > (Jj \wedge \neg Jj)) \supset (\neg\exists\, x Hx > \bot))$
(Substitution of Intensional Equivalents in the Consequent)
$(\neg\exists\, x Hx > (Hj \wedge \neg\, Hj)) \supset (\neg\exists\, x Hx > \bot)$
(Tautological Closure *and* D eduction within Conditionals)
$((\neg\exists\, x Hx > Hj) \wedge ((\neg\exists\, x Hx \wedge Hj) > \bot)) \supset (\neg\exists\, x Hx > \bot)$
(Restricted Transitivity)
$((Hj \wedge \neg Hj) > \neg\exists\, x Hx) \wedge (\neg\exists\, x Hx > (Hj \wedge \neg Hj)) \wedge ((Hj \wedge \neg Hj) > \bot))$
$\qquad \supset (\neg\exists\, x Hx > \bot)$ (CSO)
$\Box\exists\, x Hx \equiv (\neg\exists\, x Hx > (Hj \wedge \neg Hj))$ ($\Box$-Equivalence)
$\Diamond\neg\exists\, x Hx \equiv \neg (\neg\exists\, x Hx > (Hj \wedge \neg Hj))$ ($\Diamond$-Equivalence)
$(\neg\exists\, x Hx > (Hj \wedge \neg Hj)) \rightarrow (\Diamond\neg\exists\, x Hx \rightarrow \Diamond (Hj \wedge \neg Hj))$ ($\Diamond$-Closure)

Next, consider Dr ('Rex is a dragon'). Being an atomic sentence, it gets translated into itself, and its translation is true in the model. $\exists x Dx$, on the other hand, gets translated into $\exists x(Iw\, @ \wedge Dx)$ ('There is a dragon in the actual world'), and its translation is false in the model. The translations of the following instances of And-to-If and Counterfactual Modus Ponens, then, are false in the model:

$(Dr \wedge \neg\exists\, x Dx) \supset (Dr > \neg\exists\, x Dx)$
$(Dr > \exists\, x Dx) \supset (Dr \supset \exists\, x Dx).$

Let us briefly return to L2. According to L2,

$$(\varphi > \psi)^w := \quad \neg \exists v \exists x_1 \ldots \exists x_n \, (Cx_1 \ldots x_n t_1 \ldots t_n v \wedge \varphi^v \, [x_1 \ldots x_n / t_1 \ldots t_n]) \vee$$
$$\exists v \exists x_1 \ldots \exists x_n \, (Cx_1 \ldots x_n t_1 \ldots t_n v \wedge \varphi^v \, [x_1 \ldots x_n / t_1 \ldots t_n]) \wedge$$
$$\forall u \, \forall y_1 \ldots \forall y_n \, ((u \leq_w v \wedge Cy_1 \ldots y_n t_1 \ldots t_n u) \supset$$
$$(\varphi \supset \psi)^u \, [y_1 \ldots y_n / t_1 \ldots t_n])),$$

where $t_1 \ldots t_n$ are all of the singular terms with free occurrences in $\varphi > \psi$. We adopt the same convention for the case of zero free occurrences as in connection with L1, so in that case the two translations deliver the same result. Like L1, L2 fails to validate each of the principles from §5.1 discussed in this section so far, but unlike L1, L2 also fails to validate Agglomeration. While the same instances and the same model suffice to demonstrate the invalidity of the other principles on L2, to demonstrate the invalidity of Agglomeration on L2, we will have to consider a different model of $CT_\leq$. In this model there are (to put it casually) three worlds. Jones and Rex are as in the model we have described. In each world there are humans, but in the first world, which is actual, Jones has a counterpart, Rex doesn't have a counterpart, and there are dragons; in the second world, which is the unique world closest to the actual world in which Rex has a counterpart, there are dragons; in the third world, which is the unique world closest to the actual world in which both Jones and Rex have counterparts, there are no dragons. In this model, then, both the L2-translation of

$$\exists x Hx > (Hj \wedge \exists x Dx)$$

and the L2-translation of

$$\exists x Hx > (Dr \wedge \exists x Dx)$$

are true, while the L2-translation of

$$\exists x Hx > ((Hj \wedge \exists x Dx) \wedge (Dr \wedge \exists x Dx))$$

is false (because L2 requires us to look at worlds where both Jones and Rex have counterparts and in which there are humans), so the L2-translation of the following instance of Agglomeration is false in the model.

$$((\exists x Hx > (Hj \wedge \exists x Dx)) \wedge (\exists x Hx > (Dr \wedge \exists x Dx)))$$
$$\supset (\exists x Hx > ((Hj \wedge \exists x Dx) \wedge (Dr \wedge \exists x Dx)))$$

Some audiences have worried that our counterexamples involving Rex might require questionable assumptions about what can be named. (Perhaps a counterpart theorist should maintain that we could not introduce a singular constant for a dragon that is in some other world?) The worry is misplaced. What we have shown is And-to-If and Counterfactual Modus Ponens translate into non-theorems of $CT_\leq$ under L1, and these as well as Agglomeration translate into non-theorems of $CT_\leq$ under L2. These are mathematical facts that have nothing to do with what can be named.

A second common worry concerns the absence of singular constants from the language of Lewis's 1968 paper: perhaps we are somehow departing from the spirit of the counterpart-theoretic translation program in deploying the singular constant r? The issue is neither here nor there, since in 1968 Lewis is explicit that the instances of the schematic principles he is interested in include not only what we usually call 'sentences' but also formulas with free occurrences of variables (Lewis calls both kinds of expression 'sentences'). We can obtain the same result by replacing r with a variable.

Here is an interesting further fact: the universal generalizations of the formulas that figure in our counterexamples to Counterfactual Modus Ponens, And-to-If, and Agglomeration (whether using singular constants or freely occurring variables) are validated by both L1 and L2. That both translations validate, for some φ, $\forall x \varphi$ but not $\varphi[t/x]$, and therefore fail to validate Universal Instantiation ($\forall x \varphi \supset \varphi[t/x]$), is not in itself a strike against either on its own terms. Universal Instantiation is not valid in free logics, and counterpart theorists ought to be free logicians—a theme to which we will return in §5.7 (see note 21).

We haven't exhibited and will not attempt to exhibit the full range of interesting consequences of the translations. But perhaps it is worth making an observation about a connection between the translations and a principle that Stalnaker but not Lewis is sympathetic to: Counterfactual Excluded Middle:

CEM: $(\varphi > \psi) \vee (\varphi > \neg \psi)$.

The natural way to try to keep CEM in a possible worlds semantics is by imposing the condition that each set of worlds contains a unique world closest to any given world,[19] but the method of translation to $CT_\leq$ is not as

---

[19] This is equivalent to the conjunction of what Lewis labels the 'limit assumption' (see Lewis 1973: §1.4) and the assumptions that there are no ties in similarity between worlds—assumptions that Lewis notably rejects.

flexible. Most remarkably, not only do the Lewis-style translations fail to validate CEM, but they will fail to validate it even if we add the assumption that each set of worlds contains a unique world closest of all given worlds to $CT_\leq$. This is for the simple reason that there are models in which the unique closest world containing a counterpart of x that is F is a world that contains both a counterpart of x that is F and G and a counterpart of x that is F and not G. CEM-lovers like Stalnaker thus have additional reason to be suspicious of the translations. (Although the disastrous results outlined above are more than reason enough.)

Are there any widely accepted principles of counterfactual logic that survive the translations? We were a bit selective in drawing up our initial list, in that we chose only principles that at least one of the translations fails to validate. However, we did not need to be very selective, since very few interesting principles survive. Only three of Lewis's six principles concerning > survive:

$\varphi > \varphi$ (Lewis's axiom (3))

$(\neg\varphi > \varphi) \supset (\varphi > \varphi)$ (Lewis's axiom (4))

$(\varphi > \neg\psi) \vee (((\varphi \wedge \psi) > \chi) \equiv (\varphi > (\psi \supset \chi)))$ (Lewis's axiom (5)).

Another notable surviving principle that has the status of a theorem in Lewis's system, which we will come back to, is the principle that the strict conditional is at least as strong as the counterfactual conditional:

Strict-to-Would

$\Box(\varphi \supset \psi) \supset (\varphi > \psi)$.

In sum, the logic that survives the translation is radically weaker than the logic recommended by Lewis himself.

5.3 Two dead ends

5.3.1 Quasinecessitism?

It bears emphasis that all of the above counterexamples to principles of VC that arise on Lewis's translations exploit the fact that $CT_\leq$ allows things that are in worlds to lack counterparts in other worlds. The other distinctive features of Lewis's counterpart theory—that it allows a thing to have more than one counterpart in a world, and that it allows many things to have a single counterpart in a world—played no role in the failures of standard principles of counterfactual logic. In response to the problems we have raised so far, then, one might be tempted to add to $CT_\leq$ an axiom that says that anything that is in a world has a counterpart in every world:

$$\forall x \forall w \forall v (Ixw \supset \exists y Cytv).$$

Call the resulting theory *quasinecessitism*.[20] Quasinecessitism, however, is a radical solution that does little to help restore logical order when combined with Lewis's translations.

To begin with the radicalism, it bears emphasis how wildly quasinecessitism departs from the spirit of Lewis's vision and indeed the vision of most other counterpart theorists that we have encountered. Here's a natural way to flesh out the theory: in every world there are one or more non-concrete things that are counterparts of all of the otherworldly things that, under Lewis's original vision, would have no counterparts in that world. Thus, for example, Timothy Williamson's concrete counterparts are whatever they were under the original vision, but in any world in which TW has no concrete counterparts he has at least one non-concrete counterpart. There are two main ways to further flesh out the view. One would be to have some special-purpose non-concrete entities, different from the familiar ones like 0, to serve as the new counterparts. (Familiar entities like 0 won't do as unique counterparts because we don't want sentences like 'If TW had never been born, he would have been the predecessor of 1' to translate into truths of quasinecessitism.) Another way would be to count *all* non-concrete entities in a world as counterparts of each thing that has no concrete counterparts in that world. (That will fix the problem just noted, since not all non-concrete entities are predecessors of 1.) The first option involves ontological postulates that are alien to standard counterpart theory and that would require some justification—recall that counterpart theory is supposed to be a true metaphysical theory, not simply a formal tool for defining a modal or counterfactual logic. The second option yields oddities given Lewis's

---

[20] Quasinecessitism is to be sharply distinguished from *necessitism*, the thesis that it is necessary that everything is necessarily identical to something, in the sense of $\Box \forall x \Box \exists y\, x = y$ (see Williamson 2013). As Lewis himself notices in his 1968 paper, necessitism in this sense is validated by his translation scheme (Lewis 1968: 119). Yet Lewis's 1968 axiomatization of counterpart theory does not require everything to have a counterpart in every world.

translation clause for ◊ (see (T2j)): it forces us to accept that TW could have been the predecessor of 1. But more seriously still, both options involve giving up the similarity-theoretic approach to counterpart theory that drives Lewis's vision. After all, the non-concrete entities that are TW's counterparts in a world where he has no concrete counterparts are so radically dissimilar from TW that they would not be counted as TW's counterparts by any reasonable similarity heuristic. In a world that contains a human very much like Napoleon but nothing remotely like TW, it seems that the Napoleon-like figure is more similar to TW than any non-concrete thing, by any relevant standard of similarity.

Now let's consider the logic that results when quasinecessitism is combined with either L1 or L2. While these combinations restore some of VC, they still fail to validate two out of the three principles of VC listed at the beginning of §5.1: Counterfactual Modus Ponens and And-to-If. For consider a model of quasinecessitism in which there are two worlds with one inhabitant each: Rex, who is a red (R) dragon in the non-actual world, and Bex (b), who is a green (G) dragon in the actual world. Since this is a model of quasinecessitism, Rex and Bex are counterparts of each other, and the following instances of Counterfactual Modus Ponens and And-to-If translate, on either translation, to sentences that are false in the model, and therefore do not translate to theorems of quasinecessitism, which is to say that they are not validated by the translations:

$(Dr > Gr) \supset (Dr \supset Gr)$

$(Dr \wedge Rr) \supset (Dr > Rr).$

In summary, quasinecessitism delivers little logical help at a great metaphysical cost.

5.3.2 Who cares?

Of course, one might also consider simply giving up on counterfactual logic and trying to use counterpart theory directly to do all the cognitive work we are accustomed to doing with counterfactuals. By 1986, Lewis had adopted a similar attitude towards modal logic, declaring that the answer to the question 'What is the correct counterpart-theoretic translation of the modal formulas of the standard language of quantified modal logic?' is

'Who cares?'[21] One might take the view that the foregoing considerations show that the counterfactual conditional connective is not logically well-behaved, and that this is no cause for concern given that it belongs to a family of concepts that only give us a rough purchase on the counterpart-theoretic metaphysical reality anyway. It would be poignant if Lewis's counterpart theory served to fatally undermine the counterfactual logic that he himself pioneered. But, quite apart from that, we ourselves are loath to take a 'Who cares?' attitude toward well-entrenched principles of counterfactual reasoning. If adopting the counterpart-theoretic approach requires us to regard as invalid virtually all well-entrenched principles of counterfactual reasoning, then that is a cost that needs to be clearly in view, and it is one that many (including ourselves) will regard as not worth paying.

5.4 A new translation

Lewis's translation (on either construal) was getting the wrong results for two reasons. First, Lewis's translation of 'Jones is human and Jones is not human' behaves very differently from $\perp$ when embedded the consequent of a counterfactual, owing to the fact that while there are no worlds where $\perp$ (so to speak), there are plenty of worlds where every counterpart of Jones is both human and not human, since there are plenty of worlds where Jones has no counterparts. Second, while embedding Lewis's translation of 'Rex is red' in the antecedent of a counterfactual introduced existential quantification over counterparts of Rex, the truth of the unembedded translation is independent of the color of any counterparts of Rex other than Rex himself, and indeed of whether Rex has any counterparts other than himself.

The notion that will figure centrally in what follows is that of a counterpart function at a world (expressed by $CF(g, w)$ in what follows). A counterpart function at a world w takes each thing to one of its counterparts in w—if it has a counterpart in w—and otherwise takes it to itself. (Note that since things in w have only themselves as counterparts in w, every counterpart function at w will take each thing in w to itself.) Obviously a function may be a counterpart function at some world while not being a counterpart function at some other world. For example, if Lex is Rex's unique counterpart in w_1 and Hex is Rex's unique counterpart in w_2, then a

---

[21] Lewis (1986: 13).

function that takes Rex to Lex will not be a counterpart function at w_2 (while it could be a counterpart function at w_1)

To get an intuitive feel for how our translation works, we can adapt some Lewisian terminology. Let's say that a sentence is *vicariously true* at a world just in case it is true relative to some counterpart function at that world. And let's say that a sentence is *vicariously supertrue* at a world just in case the sentence is true relative to every counterpart function at that world. Deploying the ideology of vicarious truth, we say that a claim of the form $\varphi > \psi$ is true at a world w just so long as either there is no world at which φ is vicariously true or else there is some world at which φ is vicariously true and which is such that the material conditional $\varphi \supset \psi$ is vicariously supertrue at any world at least as similar to w as it.

A crucial feature of our approach is that atomic formulas themselves get a counterpart-theoretic translation, while on Lewis's approach they were unaffected by the translation. Consider, for example, the atomic sentence 'Rex is a dragon'. Our key idea is that such a sentence is true at a world just so long as it is vicariously supertrue at that world and that for it to be true at a world relative to a counterpart function of that world, the counterpart function takes Rex to something that is in that world and is a dragon. The problems introduced by Rex are thereby solved. Consider the counterfactual 'If Rex had been a dragon there would be dragons'. On Lewis's translation scheme this made trouble for Counterfactual Modus Ponens. But on our translation it does not, because we translate 'Rex is a dragon' into something false when Rex has no counterparts in the actual world. Or consider 'If Rex had been a dragon, Rex would have been green'. On Lewis's translation scheme, this too made trouble for Counterfactual Modus Ponens, but not on ours, because we translate 'Rex is green' into something true when Rex does have counterparts in the actual world.

The other basic problem for Lewis had to do with the fact that 'Jones is human and Jones is not human' behaves very differently from $\bot$ when embedded in the consequent of a counterfactual. But that problem is also circumvented by insisting that the vicarious truth of an atomic sentence at a world requires that the referents of all singular terms with free occurrences in the sentence have counterparts in that world. For example, at a world where John has no counterparts 'John is happy' is not vicariously supertrue, since no counterpart function at that world will take John to a thing that is in that world and is happy. Consider now

There are no humans > (John is happy $\land \neg$ John is happy).

This counterfactual does not come out true on our translation. A world where there are no humans will not be a world where the material conditional

There are no humans $\supset$ (John is happy $\land\neg$ John is happy)

is vicariously supertrue. In fact, it is not even vicariously true at such a world. The antecedent will be true relative to every counterpart function at that world and the consequent true relative to none, since the consequent will not be vicariously true relative to any counterpart function at that world, since no counterpart function at any world will take anything to something that is in that world and is both happy and not happy.

Of course these casual remarks are no substitute for a systematic translation scheme, so we will now turn to a more precise statement of our translation.

(Presentationally, the new translation is not quite in the spirit of Lewis's program, which requires working only with first-order theories: the quantification over counterpart functions is second-order. But this is easily remedied by defining functions as ordered pairs in set theory in the usual way, and then by supplementing $CT_\leq$ with the relevant set-theoretic axioms.)

Here is a more precise statement of our translation. First we define a counterpart function at a world:

$$CF\,(g, w) = \forall x(Cg(x)\,xw \lor (\neg\exists yCyxw \land g(x) = x)).$$

Then we define the translation φ^* of a quantified counterfactual logic (QCL) formula φ into CT as:

$$\varphi\,{}^* := \forall g(CF\,(g, @) \supset \varphi^{@,g}),$$

i.e., as

$$\forall g(CF\,(g, @) \supset \varphi^{@,g}).$$

Next we define $\varphi^{w,g}$ by induction:

$$(F\,t_1 \ldots t_n)^{w,g} := Ig(t_1)\,w \land \ldots \land Ig(t_n)\,w \land Fg(t_1) \ldots g(t_n)$$

$(\neg\varphi)^{w,g} := \neg(\varphi^{w,g})$

$(\varphi \land \psi)^{w,g} := \varphi^{w,g} \land \psi^{w,g}$

$(\varphi \lor \psi)^{w,g} := \varphi^{w,g} \lor \psi^{w,g}$

$(\varphi \supset \psi)^{w,g} := \varphi^{w,g} \supset \psi^{w,g}$

$(\varphi \equiv \psi)^{w,g} := \varphi^{w,g} \equiv \psi^{w,g}$

$(\forall x\varphi)^{w,g} := \forall x(Ixw \supset \varphi^{w,g})$

$(\exists x\varphi)^{w,g} := \exists x(Ixw \land \varphi^{w,g})$

$(\varphi > \psi)^{w,g} := \neg\exists\, v\exists h(CF(h, v) \land \varphi^{v,g})$

$\lor\exists\, v\,\exists h\, (CF(h, v) \land \varphi^{v,h} \land \forall\, u\,\forall f((u \geq_w v \land CF(f, u)) \supset \neg(\varphi \land \neg\psi)^{u,f})).$

All principles of the logic of counterfactuals from §5.1 get validated, but not only that: the new translation yields a propositional logic of counterfactuals that includes Lewis's 1973 minimal logic VC.[22]

Some readers may be wondering why we didn't adopt something less radical when it comes to atomic formulas. After all, we could have blocked the Rex problem as stated by simply imposing a *being constraint* in our translation of atomic formulas rather than translating them in a fully counterpart-theoretic way.[23] The being constraint is one that translates atomic formulas not homophonically but by adding, for each singular term t occurring in an atomic formula, a conjunct that says that the referent of t is in the world at issue:

$(Ft_1 \ldots t_n)^{w,g} := It_1w \land \ldots \land I\, t_nw \land Ft_1 \ldots t_n.$

Thus, an alternative proposal is to gloss 'Rex is a dragon' as true at w just in case Rex is in w and is a dragon. The trouble is that if this approach is taken, then other sentences provide difficulties. In general what causes trouble is that counterfactuals introduce quantification over counterpart functions, but on the proposed translation scheme atomic sentences don't. Consider the following kind of model. There are three worlds, @, w, w^*. It is raining in @ and w but not in w^*. John is in @, Johannes is in w, John is Johannes's only counterpart in @ and vice versa in w. In w^*, Bob is John's unique counterpart and Tim (who is not Bob), is Johannes's unique counterpart. Now

---

[22] While our logic is stronger than Lewis's, it does not include CEM. If you're a CEM-lover, you will have to depart from Lewis's 1973 translation in more radical ways.

[23] We take the term 'being constraint' from Williamson (2013: §4.1), who uses it with a different but similar meaning.

'John ≠ Johannes' comes out true on the being constraint approach. This is because Johannes is not in @. Consider the counterfactual

John ≠ Johannes > ¬it is raining.

There is only one world where 'John ≠ Johannes' is vicariously true: w^*. Moreover, at w^* and all closer ones the material conditional

John ≠ Johannes ⊃ ¬it is raining

is vicariously supertrue, so the counterfactual is true, but on the being constraint approach, the antecedent is true as well, so we have a counter-example to Counterfactual Modus Ponens, since the consequent is false.[24] So the less radical fix to the Rex problem does not adequately generalize.

5.5 Modal logic within counterfactual logic

There is more work to be done. If we combine the new translation with Lewis's 1968 translations of $\Box\varphi$ and $\Diamond\varphi$, we make a mess of the interaction of $\Box$ and $\Diamond$ with >: we fail to validate $\Box$-Reducibility, $\Diamond$-Reducibility, and Strict-to-Would. The natural thing to do here is to follow Lewis himself and to treat the counterfactual conditional as the only primitive intensional operator, with $\Box$ and $\Diamond$ both defined in terms of it, and this is just what we will do. We will adopt the definitions:

$$\Box\varphi := \neg\varphi > \bot$$
$$\Diamond\varphi := \neg\Box\neg\varphi$$

As the reader can check, these definitions give the following welcome results:

$$(\Box\varphi)^{w,g} \equiv \forall w \forall g (CF(g, w) \supset \varphi^{w,g})$$
$$(\Diamond\varphi)^{w,g} \equiv \exists w \exists g (CF(g, w) \land \varphi^{w,g})$$

---

[24] The point could have been made without using identity. Keep all the counterpart-theoretic facts the same and have it that John and Johannes are slightly different in height and Tim and Bob have different heights. The sentence '¬ John is the same height as Johannes' is vicariously true at one world only: w^*. So it will turn out that '¬ John is the same height as Johannes >¬ it's raining' will come out true, and once again we have a counterexample to Counterfactual Modus Ponens.

And in fact these definitions give us all of the results we want: the combined propositional logic of counterfactuals and metaphysical modality includes the logic **VC** that is characterized by Lewis's 1973 semantics, with $\Box$ and $\Diamond$ defined in Lewis's way.

As an added bonus,[25] we also get **S5** as the logic of $\Box$, which Lewis's (1968) translation did not. It will do to check a single case, the characteristic axiom of **S5**:

5: $\Diamond\varphi \supset \Box \Diamond\varphi.$

Our translation of the consequent of **5** is

$$(\Box \Diamond\varphi)^* = \forall w\, \forall g\, (CF\, (g,\, w) \supset (\neg\Box\neg\varphi^{w,g}))$$
$$= \forall w\, \forall g\, (CF(g,\, w) \supset \neg\forall\, v\, \forall h(CF(h,\, v) \supset \neg\varphi^{v,h})),$$

which is logically equivalent to our translation of its antecedent, since

$$(\Diamond\varphi)^* = (\neg\Box\, \neg\varphi)^* = \neg\forall\, w\, \forall g\, (CF\, (g,\, w) \supset \neg\varphi^{w,g}).$$

Any instance of **5**, then, translates into a theorem of logic, and therefore of $CT_\leq$. For the same reason, any instance of $\Box\varphi \equiv (\Box/\Diamond)\Box\varphi$ and of $\Diamond\varphi \equiv (\Box/\Diamond)\, \Diamond\varphi$, where $(\Box/\Diamond)$ is any finite string of boxes and diamonds, now translates into a theorem of logic, because all world quantifiers and all counterpart function quantifiers in the translation of an iterated modal formula $(\Box/\Diamond)\Box\varphi$ except for at most the innermost ones bind nothing in the translation of φ. The translation of an iterated modal formula is either equivalent to

$$\forall w\, \forall g\, (CF\, (g,\, w) \supset \varphi)$$

or to

$$\neg\forall\, w\, \forall g(CF(g,\, w) \supset \neg\varphi)$$

---

[25] A bonus by our lights anyway. There are, of course, philosophers who are altogether so taken by puzzles about the originating matter of tables that they have managed to convince themselves that their intuitions about such puzzles should trump all of the abductive considerations in favor of an **S4** (and therefore an **S5**) logic for metaphysical necessity (e.g., Salmon 1989, following Chandler 1976). See Dorr, Hawthorne, and Yli-Vakkuri (2020) for a reply to such philosophers and see Goodsell and Yli-Vakkuri (2020) for a defense of **S5**. We will not be pursuing the question of how to adapt our translation to accommodate **S4**-denial. (Thanks to Ted Sider for discussion here.)

where both of the initial occurrences of $\forall w$ and $\forall g$ bind nothing in φ, and thus each is logically equivalent to φ itself.

5.6 Basic modal logic lost and restored

It is a relief that the new translation delivers S5, because Lewis's 1968 translation delivers virtually no propositional modal logic. Here are some completely uncontentious principles, in decreasing order of strength in standard possible worlds semantics:

T: $\Box\varphi \supset \varphi$

('What is necessary is true.')

D: $\Box\varphi \supset \Diamond\varphi$

('What is necessary is possible.')

K: $\Box(\varphi \supset \psi) \supset (\Box\varphi \supset \Box\psi)$

('Any necessary consequence of a necessary truth is also necessary.' Or, put another way: 'Anything that follows by *modus ponens* from necessary truths is also necessary.')

K is valid on any relational possible worlds semantics, D is valid on any whose accessibility relation relates every world to some world, and T is valid on any whose accessibility relation relates each world to itself.

As shown in Yli-Vakkuri (2020), Lewis's (1968) translation validates none of these, because it turns $\Box$ into a hyperintensional operator in the sense that it fails to validate the principle of *intensionality*:

I: $\Box(\varphi \equiv \psi) \supset (\chi \supset \chi\,[\varphi/\psi])$.

We should not expect I to hold in every language, but, by definition, it does hold in any language with no hyperintensional operators, and QML has none.

   To show that Lewis's translation fails to validate each of T, D, K, and I, it suffices to show there is a model of CT that fails to model some instance of each of T, D, K, and I. Here is one such model: The domain is $\{0, 1, 2, 3\}$ (for mnemonic purposes: $\{w_@, w_1, o_a, o_b\}$). The model interprets W as $\{w_@, w_1\}$, I as $\{\langle o_a, w_@\rangle, \langle o_b, w_1\rangle\}$, A as $\{o_a\}$, and C as $\{\langle o_a, o_a\rangle, \langle o_b, o_b\rangle\}$. To falsify translations of instances of T, D, K, and I, the model interprets the

1-place predicates F and G, respectively, as $\{o_a\}$ and $\{o_b\}$, and the singular constants a and b, respectively, as o_a and o_b.

The model is not a model of

$$\exists w \, (\forall x(Ixw \equiv Ax) \wedge (\forall v \forall x(Cxbv \supset Gx \supset \exists x \, (Ixv \wedge Gx))) \supset (Gb \supset \exists x(Ixw \wedge Gz))),$$

which is Lewis's translation of the following T-instance.

$$\Box(Gb \supset \exists xGx) \supset (Gb \supset \exists xGx)$$

The model is also not a model of

$$\forall w \, \forall x \forall y \, (Cxyabw \supset (Fx \wedge Gy)) \supset \exists w \, \exists x \exists \, y(Cxyabw \wedge Fx \wedge Gy),$$

which is Lewis's translation of the D-instance

$$\Box(Fa \wedge Gb) \supset \Diamond \, (Fa \wedge Gb).$$

Nor is it a model of

$$\forall w \, \forall x(Cxaw \supset Fx \supset \exists y(Iyw \wedge Fy)) \supset (\forall w \forall x \, (Cxaw \supset Fx) \supset \forall w \exists x \, (Ixw \wedge Fx)),$$

which is Lewis's translation of the K -instance

$$\Box(Fa \supset \exists xFx) \supset (\Box Fa \supset \Box \, \exists xFx).$$

Finally, while the translation of

$$\Box(\neg \exists xFx \equiv (Fa \wedge \neg \, Fa))$$

is true in the model, the translation of

$$\Box(\neg \exists xFx \supset \bot)$$

is not. The model, then, is not a model of Lewis's translation of the I-instance

$$\Box((Fa \wedge \neg Fa) \equiv \bot) \supset (\Box(\neg \exists xFx \equiv (Fa \wedge \neg \, Fa)) \supset \Box(\neg \exists xFx \supset \bot)).$$

5.7 Identity and existence

Lewis rejects quasinecessitism but his translation validates, as he himself notes

N∃: $\forall x \Box \exists y\, x = y$

('Everything is necessarily something').

It also validates what is nowadays called *necessitism*:

NN∃: $\Box \forall x\, \Box \exists y\, x = y$

('Necessarily everything is necessarily something').

The reason is that if an individual has no counterpart in a world, then it's vacuously true that every counterpart of that individual is such that there is something in that world that is identical to it.

   Our proposal entails neither quasinecessitism nor necessitism. This is a welcome result from the point of view of a counterpart theorist who thinks that some things in some worlds lack counterparts in some other worlds, and counterpart theorists should think that. Consider a world—however construed—in which there are three pebbles and nothing else concrete. Non-necessitist non-counterpart theorists who think of worlds as states of affairs will be inclined to think that Abraham Lincoln is not identical to anything in that world, and to regard that world as a counterexample to both NN∃ and N∃. Counterpart theorists who share that intuition would express it in their language by saying that nothing in that world- *cum* -physical-universe is a counterpart of Lincoln, and they should think that that world is—just as our translation has it—a counterexample to the counterpart-theoretic translations of both NN∃ and N∃.

   While our translation gives salutary results when it comes to existence, its results for identity and distinctness take some getting used to. It fails to validate both the principle of the quantified necessity of distinctness:

ND: $\forall x \forall y (x \neq y \supset \Box\, x \neq y)$

and the principle of the schematic necessity of distinctness:

SND: $a \neq b \supset \Box\, a \neq b.$

For example, suppose that Bill and Ben are distinct actual things with a common counterpart,

Ben*, in w^*. Then our translation of 'Bill ≠ Ben' comes out true because all counterpart functions at the actual world assign Bill and Ben to themselves, but our translation of '□ Bill ≠ Ben' comes out false because some counterpart function at w^* assigns Ben* to both Bill and Ben. w^* is a counterexample to both ND and SND. Might order be restored by amending the definition of a counterpart function so that such a function never assigns the same individual to distinct individuals? Not only does this seem contrary to the spirit of Lewis's counterpart theory, but on closer inspection it is inconsistent. For suppose that Lex in w_1 has Rex as its unique counterpart in w_2. Any counterpart function at w_2 will assign Rex to Rex in w_2 and will furthermore assign anything that has a counterpart in w_2 to one of those counterparts, so it will also assign Lex to Rex in w_2, which is disallowed by the proposed amendment.

What about the quantified necessity of identity:

NI: $\forall x \forall y (x = y \supset \Box x = y)$

and schematic necessity of identity:

SNI: $a = b \supset \Box\, a = b$?

Our translation validates neither. Any world in which Hesperus has no counterparts is a counterexample to the translations of both NI and SNI, because the translation of 'Hesperus = Phosphorus' with respect to w, g includes a conjunct that say that Hesperus is in w and that Phosphorus is in w. Indeed, even

Hesperus = Hesperus $\supset$ □Hesperus = Hesperus

is invalidated by the translation for the same reason. The deployment of distinct singular terms was not essential to the counterexample.

Now one might wonder whether there is some natural way of adding a special clause for identities that restores more familiar logical order. There isn't. First, we could try combining Lewis's homophonic treatment of identities,

$(t_1 = t_2)^{w,g} := t_1 = t_2,$

COUNTERPART THEORY AND COUNTERFACTUALS 157

with our treatment of other atomic formulas. This has the effect of validating each of NI, SNI, ND, SND, as well as their necessitations:

NNI: $\Box \forall x \, \forall y \, (x = y \supset \Box \, x = y)$

NSNI: $\Box (a = b \supset \Box \, a = b)$

NND: $\Box \forall x \, \forall y \, (x \neq y \supset \Box \, x \neq y)$

NSND: $\Box (a \neq b \supset \Box \, a \neq b).$

This is because the homophonic option renders all world quantifiers and all counterpart function quantifiers in the translations of all of the principles vacuous, making those translations truths of quantification theory and so *a fortiori* theorems of $CT_\leq$. But this gain comes at a depressing cost. For example, in adopting the homophonic approach to identities we invalidate the following elementary principle of quantification theory.

(∃!) $(\exists! \, xFx \wedge Fa \wedge Fb) \supset a = b$

('If there is exactly one F, and a is F and b is F, then a = b.')

After all, a and b may be distinct otherworldly individuals that have the same counterpart in the actual world, and the translation under consideration takes the antecedent of (∃!) to a conjunction of generalizations about the actual counterparts of a and b while leaving its consequent untouched.

A less flat-footed approach is to drop the being constraint from the translations of identities:

$$(t_1 = t_2)^{w,g} := g(t_1) = g(t_2).$$

This would avoid the particular problem for NI that our original translation faces, but it does no better with SNI. For suppose that Rex and Tex are denizens of a non-actual world w and share Lex as their mutual and only actual counterpart in the actual world. 'Rex = Tex' comes out true under the translation, but '□Rex = Tex' does not, because at w all counterpart functions assign Rex and Tex to themselves and thus to distinct objects.

Thus we by no means restore logical order by dropping the being constraint for identity. It should be noted, however, that there is a cost to keeping the being constraint: in doing so we invalidate the axiom *schema* of the reflexivity of identity $(t = t)$. Our translation of $t = t$ is

It@ $\wedge$ $t = t$,

which is clearly not a theorem of $CT_{\leq}$ (it is false in any model of $CT_{\leq}$ that interprets t by an individual not in the extension of A). Of course, our translation does validate the *axiom* of the reflexivity of identity:

$\forall x\ x = x$,

and its necessitation:

$\Box \forall\ x\ x = x$.

It may be felt that merely validating the axiom but not the axiom schema is not good enough. We nevertheless recommend our translation to counter-part theorists. This is because their quantified modal logic ought to be a free logic—that is, a logic in which Existential Generalization ($\varphi\ [\ t/x] \supset \exists\ x\ \varphi$) is not valid—and the invalidation of the axiom schema of the reflexivity of identity is a 'feature', not a 'bug', of an important class of semantic treat-ments of free logics (so-called negative semantics).[26] Indeed, it is a feature of one of the two semantic treatments of quantified modal logic considered in Kripke's classic paper 'Semantical Considerations on Modal Logic' (1963). As Kripke himself explains the feature:

> It is natural to assume that an *atomic* predicate should be *false* in a world . . .
> of all those individuals not existing in that world . . .[27]

In his mature philosophical work, Kripke is similarly open to the idea that individuals might fail to be identical to themselves in worlds in which they do not exist. In 'Identity and Necessity' he writes:

> Well, for example, am I myself necessarily self-identical? Someone might argue that in some situations which we can imagine I would not even have existed and therefore the statement "Saul Kripke is Saul Kripke" would have been false or it would not have been the case that I was self-identical.

---

[26] Since Existential Generalization is equivalent to Universal Instantiation, the latter is also not valid in any free logic.

[27] Kripke (1963: 86, n. 1, emphasis in the original). The language of Kripke's 1963 paper does not have an identity predicate, but the next quoted passage makes it clear that he took seriously the idea that identity should not be exempted from this treatment.

Perhaps it would have been neither true nor false, in such a world, to say
that Saul Kripke is self-identical. Well, that may be so...

(Kripke 1971: 164).

For this reason, in his famous discussion of the necessity of identity,
from which the above words are quoted, Kripke proposes to 'interpret
necessity...weakly', so that we 'count statements as necessary if whenever
the objects mentioned therein exist, the statement would be true' (*ibid.*).[28]
While we ourselves are partial to the reflexivity of identity, we find giving it
up—especially for the reasons discussed by Kripke—to be a much less
serious cost than those incurred by the alternative translations. Our translation sustains the thought that to stand in a relation is to be—with no
exceptions, not even for the relation of identity. A reader who likes that
thought should be skeptical of the tweaks to our translation entertained here.
That said, if the reader cannot learn to live with the invalidation of schematic
reflexivity of identity, we recommend the option of exempting identities
from the being constraint.

5.8 A semantic anomaly

While our translation yields a reasonable classical quantified modal *logic*, in
one sense it yields a non-classical *semantics* for the language QCL: whenever
φ is an atomic QCL-sentence with at least one occurrence of a singular term,
there are models of $CT_\leq$ in which both our translation of φ and our
translation of ¬φ are false. For example, our translations of 'Rex is happy'
and '¬ Rex is happy' assert, respectively, the happiness of all of Rex's actual
counterparts and the unhappiness of all of Rex's actual counterparts, and
thus a model in which the actual world contains two counterparts of Rex,
one happy and the other unhappy, is one in which both translations are
false. (Note that it does not follow that our translations of the negations of
these sentences are true in such a model—they are not! Since our translation
of '¬¬ Rex is happy' asserts the non-unhappiness of all of Rex's actual

---

[28] A little-noticed consequence of Kripke's 1971 interpretation of the necessity operator is
that it yields an even *worse* modal logic than Lewis's 1968 translation. It invalidates T, D, K, and
I, but it additionally invalidates the one uncontested modal principle that Lewis's translation
manages to validate: **NEC**—a feature it shares with the Kaplan translation (see section 5.9). We
find the interpretations of the necessity operator in Kripke's less well-known 1963 paper to be
far preferable to the one used in his celebrated discussion of the necessity of identity.

counterparts, the falsehood of our translation of a QCL-sentence in a model is not equivalent to the truth of our translation of its negation in that model.) This would be a serious problem if our ambition had been to produce a translation that yields not just a reasonable logic but a reasonable semantics—in the sense of truth conditions—for QCL, but that was never our ambition. In any case, there is a simple fix we recommend for those who are bothered by this semantic anomaly: instead of defining CF (g, w), treat it as a primitive and add to $CT_\leq$ (i) the definiens of our definition of $CF(g, w)$ as an axiom about counterpart functions (that is: $\forall g \forall w \, (CF \, (g, w) \supset \forall x \, (Cg \, (x) \, xw \vee (\neg\exists \, yCyxw \wedge g(x) = x))))$) and (ii) an axiom that says that there is exactly one counterpart function at each world.[29,30] It is natural to further suppose that while there is determinately exactly one counterpart function at each world, there are worlds for which nothing is determinately its counterpart function. (Cf.: there is determinately a height in millimeters that is the cutoff for being tall, but there is no height n in millimeters such that determinately n is the cutoff for being tall.) This further idea, however, cannot be expressed in counterpart theory, because its expression would require the use of the nonextensional operator 'determinately'.

5.9 The Kaplan translation

It's worth comparing our translation to one that according to Lewis was entertained by David Kaplan, which we'll call the *Kaplan translation*:

$$(\Box\varphi)^w := \forall v \, \exists x_1 \ldots \exists x_n \, (Cx_1 \ldots x_n t_1 \ldots t_n v \wedge \varphi^v \, [x_1 \ldots x_n/t_1 \ldots t_n])$$
$$(\Diamond\varphi)^w := \exists v \forall x_1 \ldots \forall x_n \, (Cx_1 \ldots x_n t_1 \ldots t_n v \supset \varphi^v \, [x_1 \ldots x_n/t_1 \ldots t_n]).$$

There are two important similarities between this and our original translation.

---

[29] Alternatively, one could add to CT an axiom that says that everything has at most one counterpart in each world. Note that this does not require giving up the similarity-based conception of ≤: when there are ties for similarity, we can simply say that it is indeterminate which is the counterpart rather than saying that there are several counterparts.

[30] It's worth noting here that this amendment, when combined with the most natural translation for the actuality operator *Act* (namely, $(Act \, \varphi) = \forall g(CF(g, @) \supset \varphi)$) also overcomes the problems Williamson and Fara (2005) raise for counterpart-theoretic treatments of *Act*. See Russell (2013) and Bacon (2014: §2) for similar solutions to Williamson and Fara's problems.

First, the Kaplan translation imposes a kind of being constraint, and so avoids validating necessitism.

Second, since the Kaplan translation has no special clause for identity, the imposition of the being constraint invalidates the necessity of identity. That said, we are not especially inclined to regard the Kaplan translation as a worthy competitor. Lewis himself complains that

$$\lozenge \exists x x \neq x$$

comes out consistent on the Kaplan translation[31]—a feature it shares with our translation—but that is hardly its worst consequence. In fact, the Kaplan translation is the only translation we have seen discussed in the literature that does worse than Lewis's at validating uncontested principles. Like Lewis's translation, it validates neither **T**, **D**, **K**, nor **I** —below is an instance of each that it takes to a non-theorem of CT.

(1) $\square(Fa \supset \exists x Fx) \supset (Fa \supset \exists x Fx)$

(2) $\square Fa \supset \lozenge Fa$

(3) $\square(Fa \supset \exists x Gx) \supset (\square Fa \supset \square \exists x Gx)$

(4) $\square(\top \equiv Fa) \supset (\lozenge \top \supset \lozenge Fa)$.

(For (1), consider a model of CT in which a is non-actual, is F, and has counterparts in every world, and none of a's counterparts other than a itself inhabits a world in which anything is F. For (2) and (4), consider a model of CT where a has an F counterpart in every world and in one world a has a non-F counterpart. For (3), consider a model of CT with two worlds: in one all of a's counterparts are F and there are Gs, while in the other each a has an F and a non-F counterpart and there are no Gs.) But unlike Lewis's translation, the Kaplan translation also invalidates the rule of necessitation,

NEC: If $\vdash \varphi$ then $\vdash \square \, \varphi$,

which, together with **K**, is one of the two defining features of normal modal logics. What's more, the Kaplan translation invalidates **NEC** in an especially disastrous way, allowing tautologies to be counterexamples to it: if φ is any

---

[31] Lewis (1968: 119).

tautology in which a singular term t occurs free, the Kaplan translation takes φ to a theorem and $\Box$ φ to a non-theorem of CT. For example, $\Box(Fa \supset Fa)$ is taken to a non-theorem, because there are models of CT in which a does not have a counterpart in every world.

It should come as no surprise that the Kaplan translation also performs poorly when combined with either interpretation (L1 or L2) of Lewis's 1973 translation of counterfactuals. That combination invalidates two of the three principles governing the interaction of $\Box$ with > from §5.1 ($\Box$-Reducibility, ◇-Reducibility) as well as—like L2 but unlike L1—Strict-to-Would. For suppose at every world in which there are humans Rex has a happy counterpart but at the closest world where there are humans Rex also has a counterpart that is not happy. Then

$\Box(\exists x \ x$ is human $\supset$ Rex is happy)

is true but

$\exists x \ x$ is human > Rex is happy

is false. One could try to remedy this by changing the translation of the counterfactual so as to merely require a single counterpart witness to the consequent for each singular term that occurs freely in it. Out of the frying pan and into the fire! We now have

$\exists x \ x$ is human > Rex is happy

and

$\exists x \ x$ is human > ¬Rex is happy

both being true while

$\exists x \ x$ is human > (Rex is happy $\land$ ¬Rex is happy)

is false. In short, we will have rampant failures of Agglomeration. Counterfactual Modus Ponens and And-to-If are also invalidated.

The prospects for a translation based on Kaplan's idea that yields an acceptable propositional modal and counterfactual logic appear to be bleak.

5.10 Concluding remarks

Let us take stock of the overall logical situation. Lewis's 1968 and 1973 translations fit poorly with standard propositional counterfactual and modal logics, failing to validate many widely accepted principles in those areas, including three key principles of Lewis's own axiomatization of his 1973 logic of counterfactuals. We have proposed a counterpart-theoretic translation that is altogether Lewisian in spirit and that validates all of the uncontested principles of propositional modal and counterfactual logic we have surveyed. There is, admittedly, a cost to adopting our translation. While our translation and Lewis's both give up the necessity of distinctness—a move that is quite natural for the counterpart theorist who allows two things to share a counterpart in a world—adopting our translation requires taking the more radical step of also rejecting the necessity of identity and the axiom schema of the reflexivity of identity: $t = t$ (while it does not require the rejection of the axiom of the reflexivity of identity: $\forall x\, x = x$). But this, by our lights, is a much smaller cost than the radical departure from standard modal and counterfactual logic that results from Lewis's translation. After all, as we have seen, both principles can reasonably be questioned, following Kripke, on the grounds that perhaps (i) not everything necessarily exists, and perhaps (ii) there could have been things that don't actually exist. For the counterpart theorist, it is natural to translate (i) into the claim that (i′) not everything in the actual world has a counterpart in every world and (ii) into the claim that (ii′) not everything in every world has a counterpart in the actual world. And the models of counterpart theory in which conditions (i′) and (ii′) hold are those that witness the invalidity of the axiom of the necessity of identity and the axiom schema of the reflexivity of identity on our translation. (The counterpart theorist who nevertheless wishes to hold on to the axiom schema of the reflexivity of identity can do so by exempting identities from the being constraint.)

We'll put our cards on the table: We are not counterpart theorists, and in this chapter we have been, to use Quine's memorable phrase, 'in the position of a Jewish chef preparing ham for a gentile clientele'.[32] But whatever problems there are with counterpart theory—and there are plenty[33]—the

---

[32] Quine (1977: 7), quoted in Kripke (2011: 231).

[33] For the record, our main objections to the counterpart-theoretic approach to modality are that (i) we see no evidence whatsoever for the truth of any extensional theory that posits a concrete universe that contains Fs for a broad range of properties F, such as *being a talking*

absence of a translation of the language of quantified counterfactual and modal logic into it which yields a plausible quantified logic of counterfactuals and metaphysical modality is not one of them. We recommend our ham without reservation to those with a taste for pork.

References

Bacon, Andrew (2014). 'Representing Counterparts', *Australasian Journal of Logic*, 11 (2): 90–113. Available at: <https://ojs.victoria.ac.nz/ajl/article/view/2143>. Date accessed: 14 Dec. 2019. doi: https://doi.org/10.26686/ajl.v11i2.2143.

Blackburn, Patrick, Maarten de Rijke, and Yde Venema (2001). *Modal Logic*. Cambridge: Cambridge University Press.

Chandler, Hugh S. (1976). 'Plantinga and the Contingently Possible', *Analysis*, 36/2:107–9.

Cresswell, M. and G. E. Hughes (1996). *A New Introduction to Modal Logic*. London: Routledge.

Dorr, Cian (2005). 'Propositions and Counterpart Theory', *Analysis*, 6 5: 210–18.

Dorr, Cian, John Hawthorne, and Juhani Yli-Vakkuri (2020). Living on the Edge: Puzzles of Modal Variation. Unpublished manuscript, draft dated August 17th, 2020.

Goodsell, Z. and J. Yli-Vakkuri (2020). Higher-Order Logic as Metaphysics. Unpublished manuscript.

Hazen, Allen (1979). 'Counterpart-Theoretic Semantics for Modal Logic', *Journal of Philosophy*, 76: 319–38.

Kaplan, David (1989). 'Demonstratives.' In J. Almog at al., eds., *Themes from Kaplan*, 481–563. Oxford: Oxford University Press.

Kripke, Saul (1963). 'Semantical Considerations on Modal Logic', *Acta Philosophica Fennica*, 16: 83–94.

Kripke, Saul (1971). 'Identity and Necessity.' In M. K. Munitz, ed., *Identity and Individuation*, 135–164. New York: New York University Press.

donkey and *being a golden mountain*, whenever (pretheoretically speaking) there could have been *F*s, and that (ii) even if some such theory is true, that would be extraordinarily weak evidence for the hypothesis that some translation of quantified counterfactual and modal logic into it preserves meaning. (If our best cosmology ended up entailing the existence of such a pluriverse, why should we think that it is metaphysically necessary that that there is such a pluriverse?)

Kripke, Saul (1980). *Naming and Necessity*. Cambridge, MA: Harvard University Press.

Kripke, Saul A. (2011). *Philosophical Troubles*. O xford: Oxford University Press.

Lewis, David (1968). 'Counterpart Theory and Quantified Modal Logic', *Journal of Philosophy*, 65: 112–26.

Lewis, David (1973). *Counterfactuals*. Oxford: Blackwell.

Lewis, David (1983). Postscripts to 'Counterpart Theory and Quantified Modal Logic'. In David Lewis, *Philosophical Papers*, Vol. 1, 39–46. Oxford: Oxford University Press.

Lewis, David (1986). *On the Plurality of Worlds*. Oxford: Blackwell.

Montague, Richard (1963). 'Syntactical treatments of modality, with corollaries on reflexion principles and finite axiomatizability', *Acta Philosophica Fennica*, 16: 153–67.

Quine, W. V. (1955). 'Three Grades of Modal Involvement', *Journal of Symbolic Logic*, 20: 168–9.

Quine, W. V. (1977). "Intensions Revisited", *Midwest Studies in Philosophy*, 2(1): 5–11.

Russell, Jeffrey Sanford (2013) 'Actuality for Counterpart Theorists', *Mind*, 122: 85–134.

Salmon, Nathan (1989). 'Illogical Belief', Philosophical Perspectives, 3: 243–85.

Stalnaker, Robert (1968). 'A theory of conditionals.' In N. Rescher, ed., *Studies in Logical Theory*, 98–112. Oxford: Blackwell.

Williamson, Timothy (2007). *The Philosophy of Philosophy*. Oxford: Oxford University Press.

Williamson, Timothy (2010). 'Modal Logic within Counterfactual Logic'. In B. Hale and A. Homan, eds., *Modality: Metaphysics, Logic, and Epistemology*, 81–96. Oxford: Oxford University Press.

Williamson, Timothy (2013). *Modal Logic as Metaphysics*. Oxford: Oxford University Press.

Williamson, Timothy and Michael Fara (2005). 'Counterparts and Actuality', *Mind*, 114: 1–30.

Woollaston, Lin (1994). 'Counterpart Theory as a Semantics for Modal Logic', *Logique et Analyse*, 37: 255–63.

Yli-Vakkuri, J. (2020). 'Counterpart Theory and Modal Logic'. Unpublished manuscript.

6

Essence and Thisness

Sungil Han

6.1 Introduction

Many philosophers were once skeptical about metaphysics mainly because we did not have a semantic framework with which to understand modal claims as intelligible. Against this skeptical backdrop, Saul Kripke made a significant contribution to rehabilitating metaphysics in the analytic tradition.[1] With the help of possible worlds framework, Kripke showed how modal claims in general can intelligibly be made and how certain claims of necessity are indeed plausible or even undeniable.[2] Nevertheless, Kripke has left a lacuna concerning the source of modality. In virtue of what, are necessary truths and modal truths in general true? How to ground modality is a task we need to take up if we wish to complete Kripke's project of vindicating metaphysics.[3]

Kit Fine has proposed a promising way to undertake this remaining task.[4] Since the framework of possible worlds was given, essence has often been assimilated to necessity: an object has a certain property essentially just in case the object has the property necessarily—that is, it has the property in all possible worlds in which it exists. According to Fine, however, the assimilation of essence to necessity can't be right because essence is prior

---

[1] S. Kripke, *Naming and Necessity*, (Harvard University Press, 1980).

[2] In this chapter, by 'necessity', I mean *metaphysical* necessity. And I will be concerned primarily with necessary truths about *individuals*. Kripke assumes or proposes three kinds of necessary truths about individuals: the necessity of sortal kind; the necessity of origin; and the necessity of identity. These are not universally accepted. But here I assume that they are all true.

[3] Here I set aside the view that modal truths are brute facts and the view that modal truths hold as a matter of convention. For the primitivist view about modal truths, see D. Lewis, *Counterfactuals*, (Harvard University Press, 1973); *On the Plurality of Worlds*, (Blackwell Publisher, 1986); and R. Stalnaker, "Possible Worlds," *Nous* 2 (1973), 303–314. Lewis is in a sense not a primitivist, for he claims that the notion of modality is reducible to the non-modal notion of worlds. Nonetheless, he is a primitivist in the sense that he takes facts about nonactual worlds as primitive. For the conventionalist view, see A. Sidelle, *Necessity, Essence, and Individuation: A Defense of Conventionalism*, (Cornell University Press, 1989).

[4] K. Fine, "Essence and Modality," *Philosophical Perspectives*, 8 (1994), 1–16.

Sungil Han, *Essence and Thisness* In: *Oxford Studies in Metaphysics Volume 13*. Edited by: Karen Bennett and Dean W. Zimmerman, Oxford University Press. © Sungil Han 2023. DOI: 10.1093/oso/9780192886033.003.0006

to, and the source of, necessity: every necessary truth is grounded in some essential truth. Let us call this claim 'Fine's thesis.' If Fine's thesis is true, necessary truths have their source in essential truths, which provides us with resources with which to ground modal truths in general.

If essence is prior to necessity, how is essence to be understood? For Fine, essence is conceptually primitive. This, however, does not prevent us from having a model of how the concept of essence works. Fine proposes a 'definitional' model of essence. Among properties of an object are properties that explain what it is. According to Fine, the collection of the identity-explaining properties of an object or 'the definition' of an object makes up the constitutive portion of the essence of the object, while the rest of the essence consists of the consequences of the definition. On the definitional model of essence, the essence of an object is the collection of properties that are in the definition of the object or consequences of the definition.

I accept Fine's thesis, for I believe that the project of grounding modality should be pursued along the line of Fine's thesis. But I have qualms about the definitional model. The definition of an object comprises the constitutive essence of it. This much is uncontroversial. But the definitional model suggests more than that: on this model, the definition of an object *is* the constitutive essence of it. Therein, I think, lies a problem. Socrates is identical to Socrates. That's necessary. If we are to ground this necessary truth, we must acknowledge that Socrates has a primitive individuality we cannot capture except by an act of naming—viz. his being *this* one—and that the 'thisness' of Socrates is in his constitutive essence, though it doesn't belong in the definition of him. If modality is to be grounded, the constitutive essence of an object must not be assimilated to the definition of it. This is what I aim chiefly to establish in the chapter.

The chapter has two main parts. The first is concerned with setting up the problem for the definitional model. In Section 6.2, I will look closely at the definitional model and uncover a problem. The problem is this: if Socrates being necessarily identical to Socrates is to be grounded, being-identical to Socrates or the identity property of Socrates must be essential to Socrates; but, the definitional model prevents us from regarding the identity property of Socrates as an essential property of him. In order to appreciate the problem properly, we need to consider what the basic form of modal/essence statements is. In Section 6.3, I will consider two approaches, sentential and predicational, and argue that the basic form of modal/essence statements is predicational. Once this is done, it will become clearer why the problem should be taken seriously.

The second part of the chapter will be devoted to arguing that the problem is not solvable. The problem would be solved if we could show that the definitional model, contrary to the appearance, doesn't really prevent us from regarding the identity property of Socrates as essential to him or that, even if the identity property of Socrates is not essential to him, there is an essential ground for Socrates being necessarily identical to Socrates. In Section 6.4, I will argue that neither of these is true, showing that within the definitional model, the identity property of Socrates can't be deemed an essential property of him: it is neither in the definition of him nor a consequence of the definition. And it will be argued in Section 6.5 that if the identity property of Socrates is not essential to Socrates, prospects for finding an essential ground for Socrates being necessarily identical to Socrates are extremely dim.

If I am right, the identity property of Socrates is in the constitutive essence of him though it is not in the definition of him. So, the definitional model must give way to an alternative model of essence that makes room for this kind of essential properties. The aim of Section 6.6 is to offer one such model. In some cases, the essence of an object is fully determined by the definition of it because its constitutive essence amounts to its definition, but as a general rule, this will not be the case. For concrete objects such as you and me or substances as it were, their constitutive essence involves not only their definition or whatness that makes them intelligible to the intellect but also their thisness that is not graspable without the help of the sensible intuition. To generalize, the essence of an object, I propose, should be determined in terms of the identity property of it. Finally, I will close by drawing a few distinguishing features of the alternative model.

6.2 The definitional model

Let us begin by considering Fine's view of essence in more detail. The central element of Fine's view is Fine's thesis:

Fine's thesis Every necessary truth is grounded in some essential truth or, put another way, every necessary truth has an essential ground.[5]

---

[5] If Fine's thesis is true, we can also think that necessity is reducible to essence with the help of what Gideon Rosen calls "the Grounding-Reduction link." See G. Rosen, "Metaphysical Dependence: Grounding and Reduction," in B. Hale and A. Hoffmann (eds.), *Modality: Metaphysics, Logic, and Epistemology*, Oxford University Press, 2010, 109–36.

Fine's thesis assumes that essence is prior to modality. This makes a stark contrast to the modal account of essence, according to which what it is for an object to have a certain property essentially is for the object to have that property necessarily. Before proposing Fine's thesis, Fine persuasively argues against the modal account. To use his celebrated example, Socrates necessarily belongs to {Socrates}, but that doesn't seem to be essential to Socrates, for there seems to be nothing in the essence of Socrates that indicates the existence of sets.[6] For Fine, essence cannot be understood in modal terms.

How then is essence to be understood? According to Fine, "we have an informal way of saying that an object essentially has a certain property." When we say that an object has a property essentially, we mean that "the object must have that property if it is to be the object that it is."[7] It seems to me that this accurately captures our grasp of essence, which can be formulated as follows:

The Fine equivalence   For any object x and any property F, x is essentially F if and only if x must be F to be the object that it is.

The term 'must' in the right-hand side has a pre-modal sense. When we say that x in the relevant sense must be F to be the object that it is, we are not considering how x is in all possible worlds in which it exists. We are rather focused on x and F and saying that x's *being* F or x's *having* of F is so 'strong' that x is 'inseparable' from being F.[8]

This is not to say that the Fine equivalence provides a reductive analysis of essence. The sense of 'strong' or 'inseparable' used in explaining the sense of 'must' is neither physical nor modal. It has a peculiar metaphysical sense. And it seems that we cannot understand the metaphysical sense except through the concept of essence: an essential property of an object is inseparable from the object (even in thought) not because of some physical or modal bond between them but owing to the *essential* connection of the property to the object. The metaphysical *must* on the right-hand side relies on the concept of essence. The concept of essence is after all primitive.

---

[6] Fine, "Essence and Modality," p. 5. For defenses of the modal account against Fine's objection, see S. Cowling, "The Modal View of Essence," *Canadian Journal of Philosophy* 43 (2), 248–266; and N. Wildman, "Modality, Sparsity, and Essence," *The Philosophical Quarterly* 63(253), 760–782. I assume here without argument that Fine's objection is successful.

[7] Fine, *ibid.*, p. 4.

[8] It is due to this strong metaphysical connection between x and F that we cannot separate being F from it even in thought and that what we talk about can't be x unless we think of it as being F.

Nevertheless, the Fine equivalence is not unilluminating. The concept of essence stands in relation to other primitive concepts so as to form a conceptual circle. Every single one of the concepts in the circle is not subject to reductive analysis. Yet, the circle is useful and informative: we may grasp the sense of each concept in terms of the others. The Fine equivalence illuminates one aspect of the circle of basic concepts. Fine calls the Fine equivalence 'informal' perhaps because he thinks that it is a pre-theoretic construal of essence and thus might need refinement. But, in any case, the Fine equivalence itself is unproblematic and captures our intuitive grasp of essence. The Fine equivalence is a minimal necessary condition for the concept of essence. Or so I assume.

The concept of essence is primitive. Nonetheless, we may have a model of how the essence of an object is determined. To see what Fine offers as a model of essence, we should note that, for Fine, the essence of an object divides into the constitutive portion of the essence and the rest. For any object x and any properties F and G, let us say that G is a consequence of F (or F entails G) just in case it is a logical truth, for any x, that x is G if x is F;[9] and that F is in the constitutive essence of x just in case there are no properties in the essence of x such that F is in the essence of x in virtue of being a consequence of the properties, while F is in the derivative essence of x just in case F is in the essence of x but not in the constitutive essence of x.[10]

---

[9] K. Fine, "Senses of Essence," in W. Sinnott-Armstrong, D. Raffman, and N. Asher (eds.), *Modality, Morality and Belief: Essays in Honor of Ruth Barcan Marcus*, Cambridge University Press (1994), 53–73, p. 56. Here Fine identifies consequence as *logical* consequence, while suggesting that it corresponds to the traditional relation (*flowing from*) between essences and propria (p. 57). But Fine's construal of consequence as logical consequence may be called into question as we may think that being rational flows from, and thus is a consequence of, being human, but the former is not a logical consequence of the latter. (See D. Oderberg, "Essence and Properties," *Erkenntnis* 75, 2011, 85–111; and K. Koslicki, "Essence, Necessity and Explanation," in T. Tahko (ed.), *Contemporary Aristotelian Metaphysics*, Cambridge University Press, 2012, 187–206.) Perhaps, consequence in the relevant sense is broader than Fine thinks and should be understood as follows: G is a consequence of F if and only if *either* G is a logical consequence of F *or* to be F is (partly) to be G. But, for simplicity, I will say as if consequence is logical consequence. My argument will not turn on this, for when I consider whether G is a consequence of F in the logical sense of the term, my main point will stand even with the non-logical reading of 'consequence'.

[10] K. Fine, "Guide to Ground" in F. Correia and B. Schnieder (eds.), *Metaphysical Grounding*, Cambridge University Press, 2012, 37–80, p. 79. (See also G. Rosen, "Real Definition," *Analytic Philosophy* 56 (2015), 189–209, p. 195.) It should be noted that not all consequences of essential properties of an object are in the essence of the object. For example, being such that $2=2$ may well be a consequence of some essential property of Socrates but not in the essence of him. Fine puts a general constraint on what can be in the essence of an object: a property can be in the essence of x only if the property involves no particular object extraneous to x (Fine, *ibid.*, pp. 58–61).

Both having Socrates as a sole member and having something as a member are essential to {Socrates}. Presumably, however, the former but not the latter is in the constitutive essence of {Socrates}: it is fundamental that the former is in the essence of {Socrates}, whereas the latter is in the essence of {Socrates} in virtue of being a consequence of the former. For Fine, the essence of an object consists of the constitutive and derivative essences of the object.[11]

If the essence of an object is given, we know how to determine *which* properties are in the constitutive essence of the object. But *what* properties are (candidates for inclusion) in the constitutive essence in the first place? The definition of an object has a key role to play in this matter. While the definition of a word explains what the word means, the definition of an object explains what the object is. Let us say that F explains what x is if and only if that x is F explains what x is. Among properties of an object are properties that explain what the object is. Call the collection of such identity-explaining properties the 'definition' of the object. According to Fine, the constitutive essence of an object is the definition of the object. I will call any model of essence that is committed to the assimilation of constitutive essence to definition 'the definitional model' of essence.

What is notable about the definitional model is that it puts a certain constraint on essence that is not found in the Fine equivalence. On this model, all essential properties of an object are in the definition of it or consequences of the definition. So, the essence of an object is fully determined by the definition of it. Recall that the definition of an object are its properties that *explain* its identity. At the heart of the definitional model is an explanatory constraint on essence: if a property of an object is to be an

[11] So, for Fine, the essence of an object includes mere consequences of the constitutive essence of it unless the consequences involve an extraneous object. But, instead of this 'consequentialist' conception of essence, it is possible to accept the 'constitutive' conception, according to which the essence of an object is confined to the constitutive essence of it, and mere consequences of the constitutive essence are not in a proper sense essential to it. Fine (*ibid.*, p. 58) prefers the consequentialist conception for the reason that if the essence of an object is identified with its constitutive essence and thus not closed under consequence, there is no principled way to distinguish essential properties from their logical equivalents. Fine's consequentialist conception is controversial. (See, for example, E. Nutting, B. Caplan, and C. Tillman, "Constitutive Essence and Partial Grounding," *Inquiry* 61 (2018), 137–161; H. Morvarid, "Essence and Logical Properties", *Philosophical Studies* 176 (2019), 2897–2917; and J. Zylstra, "Constitutive and Consequentialist Essence," *Thought* 8 (2019), 190–199.) But I will not go into this controversy because it will not be relevant to my main theme. Instead, I will follow Fine and assume the consequentialist conception. This should be harmless for my purposes because it will give proponents of Fine's model of essence more winning chance as they will thereby have more essential properties of an object with which to ground necessary truths.

essential one, it must explain the identity of the object or be consequential from what explains the identity. This is something beyond what the Fine equivalence suggests. Let F be a constitutive essential property of x. On the definitional model, F must explain what x is. But all the Fine equivalence implies is that x must be F to be the object that it is whether F explains what x is or not.

So, the definitional model of essence can be understood as the Fine equivalence combined with the explanatory constraint on essence. Indeed, this is how advocates of the definitional model characterize the essence of an object. For example, E. J. Lowe, a notable espouser of Fine's view on essence, understands the essence of an object as "what makes it the thing that it is,"[12] and in grounding modality along the line of Fine's proposal, Bob Hale characterizes the essence of an object X as "the property which anything must possess, if it is to be X, and possession of which makes it X."[13] It is clear that their construal of essence is based on the Fine equivalence. And, although they don't use the term 'explain', it is also clear that they assume the explanatory constraint on essence, for the intended sense of 'make' in the above characterizations is explanatory while the choice of the word 'make' is to highlight that the explanation in question is in nature metaphysical.

Fine's view of essence consists of Fine's thesis and the definitional model, while the definitional model consists of the Fine equivalence and the explanatory constraint on essence. Fine's thesis should be accepted if we are to take up the task of grounding modality. Or so I assume. But I think the definitional model is open to question. Indeed, the definitional model fits well with Fine's favored example, {Socrates}, and its ilk. The definition of the null set, Ø, is being a set with no member, while all other essential properties of it seem to be consequential from the definition. The definition of {Socrates} is being a set with Socrates as a sole member, while all other essential properties of it seem to be consequential from the definition. So, their essences are fully determined by their definitions. The definitional model seems to work very well for most or even all 'abstract' objects.

When it comes to agents or individual substances we encounter in the causal realm, however, some of their essential properties might not get caught in the net of the definitional model. What is Socrates? He is a person. Being a person

[12] E. J. Lowe, "Two Notions of Being: Entity and Essence," *Royal Institute of Philosophy Supplement 62* (2008), 23–48, p. 37.
[13] B. Hale, *Necessary Beings: An Essay on Ontology, Modality, and the Relations Between Them*, (Oxford University Press, 2013), p. 222.

belongs in the definition of Socrates and thus is in the constitutive essence of him. This much is what the definitional model correctly predicts about the essence of Socrates. Now consider this. Socrates is identical to Socrates. This is also necessarily true. Given Fine's thesis, the necessary truth requires an essential ground. What grounds it? We may plausibly think that this necessity holds because Socrates is essentially identical to Socrates—that is, because being identical to Socrates or the identity property of Socrates is essential to him.[14] On reflection, however, the definitional model doesn't seem to allow us to regard the identity property of Socrates as an essential property of him.

On the one hand, it seems that the identity property of Socrates cannot be understood except through Socrates, so it can't explain what Socrates is on pain of being circular and thus doesn't belong in the definition of him. On the other hand, it seems that the identity property of Socrates cannot be understood except through Socrates *alone*, so it can't be explained by things other than Socrates and thus isn't a consequence of the definition of Socrates either. So, within the definitional model, it seems impossible for us to regard the identity property of Socrates as an essential property of him. It seems to me that the identity property of Socrates is in the constitutive essence of Socrates though it isn't in the definition of him. Space for constitutive and yet non-definitive essential properties is a blind spot of the definitional model.

This leads us to suspect that the definitional model is tailored to abstract objects but not a general model for all objects. Of course, the suspicion is in need of much justification. Does the definitional model really prevent us from accepting the identity property of Socrates as an essential property of him? And do we really have to accept the identity property of Socrates as an essential property of him in order to ground the fact that necessarily, Socrates is identical to Socrates? Much of my subsequent discussion will be devoted to answering these questions. But before embarking on a detailed discussion, I should address one issue to set up the stage for the subsequent discussion. In the next section, I will consider what the basic form of modal/essence statements is. Once the basic form of modal/essence statements is identified, we will be in a better position to see the problem more clearly.

---

[14] For every object x, x is identical-to-x. For convenience, let me use the phrase ⌜the identity property of x⌝ to express the property of being-identical-to-x.

6.3 A clarification on the problem with the definitional model[15]

Socrates is identical to Socrates. And this is necessarily so. So, the following must be true:

(N)   Necessarily, Socrates is Socrates.

But we should note that (N) is potentially ambiguous, meaning either of the following two:

(1)   Necessarily, Socrates is self-identical.

(2)   Necessarily, Socrates is identical-to-Socrates.

To say that Socrates is self-identical is to ascribe to Socrates being-self-identical—a property shared by all objects. On the other hand, to say that Socrates is identical-to-Socrates is to ascribe to Socrates being-identical-to-Socrates—a property had by Socrates only. Given that being-self-identical and being-identical-to-Socrates are different properties, (1) and (2) must mean different things. And when I said that (N) requires an essential ground, my concern was with (2) rather than (1).

But it might be claimed that (1) and (2) mean the same. It is true that being-self-identical and being-identical-to-Socrates are different properties. Even so, the claim goes, it does not follow that (1) and (2) are not the same. In the language of the lambda calculus, 'Socrates is self-identical' and 'Socrates is identical-to-Socrates' are expressed as 'Socrates is $\lambda z(z=z)$' and 'Socrates is $\lambda z(z=\text{Socrates})$'. And 'Socrates is $\lambda z(z=z)$' and 'Socrates is $\lambda z(z=\text{Socrates})$' are logically equivalent: by the rules of lambda transformation, from 'Socrates is $\lambda z(z=z)$', 'Socrates=Socrates' is derivable, and from 'Socrates=Socrates', 'Socrates is $\lambda z(z=\text{Socrates})$' is derivable; and vice versa. If 'Socrates is self-identical' and 'Socrates is identical-to-Socrates' are logically equivalent, the two after all express the same thing: when we say that Socrates is identical-to-Socrates, we mean in a roundabout way that he is self-identical, and vice versa.

However, even if 'Socrates is self-identical' and 'Socrates is identical-to-Socrates' are logically equivalent, it does not follow that the two are

---

[15] I would like to thank Kit Fine for helpful discussion and suggestions for this section.

semantically equivalent. When we make a simple subject-predicate statement, we ascribe a property expressed by the predicate to an object regarded as the subject. If we ascribe the same property to different objects, we make different statements. If we ascribe to the same object different properties, we make different statements. It is true that in many contexts, logically equivalent statements can be used interchangeably for the purpose given in the contexts. But logically equivalent propositions are not always semantically equivalent. And I think that 'Socrates is self-identical' and 'Socrates is identical-to-Socrates' are such a case in point. Given that 'Socrates is self-identical' and 'Socrates is identical-to-Socrates' are semantically different, (1) and (2) should mean different things.[16]

Admittedly, it is controversial to claim that 'Socrates is self-identical' and 'Socrates is identical-to-Socrates' are not semantically equivalent although they are logically equivalent. It would be better for the current discussion not to rely on the controversial claim. To avoid the unnecessary controversy, let me assume, for the sake of argument, that 'Socrates is self-identical' and 'Socrates is identical-to-Socrates' are semantically equivalent. Even so, however, that doesn't undermine the claim that (1) and (2) mean different things. Although being-self-identical and being-identical-to-Socrates are different properties, when we ascribe these properties to Socrates by way of simple predication, we might end up proposing the same proposition. Or so we assumed. But in saying (1) and (2), we are ascribing these properties to Socrates by way of *modal* predication, in which case, we may be saying different things.

To see how that can be, we should distinguish two approaches to the logical form of modal statements: sentential and predicational. How is a modal statement 'Necessarily, x is F' to be understood? One approach is to take 'Necessarily' as a sentential modifier. So, in the sentential approach, in making a modal statement, 'Necessarily, x is F', we take a sentence 'x is F' first and add 'Necessarily' to the sentence to get a new one. To make explicit the logical form, 'Necessarily, x is F' may be parsed as 'It is necessary that x is F' or '$\Box$(x is F)'. So, in the sentential approach, (1) and (2) are regimented as follows:

(1') $\Box$(Socrates is self-identical).

(2') $\Box$(Socrates is identical-to-Socrates).

---

[16] David Wiggins is a notable espouser of this view. See D. Wiggins, "The De Re 'Must': A Note on the Logical Form of Essentialist Claims," in G. Evans and J. McDowell (eds.), *Truth and Meaning*, Clarendon Press, 1976, 131–160.

As assumed, to say that Socrates is self-identical is to say that Socrates is identical-to-Socrates. Then, clearly, (1') and (2') mean the same. In the sentential approach, (1) and (2) mean the same thing.

On the other hand, in the predicational approach, things are not the same. In this approach, 'Necessarily' is a predicate modifier to the effect that when we make the modal statement 'Necessarily, x is F', 'Necessarily' is added to a predicate 'F' to produce a new predicate 'Necessarily F', and we use the new predicate to make a modal statement. So, 'Necessarily, x is F' may be parsed as 'x is necessarily F' or 'x is N~F' in which case, (1) and (2) are regimented as follows:[17]

(N1)   Socrates is necessarily self-identical—i.e., Socrates is N~self-identical.

(N2)   Socrates is necessarily identical-to-Socrates—i.e., Socrates is N~identical-to-Socrates.

Clearly, being-self-identical and being-identical-to-Socrates are different properties. Then, being-N~self-identical and being-N~identical-to-Socrates should be different properties. In the language of the lambda calculus, (N1) is that Socrates is $N\sim\lambda z(z=z)$, and (N2) is that Socrates is $N\sim\lambda z(z=\text{Socrates})$. Note that the rules of lambda transformation do not license us to infer (N2) from (N1) as the rules are not applicable to 'Socrates is $N\sim\lambda z(z=z)$'. In the predicational approach, (1) and (2) mean different things.

(1) and (2) express two distinct propositions if the basic form of modal statements is predicational. But should we accept the predicational approach to modal statements? It is true that the sentential approach to modal statements is far more popular in the literature than the predicational approach. This is understandable because it is technically convenient to take the sentential approach, while in most contexts, we don't need to choose between the two approaches as it makes no significant difference for the purposes of the given context. But I think we nonetheless have good reason for thinking that the basic form of modal statements is predicational. The necessity of identity is true—that is, for any x and y, if x is y, then necessarily, x is y. And it is true as Kripke proved it. This much is familiar.

---

[17] I will henceforth use the sentence forms 'Necessarily, x is F', 'It is necessary that x is F', and 'x is necessarily F' distinctively in such a way that the first is a neutral one waiting to be disambiguated to mean either the second or the third, while the second is a construal of the first in the sentential approach, and the third a construal of the first in the predicational approach.

But a close examination shows that if we are to think that Kripke's proof goes through, we should accept the predicational approach.

Assuming that names behave like individual constants, let 'a' and 'b' be names of the same object.[18] Kripke's proof goes as follows:[19]

(A) $\Box(a=a)$.

(B) $(a=b) \supset (\Box(a=a) \supset \Box(a=b))$.

(C) $(a=b) \supset \Box(a=b)$.

The basic idea is this. If $a=b$, then any property of a including a's modal properties must be had by b. (A) tells us that a has a certain modal property. (B) tells us that if $a=b$, b also has that modal property. Given (A) and (B), (C) truth-functionally follows.

This proof seems to be intuitive and straightforward. On reflection, however, things are not so simple. What modal property is it that is ascribed to a in (A) and thereby claimed to be shared with b? Kripke takes (A) as obviously true, saying that "every object surely is necessarily self-identical."[20] This might suggest that the modal property Kripke has in mind is the property of being necessarily self-identical. However, this can't be right. If the shared modal property in question were being necessarily self-identical, it would follow only that b is necessarily self-identical. This being the case, all we can have would be this: $(a=b) \supset (\Box(a=a) \supset \Box(b=b))$, which is weaker than (B). And this does not license us to infer (C).

What then is the shared modal property? In explaining the idea behind the proof, Kripke also says that "if x and y are the same object and x has a certain property F, then y has to have the same property F...even if the property F is itself of the form of necessarily having some other property G, in particular that of necessarily being identical to a certain object..."—in

---

[18] Thanks to Zoltán Szabó for suggesting that the assumption needs to be made explicit.

[19] S. Kripke, "Identity and Necessity," M. K. Muniz (ed.), *Identity and Individuation* (New York University 1971), 135–164. Perhaps Kripke wasn't the first to come up with the proof of the necessity of identity. The thought that identity statements are necessary can go back to the pioneering work of Ruth Marcus, although the specific form of proof to be discussed above is due to Kripke. See R. Marcus, "Identity of Individuals in a Strict Functional Calculus of Second-Order," *Journal of Symbolic Logic* 12 (1947), 12–15. For a detailed historical remark on the proof, see J. Burgess, "On a Derivation of the Necessity of Identity," *Synthese* 191 (2014), 1567–1585.

[20] Kripke, "Identity and Necessity," p. 137.

particular, even if 'F' stands for the property of necessary identity with x."[21] This suggests that the shared modal property Kripke has in mind is the property of being necessarily identical to a rather than the property of being necessarily self-identical.

Kripke oscillates between the two properties perhaps because he assumes that (i) a being necessarily self-identical and (ii) a being necessarily identical to a are the same thing. However, if the proof is to get off the ground, (i) and (ii) must be distinguished. For if (i) and (ii) were the same, the proof would be open to serious question as opponents of the necessity of identity would interpret (A) as (i) and insist that all we can get is the weaker claim than (B)—i.e., $(a=b) \supset (\square(a=a) \supset \square(b=b))$.[22] So, if Kripke's proof is to go through, (i) and (ii) must be distinguished, and (ii) must be taken as the intended meaning of (A).

In the sentential approach, however, (i) and (ii) are not distinguishable. We can't distinguish the two by claiming that (i) means that a is $\lambda z \ \square(z=z)$ whereas (ii) means that a is $\lambda z \ \square(z=a)$. Clearly, 'a is $\lambda z \ \square(z=z)$' and 'a is $\lambda z \ \square(z=a)$' are logically equivalent: both come down to ' $\square(a=a)$.' If 'a is $\lambda z \ \square(z=z)$' and 'a is $\lambda z \ \square(z=a)$' are logically equivalent, as assumed for the sake of argument, 'a is $\lambda z \ \square(z=z)$' and 'a is $\lambda z \ \square(z=a)$' are semantically equivalent: (i) and (ii) mean the same thing.

On the other hand, in the predicational approach, we can properly distinguish between (i) and (ii). In the predicational approach, 'Necessarily, x is F' is parsed as 'x is ℕ~F.' So, (i) and (ii) are respectively expressed as (i*) 'a is ℕ~self-identical' and (ii*) 'a is ℕ~identical-to-a.' As has been seen, (i*) is not derivable from (ii*) and vice versa. So, (i) and (ii) are not logically equivalent. And when we say that x is ℕ~F, we say of x *being* F, the connection between x and F, that its mode is necessary.[23] (i*) is concerned with the mode of a *being* self-identical, the connection between a and the property of being self-identical, while (ii*) is concerned with the mode of a *being* identical-to-a, the connection between a and the property of being-identical-to-a. Clearly, (i) and (ii) are distinct.

Now, with the distinction between (i) and (ii) in hand, we may restate Kripke's proof as follows:

---

[21] Kripke, *ibid.*, pp. 137–138.
[22] See, for example, E. J. Lowe, "On the Alleged Necessity of True Identity Statements," *Mind* 91 (1982), 579–584.
[23] Cf. C. McGinn, *Logical Properties*, (Oxford University Press, 2000), Ch. 4.

(A*) a is $\mathbb{N}$~identical-to-a.

(B*) $(a{=}b) \supset ((a$ is $\mathbb{N}$~identical-to-$a) \supset (b$ is $\mathbb{N}$~identical-to-$a))$

(C*) $(a{=}b) \supset (b$ is $\mathbb{N}$~identical-to-$a)$.

The argument is clearly sound. And if 'b is $\mathbb{N}$~identical-to-a' is given, we may legitimately derive '$\Box(b$ is identical-to-$a)$': 'b is $\mathbb{N}$~identical-to-a' says of b's *having* of being-identical-to-a that its mode is necessary; and we may then plausibly think that the necessary mode of b's *having* of being-identical-to-a gives rise to a universal truth 'b has being-identical-to-a in all possible worlds in which it exists' or, put in sentential mode, '$\Box(b$ is identical-to-$a)$', which is equivalent to '$\Box(a{=}b)$.' So, from (C*), we can also get (C): $(a{=}b) \supset \Box (a{=}b)$.

The consideration so far strongly suggests that the basic form of modal statements is predicational. This motivates us to rethink about the basic form of essence statements too. Note that corresponding to the two approaches to modal statements, there are two approaches to essence statements: in the sentential approach, 'Essentially' is a sentential operator to the effect that 'Essentially, x is F' is parsed as 'It is essential to x that x is F' or, to use Fine's notation, '$\Box_x(x$ is F$)$'; while in the predicational approach, 'Essentially' is a predicate modifier to the effect that 'Essentially, x is F' is parsed as 'x is essentially F' or 'x is $\mathbb{E}$~F.'[24]

Fine often assumes the sentential approach to essence statements in discussing issues about essence. Perhaps it is due to this assumption of his that it became a rule of the game to assume the sentential approach in the literature. Fine's motivation is methodological. He usually adopts the sentential approach for the purpose of making essence and modal statements structurally similar and thereby making the reduction of necessity to essence smooth as we can have the following scheme:

$\underline{\Box_x/\Box\text{-Ground}}$ For any x and any F, if $\Box_x(x$ is F), then $[\Box_x(x$ is F$)]$ grounds $[\Box(x$ is F$)]$.[25]

---

[24] For more on the logical form of essence statements, see K. Fine, "Senses of Essence"; and K. Fine, "The Logic of Essence," *Journal of Philosophical Logic* 24 (2005), 241–273. And, as in the case of modal statements, I will use the sentence forms 'Essentially, x is F', 'It is essential to x that x is F', and 'x is essentially F' distinctively.

[25] Fine, "Senses of Essence," p. 55; Fine, "The Logic of Essence," p. 241. And, borrowing Rosen's notation, I will write [p] for the fact that p. (Rosen, "Metaphysical Dependence: Grounding and Reduction," p. 115.) And I did and will embed a sentence within single quotation marks to mean the proposition expressed by the sentence.

Note that Fine's assumption of the sentential approach to essence statements was made against the backdrop of the sentential approach to modal statements. If, however, the predicational approach should be preferred over the sentential approach in the case of modal statements, Fine would have no reason for holding onto the sentential approach in the case of essence statements.[26] As has been argued, we should adopt the predicational approach to modal statements. Then, we should adopt the predicational approach to essence statements for the purpose of making essence and modal statements structurally similar and thereby making the reduction of necessity to essence smooth as we can have the following scheme:

$\underline{E/N\text{-Ground}}$ For any x and any F, if x is $E{\sim}F$, then [x is $E{\sim}F$] grounds [x is $N{\sim}F$].

I am now in a better position to explain more clearly why I think the definitional model is problematic. Consider the following modal claims:

(N1) Socrates is necessarily self-identical—i.e., Socrates is $N{\sim}$self-identical.

(N2) Socrates is necessarily identical-to-Socrates—i.e., Socrates is $N{\sim}$identical-to-Socrates.

Obviously, (N1) and (N2) are true. According to Fine's thesis, (N1) and (N2) must be grounded in some essential truths. What essential truths ground them? Well, the answer is simple: (N1) and (N2) are respectively grounded in the following essentialist claims:

(E1) Socrates is essentially self-identical—i.e., Socrates is $E{\sim}$self-identical.

(E2) Socrates is essentially identical-to-Socrates—i.e., Socrates is $E{\sim}$identical-to-Socrates.

If, however, the definitional model is true, (N2) is in danger of lacking an essential ground, for on the definitional model, (E2) can't be true, and if so, no essential truth would ground (N2). If we hold onto the definitional

---

[26] Indeed, Fine is inclined to take the basic form of essence statements as predicational owing to its expressive subtlety. See Fine, "Senses of Essence," p. 55.

model, the project of grounding modality along the line of Fine's thesis is jeopardized. This calls the definitional model into serious doubt.

Let me recapitulate my worry about the definitional model as follows:

(P1)   If the definitional model is true, then it is not the case that Socrates is essentially identical-to-Socrates.

(P2)   If it is not the case that Socrates is essentially identical-to-Socrates, then the fact that Socrates is necessarily identical-to-Socrates has no essential ground.

(C)   There is an ungrounded necessary truth or else the definitional model is false.

The argument is clearly valid. So, if (P1) and (P2) are true, unless we give up Fine's thesis, we must deny the definitional model and find another model that makes room for (E2). In the ensuing two sections, I will explain in detail why I think (P1) and (P2) are true.

6.4 In defense of (P1)

Why is (P1) true? My reason is as follows. The essence of an object divides into the constitutive and the derivative essences of the object. If the definitional model is true, then the constitutive essence of an object amounts to the definition of it, so the essence of an object would consist of the definition of the object and its derivative essence. This implies that on the definitional model, if the identity property of Socrates (i.e., being-identical-to-Socrates) is in the essence of Socrates, it is either in the definition of him or in his derivative essence. However, on the definitional model, the identity property of Socrates is neither in the definition of him nor in his derivative essence. So, if the definitional model is true, Socrates is not essentially identical-to-Socrates. (P1) is thus vindicated. In what follows, I will argue for this in greater detail.

For the sake of argument, suppose, for the moment, that the definitional model is true. To defend (P1), I need only to show that the following two claims are true:

(I)   The identity property of Socrates is not in the definition of Socrates.

(II)   The identity property of Socrates is not in the derivative essence of Socrates.

Let me begin with (I). If the identity property of Socrates is to belong in the definition of Socrates, it must explain what Socrates is. Explanation of identity is "a form of explanation" and thus "must conform to a noncircularity condition and not yield an explanation of something in terms of the very thing to be explained."[27] Thus, if the identity property of Socrates is to explain what Socrates is, it must conform to a noncircularity condition. But note that the identity property of Socrates or being-identical-to-Socrates 'presupposes' Socrates—i.e., it contains Socrates as a constituent.[28] So, the identity property of Socrates can't do the explaining because it presupposes the very object to be explained. The identity property of Socrates, on pain of being circular, can't explain what Socrates is. So, it doesn't belong in the definition of Socrates.[29]

Let us say that, for any x, the identity property of x is primitive just in case it presupposes x and that x is primitive just in case the identity property of x is primitive. In arguing for (I), I have assumed that the identity property of Socrates is primitive or that Socrates is primitive. In defense of the definitional model, one might question the assumption. The identity property of $\emptyset$ appears to presuppose $\emptyset$, but it really doesn't: being-identical-to-$\emptyset$ is ultimately being a set with no member—it presupposes no individual. The

---

[27] Fine, "Unified Foundations for Essence and Ground," *Journal of the American Philosophical Association* 1 (2015), 296–311, pp. 296–297.

[28] The notion of presupposition employed here is neither epistemic nor pragmatic. It is a metaphysical notion that I borrowed from Fine. (See K. Fine, "Plantinga on the Reduction of Possibilist Discourse," in J. E. Tomberlin and P. van Inwagen (eds.), *Alvin Plantinga*, 145-186, Dordrecht: Reidel, 1985). Intuitively, to say that being-identical-to-Socrates presupposes Socrates is to say that the former involves the latter as a constituent so that the former is metaphysically explained in terms of the latter.

[29] My discussion runs against the assumption that it is true by the concept of real definition that the definition of an object *explains* the identity of the object. Two remarks in defense of the assumption are in order. Firstly, the assumption is in keeping with the traditional framework of real definition that aims at the study of things, where the study of things is pursued in terms of a study of their 'causes', one of which is a formal cause of what they are or, in other words, an explanation of their identity. One can freely use the word 'definition' in such a way that the definition of an object doesn't have to explain what it is. But that is not the sense of 'definition' intended in the present discussion. Secondly, the assumption is also in keeping with an ordinary concept of definition. One might disagree, claiming that being-odd is defined as being-not-even, and being-even is defined as being-not-odd in which case, being-odd is not explained in terms of being-not-even on pain of circularity. However, the claim doesn't seem right. What is going on is not that being-odd is defined as being-not-even and *at the same time* being-even is defined as being-not-odd but that there are two alternative systems of definitions with respect to the two concepts. We may be indeterminate as to which system is to be adopted. This is not to say that we adopt both definitions. Once we choose one system, we adopt the definition in the chosen system and reject the definition in the other system on pain of circularity. (Cf. Fine, "Ontological Dependence," *Proceedings of the Aristotelian Society* 95 (1995), 269–290, p. 285.) I would like to thank an anonymous referee for pressing me on this matter.

identity property of {Socrates} appears to presuppose {Socrates}, but it really doesn't: being-identical-to-{Socrates} is ultimately being a set with Socrates as a sole member—it presupposes some individual but not {Socrates}. Can't we think that the identity property of Socrates, despite the appearance to the contrary, is not primitive either because it presupposes no individual or because it presupposes some individual but not Socrates? If we can, why can't we think also that the identity property of Socrates belongs in the definition of him?

Let me call this defense of the definitional model 'the Denial of Primitiveness'. The Denial of Primitiveness is based on two claims: first, (i) the identity property of Socrates is not primitive; and second, (ii) it belongs in the definition of him. But the Denial of Primitiveness fails because (i) and (ii) can't be true at the same time: if (i) is true, (ii) is false. Or so I will argue. Before proceeding, we should note that the Denial of Primitiveness commits its proponents to rejecting primitive individuals altogether. This is so because if we assume that there is a primitive individual (call it 'PI'), the question of how the identity property of Socrates can be deemed as essential to him would switch to the question of how the identity property of PI can be deemed as essential to PI. Consistency should force the proponents of the Denial of Primitiveness to reject the assumption that PI is primitive.

Suppose that (i) is true: the identity property of Socrates is not primitive. This is so either because it presupposes no individual (i.e., it is ultimately qualitative) or because it presupposes some individual but not Socrates. It is hard to think that it is qualitative. Being identical-to-Socrates is partly being a person. But being identical-to-Socrates is not being a person: the former is ascribable to Socrates only, but the latter is ascribable to many. Is being identical-to-Socrates being a person whose name is 'Socrates'? No, there might have been someone other than Socrates who is a person whose name is 'Socrates'. Similarly, for any finite number n, it would not be the case that being identical-to-Socrates is being $F_1 \ldots F_n$, where $F_1, \ldots, F_n$ are all qualitative, because there is no principled reason not to think that being a person who is $F_1, F_2, \ldots,$ and F_n might have been had by someone other than Socrates.[30] So, if the identity property of Socrates is qualitative, it should be a conjunction of infinitely many (and even all) qualitative properties

[30] This is not to say that no qualitative property can be had by one possible object only. There might be a single qualitative property or a conjunction of finitely many qualitative properties that is uniquely instantiable. For example, being a God or being a null set is ultimately finitely qualitative but uniquely instantiable. But, when it comes to so-called ordinary substances, no conjunction of finitely many qualitative properties seems to be uniquely instantiable.

Socrates actually has. But this is hard to believe, for it forces us to believe that the conjunction of infinitely many or even all actual qualitative properties of Socrates are essential to Socrates. Leibniz would be happy to embrace this counterintuitive consequence for his theoretical motivation.[31] But I suspect that whatever the motivation, the proponents of the definitional model with whom I engage now are not ready to accept the Leibnizian position. We may assume that the identity property of Socrates is not qualitative.[32]

This implies that if the identity property of Socrates is not primitive, that is so because it presupposes some individual but not Socrates. Call that individual 'α'. Then, being identical-to-Socrates amounts to being in R1 to α. Recall that given the Denial of Primitiveness, there are no primitive individuals. So, the identity property of α is not primitive. On the other hand, the identity property of α is not qualitative, for the identity property of Socrates is not qualitative. So, the identity property of α presupposes some other individual α*. So, being identical-to-Socrates amounts to being in R1 to an object that is in R2 to α*. Then, for the same reason, α* is not primitive, and the identity property of α* presupposes some other individual α**. So, being identical-to-Socrates amounts to being in R1 to an object that is in R2 to an object that is in R3 to α**. And this will go on and on indefinitely. The identity property of Socrates is ultimately an indefinite property analyzed in terms of a series of indefinitely many objects: being identical-to-Socrates is being in R1 to an object that is in R2 to an object that is in R3 to an object and so on and so forth.

So, if the identity property of Socrates is not primitive, it turns out to be the above indefinite property. Once this is noted, it is hard to think that the identity property of Socrates is in the definition of him. We should note first that the indefinite property is supposed to be non-qualitative. But it is unclear how that can be. If it is non-qualitative, it contains as a constituent some particular individual. But what particular individual does it contain as

---

[31] G. W. Leibniz, "Discourse on Metaphysics," in R. Ariew and D. Garbert (eds.), *G. W. Leibniz: Philosophical Essays*, Hackett Publishing Company, 1989, 35–68, Section 8.

[32] The locus classicus for the argument against the Leibnizian position is M. Black, "The Identity of Indiscernibles," *Mind* 61 (1952), 153–164; and R. Adams, "Primitive Thisness and Primitive Identity," *Journal of Philosophy* 76 (1979), 5–26. For skeptical discussions of the argument, see I. Hacking, "The Identity of Indiscernibles," *Journal of Philosophy* 72 (1975), 249–256; and M. Della Rocca, "Two Spheres, Twenty Spheres, and the Identity of Indiscernibles," *Pacific Philosophical Quarterly* 86 (2005), 480–492. I think that the conclusion of Adams's argument is true whether the argument for the conclusion is successful or not. Fine would also agree with Adams on this matter. See K. Fine, "The Problem of Possibilia," in D. Zimmerman (ed.), *The Oxford Handbook of Metaphysics*, Oxford University Press, 2002, 161–179.

a constituent? It is not Socrates. He is defined away by α. It is not α either. It is defined away by α*. And so on and so forth. Where does the singularity of the indefinite property come from? We have no clue. This consideration strongly suggests that the indefinite property can't explain what Socrates is. I am not saying that there cannot be an indefinite property. Nor do I say that an indefinite property cannot be an essential property of an object. What is hard to accept is that an indefinite property does a *defining* job.

An explanation delivered by definition must be noncircular and definite. This is what I have assumed. The assumption should be uncontroversial. An attempt to define a word w in terms of a word or words w* would not succeed if w* presupposes w or consists of a never-ending list of many words whose whole meaning is never determined but is indefinitely deferred. A definition of an object is a real or objectual counterpart of a definition of a word. Thus, in the intended sense of 'explain' employed in the definitional model of essence, no property can explain what an object is if it presupposes the very object to be explained or consists of a never-ending list of many objects whose singularity is never determined but indefinitely deferred.[33]

The Denial of Primitiveness relies on the idea that if the identity property of Socrates is not primitive, it belongs in the definition of him as in the case of ∅ or as in the case of {Socrates}, wherein lies a problem. Proponents of the Denial of Primitiveness cannot claim that the identity property of Socrates is in the definition of Socrates as in the case of ∅: the identity property of ∅ can define ∅ because it is qualitative; but the identity property of Socrates isn't. Proponents of the Denial of Primitiveness cannot claim that the

[33] Does my argument imply that it is not possible that some objects have parts but don't have ultimate parts? The argument would be in trouble if it implies the impossibility of these objects as infinitely complex matter (i.e., matter made of quarks, made of schmarks, made of darks, ...) and gunk (i.e., an object composed of proper parts, composed of proper parts,...) seem to be possible. (For the possibility of gunk, see D. Zimmerman, "Could Extended Objects Be Made out of Simple Parts? An Argument for 'Atomless Gunk'," *Philosophy and Phenomenological Research* 56 (1996), 1–29.) But my argument does not imply the impossibility of gunk. I have a mug in front of me. Call it 'M.' My argument does not imply that M is not gunk. What it implies is only that if M is gunk, M is not defined by its parts, say, $p_1, p_2, \dots$. Suppose that M is gunk and thus that M is not defined by $p_1, p_2, \dots$. Being gunk may or may not be in the definition of M. If being gunk is in the definition of M, M is defined as an object composed of proper parts composed of proper parts and so on ad infinitum, which does not contradict that M is not defined by the *particular* parts $p_1, p_2, \dots$. If, on the other hand, being gunk is not in the definition of M, perhaps M is accidentally gunk. Then, M may have a definition that does not include being gunk: M may be defined as a cup, while it is accidentally gunk. Thanks to Dean Zimmerman for raising this issue that helps clarify my argument.

identity property of Socrates is in the definition of Socrates as in the case of {Socrates}: the identity property of {Socrates} can define {Socrates} only if Socrates is primitive so that it is definite; but given the Denial of Primitiveness, Socrates isn't primitive, so neither the identity property of {Socrates} nor the identity property of Socrates can do the defining job.

Insisting that the identity property of Socrates is not primitive doesn't support and rather undermines the claim that it belongs in the definition of Socrates. So, the Denial of Primitiveness fails. Indeed, it is hard to deny that Socrates is a primitive individual. $\emptyset$ and {Socrates} are in a sense a derivative individual. However, intuitively, Socrates is fundamental or a 'substance' as it were. This being the case, it is not surprising that being-identical-to-Socrates cannot be understood except through Socrates himself. The identity property of Socrates is primitive. So, it can't explain what Socrates is and thus doesn't belong in the definition of Socrates. This vindicates (I).

Let me turn now to (II). The identity property of Socrates doesn't belong in the definition of him. Is it then in the derivative essence of Socrates? In the remainder of this section, I will argue that the answer is 'No.' If the identity property of Socrates is in the derivative essence of him, it is in the essence of Socrates because it is a consequence of some property F in the essence of him. And if F is in the derivative essence of Socrates, that is so because F is a consequence of some other property F' in the essence of him. And the same goes for F', F'', and so on until we reach a property in the definition of Socrates in which the essentiality of F has its ultimate source. So, if the identity property of Socrates is in the derivative essence of him, it is in the essence of Socrates because it is a consequence of some property in the definition of him.[34] In what follows, I will argue that it is extremely unlikely that there is such a property in the definition of Socrates.

Being a person belongs in the definition of Socrates. Obviously, the identity property of Socrates is not a consequence of being a person. Plato is a person. But he is not identical-to-Socrates. So, it is not a logical truth, for any x, that x is identical-to-Socrates if x is a person. This helps us see that for any property, if it can be had by something other than Socrates, the identity property of Socrates is not a consequence of that property. So, if the identity property of Socrates is a consequence of some property in the definition of Socrates, the property in question must be a property that can be had by Socrates and Socrates only. What would be such a property?

[34] Recall that for properties F and G, G is a consequence of F if and only if it is a logical truth, for any x, that x is G if x is F as Fine suggests it. (See note 9.)

Perhaps, the best we can think of is the origin property of Socrates. Suppose that it is in the definition of Socrates that he came from his actual origin source O.[35] Then, since being a person is also in the definition of him, being a person who came from O is in the definition of Socrates. For simplicity, let me use the phrase 'the origin property of Socrates' to express the property of being a person who came from O, not just the property of having come from O. If the identity property of Socrates is to be a consequence of the origin property of Socrates, it must be the case that the origin property of Socrates can be had by Socrates only. But what prevents us from thinking that there might have been some person other than Socrates who came from O? If we are to think that the origin property can be had by Socrates only, we must also commit ourselves to what we may call 'the sufficiency of origin', according to which if it is possible that y came from z, it is necessary that anything that came from z is y and no other.[36]

The sufficiency of origin is contentious.[37] And I don't think it's true. But, for the sake of argument, let us assume that the sufficiency of origin is true and thus that the origin property of Socrates can be had by Socrates only. Even so, however, the identity property of Socrates is not a consequence of the origin property of Socrates. Suppose that x is a person who came from O. Given the sufficiency of origin, it follows that x is a unique person who could have come from O. Yet, this doesn't entail that x is identical-to-Socrates. If the fact that x is a unique person who could have come from O is to entail the fact that x is identical-to-Socrates, it must also be assumed that Socrates came from O. But that Socrates came from O is an actual historical fact, not a logical truth however broadly 'logical truth' is construed. Thus, even if the sufficiency of origin is assumed, it is not a

---

[35] Is this supposition true? I believe that Socrates necessarily and essentially came from O. But I don't think that Socrates's origin (having come from O) is in his definition. My worry is that if his origin is in the definition of him, he ontologically depends upon O, which jeopardizes Socrates's ontological status as an independent being. I will talk about this very briefly in the final section. But, for the sake of argument, let me put this worry to one side for the moment.

[36] The sufficiency of origin has been proposed to develop the sketchy argument for the necessity of origin Kripke offers in the celebrated note 56 of *Naming and Necessity*. See, for example, N. Salmon, "How not to Derive Essentialism from the Theory of Reference," *Journal of Philosophy* 76 (1979), 703–725; N. Salmon, *Reference and Essence*, Prometheus Books (2005); C. McGinn, "On the Necessity of Origin," *Journal of Philosophy* 73 (1976), 134–135; G. Forbes, *The Metaphysics of Possibility*, Oxford: Clarendon Press, 1985.

[37] For criticisms of the sufficiency of origin, see, for example, T. Robertson, "Possibilities and the Arguments for Origin Essentialism," *Mind* 107 (1998), 729–749; P. Mackie, *How Things Might Have Been*, Oxford University Press, 2006.

logical truth, for any x, that x is identical-to-Socrates if x is a person who came from O.

This consideration points in a direction of seeing that the identity property of Socrates is a consequence of *no* property (or properties) in the definition of Socrates. Let D be a property in the definition of Socrates. Since D is in the definition of him, D does not presuppose him (on pain of circularity). Suppose that x is D. Then this may entail that x is a unique thing that is possibly D. Even so, that does not entail that x is identical-to-Socrates unless it relies on a non-logical fact that Socrates is actually D. Thus, it is not a logical truth, for any x, that x is identical-to-Socrates if x is D. The identity property of Socrates is not a consequence of D. This shows that the identity property of Socrates is not in the derivative essence of him.

I have argued that the identity property of Socrates is not in the derivative essence of him because it is not a consequence of any property in the definition of Socrates. And the argument has operated with the following notion of derivative essence:

(DE)   A property F is in the derivative essence of an object x just in case F is in the essence of x because it is a consequence of some property G in the definition of x, where F is a consequence of G if and only if it is a logical truth, for any x, that x is F if x is G.

Proponents of the definitional model might call (DE) into question, claiming that strictly speaking, (DE) is false, and once (DE) is revised properly, the identity property of Socrates can be taken to be in the derivative essence of him. In the remainder of this section, I will consider two possible responses in this line of thought and argue that both fail.

Note that (DE) is made for the property conception of essence, according to which the essence of an object is a collection of properties of the object. But what if, instead, we adopt the proposition conception of essence, according to which the essence of an object is a collection of propositions true in virtue of the nature of the object? If we adopt the proposition conception of essence, perhaps (DE) needs to be revised in the following way:

(DE1)   A proposition P is in the derivative essence of an object x just in case P is in the essence of x because it is a consequence of some proposition Q in the definition of x, where P is a consequence of Q if and only if it is a logical truth that P if Q.

With the proposition conception of essence and (DE1) in hand, the defender of the definitional model might respond to my argument in the following line. Socrates is essentially self-identical. On the proposition conception of essence, this means that 'Socrates is self-identical' is in the essence of Socrates. Moreover, 'Socrates is identical-to-Socrates' is a consequence of 'Socrates is self-identical': it is a logical truth that Socrates is identical-to-Socrates if Socrates is self-identical. Then, according to the response, 'Socrates is identical-to-Socrates' is in the derivative essence of Socrates.[38]

However, the response does not work, for two reasons. If we assume the proposition conception of essence and (DE1), we may think that 'Socrates is self-identical' is in the essence of Socrates and that 'Socrates is identical-to-Socrates' is a consequence of 'Socrates is self-identical'. Even so, however, it doesn't follow that 'Socrates is identical-to-Socrates' is in the derivative essence of Socrates. If the responder is to conclude that 'Socrates is identical-to-Socrates' is in the derivative essence of Socrates, she must show that 'Socrates is identical-to-Socrates' is in the essence of Socrates *because* it is a consequence of 'Socrates is self-identical'.[39] But what reason is there for thinking that Socrates has being-identical-to-Socrates, the property particular to him, *because* he has being-self-identical, the property universal to all? If there is some such reason, I don't see what it is.

Moreover, the response does not work anyway because we should adopt the property conception of essence, not the proposition conception. Indeed, the two conceptions are often assumed to be interchangeable in the literature. And for some specific purposes, it might be harmless to make the assumption. However, strictly speaking, the two conceptions are not equivalent. Recall that we have adopted the predicational approach to essence statements and thus that being-self-identical and being-identical-to-Socrates are treated as two distinct essential properties of Socrates. On the proposition conception, however, corresponding to the two essential properties, there is only one essential proposition: 'Socrates is Socrates'. In order not to ignore subtle distinctions made in the predicational approach, which

---

[38] I would like to thank an anonymous referee for this line of response.

[39] Suppose that 'x is F and G' is in the essence of x. Surely, 'x is F' is a consequence of 'x is F and G'. But this doesn't imply that 'x is F' is in the derivative essence of x. It might be the case that 'x is F' and 'x is G' are each in the constitutive essence of x, and 'x is F and G' is in the derivative essence of x: it is not that 'x is F' is in the essence of x because 'x is F' is a consequence of 'x is F and G' in the essence of x but that 'x is F and G' is in the essence of x because it is a consequence of 'x is F' and 'x is G' that are each in the essence of x.

is crucial for our purposes, we should accept the property conception, not the proposition conception.

Let me turn now to the second response. Some properties of an object are in the derivative essence of the object in virtue of being consequences of some properties in the definition of it. (DE) is meant to accommodate this kind of derivative essential properties. However, according to the response, some properties enter the derivative essence of an object by the back door thanks to a logical truth. (DE) ignores this kind of derivative essential properties. So, the response goes, what we should accept is not (DE) but the following:

(DE2)   A property F is in the derivative essence of an object x just in case *either* (i) F is in the essence of x because it is a consequence of some property G in the definition of x *or* (ii) F is in the essence of x because it is an instance of some logical truth that x is F.

Given (DE2), the identity property of Socrates is in the derivative essence of him. It is a logical truth that for any z, z is identical-to-z. Then, it is an instance of the logical truth that Socrates is identical-to-Socrates. So, by (DE2), we may think that being-identical-to-Socrates is in the derivative essence of Socrates. So, according to the response, we have no difficulty in thinking that the identity property of Socrates is in the derivative essence of him.[40, 41]

At first glance, the response might sound plausible. On examination, however, it doesn't work. Consider the following logical truths:

(L1)   For every z, z is self-identical.

(L2)   For every z, z is identical-to-z.

Given (DE2), being-identical-to-Socrates is in the derivative essence of Socrates because it is an instance of (L2) that Socrates is identical-to-Socrates.

---

[40] Thanks to Kit Fine for suggesting something like this response, though his suggestion might not be the same. Thanks also to Nikolaj Pedersen for pressing me to explain why I think that this response fails.

[41] This response implies that for *every* object, the identity property of it is in the derivative essence of it, not in the definition of it. But this seems wrong. Being identical-to-$\emptyset$ is ultimately being a set with no member. Intuitively, there is no reason not to take this as the definition of $\emptyset$. Being identical-to-{Socrates} is ultimately being a set with Socrates as a sole member. Intuitively, there is no reason not to take this as the definition of {Socrates}. So, I think the response is problematic. But let me set aside this problem. Even if this problem is set aside, we will see that the response does not work anyway.

But note that (L1) and (L2) are the same as it has been assumed that z being self-identical and z being identical-to-z are the same. So, the responder amounts to claiming that being-identical-to-Socrates is in the derivative essence of Socrates because it is an instance of (L1) that Socrates is self-identical. This strongly suggests that something goes wrong in (DE2). How can we conclude that being-identical-to-Socrates, the property particular to him, is in the derivative essence of him on the ground that being-self-identical, the property universal to all, is had by Socrates?

Where does (DE2) go wrong? Condition (ii) in (DE2) assumes that derivative essential properties an object has thanks to logic are understood as properties abstracted from propositions following from logical truths. The assumption is problematic as it is not in keeping with the property conception of essence. On the property conception, if there are derivative essential properties an object has thanks to logic, those properties are derivative essential properties not because they occur in some logical proposition but because they are a consequence of some logical *property*—a property shared by all objects by logic. So, what we should accept is not (DE2) but the following:

(DE2*)   A property F is in the derivative essence of an object x just in case *either* (i) F is in the essence of x because it is a consequence of some property G in the definition of x *or* (ii) F is in the essence of x because it is a consequence of some logical property.

With (DE2*) in hand, let us see if being-identical-to-Socrates is in the derivative essence of Socrates. Consider the property of being such that for every z, z is identical-to-z.[42] This is a logical property. Call it 'the logical identity property'. Being self-identical is a consequence of the logical identity property: it is a logical truth, for any x, that x is self-identical if x is such that for every z, z is identical-to-z.[43] So, we may think by (DE2*) that being self-identical is in the derivative essence of Socrates. However, being identical-to-Socrates is not a consequence of the logical identity property: it is clearly not the case that it is a logical truth, for any x, that x is

---

[42] Under the assumption that z being identical-to-z and z being self-identical are the same, this is the same as the property of being such for every x, x is self-identical.

[43] Given that x is such that for every z, z is identical-to-z, it logically follows that x is identical-to-x, which is that x is self-identical. So, it is a logical truth, for any x, that x is self-identical if x is such that for every z, z is identical-to-z.

identical-to-Socrates if x is such that for every z, z is identical-to-z.[44] This comes as no surprise: no logical property presupposes Socrates as it is had by all objects by logic, but the identity property of Socrates presupposes Socrates. The identity property of Socrates is not a consequence of any logical property.

So far, I have argued, assuming the definitional model, that the identity property of Socrates is neither in the definition of Socrates nor in the derivative essence of him. So, if the definitional model is true, then Socrates is not essentially identical-to-Socrates. This completes my defense of (P1). Of course, this alone does not show that the definitional model is false. For it is still open for proponents of the definitional model to insist that the identity property of Socrates should be dismissed as a bogus essential property precisely because it is not identity-explaining.[45] But this will put Fine's thesis into jeopardy. If the identity property of Socrates is not in the essence of him, the necessary truth that Socrates is necessarily identical-to-Socrates turns out to be groundless. This is what I will argue in the next section.

6.5 In defense of (P2)

Consider the following modal truths:

(N1)   Socrates is necessarily self-identical—i.e., Socrates is $\mathbb{N}$~self-identical.

(N2)   Socrates is necessarily identical-to-Socrates—i.e., Socrates is $\mathbb{N}$~identical-to-Socrates.

Given Fine's thesis, they require essential grounds. What ground them? It was my proposal that (N1) and (N2) are respectively grounded in the following essential truths:

---

[44] For example, it is not a logical truth that Plato is identical-to-Socrates if Plato is such that for every z, z is identical-to-z: it is true that Plato is such that for every z, z is identical-to-z; but it is false that Plato is identical-to-Socrates.

[45] Bob Hale considers identity properties briefly and dismisses them as non-essential properties precisely because the identity property of a particular individual "tells us nothing about what it is to be that individual." (Hale, *Necessary Beings*, 222, n. 27.) Part of what I am doing here is to show that he is mistaken about this.

(E1)   Socrates is essentially self-identical—i.e., Socrates is $\mathbb{E}$~self-identical.

(E2)   Socrates is essentially identical-to-Socrates—i.e., Socrates is $\mathbb{E}$~identical-to-Socrates.

But, in the previous section, it has been argued that (E2) finds no home in the definitional model. So, unless proponents of the definitional model give up Fine's thesis, they need to find an essential ground for (N2) without relying on (E2). In this section, assuming that (E2) is not true, I will consider various attempts to do so and argue that they all fail. Of course, this will not directly show that there is *no* way for the proponents of the definitional model to ground (N2). Nevertheless, once we see how these attempts fail, we will be more certain that it is extremely unlikely for them to find an essential ground for (N2).

Let us assume, for the sake of argument, that (E2) is false. What then grounds (N2)? The proponents of the definitional model might consider four possibilities: they might appeal to an essential truth about Socrates other than (E2); an essential truth about some object other than Socrates; an essential truth about plural objects; or an essential truth about some property rather than an object. In what follows, I will consider best versions of the four possibilities and argue that they all fail.[46]

6.5.1 Is there an essential truth about Socrates other than (E2) that grounds (N2)?

On the definitional model, we have (E1). (E1) grounds (N1). And that in principle doesn't prevent (E1) from grounding (N2): one fact may ground two distinct facts. This might lead the proponents of the definitional model to the idea that (E1) grounds (N2), so we don't need (E2) in grounding (N2).

Let us take a closer look at this idea. If the proponents of the definitional model think that (E1) grounds (N2), on what basis would they think so? As far as I can imagine, what they have in mind is something like the following argument:

---

[46] I would like to thank anonymous referees for suggesting several possible attempts to ground (N2). Thanks to Youngchan Lee for suggesting that (N2) might be grounded in an essential truth about being identical-to-Socrates in particular.

(a)   [Socrates is 𝔼~self-identical] grounds [Socrates is ℕ~self-identical].

(b)   'Socrates is ℕ~self-identical' entails 'Socrates is ℕ~identical-to-Socrates'.

(c)   So, [Socrates is 𝔼~self-identical] grounds [Socrates is ℕ~identical-to-Socrates].

Is this argument sound? Recall that the following is true as a general principle:

𝔼/ℕ-Ground   For any x and any F, if x is 𝔼~F, then [x is 𝔼~F] grounds [x is ℕ~F].

Socrates is 𝔼~self-identical. So, by 𝔼/ℕ-Ground, (a) is true.

How about (b)? Clearly, 'Socrates is ℕ~self-identical' entails '□(Socrates is self-identical)' as we may think that if the former is true, the former grounds the latter: if the mode of Socrates's *being* self-identical is necessary, then it is in virtue of this fact that Socrates is self-identical in all possible worlds in which he exists. In general, we may accept the following as a general principle:

ℕ/□-Ground   For any x and any F, if x is ℕ~F, then [x is ℕ~F] grounds [□(x is F)].

And '□(Socrates is self-identical)' entails '□(Socrates is identical-to-Socrates)' as they are equivalent. So, 'Socrates is ℕ~self-identical' would entail 'Socrates is ℕ~identical-to-Socrates' if '□(Socrates is identical-to-Socrates)' entails 'Socrates is ℕ~identical-to-Socrates.' However, it is not true as a rule that '□(x is F)' entails 'x is ℕ~F', for it might be the case that x is F in all possible worlds in which x exists though the mode of x's having F is not necessary.[47]

Nevertheless, we may think that (b) is true. But if (b) is true, that is not because 'Socrates is ℕ~self-identical' entails 'Socrates is ℕ~identical-to-Socrates' as a rule but because we may infer 'Socrates is ℕ~identical-to-Socrates' independently of 'Socrates is ℕ~self-identical'. This being the case, (a) and (b) are true, but (c) doesn't follow. [Socrates is 𝔼~self-identical] grounds [Socrates is ℕ~self-identical], which grounds [□(Socrates is self-identical)] or,

---

[47] For example, it is true that □(Socrates is a member of {Socrates}), but, from this, we may not infer that Socrates is ℕ~a member of {Socrates} because □(Socrates is a member of {Socrates}) is true not because the mode of Socrates's being a member of {Socrates} is necessary but because the mode of {Socrates}'s having Socrates as a member is necessary.

equivalently, [□(Socrates is identical-to-Socrates)]. However, [□(Socrates is identical-to-Socrates)] entails but doesn't ground [Socrates is ℕ~identical-to-Socrates]. Rather, [Socrates is ℕ~identical-to-Socrates] is grounded in [Socrates is 𝔼~identical-to-Socrates].

Essential grounding is not transferable through consequence between propositions: it is not the case that (*) for propositions p and q, if [x is 𝔼~F] grounds [p], and q is a consequence of p, then [x is 𝔼~F] grounds [q]. If an essential truth grounds a necessary truth, the grounding relation tracks down the source of the necessity. (*) fails to meet this constraint on essential grounding. When [x is 𝔼~F] grounds [p], the necessity in [p] has its source in [x is 𝔼~F]. On the other hand, when p entails q, the entailment might hold owing to the necessity of q whose source lies not in [x is 𝔼~F] but in some other essential truth.

On the other hand, we may think that essential grounding is transferable through consequence between *properties* as follows:

𝔼/ℕ-Ground by PE   For any x and any F and G, if x is 𝔼~F, and G is a consequence of F, then [x is 𝔼~F] grounds [x is ℕ~G].

Indeed, 𝔼/ℕ-Ground by PE is true.[48] However, this doesn't support the claim that (E1) grounds (N2). Given 𝔼/ℕ-Ground by PE, [Socrates is 𝔼~self-identical] would ground [Socrates is ℕ~identical-to-Socrates] if being identical-to-Socrates is a consequence of being self-identical. But clearly, being identical-to-Socrates is not a consequence of being self-identical.

If there is an essential truth about Socrates other than (E2) that grounds (N2), (E1) would be the best candidate. But it is a mistake to think that (E1) grounds (N2). This plausibly suggests that no essential truth about Socrates other than (E2) grounds (N2).

6.5.2 Is there an essential truth about plural objects that grounds (N2)?

We have considered essence statements that ascribe an essential property to a single object. For example, 'Socrates is essentially a person' ascribes being a person to Socrates, which is of the form 'x is 𝔼~F.' Essence statements of this

---

[48] Suppose that x is 𝔼~F, and G is a consequence of F. Since x is 𝔼~F, and G is a consequence of F, x is 𝔼~G, for essence is closed under consequence. On the one hand, by 𝔼/ℕ-Ground, [x is 𝔼~G] grounds [x is ℕ~G]. On the other hand, [x is 𝔼~F] grounds [x is 𝔼~G]: x is 𝔼~G because x is 𝔼~F (and G is a consequence of F). So, [x is 𝔼~F] grounds [x is ℕ~G].

form are meant to express individual essences. On the other hand, there are essence statements that ascribe an essential property to plural objects. For example, 'Socrates and Eiffel Tower are essentially distinct' ascribes being distinct to Socrates and Eiffel Tower taken together, which is of the form 'x and y are $\mathbb{E}$~F.' Essence statements of this form are meant to express collective essences.

Now consider the following:

(d)   Socrates and Socrates are $\mathbb{E}$~identical.

'Socrates and Socrates are $\mathbb{E}$~distinct' is a collective essential statement of a legitimate form. And it is false. Then, (d) should be a collective essential statement of a legitimate form. And it is true. With this collective essential truth, the proponents of the definitional model might claim that (d) grounds (N2), so we don't need (E2) in grounding (N2).

However, it is unclear how (d) grounds (N2). How could they think that (d) grounds (N2)? They can't think that (d) grounds (N2) because when x and y are in $\mathbb{E}$~R, it follows that x is in $\mathbb{E}$~R-to-y or that y is in $\mathbb{E}$~R-to-x: Socrates and Eiffel Tower are $\mathbb{E}$~distinct, but it doesn't follow that Socrates is $\mathbb{E}$~distinct-from-Eiffel-Tower or that Eiffel Tower is $\mathbb{E}$~distinct-from-Socrates.[49] On what basis, then, could they think that (d) grounds (N2)?

Well, what the proponents of the definitional model have in mind after all seems to be the following argument:

(e)   [Socrates and Socrates are $\mathbb{E}$~identical] grounds [Socrates and Socrates are $\mathbb{N}$~identical].

(f)   'Socrates and Socrates are $\mathbb{N}$~identical' entails 'Socrates is $\mathbb{N}$~identical-to-Socrates'.

(g)   So, [Socrates and Socrates are $\mathbb{E}$~identical] grounds [Socrates is $\mathbb{N}$~identical-to-Socrates].

---

[49] It is not the case that Socrates is $\mathbb{E}$~distinct-from-Eiffel-Tower because nothing in the essence of Socrates indicates Eiffel Tower. And the same goes for Eiffel Tower. See Fine, "Essence and Modality," p. 5. See also F. Correia, "On the Reduction of Necessity to Essence," *Philosophy and Phenomenological Research* 84 (2012), 639–653, section 2. This is not to say that the collective essential truth that Socrates and Eiffel Tower are $\mathbb{E}$~distinct cannot be explained in terms of individual essential truths about Socrates and Eiffel Tower. Indeed, I think, *pace* Correia, that the collective essential truth in question is grounded in individual essential truths about Socrates and Eiffel Tower, although I will not go into the details here. I am not saying, though, that collective essence is reducible to individual essence or that *any* collective essential truth is grounded in some individual essential truths.

However, the argument (e)–(g) is problematic just as the argument (a)–(c) is: (g) doesn't follow from (e) and (f). If (f) is true, it is true because [□(Socrates and Socrates are identical)] entails [Socrates is $\mathbb{N}$~identical-to-Socrates]. But the former does not ground the latter: the former says of Socrates and Socrates that 'they' have the same properties in all possible worlds in which 'they' exist, which indicates nothing about which properties 'they' share, whereas the latter says of Socrates that he has the specific property of being-identical-to-Socrates, and the mode of his having the property is necessary. The latter holds in virtue of the fact that Socrates is $\mathbb{E}$~identical-to-Socrates. There is no reason for thinking that [Socrates and Socrates are $\mathbb{E}$~identical] grounds [Socrates is $\mathbb{N}$~identical-to-Socrates].

6.5.3 Is there an essential truth about an object other than Socrates that grounds (N2)?

{Socrates} essentially contains Socrates as a sole member. So, it might be thought that the following must be true:

(h)   {Socrates} is $\mathbb{E}$~λz(Socrates $\in z$ & (x)(if $x \in z$, x is identical-to-Socrates)).

Now the proponents of the definitional model might claim that (h) grounds (N2), so we don't need (E2) in grounding (N2).

Why would they think that (h) grounds (N2)? If they think that (h) grounds (N2) based on the following argument, they would be committed to the same error as before:

(i)   [{Socrates} is $\mathbb{E}$~λz(Socrates $\in z$ & (x)(if $x \in z$, x is identical-to-Socrates))] grounds [{Socrates} is $\mathbb{N}$~λz(Socrates $\in z$ & (x)(if $x \in z$, x is identical-to-Socrates))].

(j)   '{Socrates} is $\mathbb{N}$~λz(Socrates $\in z$ & (x)(if $x \in z$, x is identical-to-Socrates))' entails 'Socrates is $\mathbb{N}$~identical-to-Socrates.'

(k)   So, [{Socrates} is $\mathbb{E}$~λz(Socrates $\in z$ & (x)(if $x \in z$, x is identical-to-Socrates))] grounds [Socrates is $\mathbb{N}$~identical-to-Socrates].

Why then would they think that (h) grounds (N2)? They might do so for the following reason:

(l) {Socrates} is $\mathbb{E}$~λz(Socrates$\in$z & (x)(if x$\in$z, x is identical-to-Socrates)).

(m) Being identical-to-Socrates is a consequence of λz(Socrates$\in$z & (x)(if x$\in$z, x is identical-to-Socrates)).

(n) So, Socrates is $\mathbb{E}$~identical-to-Socrates.

(o) So, [Socrates is $\mathbb{E}$~identical-to-Socrates] grounds [Socrates is $\mathbb{N}$~identical-to-Socrates].

However, this doesn't work either. First of all, (m) is not true: it is not the case that it is a logical truth, for any y, that y is identical-to-Socrates if y is λz(Socrates$\in$z & (x)(if x$\in$z, x is identical-to-Socrates)): {Socrates} is λz(Socrates$\in$z & (x)(if x$\in$z, x is identical-to-Socrates)), but {Socrates} is not identical-to-Socrates. And even if (m) is true, from (l) and (m), (n) doesn't follow. Given (DE2*), what follows would be that {Socrates} is $\mathbb{E}$~identical-to-Socrates, which is false.

It is a logical truth that Socrates is identical-to-Socrates if {Socrates} is λz(Socrates$\in$z & (x)(if x$\in$z, x is identical-to-Socrates)). So, being such that Socrates is identical-to-Socrates if {Socrates} is λz(Socrates$\in$z & (x)(if x$\in$z, x is identical-to-Socrates)) is a logical property. If being identical-to-Socrates were a consequence of this logical property, then it would follow, by (DE2*), that being identical-to-Socrates is in the derivative essence of Socrates, which implies (n) and thus (o). But clearly, being identical-to-Socrates is not a consequence of the logical property: it is not a logical truth, for any y, that y is identical-to-Socrates if y is such that Socrates is identical-to-Socrates if {Socrates} is λz(Socrates$\in$z & (x)(if x$\in$z, x is identical-to-Socrates)).[50]

It is tempting to think that some essential truth about {Socrates} grounds (N2), but on close examination, the tempting idea is misguided. And we may plausibly think that things are not so different when we consider another object other than {Socrates}: it might be tempting to think that, for some

---

[50] An anonymous referee suggested a defense of the definitional model along the above line of thought. In an earlier version of the chapter, I responded by claiming that not (h) but something in the vicinity is true, while agreeing with the referee that (m) is true. I was mistaken to think that (m) is true or that being identical-to-Socrates is a consequence of some logical property. The above defense of the definitional model fails even if (h) is taken for granted though I still do think that my response in the previous version stands.

object, some essential truth about the object grounds (N2), but a close examination will show in a similar vein that the tempting idea is misguided.

6.5.4 Is there an essential truth about a property that grounds (N2)?

The consideration of 6.5.1 to 6.5.3 suggests that no essential truth about *objects* (whether a single object or plural ones) grounds (N2). This might lead the proponents of the definitional model to the idea that (N2) is grounded in some essential truth about entities other than objects. What if we consider, for example, essential truths about *properties*? Can't we think that (N2) is grounded in an essential truth about a property? If there were such a property in question, the best candidate would be being-self-identical or being-identical-to-Socrates. I will consider if essential truths about these properties can serve as a ground for (N2) and argue that there are no such essential truths about the properties.

Before proceeding, we should distinguish two ways of conceiving essences of properties. How is the essence of F to be understood? We may treat F as something objectual or saturated in nature, in which case, we pursue the essence of it by answering the question of what it is. On the other hand, we may treat F as something predicational or unsaturated in nature, in which case, we pursue the essence of it by answering the question of what it is to be F.[51] If properties are treated as something objectual, attempts to show that (N2) is grounded in some essential truth of some property collapse into attempts to show that (N2) is grounded in some essential truth of some object, which should fail for the reason similar to the one given in 6.5.3.[52] If

---

[51] For a perceptive observation on the distinction between the essence of a property qua something objectual (or, objectual essence) and the essence of a property qua something predicational (or, generic essence), see F. Correia, "Generic Essence, Objectual Essence, and Modality," *Nous* 40(4) (2006), 753–767. See also Fine, "Unified Foundations for Essence and Ground."

[52] Suppose, for example, that being-identical-to-Socrates is conceived as an object. Let me use 'O(being-identical-to-Socrates)' to refer to the property qua an object. O(being-identical-to-Socrates) is $\mathbb{E}\sim$a property such that anything having it is Socrates. But considering this essential property about O(being-identical-to-Socrates) gets us nowhere: first, being identical-to-Socrates is not a consequence of this property; and second, even if it were a consequence of the property, it would follow only that O(being-identical-to-Socrates) is $\mathbb{E}\sim$identical-to-Socrates, which is false. It is a logical truth that anything having O(being-identical-to-Socrates) is Socrates. Consider the logical property, being such that anything having O(being-identical-to-Socrates) is Socrates. If being identical-to-Socrates were a consequence of this logical property, it would follow, by (DE2*), that Socrates is $\mathbb{E}\sim$identical-to-Socrates. But clearly, being identical-to-Socrates is not a consequence of the logical property.

the proponents of the definitional model are to think that essences of properties do the grounding job, they must treat properties as predicational.

What is it to be F? The answer is of the form: to be F is to be $G_1 \ldots G_n$. Given this, we may think that F is E~such that for any x, x is F if and only if x is $G_1 \ldots G_n$.[53] This grounds [F is N~such that for any x, x is F if and only if x is G1 ... Gn] which in turn grounds [□(For any x, x is F if and only if x is G1 ... Gn)]. What is it to be a vixen? To be a vixen is to be a female fox. This grounds [Being a vixen is N~such that for any x, x is a vixen if and only if x is a female fox] which in turn grounds [□(For any x, x is a vixen if and only if x is a female fox)].

Now consider being self-identical. What is it to be self-identical? To be self-identical is to have all and only properties of itself. So, the following is true:

(p) Being self-identical is E~such that for any x, x is self-identical if and only if x has all and only properties of itself.

This essential truth grounds [Being self-identical is N~such that for any x, x is self-identical if and only if x has all and only properties of itself], which in turns grounds [□(For any x, x is self-identical if and only if x has all and only properties of itself]. [Being self-identical is N~such that for any x, x is self-identical if and only if x has all and only properties of itself], which in turns grounds [□(For any x, x is self-identical if and only if x has all and only properties of itself]. However, this is far from showing that (p) grounds (N2) – i.e., the fact that Socrates is N~identical-to-Socrates.

Consider being identical-to-Socrates. What is to be identical-to-Socrates? Let us say that to be identical-to-Socrates is to be $G_1 \ldots G_n$ whatever $G_1 \ldots G_n$ are. (More will be said about this in the last section.) Then, the following is true:

(q) Being identical-to-Socrates is E~such that for any x, x is identical-to-Socrates if and only if x is $G_1 \ldots G_n$.

---

[53] This is based on a principle, according to which to be F is to be G1 ... Gn if and only if it is in the essence of F that for any x, x is F if and only if x is G1 ... Gn. The principle is weaker than the proposal offered in Rosen, "Real Definition," according to which to be F is to be G1 ... Gn if and only if (assuming Weak Formality) it is in the essence of F that for any x, if x is F, then [x is F] is grounded in [x is G]. When we say that to be F is to be G1 ... Gn, in some cases, 'is' in 'To be F is to be G1 ... Gn' has an *explanatory* reading on which x being F is *explained* by x being G1 ... Gn. Rosen's principle is meant to accommodate this reading. But I think 'is' in 'To be F is to be G1 ... Gn' basically has an explanatorily neutral reading on which to say that to be F is to be G1 ... Gn does not automatically imply that [x is F] is grounded in [x is G1 ... Gn] or that [x is G1], [x is G2],..., [x is Gn] are each metaphysically prior to [x is F]. For example, we may say that to be F is to be G1 ... Gn to mean that x being F is *identical* to x being G1 ... Gn. For the identity reading and logic of 'To be F is to be G', see C. Dorr, "To be F is to be G," *Philosophical Perspectives* 30 (2016), 39–134.

This essential truth grounds [Being identical-to-Socrates is $\mathbb{N}$~such that for any x, x is identical-to-Socrates if and only if x is $G_1 \ldots G_n$], which in turn grounds [$\square$(For any x, x is identical-to-Socrates if and only if x is G1 ... Gn.)]. But this gives us no reason for thinking that (q) grounds (N2) – i.e., the fact that Socrates is $\mathbb{N}$~identical-to-Socrates.

So far, I have considered various attempts to ground (N2) without relying on (E2). If my argument is right, all fail. Are there other kind of attempts that I didn't consider? I don't know. But I suspect that if there are such attempts, they will turn out to fail for some reason like the ones I've given. In any case, the consideration so far strongly suggests that if (E2) is false, prospects for finding an essential ground for (N2) are extremely dim. This puts the definitional model into serious doubt. From the previous section, we know that we can't have (E2) in the definitional model. But if we don't have (E2), we have no way to ground (N2). (N2) is an ungrounded necessary truth, which contradicts Fine's thesis.[54] Thus, Fine's thesis is false or else the definitional model must go.

It is an open possibility to give up Fine's thesis in favor of the definitional model. But this doesn't seem to be well motivated. The principal motivation for adopting the framework of real definition is that within the framework, we can ground modality. If Fine's thesis is given up, there is not much point in insisting on the definitional model. This leaves us with only one option. The definitional model must go. Of course, this is not to say that we should reject the framework of real definition altogether. All we need to do is to find an alternative model of essence in the framework of real definition in which for objects such as you and me, some essential property of an object does not

---

[54] This is so because (N2) is a truth of *metaphysical* necessity. If (N2) is not a truth of metaphysical necessity but a truth of some other kind of necessity, (N2) would not require an essential ground. (For the view that there are various kinds of necessity, see K. Fine, "The Varieties of Necessity," in T. S. Gendler and J. Hawthorne, (eds.), *Conceivability and Possibility*, Oxford University Press, 2002, 253–282; and to see that Fine's thesis is meant to be about metaphysical necessity, see Fine, "Guide to Ground," pp. 77–78.) For example, one might think that (N2) does not require an essential ground, claiming that (N2) or the necessity of identity in general is a consequence of semantic convention on direct reference. (See E. J. Lowe, "Two Notions of Being: Entity and Essence," p. 25.) But I think that (N2) is not derivable from the theory of direct reference, though I can't go into this issue in any detail for lack of space. Here I will simply assume without argument that (N2) is a truth of metaphysical necessity. For the well-discussed point that the theory of direct reference alone is not committed to any view of metaphysically necessary truths, see D. Kaplan, "Demonstratives," in *Themes From Kaplan*, J. Almog, H. Wettstein, J. Perry, (eds.), Oxford University Press, 1989, 481–564; Salmon, "How not to Derive Essentialism from the Theory of Reference"; Salmon, *Reference and Essence*; J. Almog, "Naming without Necessity," *Journal of Philosophy* 83 (1986), 210–242; K. Fine, "Reference, Essence, and Identity," in his *Modality and Tense: Philosophical Papers*, Oxford University Press, 2005, 19–39.

explain what it is and thus doesn't belong in the definition of it but is nonetheless in its constitutive essence. In the next section, I will offer an alternative model in this line of thought.

6.6 Toward an alternative model of essence

On the definitional model of essence, the constitutive essence of an object is assimilated to the definition of it. The discussion so far suggests that the assimilation of constitutive essence to definition is problematic. On the one hand, the identity property of Socrates is in the constitutive essence of him as it is not a consequence of any other property. On the other hand, it is not in the definition of him either as it does not explain what he is. The definitional model should give way to an alternative model in which the identity property of an object may be in the constitutive essence of it though it is not in the definition of it. How then is the constitutive essence of an object to be understood if it is not regarded as the definition of it? I think we should approach the constitutive essence of an object in terms of the identity property of it.

Let's take a close look at the identity property of Socrates. What is it to be identical-to-Socrates? To be identical-to-Socrates is partly to be a person. But to be identical-to-Socrates is not just to be a person. Then what more is there? It will be instructive to imagine a situation in which someone (say, Xanthippe) encountered Socrates for the first time. Her knowledge of him is minimal: nobody told her about him, and this is the very first time she has met him. Nonetheless, she knows him to some extent. She asks herself: Who is this? This question presupposes things about him, and that much, if true, she knows about him. The 'who' of 'Who is this?' indicates that she takes him as a person. She ascribes being a person to him. If that's true, she knows that he is a person. What then does the 'this' of 'Who is this?' indicate? What it indicates seems to be that she takes him as a particular one among others. What property is it, then, that is being ascribed to him?

The property in question is not some of his sensory qualities, though those qualities might help her discern the property in question. It is not some of his historical properties about his family, friends, career and so on either: these are properties she wishes to know *further* by asking the question 'Who is this?'. Then what is it? It is no accident that she uses the demonstrative 'this' because we don't seem to have purely conceptual resources with which to express it and thus cannot capture it except by the act of naming. What she talks about when she talks about Socrates in that situation is *this* man. And the property Xanthippe ascribes to him by her use of 'this' is the irreducible individuality of the particular man or, to coin a name for it, his *thisness*. We don't have a natural language predicate for this kind of property, but we may construct one. Let $\ulcorner$is/am/are this$_c$$\urcorner$ be a predicate, where c is a schematic letter for a name, such that for any primitive object c, c is this$_c$ if and only if c has its thisness. The property in question is being this$_{Socrates}$.

This provides an opportunity to understand the identity property of Socrates: being identical-to-Socrates is being this$_{Socrates}$ person. This sheds light on how the constitutive essence of Socrates is to be understood. What is Socrates? He is a person. Socrates is definitionally a person. It is not that Socrates is an object, and on top of that, he is also a person. It is that Socrates is a person, and only in virtue of that, he is an object. The definition of Socrates is the central element of the constitutive essence of him.[55] The definitional model is right about this. But it implies that the definition of Socrates *is* the constitutive essence of him, and here it goes wrong. Being this$_{Socrates}$ person is not in the definition of Socrates because being this$_{Socrates}$ doesn't do the defining as it presupposes Socrates. Nonetheless, it is also a core element of the constitutive essence of Socrates. This naturally hints at the idea that the constitutive essence of Socrates is the identity property of him—i.e., being this$_{Socrates}$ person.

How is the constitutive essence of an object to be understood in general? My proposal is that for any object, the constitutive essence of it should be assimilated to the identity property of it. Two remarks are worth making. Having said that the definition of Socrates and the thisness of Socrates are central elements of the constitutive essence of Socrates or, equivalently, that being this$_{Socrates}$ person is partly being a person and partly being this$_{Socrates}$, I am not saying that [Socrates is a person] and [Socrates is this$_{Socrates}$]

---

[55] This view implies the essentiality of sortal kind, according to which for any x, x is essentially of the sortal kind it falls under. The essentiality of sortal kind serves as an essential ground for the necessity of sortal kinds, according to which for any x, x is necessarily of the sortal kind it falls under. The necessity of sortal kind has been widely accepted. For defenses of the necessity of sortal kind, see D. Wiggins, *Sameness and Substance Renewed*, Cambridge University Press, 2001; B. Brody, *Identity and Essence*, Princeton University Press, 1980/2014. (Cf. E. J. Lowe, *More Kinds of Being: A Further Study of Individuation, Identity, and the Logic of Sortal Terms*, Wiley-Blackwell, 2009.) Kripke also commits himself to the necessity of sortal kind. See Kripke, *Naming and Necessity*, p. 115, n. 57. The necessity of sortal kind is not universally accepted though. For example, see T. Williamson, "Necessary Existents," in A O'Hear (ed.), *Logic, Thought and Language*, 233-251 Cambridge University Press, 2002; T. Williamson, *Modal Logic as Metaphysics*, Oxford University Press, 2013; and Mackie, *How Things Might Have Been*.

are prior to [Socrates is this$_{\text{Socrates}}$ person]. Socrates is not a person independently of being this$_{\text{Socrates}}$. He is not an 'ideal' or 'Meinongian' person but an *actual* one we encounter in history—a person that is a person in virtue of being a person that is this or that person. Socrates is not this$_{\text{Socrates}}$ one independently of being a person. He is not a 'bare' particular but an *intelligible* individual—an individual that is an individual in virtue of being an instance of a certain sortal kind or in virtue of a fact about what it is. It is not that Socrates is this$_{\text{Socrates}}$ person because he is a person and he is this$_{\text{Socrates}}$ but that he is a person and he is this$_{\text{Socrates}}$ because he is this$_{\text{Socrates}}$ person. This being the case, what is (in) the constitutive essence of Socrates is being this$_{\text{Socrates}}$ person, while the definition of Socrates, being a person, and the thisness of Socrates, being this$_{\text{Socrates}}$, are in the derivative essence.[56]

In the case of Socrates, the constitutive essence of him is not the same as the definition of him. This is not to say that the definition of an object *as a rule* does not exhaust the constitutive essence of it. What is {Socrates}? It is a set with Socrates as a sole member. The definition of {Socrates} is being a set with Socrates as a sole member. What is it to be identical-to-{Socrates}? To be identical-to-{Socrates} is to be a set with Socrates as a sole member. The identity property of {Socrates} is being a set with Socrates as a sole member. Thus, in the case of {Socrates}, the constitutive essence of {Socrates} *is* the definition of {Socrates}. This may well be generalized. For any non-primitive object such as {Socrates}, the constitutive essence of it collapses into the definition of it. For any primitive individual such as Socrates, however, the definition of it does not exhaust its constitutive essence because the thisness of it is also part of the constitutive essence of it.[57]

---

[56] The term 'thisness', which is an English counterpart of the Latin word 'haecceitas', is due to Duns Scotus. But the view just characterized is not Scotist. In Scotus's view, an individual is analyzed into its general essence and its particular thisness that are formally (though not really) distinct from each other. The view suggested here is rather Suarezian: an individual is not analyzable into metaphysical constituents; it is a substance, as it were. So, the Suarezian view comes closer to Aristotle's view than the Scotist view. (For a useful historical remark, see J. Gracia, "Introduction," in J. Gracia (ed.), *Individuation in Scholasticism: The Later Middle Ages and the Counter-Reformation*, 1-19 State University of New York, 1994.)

Alvin Plantinga and Gary Rosenkrantz are notable contemporary advocates of the Scotist view. See A. Plantinga, *The Nature of Necessity*, Oxford University Press, 1974; A. Plantinga, "Actualism and Possible Worlds," *Theoria* 42 (1976), 139–160; and G. Rosenkrantz, *Haecceity: An Ontological Essay* (Dordrecht: Kluwer, 1993). For a contemporary instance of the Suarezian view, see Adams, "Primitive Thisness and Primitive Identity"; and R. Adams, "Thisness and Actualism," *Synthese* 49 (1981), 3–41.

[57] Some terminological remarks are worth making. My use of the terms 'thisness' and 'primitive' is different from Robert Adams's use of the terms. Adams uses 'thisness' to mean what I have called 'identity property'. So, in his terminology, ∅ has a thisness as it has an identity property, while in my terminology, it doesn't have a thisness though it has an identity

This way of determining the constitutive essence of an object fits well with the intuitive conception of essence behind the Fine equivalence. According to the Fine equivalence, the essence of Socrates is the collection of properties he must have to be the object that he is—that is, the collection of properties he must have *to be identical-to-Socrates*. Fine himself has recently proposed something like this.[58] His suggestion is, roughly, that essential truths about Socrates can be equated with truths required for something (an arbitrary object) to be identical to Socrates except truths involving Socrates due to the explanatory constraint—put in property talk, essential properties of Socrates can be equated with properties something must have to be identical to Socrates except properties presupposing Socrates due to the explanatory constraint. I agree with him on this proposal except that there is an essential property of Socrates that presupposes Socrates. In my view, the explanatory constraint is a constraint on definition but not a constraint on essence in general.

It might be thought that the model of essence I propose is only a little revision of the definitional model: in the case of primitive individuals, extend the constitutive essence of an object to include its thisness, and we get the new model of essence that would be otherwise indiscernible from the definitional model. Upon inspection, however, consequences of accepting this model are more significant than it might first seem. And once those consequences are noticed, it will become clearer how it is fundamentally different from the definitional model.

In keeping with Kripke's insight, we think that Elizabeth II essentially came from her parents. But we might not want to say that her origin, having come from her parents, is in the definition of her: if her origin is in her definition, she is defined by her parents, which puts her into danger of losing her ontological status as an independent being.[59] So, we might want to say

property. While Adams uses 'primitive' to distinguish non-qualitative properties from qualitative ones, I use it to distinguish identity properties of objects that presuppose the objects from identity properties that don't. So, in his terminology, {Socrates} has a primitive thisness or a primitive identity property, as the identity property is not qualitative; but in my terminology, {Socrates} does not have a primitive identity property, as the identity property does not presuppose {Socrates}.

[58] Fine, "Unified Foundations for Essence and Ground."

[59] Perhaps this is why Aquinas said in *Summa Theologica*, I, 44, art.: "Habitudo ad causam non intrat in definitionem entis quod est causatum" which in English is that the relation to a cause does not enter into the definition of the thing that is caused. The English translation is due to E. Anscombe, "Times, Beginnings, and Causes," in her *Metaphysics and the Philosophy of Mind*, University of Minnesota Press, 1981, p. 152. Of course, from the essentiality of origin, one might simply conclude that familiar objects such as Elizabeth II are all non-independent beings: she depends upon her parents, while her parents depend upon parents of their own and so on and so forth. Perhaps Spinoza has this view or something in the vicinity. (Spinoza, *A Spinoza*

that her origin is not in the definition of her. But this is not what we can do within the definitional model, for it seems hopeless to think that her origin is a consequence of her definition or of a logical property. On the other hand, the alternative model leaves open the possibility that her origin is essential to her but nonetheless not in her definition. Why could Elizabeth II not have come from different parents from her actual parents? Well, "[how] could a person originating from different parents... be *this very woman*?"[60] Perhaps, her origin is a consequence of being *this$_{Elizabeth}$*: to be *this$_{Elizabeth}$* is partly to have come from Elizabeth II's actual parents.[61]

If the alternative model is right, in the case of primitive individuals such as you and me, essences are ultimately singular, for they presuppose individuals. This departs from one traditional way of using the term 'essence', according to which 'essence' should mean something general. I have no intention to debate over terminology. If the traditional terminological convention is firmly entrenched in our philosophical culture, I would be happy to follow it. All I want to claim is that for individuals such as you and me, they have some ultimately singular and primitive properties in virtue of which some necessary truths about them hold whether those properties are called 'essential properties' or not. If my claim is right, either Fine's thesis should be restated in different terms or the traditional terminological convention should be revised. Since I hold onto Fine's thesis as Fine presents it, I chose the latter.[62]

Reader: The Ethics and other Works, ed. E. Curley, Princeton University Press, 1994, Part I. See also M. Della Rocca, *Representation and the Mind-Body Problem in Spinoza*, Oxford University Press, 1996). Thanks to Michael Della Rocca for discussion about Spinoza's view on this matter.

[60] Kripke, *Naming and Necessity*, p. 113, italics original.

[61] Three remarks are in order. (1) The relevant sense of 'consequence' is the non-logical one: to be this$_{Elizabeth}$ is (partly) to have come from the parents. (See note 9.) (2) To be this$_{Elizabeth}$ is also (partly) to have this$_{Elizabeth}$ agential power. In my view, to be identical-to-Elizabeth is to be a person with this$_{Elizabeth}$ agential power who came from the actual parents. My proposal that the origin of an object is a consequence of its non-definitive constitutive essence requires a substantive defense. It lies beyond the scope of the chapter to discuss how this can be done in detail, which is what I hope to do elsewhere. I wish only to add that if my proposal is right, the defense of the essentiality of origin should be pursued in a different line from the usual ones found in N. Salmon, "How not to Derive Essentialism from the Theory of Reference"; and G. Rohrbaugh and L. deRosset, "A New Route to the Necessity of Origin," *Mind* 113 (2004), 705–725.

[62] Perhaps the traditional convention can be traced back to Aristotle. (It should be noted, though, that it is unclear that Aristotle *always* used the term 'essence' to signify something general. While Aristotle in *Metaphysics* Z suggests that the essence of an object is general, identifying the essence of an object with its form, which is for Aristotle shareable by many objects, he also suggests that the essence of an object is singular and unshareable, identifying the essence of an object with the object qua itself. It is also worth noting that in Aristotle, definitions are of kinds and there are no definitions of individuals. In this respect, Fine's use of 'definition' is broader than Aristotle's.) However, not all philosophers follow the traditional convention.

Perhaps behind the traditional convention is an epistemological view, according to which knowledge of essence is purely intellectual. If that is the case, I should reject the traditional convention because I reject the epistemological view associated with it. And, from the post-Kripke essentialist perspective, this is as it should be. True, it is not by perceiving sensory qualities of you that I know your essence: I don't perceive being this$_{you}$ as I perceive colors, sounds, tastes, and so on. But it is also not purely by the intellect that I know your essence. If I attempt to grasp it by the intellect only, I must grasp it through its general features, but I am then doomed to miss it, for it has a *primitive* singularity. I know your essence by experiencing you as one particular person, perceiving human actions of yours, which is not possible without the help of 'sensible intuition' in Peirce's sense of the term.[63] My knowledge of your essence is ultimately experiential in a nonparochial sense of 'experience.'

The 'discovery' of a posteriori essence was a great achievement in contemporary metaphysics. Truths of identity are often considered as a paradigm case of a posteriori essence on the grounds that although it is knowable a priori that Cicero is Cicero, it is only knowable a posteriori that Cicero is Tully. But if I am right, even the fact that Cicero is Cicero is in a way knowable only a posteriori. It is knowable a priori that Cicero is Cicero if that means that Cicero *is self-identical*. If, on the other hand, that Cicero is Cicero means that Cicero *is identical-to-Cicero*, it is knowable only a posteriori that Cicero is Cicero: to know that Cicero is Cicero, we must know that Cicero is this$_{Cicero}$ person, knowing that Cicero is this$_{Cicero}$ is an experiential matter.[64]

When Locke says that "essence," in the "proper original signification" of the word, denotes "the very being of any thing, whereby it is, what it is," he seems to assume that the essence of an object is singular and unique to the object, because if the essence of an object were a general feature, it would not be the case that the object is or exists by its essence. (J. Locke, *An Essay Concerning Human Understanding*, ed. P. H. Nidditch, Clarendon Press, 1975, III, III, 15.) Spinoza might be another instance in point. (See note 60.) And Fine should have no objection to the view that singular properties can be called 'essences', as he regards the property of containing Socrates as a sole member as an essential property of {Socrates}. Thanks to Tim Clarke, Michael Della Rocca, and Ken Winkler for discussion on this matter.

[63] For helpful discussions about Peirce's view on naming and thisness, see J. R. DiLeo, "Pierce's Haecceitism," *Transactions of the Charles S. Peirce Society* 27 (1991), 79–109; and D. Boersema, *Pragmatism and Reference*, MIT Press, 2009, Ch. 4.

[64] E. J. Lowe, a prominent espouser of the definitional model, forcefully objects to Kripkean essentialism, claiming that essences are knowable a priori. See Lowe, "On the Alleged Necessity of True Identity Statements"; Lowe, "Two Notions of Being: Entity and Essence"; E. J. Lowe, "A Problem for a posteriori Essentialism concerning Natural Kinds," *Analysis* 67 (2007), 286–292. I believe that his criticism of a posteriori essentialism is based on the failure to acknowledge the essentiality of thisness which is knowable only a posteriori. But this is a larger issue that I cannot properly discuss here.

When Kripke proposed his essentialist theses, he implicitly assumed the modal account of essence. So, those theses were meant to be modal theses, not in a proper sense essentialist ones. If Fine's thesis is true, the modal account is false. But Fine's thesis should be taken not as an objection to Kripke's view but as a welcome opportunity to make it sophisticated. With Fine's thesis in hand, we can complete Kripke's project by essentially grounding modality, while reconstruing Kripke's modal theses as their essentialist counterparts. Nonetheless, it seems to me that advocates of Kripke's view have not welcomed Fine's thesis with open arms. Perhaps that is because they assumed that Fine's thesis is committed to the definitional model, while the definition model is potentially in tension with the essentialist counterparts of Kripke's theses. However, if I am right, Fine's thesis is not committed to the definitional model and even recommends denying it. I hope my discussion soothes Kripkeans' worries about Fine's thesis and helps them see how Kripke's view can be reconstrued and strengthened along the line of Fine's thesis.[65,66]

References

Adams, Robert. (1979), "Primitive Thisness and Primitive Identity," *Journal of Philosophy* 76, 5–26.

Adams, Robert. (1981), "Thisness and Actualism," *Synthese* 49, 3–41.

---

[65] I should mention that Joseph Almog proposed a construal of essence that seems to be similar to what I propose here. (J. Almog, "The Structure-in-Things: Existence, Essence and Logic," *Proceedings of the Aristotelian Society* 103 (2003), 197–225.) He objects to Fine's definitional account of essence on the grounds that the essence of an object is not exhausted by the definition of the object, while the essence of an object should be understood in terms of a generative process by which the object came into being. I find Almog's proposal insightful, but my proposal is different from his in several respects. I should note first that it is hard to tell if Almog's account is intended to account for the *notion* of essence or the *content* of the essence of an object. If he meant the former, I must disagree with him. It isn't and shouldn't be built into the concept of essence that the essence of an object arises from a generative process. I don't see that there is a generative process from which the null set or God came into being. If he meant the latter, I basically agree with him in spirit, but I disagree with him about details. He rejects the modal account of essence but nonetheless thinks that essentiality is extensionally equivalent to necessity. So, he claims that Socrates is not only necessarily but also essentially a member of {Socrates}. But the notion of essence proposed here doesn't require or recommend it.

[66] Versions of this chapter were presented at the spring meeting of the Korean Society for Analytic Philosophy (KSAP), Seoul, 2019, to the Analytic Philosophy workshop at Yonsei University, and to the conference on Truth, Metaphysics and Epistemology at Peking University. I am grateful to everyone who participated in these discussions, including my commentator, Jaeho Lee, at the meeting of KSAP. I should like to thank Tim Clarke, Michael Della Rocca, Kit Fine, Zoltán Szabó, Dean Zimmerman as well as anonymous referees for helpful comments and suggestions.

Aristotle. (1984), *The Complete Works of Aristotle* vols. I and II, ed. Jonathan Barnes, Princeton, NJ: Princeton University Press.

Almog, Joseph. (1986), "Naming without Necessity," *Journal of Philosophy* 83, 210–242.

Almog, Joseph. (2003), "The Structure-in-Things: Existence, Essence and Logic," *Proceedings of the Aristotelian Society* 103, 197–225.

Anscombe, G. E. M. (1974), "Times, Beginnings, and Causes," in her *Metaphysics and the Philosophy of Mind*, Minneapolis–St Paul, MN: University of Minnesota Press (1981), 148–162.

Aquinas, Thomas. (1948), *Summa Theologica* vol. I, trans. The Fathers of the English Dominican Province, New York: Benziger Brothers.

Black, Max. (1952), "The Identity of Indiscernibles," *Mind* 61, 153–164.

Boersema, David. (2009), *Pragmatism and Reference*, Cambridge, MA: MIT Press.

Brody, Baruch. (1980/2014), *Identity and Essence*, Princeton, NJ: Princeton University Press.

Burgess, John. (2014), "On a Derivation of the Necessity of Identity," *Synthese* 191, 1567–1585.

Cowling, Sam. (2013), "The Modal View of Essence," *Canadian Journal of Philosophy* 43(2), 248–266.

Correia, Fabrice. (2006), "Generic Essence, Objectual Essence, and Modality" *Nous* 40(4), 753–767.

Correia, Fabrice. (2012), "On the Reduction of Necessity to Essence," *Philosophy and Phenomenological Research* 84, 639–653.

Della Rocca, Michael. (1996), *Representation and the Mind-Body Problem in Spinoza*, Oxford: Oxford University Press.

Della Rocca, Michael. (2005), "Two Spheres, Twenty Spheres, and the Identity of Indiscernibles," *Pacific Philosophical Quarterly* 86, 480–492.

DiLeo, Jeffrey. R. (1991), "Pierce's Haecceitism," *Transactions of the Charles S. Peirce Society* 27, 79–109.

Dorr, Cian. (2016), "To be F is to be G," *Philosophical Perspectives* 30, 39–134.

Fine, Kit. (1984), "Reference, Essence, and Identity," in his *Modality and Tense: Philosophical Papers*, Oxford: Oxford University Press (2005), 19–39.

Fine, Kit. (1985), "Plantinga on the Reduction of Possibilist Discourse," in J. E. Tomberlin and P. van Inwagen (eds.), *Alvin Plantinga*, 145–186, Dordrecht: Reidel.

Fine, Kit. (1994), "Essence and Modality," *Philosophical Perspectives* 8, 1–16.

Fine, Kit. (1994), "Senses of Essence," in Walter Sinnott-Armstrong, Diana Raffman, and Nicholas Asher (eds.), *Modality, Morality and Belief. Essays in Honor of Ruth Barcan Marcus*, Cambridge University Press, 53–73.

Fine, Kit. (1995), "Ontological Dependence," *Proceedings of the Aristotelian Society* 95, 269–290.

Fine, Kit. (1995), "The Logic of Essence," *Journal of Philosophical Logic* 24, 241–273.

Fine, Kit. (2002), "The Varieties of Necessity," in T. S. Gendler and J. Hawthorne (eds.), *Conceivability and Possibility*, 253–282 New York: Clarendon Press.

Fine, Kit. (2002), "The Problem of Possibilia," in D. Zimmerman (ed.), *The Oxford Handbook of Metaphysics*, Oxford: Oxford University Press, 161–179.

Fine, Kit. (2012), "Guide to Ground," in Fabrice Correia and Benjamin Schnieder (eds.), *Metaphysical Grounding*, Cambridge: Cambridge University Press, 37–80,

Fine, Kit. (2015), "Unified Foundations for Essence and Ground," *Journal of the American Philosophical Association* 1, 296–311.

Forbes, Graham. (1985), *The Metaphysics of Possibility*, Oxford: Clarendon Press.

Geach, Peter (1968), *Reference and Generality*, Ithaca, NY: Cornell University Press.

Hacking, Ian. (1975), "The Identity of Indiscernibles," *Journal of Philosophy* 72, 249–256.

Hale, Bob. (2013), *Necessary Beings: An Essay on Ontology, Modality, and the Relations Between Them*, Oxford: Oxford University Press.

Kaplan, David. (1989), "Demonstratives," in J. Almog, H. Wettstein, and J. Perry, (eds.), *Themes From Kaplan*, Oxford: Oxford University Press, 481–564.

Koslicki, Katherine. (2012), "Essence, Necessity and Explanation," in T. Tahko, (ed.), *Contemporary Aristotelian Metaphysics*, Cambridge: Cambridge University Press, 187–206.

Kripke, Saul. (1971), "Identity and Necessity," in Milton K. Muniz, (ed.), *Identity and Individuation*, New York: New York University Press, 135–164.

Kripke, Saul. (1980), *Naming and Necessity*, Cambridge, MA: Harvard University Press.

Leibniz, Gottfried Wilhelm. (1968/1989), "Discourse on Metaphysics," in Roger Ariew and Daniel Garbert (eds.), *G. W. Leibniz: Philosophical Essays*, Indianapolis, IN: Hackett Publishing Company, 35–68.

Lewis, David. (1973), *Counterfactuals*, Cambridge, MA: Harvard University Press.

Lewis, David. (1986), *On the Plurality of Worlds*, Oxford: Blackwell Publishers.

Lowe, E. Jonathan. (1982), "On the Alleged Necessity of True Identity Statements," *Mind* 91, 579–584.

Lowe, E. Jonathan. (2007), "A Problem for a posteriori Essentialism concerning Natural Kinds," *Analysis* 67, 286–292.

Lowe, E. Jonathan. (2008), "Two Notions of Being: Entity and Essence," *Royal Institute of Philosophy Supplement* 62, 23–48.

Lowe, E. Jonathan. (2009), *More Kinds of Being: A Further Study of Individuation, Identity, and the Logic of Sortal Terms*, Oxford: Wiley-Blackwell.

Mackie, Penelope. (2006), *How Things Might Have Been*, Oxford: Oxford University Press.

Marcus, Ruth. (1947), "Identity of Individuals in a Strict Functional Calculus of Second-Order," *Journal of Symbolic Logic* 12, 12–15.

McGinn, Colin. (1976), "On the Necessity of Origin," *Journal of Philosophy* 73, 134–135.

McGinn, Colin. (2000), *Logical Properties*, Oxford: Clarendon Press.

Morvarid, Hashem. (2019), "Essence and Logical Properties," *Philosophical Studies* 176, 2897–2917.

Nutting, Eileen, Caplan, Ben, and Tillman, Chris. (2018), "Constitutive Essence and Partial Grounding," *Inquiry* 61, 137–161.

Oderberg, David. (2011), "Essence and Properties," *Erkenntnis* 75, 85–111.

Plantinga, Alvin. (1974), *The Nature of Necessity*, Oxford: Oxford University Press.

Plantinga, Alvin. (1976), "Actualism and Possible Worlds," *Theoria* 42, 139–160.

Robertson, Teresa. (1998), "Possibilities and the Arguments for Origin Essentialism," *Mind* 107, 729–749.

Rohrbaugh, Guy and deRosset, Louis. (2004), "A New Route to the Necessity of Origin," *Mind* 113, 705–725.

Rosen, Gideon. (2010), "Metaphysical Dependence: Grounding and Reduction," in Bob Hale and Aviv Hoffmann, (eds.), *Modality: Metaphysics, Logic, and Epistemology*, Oxford: Oxford University Press, 109–36.

Rosen, Gideon. (2015), "Real Definition," *Analytic Philosophy* 56 (3), 198–201.

Rosenkrantz, Gary. (1993), *Haecceity: An Ontological Essay*, Dordrecht: Kluwer.

Russell, Bertrand. (1912), *The Problems of Philosophy*, London: Williams and Norgate.

Salmon, Nathan. (1979), "How not to Derive Essentialism from the Theory of Reference," *Journal of Philosophy* 76, 703–725.

Salmon, Nathan. (2005), *Reference and Essence*, Amherst, NY: Prometheus Books.

Sidelle, Allen. (1989), *Necessity, Essence, and Individuation: A Defense of Conventionalism*, Ithaca, NY: Cornell University Press.

Spinoza, Baruch. (1994), *A Spinoza Reader: The Ethics and other Works*, ed. Ed Curley, Princeton, NJ: Princeton University Press.

Stalnaker, Robert. (1973), "Possible Worlds," *Nous* 2, 303–314.

Wiggins, David. (1976), "The De Re 'Must': A Note on the Logical Form of Essentialist Claims," in G. Evans and J. McDowell, (eds.), *Truth and Meaning*, Oxford: Clarendon Press.

Wiggins, David. (2001), *Sameness and Substance Renewed*, Cambridge: Cambridge University Press.

Wildman, Nathan. (2013), "Modality, Sparsity, and Essence," *The Philosophical Quarterly* 63(253), 760–782.

Williamson, Timothy. (2002), "Necessary Existents," A O'Hear, ed., *Logic, Thought and Language*, Cambridge: Cambridge University Press.

Williamson, Timothy. (2013), *Modal Logic as Metaphysics*, Oxford: Oxford University Press.

Zimmerman, Dean. (1996), "Could Extended Objects Be Made out of Simple Parts? An Argument for 'Atomless Gunk'," *Philosophy and Phenomenological Research* 56, 1–29.

Zylstra, Justin, (2019), "Constitutive and Consequentialist Essence," *Thought* 8, 190–199.

PART III

TIME, CHANGE, AND PERSISTENCE

7

Prudence and Perdurance

Kristie Miller and Caroline West

7.1 Introduction

Many nowadays are sympathetic to a view on which persisting persons, like other persisting objects, have distinct temporal as well as spatial parts, and persist by having those temporal parts located at different times. Persons, then, are collections (or sums or aggregates) of numerically distinct entities—temporal parts, or 'person-stages' as they are sometimes called—united over time by relations of causal dependence and qualitative similarity. This is the view that persons persist by perduring.[1]

Recently, there has arisen a cluster of arguments that aim to show that perdurantism is incompatible with certain obvious normative truths, and as a result should be abandoned. Many of these arguments try to show that, if true, perdurantism would lead to repugnant ethical and prudential consequences. Roughly, these arguments proceed by noting that perdurantists are committed to holding that wherever there exists a whole four-dimensional person, there also exist a plethora of shorter-lived person-like objects that are person-stages of the person (and called "subpeople" by Olson (2010), "personites" by Johnston (2017)). The claim is that these subpeople are intrinsically like people, and so have the same moral status as people. The problem is that, inevitably, subpeople will end up making sacrifices whose benefits they do not get to enjoy, since they no longer exist (Olson 2010; Taylor 2013; Johnston 2017); and will be punished for actions that occurred before they came into existence (Olson 2010; Johnston 2017).

---

[1] For defences of perdurantism see Quine (1950), Lewis (1976) and (1986), Armstrong (1980), Heller (1984) and (1990), Hudson (2001), Sider (2001), Miller (2007), Wasserman (2016), Balashov (2000) and Hales & Johnson (2003). There are other, related, views on which persons are four-dimensional but lack temporal parts (for discussion see Miller (2009b)), but we set those aside.

Kristie Miller and Caroline West, *Prudence and Perdurance* In: *Oxford Studies in Metaphysics Volume 13*. Edited by: Karen Bennett and Dean W. Zimmerman, Oxford University Press. © Kristie Miller and Caroline West 2023. DOI: 10.1093/oso/9780192886033.003.0007

This is morally and prudentially repugnant, and hence, the argument goes, we should reject perdurantism.[2]

We think such arguments are misplaced. They appear to assume that persons, conceived as we will conceive them in this chapter as four-dimensional perduring entities, are the fundamental seat of agency.[3] So, it is persons who *decide* to spend three months painstakingly learning to swim in order to reap the reward of a month swimming on the barrier reef, and it is rather unfortunate subpeople who are *forced* to spend their time learning to swim *without reaping the reward of the barrier reef trip*. Thus, on this view, agency and moral patiency come apart rather oddly: subpeople are moral patients despite not being (moral) agents.

We think this is a peculiar view to take. Persons, we think, are not the seat of agency. Persons typically have massively inconsistent beliefs, desires, and preferences. Persons typically both desire that D and not D, and believe that Q and not Q, for a large range of D and Q: they do this by having temporal parts that desire D, and others that desire not D, and temporal parts that believe Q, and others that believe not Q. Given this, it is hard to see how four-dimensional persons are an appropriate locus of reasons for action. What reasons for action could a four-dimensional person have, given their largely inconsistent beliefs and desires? Equally though, what we call person-slices (instantaneous temporal parts of a person) are too temporally thin to *deliberate*, or *act*, since each of these takes time.

So, it seems to us, it is short-lived localised clusters of deliberating temporal parts of persons—what we will call *agent-stages*—that are the locus of reasons for action. It is these agent-stages that have reasons. It is agent-stages, then, that are the fundamental seat of agency.

In turn, if there are agent-stages who decide to learn to swim they do so *on the basis of their own reasons*. They are not hapless victims, riding the wave of choices made by the person of whom they are parts.[4]

[2] For responses to these kinds of worries see Longenecker (2020a) and (2020b) and Kaiserman (2019).

[3] Exdurantism or stage-theory is the view that persons just are stages, and claims about how they were, or will be, are made true by the existence of temporal counterparts. So on such views persons are the fundamental seat of agency. But, arguably at least, arguments concerning subpeople do not arise in quite the same way within a stage-theoretic picture. In this chapter we take persons to be four-dimensional entities. But everything we say about how to think about prudence within a perdurantist framework can be adopted very naturally by stage-theorists.

[4] We do not suggest that this, alone, is sufficient to resolve the problem of subpeople, and that is not the aim of this chapter; but we do think it's an important first step.

This picture of persons, however, raises its own problems. If agent-stages are the fundamental locus of agency, then rational requirements fundamentally fall to agent-stages, not persons. The question then arises as to why such stages, that are stages of the same person, *ought* to care about one another in a distinctively prudential manner.

It is this question that we take up in this chapter. According to the normative argument against perdurantism, they have no such reason and that is why we should reject perdurantism.

We begin, in Section 7.2, by outlining the normative argument against perdurantism. In Section 7.3 we home in on the claim that we will defend in this chapter. In Section 7.4, we describe one possible approach the perdurantist could take to vindicating the axiom of prudence: the analytic approach. While we think there is something right about some of the ideas behind this approach, we argue that it fails. In Sections 7.5 and 7.6, we present several arguments which, jointly, aim to show how the perdurantist can vindicate the axiom of prudence. Finally, in Section 7.7, we consider a stronger axiom—the Strong Axiom of Prudence—and discuss how far the perdurantist can get in vindicating that axiom.

7.2 The normative argument against perdurantism

In what follows, we take prudential (or "selfish" or "egoistic") concern to be that distinctive concern we have for our own wellbeing. Prudential rationality takes the familiar consequentialist instruction to promote wellbeing, but applies it within a life rather than over distinct lives. The axiom of prudence says that a person *should promote his or her own lifetime wellbeing*. That is, a person should promote their own wellbeing over the course of their life.

Theories of prudential rationality come in different varieties. They may differ regarding whether a person should *maximise or satisfice* their own wellbeing; whether a person should *consciously aim* to maximise their own wellbeing;[5] whether a person should maximise (or satisfice) their own *objective* utility or rather their *subjective or expected* utility,[6] in what *wellbeing* consists,[7] and in whether they should promote the wellbeing of all of their selves equally, or are permitted to promote the wellbeing of some selves

---

[5] See for instance Sidgwick (1884).   [6] Slote (1989).   [7] Parfit (1984).

over others.[8] Other than where explicitly stated (later in this chapter) we aim to remain neutral on these issues.

We will take the axiom of prudence to be the claim that at any time t, a person, P, ought to promote P's wellbeing at all times. So, as a first pass we will take the perdurantist construal of the axiom to be the claim that, *necessarily*, any agent-stage, P, is rationally required to promote the wellbeing of any person-stage, P*, that is a stage of the same person as P.

Let's unpack this idea.

First, as stated, the axiom is a claim about what is necessarily the case. One could take a weaker view and think the axiom is, if true, merely contingently true: one might think that it's true of things psychologically like us, but that there are possible creatures (creatures that nevertheless count as persons) for whom it is false. Since we are going to argue that the perdurantist can vindicate the axiom of prudence, conceived as a necessary truth, everything we say will obviously also vindicate any modally weaker version of the axiom.

Second, the rational requirement here is not an all things considered requirement. An agent-stage might have other, conflicting requirements (be they moral or prudential). Rather, we take it that the axiom says that an agent-stage has a *pro tanto* reason to promote the wellbeing of all of the person-stages that are parts of the same person as it.

Third, the axiom of prudence says that we should promote lifetime wellbeing, and so far we have interpreted this as the claim that any agent-stage has a *pro tanto* reason to promote the wellbeing of *every* person-stage that is part of the same person as that agent-stage. Let's say that if P* is a person-stage of the same person as P, and if P* is later than P, then P* is a *continuer* of P's; and if P* is earlier than P, then P* is an *ancestor* of P's. More carefully, since person-stages can overlap one another, let's say that P* is a continuer of P's just in case P and P* are parts of the same person, and P* is at least *partly* later than P[9]; and P* is an ancestor of P's just in case P and P* are parts of the same person, and P* is at least *partly* earlier than P. As stated, then, the

---

[8] While most philosophers hold that near-bias (that is, more highly valuing the wellbeing of near selves over far ones simply on the basis of where those selves are located in time) is rationally impermissible (see for instance Smith (1790), Rawls (1971), and Sidgwick (1884, 380–381)), many hold that it is rationally permissible (or even obligatory) to more highly value the wellbeing of future selves over past selves (see for instance Prior (1959), Hare (2007) and (2013), and Pearson (2018))—though also see Dougherty (2011) and (2015), Greene and Sullivan (2015), Sullivan (2018), and Brink (2011) for views to the contrary.

[9] That is, at least some of P*'s parts are later than any of P's parts.

axiom of prudence says that every agent-stage should promote the wellbeing of each of its ancestors and continuers.

Insofar as one thinks of promoting wellbeing as *causally* promoting wellbeing, this should strike one as too strong a claim. Many worlds lack backwards causation, and in such cases agent-stages will be unable to causally promote the wellbeing of any (let alone all) their ancestors.

Now, on some views of wellbeing it is possible for agent-stages to promote the wellbeing of some of their ancestors in virtue of satisfying those ancestors' desires.[10] But even if one accepts this kind of view (which is in itself controversial) it will not always be possible for an agent-stage to promote the wellbeing of an ancestor: namely in cases in which that ancestor has no desires that the agent-stage in question can satisfy.

Given that agent-stages can only be rationally required to do what they can do, and given that we want to (largely) remain neutral about theories of wellbeing, we will suppose that the sense in which persons should promote their own lifetime wellbeing is the sense in which, at any time, a person should promote the wellbeing of itself at all times to which it has causal access. Thus, in worlds without backwards causation this amounts to saying that any agent-stage has a *pro tanto* reason to promote the wellbeing of all of its *continuers*. This is the version of the axiom that we will focus on, though everything we say can be applied to any ancestors an agent-stage has, whose wellbeing can be causally promoted.

Fourth, what is it to promote wellbeing? Recall that we are remaining neutral on what wellbeing consists in. Still, we want to distinguish what we might call *partial* wellbeing from *overall* wellbeing. To get a handle on this distinction let's imagine for a moment that wellbeing consists in being healthy, wealthy, wise and attractive. Then an agent-stage partially promotes wellbeing if it promotes *any* of these aspects of wellbeing. It promotes overall wellbeing if it promotes *all* of these aspects of wellbeing.[11] In what follows when we talk about promoting wellbeing we mean partially promoting wellbeing unless we say otherwise.

So, as we will interpret the axiom of prudence, it says the following:

Perdurantist Axiom of Prudence: necessarily, any agent-stage is rationally required to partially promote the wellbeing of each of its continuers.

[10] See for instance Dorsey (2018).
[11] Notice this is distinct from the question of whether one maximises (or not) overall or partial wellbeing.

A stronger axiom of prudence says the following:

Strong Perdurantist Axiom of Prudence: necessarily any agent-stage is rationally required to promote the *overall* wellbeing of each of its continuers.

We will consider the stronger version of the axiom in Section 7.7, but for the remainder of the chapter we focus only on the weaker axiom. That is because even the weaker axiom is imperilled by the normative argument against perdurantism.

To see why, notice that there are broadly two accounts of what grounds the truth of the axiom of prudence. According to Humean or instrumental views of rationality, what grounds its being true that at any time t, a person P ought to promote P's wellbeing at all times, are P's desires.[12] *Strict* views of instrumental rationality will say that it is P's actual desires, while *idealised* views of instrumental rationality will say that it is P's counterfactual desires; in particular, it is usually thought to be P's (subjectively) ideal desires—i.e., what P would want for herself for its own sake (i.e. non-instrumentally) if P were in (what P takes to be) more ideal conditions of reflection.[13] For example, suppose that, being unaware of the joys that canine companionship would bring me, I currently have no desire to acquire a pet dog. However, if I fully and accurately foresaw (both intellectually and emotionally) the delights of canine companionship, I would want to acquire a canine companion for myself. According to an idealised view of instrumental rationality, although acquiring a canine companion does not satisfy any actual desire of mine, I nevertheless have prudential reason to acquire a canine companion (and hence to form a desire to acquire one) inasmuch as under these more ideal conditions of reflection—say, where I possessed fuller knowledge of the joys of canine companionship—I would desire this for myself.[14]

By contrast, according to non-Humean/non-instrumental views of rationality there exist *sui generis prudential reasons*: reasons that are not

---

[12] More carefully, the ultimate grounds will be P's non-instrumental desires.

[13] For defences of Humeanism about instrumental reason see Schroeder (2007), Markovits (2014), Williams (1981), and Lin (2015).

[14] The view we have in mind is one on which not only can the idealisation process change which instrumental desires one has, as one might think is occurring in the case of the canine companion (where I non-instrumentally desire to be, say, happy, and a canine companion would satisfy this desire); but it can also change one's non-instrumental desires. That is, under conditions I take to be better, I would have diffeerent non-instrumental desires.

moral reasons, nor reasons arising from P's (actual or ideal) desires, and these ground the truth of the axiom of prudence.[15]

Many philosophers have thought that instrumental rationality, in either its strict or its idealised versions, cannot ground the truth of the axiom of prudence, because there are possible agent-stages who have a pattern of desires which fails to make it true that they should promote the wellbeing of all of their continuers.

Consider an agent-stage of Jeremy at age 13. One can imagine that this stage, Jeremy-at-13, has a pattern of desires that do not ground his having reason to promote the wellbeing of a person-stage of Jeremy at 89. We can imagine that Jeremy-at-13 simply does not care what happens to him in old age. So, Jeremy-at-13's actual desires do not ground his having reason to promote the wellbeing of Jeremy-at-89. Likewise, we seem able to imagine that Jeremy-at-13 is such that even his subjectively idealised desires are such that they fail to give him reason to promote the wellbeing of Jeremy-at-89. In that case, if there are only instrumental reasons it follows that Jeremy-at-13 *has* no reason to promote the wellbeing of Jeremy-at-89 and hence that the axiom of prudence is false.[16]

This has prompted many to conclude that the axiom of prudence must be grounded in *sui generis* prudential reasons. This has been taken to present special problems for the perdurantist. For, the thought goes, the only thing that could ground there being such *sui generis* prudential reasons is numerical identity. The reason why P at t should care about P at all future times in this distinctively prudential manner—and should do so regardless of P's own desires—is that P at t is numerically identical with P at each of these times. P should care about *itself*, and so the obtaining of numerical identity over time grounds the obtaining of *sui generis* prudential reasons.

By contrast, non-identity relations do not seem able to ground there being such reasons. For the sorts of non-identity relations that obtain between P at one time and P at another time are similar to those that obtain between P at one time and Q at some other time. Yet we do not want to say that P has *prudential* reason to care about Q. The problem facing perdurantism, then, is that because the view renders the connection between stages of the *same* person as similar in kind to the connection between stages of *different* persons, it undermines there being any *sui generis* prudential reasons. Here is Sidgwick back in 1884:

[15] For defences of this view see Parfit (1984), Sullivan (2018), and Fletcher (2021).
[16] See for instance Parfit (1984) and Fletcher (2021).

Grant that the Ego is merely a system of coherent phenomena, that the permanent identical 'I' is not a fact but a fiction, as Hume and his followers maintain; why, then, should one part of the series of feelings into which the Ego is resolved be concerned with another part of the same series, any more than with any other series?   (418–419).[17]

Schechtman expresses similar sentiments when she notes that self-interested concern is an emotion that is appropriately felt only towards *my own self and not towards someone like me* (Schechtman 1996, 52).[18] She notes that it "doesn't matter if the person who gets my paycheck is more *like* me than someone else; I am only compensated if *I* get the money" (Schechtman 1996, 52–53).[19, 20]

So, the problem for perdurantists who, like us, take agent-stages (rather than whole four-dimensional persons) to be the fundamental locus of agency, is that it is not possible to appeal to numerical identity to ground there being *sui generis* prudential reasons, since the agent-stages of persons are numerically distinct from one another. But, as we noted earlier, it is these

---

[17] Though in fact Sidgwick (1884, 418) thinks a similar problem arises even if persons endure.

[18] Sentiments such as this go back at least as far as Butler (1784).

[19] Rather ironically, the idea that persons perdure has been used to argue that liberals can legitimately intervene in cases otherwise conceived of as self-harm (and hence falling under the banner of 'autonomy') precisely because the relelvant future selves that bear the harm are numerically distinct from the self perpetuating the harm. See for instance Kleinig (1983) and (2009), Reagan (1983), Kogan (1976), and Carter (2018).

[20] The claim that persons do not have these kinds of *sui generis* prudential reasons to promote the welfare of other person-stages is often known as the extreme claim. See Parfit (1984, 307) for discussion. That claim is often marshalled not against perdurantist views of persistence, but more broadly against reductionist views of personal identity (views on which personal identity reduces to the obtaining of certain mental and physical properties of person-stages, and the relations between said stages). See for instance Parfit (1984); Schechtman (1996), (2005), (2014); and Butler (1784). The dialectic here is a little murky. Sometimes these kinds of objections to reductionist views seem to simply suppose that reductionists must in fact be committed to something like perdurantism, on the grounds that the continuity relations that reductionists appeal to clearly are not identity relations. Certainly, there are those who argue that endurantists cannot endorse reductionism precisely because identity does not reduce to, or consist in, the obtaining of these other relations (see for instance Merricks (1999)). On the other hand, some reductionists clearly do seem to think that their view is consistent with strict identity over time (at least as long as the account includes a non-branching rquirement), and take themselves to be giving an account of what that identity consists in (see for instance Parfit (1984)). But if numerical identity over time in some sense consists in the obtaining of these kinds of continuity relations, then it's unclear why reductionists have any more of a problem than non-reductionists in explaining what grounds prudential rationality. At any rate, we are interested in this argument as it pertains to perdurantism, rather than as it pertains to reductionist views in general.

agent-stages that are the fundamental locus of agency, and hence of rational requirement, even if persons themselves are four-dimensional objects.

Thus, the perdurantist is faced with the normative argument against perdurantism.[21] That argument proceeds as follows. The axiom of prudence is true. But the axiom can be true only if P at one time has *sui generis* prudential reasons to promote the wellbeing of P at future times. That is because mere instrumental reasons cannot ground the truth of the axiom of prudence. P at one time, however, can only have *sui generis* prudential reasons to promote the wellbeing of P at any future time if P at t is numerically identical with P at each of those future times. But, according to perdurantism, P at t is numerically distinct from P at each of these times. Hence, perdurantism is incompatible with the truth of the axiom of prudence, and since the axiom is true, perdurantism is false.

In fact, we do not endorse the idea that *sui generis* prudential reasons must be grounded by numerical identity. Hence, we do not accept that the perdurantist cannot appeal to such reasons.[22] In this chapter, however, we are primarily interested in showing that the perdurantist axiom of prudence can be vindicated by appealing only to instrumental reasons.

7.3 Prudence and Humeanism

We will say that P has a *strict instrumental reason* to promote the wellbeing of P* iff (a) P and P* are temporal parts of the same person and (b) promoting the wellbeing of P* is a way to satisfy P's actual desires. Another way to put this is to say that P has an instrumental reason to promote the wellbeing of P* iff (i) P and P* are temporal parts of the same person and (ii) the combination of P's total set of non-instrumental desires, what is logically and instrumentally entailed by those desires, and the non-normative facts grounds P having a reason to promote P*'s wellbeing.

We will say that P has an *idealised instrumental reason* to promote the wellbeing of P* iff (a) P and P* are parts of the same person and (b) promoting

---

[21] Something *like* this argument has been offered by, *inter alia*, Schechtman (1996), Butler (1784), and Wolf (1986, 719); and perhaps underlies some of Korsgaard's comments in Korsgaard (1989, 113–114). It has motivated some to suggest that while in general objects perdure, persons are special and persist in some other manner. See, for instance, Miller (2010).

[22] Indeed, whether numerical identity over time really is sufficient to ground *sui generis* prudential reasons is open to debate. Whiting (1986), Beck (2013), Sidgwick (1884, 418), and Miller (forthcoming) do not think so.

the wellbeing of P* is a way to satisfy P's subjectively idealised desires. Another way to put this is to say that P has an instrumental reason to promote the wellbeing of P*, iff P and P* are temporal parts of the same person, and P's total set of subjectively idealised non-instrumental desires, and what is logically and instrumentally entailed by those desires in combination with the non-normative facts, ground P's having a reason to promote P*'s wellbeing.

Then we will say that P has an instrumental reason to promote the wellbeing of P* iff P has either a strict or an idealised instrumental reason to do so.

So, for instance, in the most obvious case, P has an instrumental reason to promote the wellbeing of its continuers when P has a desire (instrumental or otherwise) to do so. But it need not be that P's reasons to promote the wellbeing of some particular person-stage, P*, issue from P's desiring to promote P*'s wellbeing. It could be that P has other desires whose satisfaction gives P instrumental reason to promote P*'s wellbeing.

The problem with grounding the perdurantist axiom of prudence in instrumental reasons is that it seems obvious that there are possible agent-stages, P and P*, such P* is P's continuer, and yet P's desires provide P with no reason to promote P*'s wellbeing. This is what we call the Possibility Claim:

Possibility Claim: It is (metaphysically) possible that there are agent-stages P and P* such that P* is P's continuer, and promoting P*'s wellbeing is not a way to satisfy P's actual/subjectively idealised desires.

The Possibility Claim seems very plausible. If it's true, though, the truth of the axiom of prudence cannot be grounded in instrumental reasons, and hence if those are the only reasons to which the perdurantist can appeal, it follows that if the axiom is true, then perdurantism is at the very least actually false (and with not much argument one might try to show that it is necessarily false).

In fact, you might even think that a much weaker claim is also true. Call this the Psychological Claim.

Psychological Claim: It is psychologically possible that there are agent-stages P and P*, that that P* is P's continuer, and promoting P*'s wellbeing is not a way to satisfy P's actual/subjectively idealised desires.

If the Psychological Claim is true then the perdurantist cannot even retreat to a weaker reading of the axiom of prudence on which it is, if true, psychologically necessary (say).

In what follows we focus on the Possibility Claim, since we are interested in the more modally robust version of the axiom.

We want to distinguish two possibilities, each of which would render the Possibility Claim true. We distinguish these because different resources need to be brought to bear to show why neither is in fact possible. To do so, we introduce the idea of an *adjacent agent-stage*.

Consider an agent-stage, P, which exists throughout a short temporal interval T, where T is composed of instants T_1 to T_{10}. P^* is an agent-stage that exists throughout the interval composed of T_{11} to T_{21}. Call P^*, P's *adjacent agent-stage continuer*. P^* is, at it were, the 'very next' agent-stage continuer of P's which does not overlap any of P itself.[23]

Then the Possibility claim will be true if it is possible that there is an agent-stage that has an adjacent agent-stage continuer such that that stage's desires do not provide it with reason to promote the wellbeing of that adjacent continuer. We will call this the Adjacent-Stage Possibility Claim.

Adjacent-Stage Possibility Claim: it is possible that there is an agent-stage P, such that P^* is P's adjacent continuer, and P's actual/idealised desires do not provide P with any reason to promote the wellbeing of P^*.

The Possibility claim will also be true if it is possible that there is an agent-stage that has a continuer that is more temporally distant than an adjacent continuer, and where that stage's desires do not provide it with a reason to promote the wellbeing of that more temporally distant stage.

Non-Adjacent-Stage Possibility Claim: it is possible that there is an agent-stage P, such that (i) P^* is P's continuer, (ii) P^* does not overlap P's adjacent continuer, and (iii) P's actual/idealised desires do not provide P with any reason to promote the wellbeing of P^*.

Non-adjacent agent-stages, then, are continuer stages that are entirely distinct from adjacent agent-stages (i.e., they do not overlap adjacent agent-stages). Some such stages might be relatively temporally near to the agent-stage in question, while others might be temporally quite far (as when we consider a particular agent-stage of Jeremy at 13, and another of Jeremy at 89).

---

[23] Where time and personal time come apart, continuers and adjacent continuers (etc.) shoud be defined in terms of personal-time, not time itself. We leave these complications aside.

Our aim will be first to show that the Adjacent-Stage Possibility claim is false, and, from there, to show that the Non-Adjacent-Stage Possibility Claim is false. First, however, we turn to consider a view that promises to straightforwardly show that the Possibility Claim is false. Ultimately, we will argue that this view fails—or, at least, that the version that succeeds may not be very attractive. But we think that some of the lessons learned here will be useful later when we come to present our own arguments against the Possibility Claim.

7.4 The analytic approach

According to one view of persons, person-stages count as stages of a persisting person only insofar as they desire to promote the wellbeing of the person of which they are stages. Very roughly, on such views it is partly *constitutive* of P*'s being a continuer or ancestor of P's, that P directs certain attitudes towards P*: in particular, that P directs attitudes of prudential concern towards P* (that is, P desires to promote P*'s wellbeing). Thus, on this view it is analytic that P and P* are agent-stages of the same person if and only if P and P* desire to promote each other's wellbeing in a distinctively prudential sort of way. So, on this view, it is constitutive of P*'s being a continuer or ancestor of P that P has the right sorts of desires to ground P's having reason to promote P*'s wellbeing, and hence the Possibility Claim is false.

Whiting (1986) defends a view like this. More generally, *conventionalists*[24] about personal identity hold that the personal-identity relation—that is, the relation that obtains between person-stages that are stages of the same person—is in part determined by the obtaining of certain kinds of attitudes of prudential concern between the stages in question.

We are broadly sympathetic to *something* like this view. But there is a worry that a version of conventionalism that can resist the Possibility Claim in this manner is not very plausible. For it will turn out that if person-stage P does *not* care prudentially about P*, then regardless of which other relations obtain between P and P*, P* is not an ancestor or a continuer of P*.

---

[24] Views of this kind have been defended by Kovacs (2016), (2020); Zimmerman (2012); Johnston (2010, 5); and Whiting (1986). They are sometimes known as conventionalist (see Kovacs (2016) and (2020), Braddon-Mitchell and Miller (2004), Miller (2009a), Longenecker (2022), and Schechtman (2014)) or conativist (see Braddon-Mitchell and Miller (2020a), (2020b)) or practice-dependent (see Braddon-Mitchell and West (2001), and West (1996)).

So, if an agent-stage of 13-year-old Jeremy does not care, prudentially, about an agent-stage of 89-year-old Jeremy, then it just turns out that the latter is not a continuer of the former. There are 'two Jeremys', one who begins life as a child and ceases to exist before old age, and another who comes into existence later in life and lives to be old. But, you might think, this is not overly plausible. That is why many versions of conventionalism appeal to attitudes of prudential care in a more subtle manner than this.

For instance, some versions of conventionalism hold that what determines which continuers are P's are the overlapping chains of (*inter alia*) attitudes of self-concern emanating from P. On this kind of view, it is constitutive of P* being an adjacent agent-stage continuer of P's that P direct certain sorts of prudential attitudes towards P*. So, this kind of view is one on which the Adjacent-Stage Possibility Claim is false. Necessarily, if P* is an adjacent agent-stage continuer of P's, then P is rationally required to promote the wellbeing of P*. What this view does not seem able to do (at least by appealing directly to these attitudes) is to make false the Non-Adjacent-Stage Possibility Claim. For we can stipulate that there are such chains connecting an agent-stage of Jeremy at 13 with an agent-stage of Jeremy at 89. Then, according to this view, these two agent-stages are stages of the same person. Yet the former stage does not care prudentially about the latter. So if it is just the presence of these attitudes that grounds the truth of the axiom of prudence, then the axiom is false.

Perhaps a version of this view could appeal to the idealised desires of agent-stages, rather than just their actual attitudes, in order to resist the Non-Adjacent-Stage Possibility Claim. For now, we simply note that, on its face, this version of conventionalism will not do.

Still other versions of conventionalism hold that what matters is not to which *particular* stages P directs its attitudes of prudential concern; but, rather, around which relation P 'organises' those attitudes.[25] If, for instance, P *typically* directs prudential concern only towards stages with which P is psychologically continuous, then all and only stages that are psychologically continuous with P are its ancestors or continuers.

This view, however, is one that leaves us with no obvious way to resist either the Adjacent-Stage or Non-Adjacent-Stage Possibility Claims. To see this, suppose that P organises its practices around the relation of psychological continuity. If this is so then, for the most part, P cares prudentially

---

[25] See for instance Braddon-Mitchell and West (2001), Braddon-Mitchell and Miller (2020a) and (2020b), and Miller (2009a).

about stages that are connected to P via psychological continuity. Still, this does not entail that P cares prudentially about *all* such stages. It is consistent with the view that there are both adjacent and non-adjacent stages that P does not prudentially care about. Then P's actual attitudes of prudential concern do not ground its being rationally required for P to promote the wellbeing of these stages, be they adjacent or non-adjacent.

The general problem here is that the more plausible the version of conventionalism as an account of personal identity, the more likely it is that there are possible cases in which P* counts as being a continuer of P's, and yet P has (actual) prudential attitudes that do not ground P's having a reason to promote P*'s wellbeing.

In what follows we begin by trying to show that the Adjacent-Stage Possibility Claim is false. We will then use this to argue that the Non-Adjacent-Stage Possibility Claim is false.

7.5 Against the Adjacent-Stage Possibility Claim

In what follows we present two arguments against the Adjacent-Stage Possibility Claim. The first of these is inspired by the conventionalist idea that it is constitutive of P*'s being an adjacent continuer of P's that P has certain desires, which ground P's having reason to promote P*'s wellbeing.

Here is the idea. We take it to be uncontroversial that, necessarily, an agent-stage has instrumental reason to promote the wellbeing of agent-stages that satisfy that stage's actual desires. Call the stage that satisfies an agent-stage's desire the *desire-satisfying stage*. So, where P* satisfies P's desire, P has reason to promote P*'s wellbeing. (Remember that we are talking here only about the promotion of wellbeing, not the promotion of *overall* wellbeing. It may be that the fact that P* satisfies that desire does not give P a reason to promote P*'s overall wellbeing, for perhaps there are aspects of P*'s wellbeing that are irrelevant to its capacity to satisfy that desire. We return to think about overall wellbeing in Section 7.7).

We will argue that necessarily, for any agent-stage, if that agent-stage has an adjacent agent-stage then that adjacent-stage continuer satisfies at least some of its desires. If this is true, then it entails that the Adjacent-Stage Possibility Claim is false.

Why think that, necessarily, for any agent-stage, if that agent-stage has an adjacent agent-stage continuer then that adjacent-stage continuer satisfies at least some of its desires? The truth of this claim hinges on a further claim about what it is to be an agent-stage. Here is where the idea is loosely inspired by conventionalist views of personal-identity. We think it is *constitutive* of being an agent-stage that agent-stages have *future-directed desires*. We will say that an agent-stage P has a future-directed *desire* just in case P has a desire that can only be satisfied by some continuer of P's.[26]

Something that lacked these would, we say, fail to be an agent-stage. Agent-stages are, of necessity, things that deliberate, intend, and act. As such, they will, of necessity, have future-directed desires. Moreover, we think it is necessary that at least some of an agent-stage's future directed desires are satisfied by their adjacent agent-stages.

Now, you might think that there are possible agent-stages whose only future-directed desires are ones that are satisfied by more distant (non-adjacent) agent-stages. We don't think that such agent-stages are possible. To be sure, an agent-stage can have a single non-instrumental desire, such as the desire to play a symphony in 10 years' time. And that non-instrumental desire can be satisfied only by a non-adjacent stage. But that desire must give rise to a host of instrumental desires, and those instrumental desires will be such that at least some of them are satisfied by adjacent agent-stages. For in order to have desires about how things go at later times, an agent-stage must have at least *some* desires for how things go at temporally near times. For instance, suppose that a current agent-stage only non-instrumentally cares about performing a piano symphony at the royal gala in three years' time. She has no non-instrumental desires about what happens in the interim. Still, we say, she must have *some* instrumental desires about what happens in the interim: she must at the very least desire to *survive* during the intervening period, which entails having desires to eat, move, and so on. And at least some of those desires are ones that can only be satisfied by an adjacent stage (for instance, the adjacent agent-stage must survive if later ones are to survive).

Now, perhaps as stated this is not quite right. Suppose that an agent-stage falsely believes that it will not persist beyond two hours' time. Now consider the agent-stage that exists just prior to the moment when it *believes* death will come. Perhaps that agent-stage has no forward-looking non-instrumental desires, and hence no desires that could ground its having reason to promote the wellbeing of its adjacent agent-stage continuer.

The tempting thing to say here is that the agent-stage in question nevertheless has *conditional* desires: were it to believe that it will survive (as in fact

---

[26] For discussion of desires such as these see Brink (1997), Perry (1976), and Hurley (1989).

it will), it *would have* various desires that would ground it having such reasons. (In particular, one might think that it's the desires that an agent-stage would have, if it had true beliefs, that are relevant here). One might worry, though, that appealing to conditional desires takes us away from a view on which it is our actual desires that ground our instrumental desires. After all, conditional desires are just the desires we *would* have, if we had different beliefs. So it's worth noting that in appealing to conditional desires, the resulting view comes a little closer to the view that it is our idealised non-instrumental desires that ground our instrumental reasons. Having said that, it's still the way the agent-stage is that grounds her having the reasons she does: after all, she really is such that she is disposed to have that desire, conditional on believing that she will live past two hours.

To put the point in a somewhat different way, most accounts of personal identity are ones on which certain kinds of causal connections between person-stages are necessary for those stages to be parts of the same person.[27] So, part of what makes it the case that agent-stage P* is the (future) adjacent continuer of agent-stage P, is that P's desires are causally efficacious in bringing about P*'s actions. For instance, part of what makes it the case that P* is P's adjacent continuer is that P's tiredness, and desires to sit, causes it to be the case that P* sits down and takes a rest.[28] On this picture, the fact that P* satisfies P's desires is (in part) what makes it the case that P* is P's adjacent continuer. So, we say, it is of the nature of agent-stages that they have future-directed desires, and, in part, what makes it the case that P* is an adjacent continuer of P is that (some of) P's immediate desires are satisfied by P*.

In turn, it follows that, necessarily, for any agent-stage P, P will have some desires that are satisfied (and can only be satisfied by) P's adjacent continuer. These desires, in turn, ground its being the case that, necessarily, P has reason to promote the wellbeing of its adjacent continuer. Hence the Adjacent-Stage Possibility Claim is false.

That is our first argument against the Adjacent-Stage Possibility Claim. Here is our second. So far, we have only appealed to the actual desires of agent-stages. In what follows we move to appealing to their subjectively idealised desires. Here is the idea. We'll begin by introducing the *principle of reflection for desires*. That principle is analogous to an amended version of

---

[27] Though see Duncan and Miller (2015) who defend the view that mere similarity might do the trick.
[28] Thanks to Antony Eagle for this suggestion.

the principle of reflection for beliefs, first introduced by van Fraassen (1984). Reflection for beliefs says that you should defer to the beliefs that you anticipate having in the future: that is, if you're going to come to believe Q (or have credence z in Q) then you should believe that Q (or have credence z in Q) now. (Importantly, Q is a proposition, and hence is taken to be fully specific. So, if at t Jeremy believes that it is raining, then what Jeremy believes is that *it is raining at t*. This matters; if the content of Jeremy's belief, at t, were simply *it is raining* then it needn't automatically be rational for Jeremy, at some earlier time, to believe *that* proposition. After all, at the earlier time it may not be raining. So, belief reflection is the claim that if Jeremy now believes that he will believe *that it is raining at t,* then he should, now, believe *that it is raining at t.* Modified versions of reflection for belief say that you should defer to the beliefs that you anticipate having in the future, unless you believe that in the future you will be irrational or will have lost evidence. Modified versions of belief reflection are widely endorsed, because agents for whom (modified) belief reflection is false can be turned into money pumps.[29]

Similar considerations motivate modified desire reflection.[30] Modified desire reflection says that you should defer to the desires that you anticipate having in the future. That is:

Modified Reflection for Desires: If you believe, or anticipate, that you will come to desire Q, then you should desire that Q now, as long as you do not anticipate that in the future you will be irrational or will have lost evidence.[31]

(Again, it's important here that Q is a maximally specific proposition. Consider Jeremy again. Suppose he's just eaten a huge breakfast and is completely full, but he believes that by noon he will desire smashed avocado on toast. Clearly Jeremy does not, now, have reason to desire the smashed avocado on toast (given that he is full). Rather, modified desire reflection says that, given that Jeremy believes he will desire smashed avocado on toast at noon, he should now desire smashed avocado on toast at noon).

---

[29] See Van Fraassen (1984).   [30] See Arntzenius (2008).

[31] Following Harman (2009) an even weaker version of reflection for desires which appeals to what one *reasonably* believes, and to what one's future self's *reasonable* desires are, yields the following:

Reflection for Desires: If P reasonably believes that P's future self will reasonably prefer that x be true, and if P reasonably believes that P's future self will not be in a worse epistemic or evaluative position at that time, then P should now prefer that x be true.

Agents for whom modified desire reflection is false can be turned into money pumps. Suppose that Freddie's default dinner meal is beef. Now suppose that as of today (Monday) Freddie would prefer kangaroo to beef for dinner in two days' time (Wednesday). Suppose he thinks it is worth $1.00 to make sure that he gets the kangaroo, not the beef on Wednesday. Now suppose Freddie also believes that tomorrow, he will prefer that on Wednesday he will have beef rather than kangaroo. Tomorrow, he will pay $1.00 to get the beef, not the roo on Wednesday. Then Freddie can end up paying $2.00 to gain nothing.

Modified Reflection for Desires talks about what *you* believe or anticipate that *you* will come to desire. Since we are taking agent-stages to be the fundamental locus of agency, it's perhaps not true that an agent-stage believes that, or anticipates that, *it* will have certain desires, since it may not be around to have those desires. Nevertheless, since surely agent-stages do anticipate things being thus and so even after they have ceased to exist, we can amend reflection for desires to say the following:

New Modified Reflection for Desires: If agent-stage P anticipates[32] pre-ferring that x be true, then P should now prefer that x be true as long as P does not think that this preference will be the product of irrationality or lost evidence.

Of course, modified reflection for desires is controversial.[33] And, you might think, it's not a principle that any instrumentalist about rationality is likely to endorse, at least as a fully general claim about what agent-stages should prefer. For if we are instrumentalists about rationality then the only grounds for the truth of such a principle will be agent-stages' actual or idealised desires. And perhaps some agent-stages have actual or idealised desires that fail to give them a reason to accept reflection for desires.

Certainly, we think that an appeal only to the actual desires of agent-stages cannot ground all agent-stages' having reason to accept reflection for desires. Nor can we hope to completely convince you that the idealised desires of any possible agent-stage will ground the truth of that principle for that agent-stage. In fact, though, we think that insofar as the principle is plausible at all, it's plausible for all possible agent-stages.

---

[32] Or, if you prefer, reasonably anticipates reasonably desiring.
[33] See for instance Harman (2009), who denies it.

One might initially think that only agent-stages who care about becoming money pumps will have reason to accept reflection for desires, and that some agent-stages won't care about this. But, arguably at least, agents for whom desire reflection is false can be turned into pumps for *whatever it is that they do care about*. Suppose that Freddie has three non-instrumental desires: a desire for roo, beef, and running. Suppose that as of today (Monday) Freddie would prefer kangaroo to beef for dinner in two days' time (Wednesday). Then it is not so implausible to think that there is *something* that is valuable to Freddie (even if only a very small amount of that thing) that he will trade to make this so. Suppose that Freddie is willing to trade 50 seconds of running to bring it about that he gets the kangaroo, not the beef, on Wednesday. Now suppose Freddie also believes that tomorrow, he will prefer that on Wednesday he will have beef rather than kangaroo. Tomorrow, he will trade 50 seconds of running to get the beef not the roo on Wednesday. Then Freddie can end up having forgone 100 seconds of running to be no better off at all. Overall, he will be worse off with regard to satisfying his desires, since he desires to run.

As long as there is something of value that Freddie is prepared to trade in order to bring about his preference, he can be turned into a pump for that thing (in this case running). Since Freddie values the thing he trades, he surely will have idealised desires not to be pumped of that thing, and hence his idealised desires will ground his having reason to accept reflection for desires. What is true of Freddie is true for us all.[34]

So, suppose that reflection for desires is true. Then consider P, and P's adjacent continuer, P*. Let's stipulate that P* desires its own wellbeing. We will return to this stipulation shortly. Then New Modified Reflection for Desires says that insofar as P anticipates having these desires—or anticipates preferring that things are thus and so—then P ought, now, to have those desires/preferences. For now, let's make another supposition: that P *does* anticipate having the desires/preferences in question. Then it follows by New Modified Reflection for Desires that P *ought* to have certain desires, now, regarding how things are for P*. The idealised instrumentalist about rationality can then say that it is the desires that P ought to have which ground P's having reason to promote P*'s wellbeing.

---

[34] If you think there are possible agent-stages whose even idealised desires will not be such that they care about lost evidence, or irrationality, then those aspects of the principle could be jettisoned for our purposes.

So, if New Modified Reflection for Desires is true for all agent-stages, then it follows that, necessarily, for any agent-stage P and adjacent stage P*, if P* desires its own wellbeing, and if P anticipates having (certain of) P*'s desires/preferences, then P has a reason to promote P*'s wellbeing.

This is all well and good. But it only follows that the Adjacent Possibility Claim is false if it's both the case that: (a) necessarily, for any agent-stage P and adjacent agent-stage P*, P anticipates having (certain of) P*'s desires/preferences; and (b) necessarily, any agent-stage P* desires its own wellbeing. But these are both surely very controversial claims. Let's start with (a). We will argue that (a) is true.

Everything we have said so far can be used to argue for the claim that, necessarily, for any agent-stage P and adjacent agent-stage P*, P anticipates having (certain of) P*'s desires/preferences. We've already argued for a view on which P* is an adjacent agent-stage continuer of P's in part because P* fulfils/carries through P's immediate desires and intentions. Part of what it is for P to have those immediate desires and intentions is to anticipate their satisfaction/fulfilment. It's hard to see what sense can be made of the idea of P intending to, say, sit down, without its also being the case that P *anticipates* sitting down. And perhaps it's also hard to see what can be made of the idea of P having an immediate desire to sit down, without its being the case that P anticipates sitting down. So, we think it plausible that it is constitutive of P*'s being P's adjacent agent-stage continuer that P anticipates at least some of P*'s experiences, desires, and preferences.

But what of (b), the claim that, necessarily, any agent-stage P* desires its own wellbeing? That claim, one might think, is surely false. And if an agent-stage has reason to promote a continuer stage's wellbeing only conditional on that continuer itself's desiring to do so, then sometimes agent-stages won't have such reason (at least, not arising from reflection).

Now, the perdurantist might, at this stage, say that she was concerned to show that there is no particular *diachronic* problem of prudence arising from endorsing perdurantism. She might point out that if we endorse reflection, then it follows that insofar as the person-stages of a person are each concerned with their *own* wellbeing, they thereby have reason to be concerned with *one another's* wellbeing. And this would still, we think, reflect significant inroads here.

Nevertheless, the axiom of prudence does not merely say that a person-stage has reason to promote the wellbeing of its continuer stages conditional on those stages' desiring their own wellbeing. So the question arises whether the perdurantist can do better here. We think she can, but only if she no longer remains neutral regarding a theory of wellbeing.

Suppose the perdurantist were to adopt a desire-satisfaction theory of wellbeing, according to which wellbeing consists in the satisfaction of desires.[35] Now, to be clear, we are not going to defend this view of wellbeing here. Rather, our aim is just to show that if one endorses such a view, then one can show that necessarily, any agent-stage P* desires its own wellbeing. Moreover, insofar as the desire-fulfilment theory has a claim to be "the dominant view of welfare among economists, social-scientists and philosophers, both utilitarian and non-utilitarian,"[36] this argument may have wide appeal.

How does the satisfaction of desires contribute to wellbeing, and to whose wellbeing does it contribute? Well, suppose that the *time-of-desiring* is the time at which a desire is held. Suppose the *time-of-satisfaction* is the time at which a desire is satisfied. Suppose the *time-of-wellbeing* is the time at which a person-stage is made better or worse off by the desire's being satisfied.

According to *concurrentism* a desire is not satisfied when the time-of-desiring and the time-of-satisfaction come apart and so no wellbeing accrues. According to the *time-of-satisfaction view*, the person-stage who benefits from a desire's being satisfied is the person-stage that exists at the time-of-satisfaction. So on this view, if P1 desires to sit down and it is P2 who sits, then it is P2 whose wellbeing is promoted. Finally, on the *time-of-desiring view*, the person-stage who benefits from the desire being satisfied is the person-stage whose desire it is that is satisfied.[37] So on this view, since it is P1 who desires to sit, and P2 who satisfies this desire, it is P1 whose wellbeing is promoted.

Suppose one endorses the time-of-desiring view. Now suppose that P* is P's adjacent continuer, that P* has a bunch of desires, and that satisfying those desires constitutes promoting P*'s wellbeing. Consider one such desire, D. According to reflection, P should desire D. Now, it is likely that P cannot itself satisfy D (assuming that D is a future-directed desire of P*'s, and not a past-directed one). Still, even if D is a future-directed desire of P*'s, P can promote the satisfaction of D. P can act, and plan, in such a way that the satisfaction of P is more, or less, likely. And since P desires D, P clearly has reason to promote the satisfaction of D. But notice that promoting the satisfaction of D just is promoting P*'s wellbeing, since

[35] See Harsanyi (1977), von Wright (1963), Barry (1965), Brandt (1966), Ramsey (1926), Singer (1979), and Hare (1981).
[36] Shaw (1999, 53).   [37] Dorsey (2013) endorses this view.

satisfying D just is (partially) promoting P*'s wellbeing according to the desire-satisfaction theory.

Putting all this together, then, necessarily, P* is P's adjacent agent-stage continuer only if P anticipates at least some of P*'s experiences, desires, and preferences. P's desires, whatever they are, ground P's having reason to endorse modified desire reflection. So, if P anticipates at least some of P*'s experiences, desires, and preferences, then P ought, now, to have those desires (by desire reflection). If P ought, now, to have those desires, then this is to say that P subjectively ideally has those desires. P's subjectively ideally having those desires amounts to P's subjectively ideally desiring that P*'s desires are satisfied (since P's subjectively idealised desires just are P*'s desires, and P of course desires that its own desires are satisfied). This gives P reason to promote the satisfaction of those desires. But by promoting the satisfaction of those desires, P just is promoting P*'s wellbeing, since P*'s wellbeing just consists in its desires being satisfied. So, necessarily, if P* is P's adjacent continuer, then P has a reason to promote P*'s wellbeing.

Thus, we have provided two arguments for the conclusion that the Adjacent-Stage Possibility Claim is false.

To be clear, we don't think these arguments are unassailable. One might deny that reflection for desires is true. Or one might think it's true for most agents, but that there are at least *possible* agents whose desires do not ground that principle's truth. One might deny that, necessarily, agent-stages anticipate (at least some) of the desires/experiences of their adjacent agent-stages. Or you might deny that desire-satisfaction theories are the right accounts of wellbeing. We think these claims are plausible, but others may not.

If you deny one or more of the above claims then it will not be possible to vindicate the perdurantist axiom of prudence by appealing only to instrumental reason. Still, the perdurantist who takes this route might argue that, although there are possible agent-stages for whom reflection is false, or possible agent-stages that do not anticipate any of the experiences/desires of their adjacent continuer; nevertheless, such agent-stages will be psychologically *very* different indeed from you and me. The perdurantist might then take the view that although the axiom of prudence is not a necessary truth, it is nevertheless true of all persons/agents that are anything at all like you and me: it is at least psychologically necessary. So, she might say, she can vindicate a modally weaker version of the axiom of prudence and, she might try to argue, that is sufficient. Indeed, she might suggest that it is unclear whether agent-stages that are so radically different from you and me really do have a *pro tanto* reason to promote the wellbeing of their continuers.

This is not the view we take. In what follows, we will proceed on the assumption that the Adjacent-Stage Possibility Claim is false, and use that to argue for the falsity of the Non-Adjacent Possibility Claim.

7.6 The Non-Adjacent-Stage Possibility Claim

Let's suppose that P1 through P4 are agent-stages of the same person, and that P2 is the adjacent continuer of P1, and P3 is the adjacent continuer of P2, and so on. If the Adjacent-Stage Possibility claim is false, it follows that P1 has a reason to promote the wellbeing of P2, and P2 has a reason to promote the wellbeing of P3, and P3 has a reason to promote the wellbeing of P4. But, of course, it does not follow from this that P1 has a reason to promote the wellbeing of P3 or P4.

In what follows we offer two arguments that aim to show that if the Adjacent-Stage Possibility Claim is false, then so too is the Non-Adjacent-Stage Possibility Claim: if P1 has reason to promote P2's wellbeing, and P2 has reason to promote P3's wellbeing, then P1 has reason to promote P3's wellbeing (and so on).

Here is the first such argument.

Recall part of the story we previously told: the reason why P1 has reason to promote P2's wellbeing is that P1 anticipates at least some of P2's experiences and desires because, necessarily, any agent-stage anticipates at least some of its adjacent continuer's experiences and desires. Given this, we know that P2 anticipates at least some of P3's experiences and desires. Let's take the limiting case of anticipation, in which P1 simply anticipates "being in P2's position" in the sense of anticipating all of P2's experiences and desires. Suppose P2 is similarly related to P3 (and so on down the line). Then we could say that P1 anticipates being P2, and that P2 anticipates being P3. Now suppose we put P1 in an epistemic position in which P1 knows these facts. What desires can we expect P1 to form? Well, P1 will surely desire *not* to *anticipate anticipating* unpleasant events. That is, P1 has subjectively idealised desires not only that things go well for P2, but also that things are such that P2 anticipates things going well for P3. That is, P has subject-ively idealised desires not to anticipate anticipating unpleasant events. That being so, P1 has subjectively idealised desires that ground its having reason to promote P3's wellbeing. And, *mutatis mutandis*, for P4.

Suppose, though, that P1 does not anticipate *all* P2's experiences/desires, and likewise for P2 with respect to P3. Then it might be that although P1 anticipates certain of P2's experiences/desires, and P2 anticipates certain of P3's experiences/desires, P1 does not anticipate anticipating *any* of P3's experiences/desires (for the experiences/desires of P2's that P1 anticipates are not ones that include an anticipation of P3's experiences/desires). But then P1's desires do not ground P1's having reason to promote P3's wellbeing. And if so, there's a possible agent-stage (P1) whose desires do not ground its having reason to promote the wellbeing of all of its non-adjacent continuers: the Non-Adjacent-Stage Possibility Claim is true.

What should we say of such a case? Let's introduce the idea of a *subjectively idealised conative state*. These are relevantly like subjectively idealised desires, except that they apply to other sorts of conative states such as hopes, fears, anticipations and the like. Then we are inclined to say that P1's subjectively idealised anticipatory states (one kind of subjectively idealised conative state) are such that P1 will ideally anticipate *all* the experiences/desires of its adjacent agent-stage. To be clear, by this we mean that P1 will anticipate having *whatever* P2's experiences are and having *whichever* desires P2 has). Why think so?

Suppose that P1 desires and intends to sit down, and that it is P2 who sits. As part of desiring and intending to sit, P1 anticipates sitting. So, P1 anticipates *some* of P2's experiences. Now suppose that while P2 sits, as a matter of fact P2 spills some hot coffee on its leg. Suppose that we inform P1 of this. Will P1 come to anticipate being (mildly) burned? Surely it will. Once we idealise P1's relevant conative states, they will include the anticipation of mild coffee-induced burning. What of other experiences of P2's? Suppose that we inform P1 that while sitting down, P2 is hungry. Will P1 anticipate being hungry while sitting down? Surely it will. Likewise for any other experience of P2's that we can list.

Now suppose we tell P1 that as P2 is sitting down, it desires a muffin. Will P1 come to anticipate having this desire? Surely the answer is yes. So, we say, the following is true. Necessarily, if an agent-stage, P, anticipates some of the experiences/desires of a continuer P*, then P's subjectively idealised conative states will be such that P anticipates *all* the experiences/desires of that continuer. Since we've already argued that, necessarily, an agent-stage P anticipates some of the experiences/desires of its adjacent agent-stage; it follows that, necessarily, an agent-stage has subjectively idealised conative states of anticipating all the experiences/desires of its adjacent continuer. Given this, it follows that if P1 has reason to promote the wellbeing of adjacent agent-stage P2, then it also has reason to promote the wellbeing of all its non-adjacent continuers. Since we've argued that P1 does have reason to promote the wellbeing of its adjacent agent-stage, it follows that it has reason to promote the wellbeing of all its non-adjacent continuers.

Here is our second argument for the falsity of the Non-Adjacent-Stage Possibility Claim. Again, we need to back off from our claim that we will remain neutral regarding which theory of wellbeing is the right one. Suppose, again, we were to adopt a desire-satisfaction theory of wellbeing according to which wellbeing consists in the satisfaction of desires.[38] And suppose, again, that one thinks that the person-stage who benefits from a desire's being satisfied is the person-stage that exists at the time-of-satisfaction. So if it is P1 who desires to sit, and P2 who satisfies this desire, it is P1 whose wellbeing is promoted. If one endorses this view, then adjacent agent-stages such as P2 promote the wellbeing of earlier stages, such as P1, when they satisfy their desires. This means that P1's wellbeing in part depends on the wellbeing of P2, since it is P2 who can promote P1's wellbeing. Indeed, P3's wellbeing depends in part on that of P4, and P2's on P3, as P1's on P2. So, if there is a chain of adjacent continuers, then any stage in that chain has reason to promote the wellbeing of *any* continuer in that chain, because any agent-stage has a reason to promote the wellbeing of its adjacent continuer and promoting the wellbeing of later continuers is a way to promote the wellbeing of adjacent continuers, and so there is a chain of reasons that 'percolate backwards' from later to earlier stages.

So, insofar as theories of wellbeing are, if true, necessarily true, it follows that necessarily, for any agent-stage P such that P* is P's continuer and P* does not overlap P's adjacent continuer, P's actual/idealised desires provide P with a reason to promote the wellbeing of P*. The Non-Adjacent-Stage Possibility Claim is false.

Again, we do not claim that one cannot resist these arguments. Clearly one can: one can deny that the right account of wellbeing is desire satisfaction; and one can deny that it is the stage whose desires are satisfied whose wellbeing is promoted; and one can deny that, necessarily, stages will have subjectively idealised anticipations of all the desires/experiences of their adjacent continuers. With regard to this last claim the perdurantist might, again, retreat to a weaker version of the axiom and argue that persons that are at all psychologically like us do have these patterns of anticipations (or at least, ideally do) and that this means that any person remotely like us has reason to promote the wellbeing of all its non-adjacent continuers.

---

[38] See Harsanyi (1977), von Wright (1963), Barry (1965), Brandt (1966), Ramsey (1926), Singer (1979), and Hare (1981).

7.7 Overall wellbeing

Recall that the strong perdurantist axiom of prudence says the following:

Strong Perdurantist Axiom of Prudence: necessarily any agent-stage is rationally required to promote the *overall* wellbeing of each of its continuers.

Nothing we have said so far vindicates this axiom. Indeed, we are sceptical that anything as strong as this axiom can be vindicated by appealing only to instrumental reasons. Still, perhaps the perdurantist can vindicate something in the rough vicinity of this axiom. And, you might think that capturing something close to this axiom is important, because the account we have so far offered is not really faithful to how we think about our reasons to promote wellbeing.

To see this, consider agent-stage P. Suppose that P desires to sit down, and that it is P* who will satisfy that desire. Then, we say, P has a reason to promote P*'s wellbeing. But of course, it's entirely open that P's desires might make it rational for P to retard P*'s wellbeing in a host of non-sitting-down-relevant ways. Yet this will no doubt seem wrong to most of us. Moreover, it does not seem true to our lived experience. We don't simply promote the wellbeing of our continuer stages because they satisfy our desires, and we don't take ourselves to have reason to promote their wellbeing *only* insofar as they satisfy our desires.

We think that what is wrong with this picture is not that we all have, and take ourselves to have, reasons to promote the wellbeing of our continuers that do not issue from our desires, but rather, that the picture presents a tremendously impoverished view of our desires.

There are multiple kinds of desires that agent-stages can have. An agent-stage can have impersonal desires.[39] I impersonally desire world peace if I care that there will be world peace, and I don't care whether the agent-stages who bring it about are my continuers or someone else's. Sometimes, as Perry (1976) notes, as a matter of empirical fact the agent-stages best placed to satisfy these kinds of desires are one's own continuers. So perhaps I desire that a certain project come to fruition, a project that I care about, and have begun already and spent many years on. If I impersonally desire that the project be completed, then I don't care that I am the one to complete

---

[39] Following the terminology of Whiting (1986).

it. Still, given the way the world is, it is much more likely that the project will be completed if my continuers complete it. And this, says Perry, gives me reason to promote the wellbeing of those continuers. Perry attempts to marshal this idea to explain why we have reason to promote the wellbeing of our continuers. He's prepared to concede that insofar as our projects can be completed without our promoting the wellbeing of certain future continuers, then we have no reason to promote the wellbeing of those continuers.

Importantly though, many of our desires are not impersonal in this manner. I desire that Annie (a labradoodle) be walked. But I also desire that I, myself, take Annie for a walk. Parents desire that their children are cared for; most of them desire that they are the ones doing the caring. We will call such desires *personal desires*. While some desires can be either personal or impersonal, such as the desire that one's children are taken care of, some desires seem to be necessarily personal. The desire for food is not the desire that someone, somewhere, eat. It's a desire that one has continuers that eat. Many of our desires are like this: they can be satisfied only by our continuers.

This is important, since it often seems, from a first-personal perspective, as though we have reason to promote the wellbeing of our continuers even if they will not be best placed to satisfy our impersonal desires. And that, of course, is right: it is right because it is only they that can satisfy our personal desires.

That, however, cannot be the full story, for it often seems to us as though we have reason to promote the wellbeing of (at least adjacent) continuers, *regardless of whether they satisfy our desires.* This is the sense in which you might think that we take ourselves to have reason to promote the *overall* wellbeing of our continuers rather than simply reason to promote their wellbeing insofar as doing so satisfies our own desires.

We think that there is something clearly right about this. But we think that this is because many, and perhaps most, of our desires are in fact personal ones and because many of those personal desires, motivated by anticipatory states, are desires that continuers have certain sorts of experiences and lack others. As a matter of fact, we want our continuers to have pleasant experiences (*inter alia*) precisely because we anticipate those experiences.

Indeed, if we are right and, necessarily, agent-stages ideally anticipate all of the experiences/desires of their adjacent stages, then it's hardly surprising that we aim to promote something *like* their overall wellbeing. At the very least we desire that things go well for our continuer stages, in ways that outstrip merely caring that they go well so that those stages can satisfy what we might think of as our 'local' or 'specific' desires—desires such as eating, or sitting down, or finishing a paper. Rather, we have much more general, personal desires that things go well for our continuers, and this gives us reason to promote something that looks closer to their overall wellbeing.

Given this, something a bit like the strong axiom is true. It's *not* that all agent-stages have reason to promote the overall wellbeing of their continuer stages. But agent-stages that are at all psychologically like us in anticipating the experiences of continuer stages will have instrumental reason to promote the wellbeing of all of their continuer stages in a much fuller and more general sense. And, we think, this may well be enough to capture what is attractive about the strong axiom.

7.8 Conclusion

We have argued that any agent-stage has instrumental reason to promote the wellbeing of all its continuers. Hence, purely instrumental rationality can ground perdurantist prudence. Perhaps there are also *sui generis* prudential reasons, and the perdurantist can avail herself of these. But, we say, it does not matter if there are not, and she cannot. For appeal to instrumental reasons will suffice. Hence perdurantism cannot be dismissed on the grounds that it cannot account for prudential rationality.

References

Arntzenius, F. 2008. No Regrets, or: Edith Piaf Revamps Decision Theory. *Erkenntnis* 68(2): 277–297.

Barry, B. 1965. *Political Argument*. London: Routledge & Kegan Paul.

Beck, S. 2015. The Extreme Claim, Psychological Continuity and the Person Life View. *South African Journal of Philosophy* 34(3): 314–322.

Braddon-Mitchell, D. and Miller, K. 2004. How to be a Conventional Person. *The Monist* 87(4): 457–474.

Braddon-Mitchell, D. and Miller, K. 2020a. Conativism about personal identity. In *Derek Parfit's Reasons and Persons: An Introduction and Critical Inquiry*, ed. A. Sauchelli, London: Routledge, 129–159.

Braddon-Mitchell, D. and Miller, K. 2020b. Surviving, to Some Degree. *Philosophical Studies* 177: 3805–3831.

Braddon-Mitchell, D. and West, C. 2001. Temporal Phase Pluralism. *Philosophy and Phenomenological Research* 62(1): 59–83.

Brandt, R. B. 1966. The Concept of Welfare. In *The Structure of Economic Science*, ed. S. R. Krupp, Englewood Cliffs, NJ: Prentice-Hall, 257–276.

Brink, David O. 1997. Rational Egoism and the Separateness of Persons. In *Reading Parfit*, ed. Jonathan Dancy. Oxford: Blackwell, 96–134.

Brink, David O. 2011. Prospects for Temporal Neutrality. In *The Oxford Handbook of Philosophy of Time*, ed. Craig Callender. Oxford: Oxford University Press, 353–381.

Butler, Joseph. 1975. Of Personal Identity. In *Personal Identity*, ed. J. Perry. 99–105. First published in 1736. Oakland: University of California Press

Carter, Ian. 2018. Equal Opportunity, Responsibility, and Personal Identity. *Ethical Theory and Moral Practice* 21: 825–839.

Dietz, A. 2020. Are My Temporal Parts Agents? *Philosophy and Phenomenological Research* 100 (2): 362–379.

Dorsey, D. (2013). Desire-satisfaction and Welfare as Temporal. *Ethical Theory and Moral Practice*, 16(1): 151–171.

Dorsey, D. 2018. Prudence and Past Selves. *Philosophical Studies* 175(8): 1901–1925.

Dougherty, T. 2011. On Whether to Prefer Pain to Pass. *Ethics* 121(3): 521–537.

Dougherty, T. 2015. Future-Bias and Practical Reason. *Philosophers' Imprint* 15/30: 1–16.

Enoch, D. 2006. Agency, Schmagency: Why Normativity Won't Come From What Is Constitutive of Action. *Philosophical Review* 115(2): 169–198.

Fletcher, G. 2021. *Dear Prudence: The Nature and Normativity of Prudential Discourse*. Oxford: Oxford University Press.

Greene, P. and Sullivan, M. 2015. Against Time Bias. *Ethics* 125/5: 947–970.

Hare, C. 2007. Self-Bias, Time-Bias, and the Metaphysics of the Self and Time. *Journal of Philosophy* 104: 350–73.

Hare, C. 2008. A Puzzle about Other-Directed Time-Bias. *Australasian Journal of Philosophy* 86: 269–77.

Hare, C. 2013. Time—The Emotional Asymmetry. In *A Companion to the Philosophy of Time*, ed. A. Bardon and H. Dyke. Oxford: Wiley Blackwell: 507–520.

Hare, R. M. 1981. *Moral Thinking*. Oxford: Clarendon Press.

Harman, E. 2009. I'll be glad I did it. Reasoning and the Significance of Future Desires. *Philosophical Perspectives* 23(1): 177–199.

Harsanyi, J. 1977. Morality and the Theory of Rational Behavior. *Social Research* 44: 623–56.

Hedden, Brian. 2015. *Reasons without Persons: Rationality, Identity, and Time.* Oxford: Oxford University Press.

Hurley, Susan. 1989. *Natural Reasons.* New York: Oxford University Press.

Jackson, Frank. 1987. Group Morality. In *Metaphysics and Morality*, ed. Philip Pettit, Richard Sylvan, and Jean Norman. Oxford: Blackwell, 91–110.

Johnston, M. 2017. The Personite Problem: Should Practical Reason be Tabled? *Noûs* 50: 617–644.

Johnston, M. 1989. "Relativism and the Self". In *Relativism: Interpretation and Confrontation*, ed. M. Krausz. Notre Dame, IN: Notre Dame University Press, 441–472.

Johnston, M. 2010. *Surviving Death.* Princeton, NJ: Princeton University Press.

Kaiserman, A. 2019. Stage Theory and the Personite Problem. *Analysis* 79: 215–222.

Kleinig, John. 1983. *Paternalism.* Totowa, New Jersey: Rowman & Allanheld.

Kleinig, John. 2009. Paternalism and Person Identity. *Jahrbuch für Wissenschaft und Ethik* 14: 93–106.

Kogan, Terry S. 1976. The Limits of State Intervention: Personal Identity and Ultra-Risky Actions. *Yale Law Journal* 85: 826–846.

Korsgaard, Christine M. (1989). Personal identity and the unity of agency: A Kantian response to Parfit. *Philosophy and Public Affairs* 18 (2): 103–31.

Kovacs, D. 2016. Self-Made People. *Mind* 125: 1071–1099.

Kovacs, D. 2020. Diachronic Self Making. *Australasian Journal of Philosophy* 98: 349–362.

Kovacs, D. (2022). Self-making and subpeople. *The Journal of Philosophy* 119(9): 461–488.

Lin, E. 2015. Prudence, Morality and the Humean Theory of Reasons. *Philosophical Quarterly* 65: 220–40.

Longenecker, M. 2020a. Perdurantism, Fecklessness and the Veil of Ignorance. *Philosophical Studies* 177: 2565–2576.

Longenecker, M. 2020b. Is Consequentialist Perdurantism in Moral Trouble? *Synthese* 198(11): 10979–10990.

Longenecker, M. 2022. Community-Made Selves. *Australasian Journal of Philosophy* 100(3): 459–470.

Markovits, J. 2014. *Moral Reason*. Oxford: Oxford University Press.

Martin, R. 2008. *Self-Concern: An Experiential Approach to What Matters in Survival*. New York: Cambridge University Press.

McCall, S. and Lowe, D. J. 2002. 3D/4D Equivalence, the Twins Paradox and Absolute Time. *Analysis* 63: 114–123.

Merricks, T. 1999. Endurance, Psychological Continuity, and the Importance of Personal Identity. *Philosophy and Phenomenological Research* 59: 983–997.

Miller, K. 2007. *Issues in Theoretical Diversity: Persistence Composition and Time*. New York: Springer.

Miller, K. 2009a. Deciphering Personal-identity Conventionalism. Special Issue of *Rivista di Estetica "Convenzioni"*, (eds. Elena Casetta and Achille Varzi) 44: 59–85.

Miller, K.2009b). Ought a four-dimensionalist to believe in temporal parts? *Canadian Journal of Philosophy* 39: 619–646.

Miller, K. 2010. Persons as *Sui Generis* Ontological Kinds: Advice to Exceptionists. *Philosophy and Phenomenological Research* 81: 567–593.

Miller, K.2013. Personal identity minus the persons. *Philosophical Studies* 166: 91–109.

Miller, K., & Duncan, M. 2015. Modal Persistence and Modal Travel. *Ratio*, 28(3): 241–255.

Nozick, Robert. 1981. *Philosophical Explanations*. Cambridge, MA: Harvard University Press.

Olson, Eric T. 2002. Thinking Animals and the Reference of 'I'. *Philosophical Topics* 30: 189–207.

Olson, Eric T. 2007. *What Are We? A Study in Personal Ontology*. Oxford: Oxford University Press.

Olson, Eric T. 2010. Ethics and the Generous Ontology. *Theoretical Medicine and Bioethics* 31: 259–270.

Parfit, Derek. 1984. *Reasons and Persons*. Oxford: Oxford University Press.

Pearson, O. 2018. Appropriate Emotions and the Metaphysics of Time. *Philosophical Studies* 175: 1945–1961.

Perry, J. 1976. The importance of being identical. In *The Identities of Persons*, ed., A. O. Rorty. Berkeley, CA: University of California Press.

Prior, A. N. 1959. Thank Goodness That's Over. *Philosophy* 34: 12–17.

Ramsey, F. P. 1931. Truth and Probability. In *Foundations of Mathematics and Other Essays*, ed. R. B. Braithwaite. London: Kegan, Paul, Trench, Trubner, & Co., 156–198. [Originally published in 1926]

Rawls, J. 1971. *A Theory of Justice*. Cambridge, MA: Belknap.

Reagan, Donald H. 1983. Paternalism, Freedom, Identity, and Commitment. In *Paternalism*, ed. Rolf E. Sartorius, 113–138. Minneapolis, MN: University of Minnesota Press.

Rovane, Carol. 1998. *The Bounds of Agency: An Essay in Revisionary Metaphysics*. Princeton, N J: Princeton University Press.

Schechtman, M. 1996. *The Constitution of Selves*. Ithaca, NY: Cornell University Press.

Schechtman, M. 2005. Experience, Agency, and Personal Identity. *Social Philosophy and Policy* 22: 1–24.

Schechtman, M. 2014. *Staying Alive: Personal Identity, Practical Concerns and the Unity of a Life*. Oxford: Oxford University Press.

Schroeder, M. 2007. *Slaves of the Passions*. Oxford: Oxford University Press.

Sebo, Jeff. 2015a. The Just Soul. *Journal of Value Inquiry*, 49: 131–143.

Sebo, Jeff. 2015b. Multiplicity, Self-Narrative, and Akrasia. *Philosophical Psychology* 28: 589–605.

Shaw, W. 1999. *Contemporary Ethics*. Malden, MA: Blackwell Publishers.

Shoemaker, David. 1999. Selves and Moral Units. *Pacific Philosophical Quarterly* 80: 391–419.

Sidgwick, H. 1884. *The Methods of Ethics*. London: Macmillan.

Singer, P. 1979. *Practical Ethics*. Cambridge: Cambridge University Press.

Slors, M. 2004. Care for One's Own Future Experiences. *Philosophical Explorations* 7: 183–195.

Slote, M. 1989. *Beyond Optimizing. A Study of Rational Choice*. Cambridge, MA: Harvard University Press.

Smith, A. 1790. *The Theory of Moral Sentiments*. Oxford: Oxford University Press.

Sullivan, M. 2018. *Time Biases: A Theory of Rational Planning and Personal Persistence*. Oxford: Oxford University Press.

Taylor, A. P. 2013. The Frustrating Problem for Four-Dimensionalism. *Philosophical Studies* 165: 1097–1115.

Taylor, A. P. 2020. The Painful Implications of Four-Dimensionalism. *Ethics, Medicine and Public Health* 13: 1–10.

Unger, P. 1990. *Identity, Consciousness and Value*. Oxford: Oxford University Press.

Van Fraassen, Bas. 1984. Belief and the Will. *The Journal of Philosophy* 81: 235–256.

Von Wright, G. H. 1963. *The Varieties of Goodness*. New York: The Humanities Press.

West, C. 1996. *Surviving Matters*. PhD Dissertation, Australian National University.

White, S. 1989. Metapsychological Relativism and the Self. *Journal of Philosophy* 86: 298–325.

Whiting, J. 1986. Friends and Future Selves. *Philosophical Review* 95: 547–580.

Williams, B. 1981. Internal and External Reasons. In his *Moral Luck*. Oxford: Oxford University Press, 101–113.

Wolf, S. 1986. Self-Interest and Interest in Selves. *Ethics* 96: 704–720.

Zimmerman, D. 2012. Personal identity and the survival of death. In *The Oxford Handbook of Philosophy of Death*, eds. B. Bradley, F. Feldman, and J. Johansson. Oxford: Oxford University Press, 97–154.

8

The Situationalist Account of Change

Martin Pickup

What is happening when things continue to exist over time? In particular, what happens when entities persist through change? There are many different answers to this question. In this chapter, I wish to offer a new one. I will claim that, when things change, parts of reality are irreducibly conflicting and that reality as a whole is therefore radically unsettled about how the world is. In other words, change involves disagreement between parts of the world and thereby introduces metaphysical indeterminacy in the world as a whole.

The idea that reality might not all be 'of a piece' has been explored in different ways in different contexts. One example is in Fine's (2005, 2006) fragmentalism, with more recent papers from Lipman (2015, 2016), Loss (2017) and Simon (2018) developing versions of the view. Moore (1997, 2019) also explores the possibility that reality is disunified. In other places, I have offered solutions to other problems which deploy underlying notions of the same sort (Pickup 2016, Darby, Pickup, and Robson 2017, Darby and Pickup 2021). In this chapter I intend to show how the persistence of material objects through change can be given a similar treatment to those other puzzles, with similar results. I believe there are advantages to doing so, though I will also highlight some costs of going this way.

While my approach joins these others in rejecting a standard view of reality as a straightforward composition of compatible parts, the positive account is distinctive in several ways. It treats reality's disunity as a matter of its being divided into parts, rather than being perspectival. It invokes metaphysical indeterminacy about what is the case in reality as a whole, and it is a tenseless, B-theoretic view. Comparisons with (extension of) existing views will be discussed in more detail in Section 8.5.

Change has a long history as a topic of philosophical reflection and as a source of puzzlement. When something changes, it seems to first have a property and then lack it. But how could one and the same thing both have

Martin Pickup, *The Situationalist Account of Change* In: *Oxford Studies in Metaphysics Volume 13*.
Edited by: Karen Bennett and Dean W. Zimmerman, Oxford University Press. © Martin Pickup 2023.
DOI: 10.1093/oso/9780192886033.003.0008

and lack a property? The answer, of course, involves *time*. But exactly how time enters the picture is contentious.

This initial concern has been framed as a problem: hence 'The Problem of Change'. In contemporary metaphysics, a particular version of this problem—the problem of temporary intrinsics—was raised by Lewis in a few pages of his *On the Plurality of Worlds* (1986, p202–205). As the name suggests, he focused on intrinsic properties which are only had temporarily. A series of papers (Hofweber 2009, Hansson 2007, Rychter 2009) have argued that there is nothing in the vicinity worthy of the title of a *problem*, as constructing an argument along these lines will involve at least one premise that shouldn't be even *prima facie* acceptable. Nevertheless, there is a variance of philosophical opinion on how to theorise about objects' existence over time which is highlighted by the different ways they treat change. I intend to describe a novel account within this debate.

I will proceed as follows. First, I will give my take on the phenomenon to be explained and some constraints on an explanation. These will generate a problem. I will then give a brief account of *situations*, which will be a tool for expressing my view. Situations, in short, are portions of possible worlds. Third, I will express my account of change in terms of what is true in different situations. This will involve accounting for what is true when different situations are put together, at which point indeterminacy will be introduced. In the fourth section (8.4), I will address some worries that naturally arise about the account. Finally, I will compare my view with a few alternatives before concluding.

8.1 Change

Change is the phenomenon by which an object first has and later lacks a certain property (or *vice versa*). Consider an orange which changes from not being ripe to being ripe. We can label the orange o, the property of being ripe F and the earlier and later times t and t' respectively. The following statements are then true:

(1)   It is not the case that o is F at t

(2) o is F at t'

This much is uncontested. How to interpret (1) and (2), however, is very much contested. I will propose that there are certain constraints on interpreting (1) and (2). These constraints will not be universally accepted, as they rule out various other options in the literature. But, nevertheless, I think they are plausible.

The first constraint is that it is the *orange* which is changing. More generally, there is a single individual which is the subject of change. The most natural way to cash this out is to say that the thing which bears (or doesn't bear) the property at the earlier time is numerically identical to the thing which doesn't bear (or bears) the property at the later time. This pushes us towards an endurance view: the thing at the earlier time is numerically identical to the thing at the later time. But not quite: the worm-theoretic temporal parts account could say that there is indeed a single thing which is the subject of change, namely the worm which is the sum of the temporal parts.[1] However, a stricter version of this idea cannot be given a temporal-parts treatment. The stricter version claims that there is a single individual which is the *primary* subject of change. This can be cast in terms of grounding or fundamentality: the fundamental bearer of the property before and after the change is numerically identical. The motivation for such an explanatory constraint is that if the primary subject of change is not numerically identical then there is no one thing (at the fundamental level) which has changed.

Thus I take it that the following is a constraint on explaining (1) and (2):

Endurance: the ultimate subject of predication before the change is numerically identical to the ultimate subject of predication after the change.

The second constraint is that it is *ripeness* which the orange both lacks at the earlier time and has at the later time. In more general terms, it is one and the same property which the subject has and lacks: the property the individual has is precisely the property the individual lacks.[2] The motivation for this constraint is that if the individual has and lacks numerically *different*

---

[1] This might seem to undermine temporal parts as a solution to the problem of change, for if the worm both has and lacks the property (tenselessly), then we have a contradiction. This connects to the criticism that temporal-parts theory involves replacement rather than change (see, e.g., Oderberg 2004). I'll set aside this worry for now.

[2] Lewis's version of the problem uses intrinsic properties, properties such that nothing external to the object is involved in their instantiation. In other words, if a property is intrinsic then whether an object has it or not does not depend on anything apart from the object and the property. I am giving a more general constraint along these lines, such that the adicity of a relation cannot be higher than the number of individuals subject to the change with respect to that relation.

properties, it hasn't changed.[3] In a similar move to the one just considered, the relational properties view could arguably satisfy such a constraint if there is a higher-level property, e.g. ripeness, which can be had or lacked in virtue of distinct lower-level properties (such as ripeness-at-t) being instantiated. In such a case there could be a single property had and lacked by an individual: the higher-level property. But, in line with our first constraint, a stricter version of the second constraint can be given on which the *ultimate* property an individual has and lacks in a case of change must be one and the same. Thus:

Property Identity: the ultimate property predicated of the subject before (after) the change is numerically identical to the ultimate property the subject lacks after (before) the change.

A third constraint is that what it is for the orange to *be* ripe is the same at the earlier and later times. The tie between the orange and ripeness which holds at the later time is precisely the tie that is lacking at the earlier time. The constraint, in other words, concerns the instantiation of the property by the changing individual. Whatever instantiation is (and luckily we don't have to settle that question here) this constraint requires it to be the same before and after the change. The motivation is that change involves something coming to be the case which was not the case beforehand. If the tie lacking between property and object is not the same as the tie that obtains when the object has the property, what fails to be the case before the change is not what *is* the case after the change.[4]

Once more, we can speak of the primary or fundamental here. Otherwise we don't rule out a view whereby there is a single higher-level instantiation relation which can hold in virtue of distinct lower-level instantiation relations. This higher-level relation would then be numerically identical across a change even if the lower-level relations are distinct. To rule this out, we specify again that *ultimate* instantiation relations are our target in the constraint.

Instantiation Identity: the ultimate connection between property and subject before (after) the change is numerically identical to the ultimate connection lacking between property and subject after (before) the change.

---

[3] See Rodriguez-Pereyra (2003) for a clear articulation of this concern.
[4] This connects to the demand that objects have properties *simpliciter*, which Giberman (2017) develops powerfully in a recent paper. This, I think, is the core of Lewis's objections to adverbialism and the like (see his 2002).

The final constraint will be more of a stipulation. I am working with a B-theoretic structure so wish the times involved in a case of change to be treated equally. There are arguments for the B-theory (and of course responses too).[5] I won't rehearse these here.

The fourth constraint is therefore:

B-theory: all times are metaphysically on a par.

The B-theory therefore sees no time as privileged above the others. In particular, the question of which time is the present doesn't have a metaphysically weighty answer. This means that all times are equally authoritative about how reality is.

* * *

This completes the four constraints I will adopt on an explanation of the phenomena of change. Now, as I mentioned, most current views reject one of these, so protagonists of such positions are unlikely to grant that these are all reasonable constraints. The final constraint is stipulated, and I shall not dwell on it. I have given indicative motivations for the other three constraints, and I hope this will supply some initial plausibility to each of them. But I do not expect these to be persuasive for those who already accept a view which breaches one of these constraints. So let me make a few brief dialectical points to appeal to such readers.

Firstly, I think it should be accepted that each account of change has its challenges. Some of the challenges with the account I am proposing will be explained in Section 8.4 (and readers will no doubt find others). The voluminous literature on persistence provides a great range of difficulties for each of the established positions which, although they may be solvable, need to be addressed. In effect, in adopting these constraints I am trying to see what can be done if the negative arguments in the literature against each major view are successful.

Secondly, in giving these constraints I am not at all suggesting that they are non-negotiable metaphysical principles. Each of them might turn out to be false, even if they are initially attractive. So if no satisfactory account of change can be furnished while we accept all of the constraints, we have a

---

[5] As starting points in this vast literature, see Markosian (2016), esp. sections 5 and 6, Mellor (1998), Zimmerman and Smart's debate in Sider, Hawthorne and Zimmerman (2008), ch. 5, and ch. 5 of Ney (2014), along with their respective references and bibliographies.

choice. We could either say that change is incomprehensible (perhaps even impossible), or we could give up a constraint. I would strongly favour the second approach. I take it that, at least with respect to the first three constraints, this would be revisionary (even if acceptably so). I suggest, therefore, that B-theory accounts which breach a constraint are revisions of our understanding of change.[6] To emphasise: this might be perfectly OK. Lewis's perdurance, for example, is plausibly a revision of our normal understanding of how objects persist. Revising our metaphysics when required is a sensible approach, and my own proposal might be seen as revisionary in a different way.

These both connect to a final point. Even if one or more of the constraints I adopt is unreasonable, and can be plausibly denied, it is still an interesting project to establish whether a coherent account of change can be found which *does* accept all of these constraints. It is, I think, typically believed that at least one of the constraints I have outlined needs to be rejected in order to make space for the possibility of change. If I am right, then change is possible even if all these constraints are adopted. This is worth investigating. In particular, I suggest it is worth seeing whether the B-theorist needs to breach one of the first three constraints to account for change: I will argue that there is an alternative which does not.

*   *   *

I am now in a position to demonstrate the issue for providing a satisfactory explanation of change. Our change case involving the orange's ripeness was captured by the following two statements:

(1)   It is not the case that o is F at t

(2) o is F at t'

We need to explain how to interpret these statements. The issue can be constructed as a paradox. The indiscernibility of identicals states that if x is (numerically) identical to y, then any property y has x also has (and

---

[6] Certain A-theorists will also face a variant of the problem under consideration. If, for instance, all past times are metaphysically on a par then the A-theorist will need an account of how past change is possible. This looks relevantly similar to the B-theorist's challenge in accounting for all change across metaphysically equal times. (Thanks to Stephen Williams for pointing this out to me.)

vice versa). The indiscernibility of identicals is rarely disputed.[7] Using it, however, seems to lead to a problem. From *B-theory* it follows that times *t* and *t'* are on a par: the claims both make about the world must be taken equally seriously. We cannot prioritise one over the other. So it not being the case that *o* is F and it being the case that *o* is F are on an even footing. *Instantiation Identity* tells us that the connection between F and *o* which holds at *t'* is precisely the same connection as that which is lacking at *t* between the two: there is a univocal sense of 'having' across those times such that the indiscernibility of identicals straightforwardly applies. *Property Identity* tells us that it is precisely the same property which is had at *t'* and lacked at *t*.

But *Endurance* tells us that the thing at *t* is numerically identical to the thing at *t'*. Thus, from the indiscernibility of identicals, we can conclude that the thing at *t* has all the same properties as the thing at *t'*. So the orange has the very same property (namely ripeness) that it lacks; it has this property in the same way that it lacks it and there is no metaphysical priority or distinction between its having and its lacking the property. This is a contradiction.

This sketch will not satisfy everyone that there is a problem of change.[8] Nevertheless, I hope it shows that there is an issue about interpreting the statements of change, like (1) and (2), in a way that avoids difficulties. To put it differently: time needs to enter the picture to stop change cases being contradictory. Given our explanatory constraints, how can it do so? Time can't enter into the object, property, instantiation relation or the metaphysical status of the statement. Where else can it go?

Before addressing this question, I'll first need to quickly introduce some machinery to articulate my suggested answer.

---

[7] Rarely, but not never. See, for instance, Williams (forthcoming; sect. 14) for an interesting discussion of loose identity and its connection with the indiscernibility of identicals. The indiscernibility of identicals is also tinkered with by those who have non-canonical views on identity, for instance that it is relative (e.g. Geach 1967) or occasional (e.g. Gallois 1998).

[8] As previously mentioned, see Hofweber (2009), Hansson (2007), and Rychter (2009) for criticisms that this argument warrants the title of a 'problem'. There are responses (e.g. Raven 2011, Einhouser 2012). My own view is that those 'dissolving' the problem of change are doing nothing of the sort: they are *solving* the problem by invoking adverbialism. (This is particularly clear in Hansson's paper, where he explicitly refers to adverbialism (p271)). But it is not a dissolution of a problem to appeal to an existing but contentious solution to that problem. Adverbialism, which tinkers with instantiation, is at least a revision of our conceptual scheme. I don't have space to fully defend my views on this here, but see Pickup (2021).

8.2 Situations

As already mentioned, I will be using situations as a tool for expressing the metaphysical position I wish to propose. I do not think that they are essential to the picture I present, but rather a useful mechanism by which to do so. Situations can be conceived as parts of possible worlds, though in situation theory it would be more accurate to say that possible worlds are special sorts of situations.[9] What situations allow us to do is deal with portions of worlds which are less than maximal. This is in the same vein as views emerging from Austin's work (Austin 1950) and running through to Yablo's *Aboutness* (2014) and the truthmaker semantics of Fine (2014). Situation semanticists use situations rather than worlds as the entities with respect to which propositions are evaluated, and there are a number of claimed advantages of doing so (see, e.g., Kratzer 1989, 2019, Heim 1990, Elbourne 2005, 2013).

For my purposes, I will mention a few features of situations. They are typically partial, giving answers to some but not all questions (contrast this with possible worlds, which give an answer to every question). Because they don't settle every question, some propositions are neither true nor false in certain situations.[10] Situations bear mereological relations to one another, so that one situation can be part of another. Truth is evaluated with respect to situations: what is true in one situation might not be true in another. Accordingly, there is no straightforward notion of truth *simpliciter*.[11]

As an example, consider what is occurring in New York City on the 31st December 2021. There is a situation corresponding to this place and day. Some things will be true in this situation, for instance that people are celebrating, that Thea has eggs for breakfast, that the air temperature is

---

[9] There are several situation-theoretic choices to make which I will be suppressing here. One is whether there are world-sized situations. If not, then there will be no possible worlds. Another is whether there are merely possible situations or only actual ones. If there are only actual ones, there will be exactly one possible world, namely the actual world. See Barwise (1988) for discussion of some of the choice points in situation theory.

[10] This is another choice point: one could alternatively take propositions to be false when the situation doesn't settle the relevant question. As I will be using them, however, situations allow propositions to lack truth-values.

[11] One might be tempted to construct such a notion, for instance by saying that what is true in the maximal situation corresponding to the (actual) world is what is true *simpliciter*. Or, alternatively, by saying that what is true in all actual situations is true *simpliciter*. Or by saying that what is true in *any* actual situation is true *simpliciter*. I won't follow any of these paths for reasons which may become clearer in the next sections. At any rate, I see no compulsion to generate a notion of truth *simpliciter* within situation theory: we can do without it.

cold. Some other things will be false in this situation, for instance that no-one is sad, that Thea has cereal for breakfast, that Times Square is quiet. There are further things which the situation says nothing about, for instance that the assassination of Franz Ferdinand caused World War I, that Danny had eggs for breakfast (Danny was in London on 31st December 2021), that it is a hot summer in NYC in 2022. These are example of propositions I take to be neither true nor false in the situation we are considering.

The situation corresponding to what's going on in NYC on the 31st December 2021 is part of many other situations, including the situation of what's going on in New York State on the 31st December 2021, the situation of what's going on in NYC throughout 2021 and the situation (if there be any such situation) of the actual world. It has many other situations as parts, including the situation of what's going on in Times Square on 31st December 2021, the situation of what's going on in NYC between 11.00pm and 11.55pm on the 31st December 2021 and so on. It is also disjoint from many other situations, such as the situation of World War I or the situation of a party in a house in the suburbs of Tokyo on 31st December 2021.

This completes the general introduction to situations. Before going on, it might be worth being explicit about the role situations will play in what is to come. My task in this chapter is to articulate a metaphysical picture, rather than to furnish a semantics.[12] I will not, therefore, be using situations primarily to give an account of the *meaning* of statements of change, nor the formal, inferential or truth-conditional roles of such statements. Rather, situations are a tool for getting a grip on the notion of a fine-grained portion of reality which allows me to spell out a view of how the world might be. In order to express the new metaphysical account of persistence I wish to present, I use situations as a means of discriminating the chunks of reality which are interestingly heterogenous with respect to what is the case. To explain this comment, which is somewhat cryptic at this stage, I now move on to describe the situationalist's understanding of persistence.

---

[12] I deal in a little more detail with the semantic issues in earlier work (see especially the Appendix to Pickup 2016), but a full semantics is a future project. There are interesting questions here, variants of which are under current discussion in the literature (see, e.g., work by Yablo (2014, 2017) and Fine (2014, 2020). But I restrict my focus to the metaphysical issues in this chapter.

8.3 Change in terms of situations

So, how can we use situations to model our new way of addressing the challenge of change? I call it the situationalist approach, and it begins by reframing the scenario in terms of situations. Let *s* be the situation before the change and *s'* the situation after the change. Because all truth is relative to a situation, we should list what is true in *s* and *s'*.

In *s*: it is not the case that *o* is F

In *s'*: *o* is F

To be clear, the proposition that *o* is F is false in *s* and true in *s'*. So far, this seems straightforward and unproblematic. What *does* seem to raise an issue is when *s* and *s'* are combined. Suppose there is a further situation *s** which has both *s* and *s'* as parts.[13] What is true in *s**?

There are choices to make here. If *s** contains all truths from *s* and *s'* then we have a contradiction: it both is and is not the case that *o* is F. The view I'm proposing rejects this, and instead takes the proposition that *o* is F to be neither true nor false in *s**.[14] So, on the situationalist account it is neither true nor false that the orange is ripe in a situation containing both *s* and *s'*. It is, in other words, indeterminate whether the orange is ripe in such situations. More generally, when something changes the situationalist allows that there are some situations in which it determinately has the relevant property, some situations in which it determinately lacks the relevant property, and some situations in which it is indeterminate whether it has the property and indeterminate whether it lacks it.

What this means is that certain situations have truth-value gaps. This, by itself, is not surprising when using situations: situations are incomplete and so plausibly fail to determine a truth-value for some propositions. What *is* surprising is that a situation can lack a truth-value for a proposition when parts of that situation do give a truth-value to it. I shall first spell out how this might be cashed out metaphysically before applying the situationalist

[13] If *s* and *s'* are actual, then presumably *s** will be as well. (Though see Darby and Pickup (2021) sect. 4.3 for a possible challenge to this presumption.)
[14] I will later, in Section 8.5(a), discuss in more detail whether truth in a part of a situation entails truth in the whole situation. There are reasons to think that this is not the case, i.e. that situations are not always monotonic.

solution directly to interpretation of the statements of change (1) and (2) while upholding the constraints I've specified.

Indeterminacy is not a feature that is usually welcomed: it complicates matters. While it might be tolerated at the level of representation (for instance, in the application of vague predicates), it is certainly unpopular when *non*-representational, i.e. when it is claimed of the target phenomenon rather than of the description of the phenomenon.[15] Nevertheless, I propose to understand this indeterminacy as metaphysical indeterminacy: the world itself being unsettled about how things are. This is in line with addressing the nature of change at the metaphysical rather than the semantic level. If we are concerned with what the world is like when things change, it is not enough to provide a semantics which avoids contradiction without saying what underlying reality the semantics corresponds to. Having a satisfying description of change is only salutary when that description is an accurate one. While there would be ways of accepting the assignment of truth-values I've detailed without the particular metaphysical reading I will offer, and I welcome such alternatives, I will focus on a straightforward interpretation of what could warrant a semantic outcome as described.

The natural way to connect truth in a situation with what reality is like or, in other words, to connect our semantics and metaphysics, is to take truth in a situation to give what is the case there. Situations are portions of reality.[16] What is true is different in different situations, so what is the case is different in different portions of reality. What the situationalist account of change therefore suggests is that when two different portions of reality which jointly describe a change are put together, unsettledness arises in the resulting portion of reality. There is no answer to the question: 'is the orange ripe?' in a part of the world which contains a change with respect to the orange's ripeness. We *can* say that the orange is unripe in a specified portion of reality before the change, and that it is ripe in a distinct portion of reality after the change. What we *cannot* say is whether it is ripe or not in a part of the world which encompasses both of these scenarios.

On one way of understanding this, it is a fairly banal claim. Everyone, presumably, would accept that what is the case is different in different parts of the world (assuming that the world is not homogenous). What the situationalist is asserting is more radical, however. It is that how things are in one part of reality *conflicts* with how they are in another. What is the case

---

[15] This will be discussed in more detail in part (b) of the next section.

[16] If we allow there to be merely possible situations, these will be possible portions of reality.

in one situation rules out what is the case in another situation, and yet both situations are actual. In the case of the orange, *s* tells us, unequivocally and in an unrelativised way, that it is not F. Within *s*, it is a bare and primitive fact that this is so. Conversely, *s'* tells us in precisely the same way that the orange is indeed F. Furthermore, *s* and *s'* are parts of reality which have equal status.[17]

It is tempting to relativise any such conflict away.[18] But the project of situationalism is to see what happens when reality is taken to *genuinely* conflict. The answer the situationalist offers is that genuine conflict leads to reality itself being unsettled. The combined situation *s**, to speak metaphorically, goes fuzzy at the point of conflict.

The situationalist's account of objects persisting through change is therefore the following: when an object changes with respect to some property over time, reality is divided.[19] While it is true in one situation that the object has the property, it is false in some other situation that the same object has the same property. When the situations are put together, the status of the object with respect to that property is indeterminate: there is no fact of the matter about whether the object has the property in the larger situation. Persisting through change, then, is a case of an object existing in different, incompatible portions of the world which are equally part of reality. Correlatively, change is a phenomenon which gives rise to the division of reality into these incompatible parts.

What this suggests is that reality is fundamentally in pieces: reality is composed of parts which irreconcilably disagree. When these disagreeing parts of reality are combined, indeterminacy results. What is determinate in smaller parts of reality can become indeterminate in larger parts of reality. Situationalism contends that change is a phenomenon which introduces indeterminacy into the world in virtue of the irreconcilable

---

[17] One way to think about this is by parallel to possible worlds. Imagine that there is more than one concrete possible world (akin to a sub-class of the Lewisian pluriverse). Furthermore, imagine that entities are transworld identical across (some of) these worlds, and that some such individuals vary in properties between worlds. What is the case across worlds would be akin to what the situationalist claims to be the case across change in a single world.

[18] See Goodman (1978 ch. 7), (1984 ch. 2) for a rejection of the relativisation strategy and an acceptance of reality's pluralism, but with a very different underlying metaphysical picture. Goodman's view informs Moore's discussion (see this chapter, 8.5 (c)).

[19] To forestall confusion: it is not that reality *becomes* divided in any loaded sense. Situationalism is B-theoretic, so there is no absolute becoming involved. Rather, change involves reality's just being divided into these conflicting parts, in a way that privileges no time over others.

parts which are required for something to genuinely change. Change breaks the world into pieces.[20]

The fact that smaller portions of the world are determinate while larger portions composed of them are not encourages us to think that these smaller portions are more fundamental. In particular, the irreconcilable chunks of the world seem to offer a decomposition of reality into *natural* (or more natural) parts. It is therefore plausible to take situations which are determinate as a guide to a privileged carving of the world into its parts, and given that change is a mechanism for introducing fundamental disagreement, it also marks out the edges of natural decompositions. But I want to mention three brief points of nuance: firstly, there may be other mechanisms of introducing such disagreement,[21] secondly, substantive questions about the relationship between change and time will need to be settled before we can say situations corresponding to times are natural,[22] and finally, I take this additional metaphysical overlay involving 'naturalness' or 'fundamentality' to be attractive but strictly optional for a situationalist.[23]

This view I have sketched is a substantive, controversial and far-reaching metaphysical position. Situationalism is by no means an easy answer to the question of how things persist. But, I think, it does allow us to satisfy the four constraints I have detailed on an account of change. That is what I intend to now show.

The statements of change, recall, are:

(1) It is not the case that o is F at t

(2) o is F at t'

The challenge is to interpret them while maintaining all of:

Endurance: the ultimate subject of predication before the change is numerically identical to the ultimate subject of predication after the change.

---

[20] Change is not the only means by which indeterminacy and fragmentation can be introduced. See, for instance, Pickup (2016), Darby, Pickup and Robson (2017) and Darby and Pickup (2021) for other examples including the Ship of Theseus, fictional indeterminacy and quantum indeterminacy.

[21] See the previous footnote.

[22] For instance, if it is metaphysically possible for changing objects to time-travel to a time at which they already exist then change seems to fracture space as well as times. Heterogeneous extended simples might also encourage a spatial fracturing view. As another example of the way the interaction of time and change can matter here, notice that if time can pass without change, then situations corresponding to distinct times might well display no disagreement.

[23] Thanks to a referee for encouraging me to discuss the issues in this paragraph explicitly.

Property Identity: the ultimate property predicated of the subject before (after) the change is numerically identical to the ultimate property the subject lacks after (before) the change.

Instantiation Identity: the ultimate connection between property and subject before (after) the change is numerically identical to the ultimate connection lacking between property and subject after (before) the change.

B-theory: all times are metaphysically on a par.

The situationalist account, given earlier, interprets (1) and (2) as stating respectively that it is not the case that the orange is ripe and that it is the case that the orange is ripe. But (1) is true in a situation at *t*, while (2) is true at a situation at *t'*. It is part of the view that truth is evaluated with respect to a situation: (1) tells us that '*o* is F' is false with respect to some situations at *t*, while (2) tells us that '*o* is F' is true with respect to some situations at *t'*.[24] What is true or false in these situations is the straightforward proposition that *o* is F. Thus the orange is unripe in some portions of the world, and ripe in others. This means that the situationalist can maintain that the ultimate subject of predication is *o* at both *t* and *t'*, and she can maintain that the property predicated at both *t* and *t'* is F, and that the relation holding between *o* and F at *t'* is the same as the relation lacking between them at *t*. Furthermore, she can hold that *t* and *t'* (and their corresponding situations) are metaphysically equal. The worry that a contradiction is thereby generated is avoided by introducing indeterminacy in situations which include both parts where the proposition is true and parts where the proposition is false.

So the situationalist maintains all of the constraints but doesn't end up with a contradiction. This is because there is no situation in which the orange is as described by (1) *and* as described by (2). The orange has the property of being ripe in some situations and lacks it in others, but in no situation is it the case both that the orange is ripe and that it is not ripe. But how is this so, given the argument that the four constraints jointly create a problem? The answer is that, as noted, truth is situation-relative for the situationalist. Thus what (1) is saying is true of or in only some portions of reality, not all. Likewise with (2). What is the case (unconditionally) depends on what part of reality we are considering. Reality as a whole, for reasons I've

---

[24] There will be further situations in which the proposition is respectively false and true, e.g. it is false a microsecond before *t* and true a microsecond after *t'* (assuming it doesn't change in the interim).

given, does not provide a univocal account of how the orange is. The incompatibility between what is the case in different situations is, so to speak, domesticated by a situation theory which doesn't require larger situations to contain all the truths of their parts. But the different situations are still genuinely incompatible because it cannot be the case in any situation that what they both say is true.

Change is often described as requiring incompatibility.[25] The existing solutions which breach one of the four constraints above arguably, by doing so, remove genuine incompatibility. There is nothing incompatible about two different objects having and lacking a property. Nor is there about an object having and lacking different properties. Nor again is there about a certain relationship holding between an object and a property and a different relationship not holding between them. Finally, there is no incompatibility about an object having a property in a privileged or genuine way while not having it in a derivative or attenuated sense. Situationalism, by contrast, *does* maintain genuine incompatibility. To underline this point, and to emphasise that the situationalist's account really is an account of *change*, it's worth comparing the change case with what the situationalist will say about variation across space.[26]

Suppose a road is wide in town and narrow in the suburbs. There will be situations in which 'the road is wide' is true and situations in which 'the road is wide' is false. In larger situations containing both stretches of the road where it is wide and stretches where it is narrow, it's plausible to think there's no straightforward answer to the question: 'Is the road wide?' It is wide in some places, narrow in others. In other words, the proposition that the road is wide can be indeterminate in a larger situation s^*, while determinately true in some sub-situation s and determinately false in some sub-situation s'. This gives the situationalist's B-theoretic account of change over time a natural parallel with variation across space. This can be considered an advantage, as B-theorists typically take space and time to be at the very least closely analogous.[27]

---

[25] Mortensen (2016) is a resource for looking into this claim, which is made extensively.

[26] I am grateful to two referees for their quite different and equally helpful comments on the potential alignment/contrast between time and space in the situationalist picture.

[27] The attitude that relativity (whether special or general) has shown that space and time are but indistinguishable elements of a more fundamental spacetime is widespread, but a little too quick. Even though taking the physics seriously plausibly requires viewing spacetime as more ontologically basic than space and time, there are nevertheless interesting asymmetries between, for instance, regions in the absolute past, absolute future and absolute elsewhere of a particular event.

But this very parallel is also the source of a worry. If the situationalist's account of change is equivalent to variation across space, in what sense is it really a robust account of *change*? The response to this worry is to highlight a crucial difference between these two for a situationalist. As I have been arguing, situationalist change involves real incompatibility: when something changes there is a deep and irreducible conflict about how things are in different parts of reality. This is because the changing entity, the ultimate subject of predication, is numerically identical in the conflicting situations. But this is not the case for variation over space: the road which is wide in town is wide there because it has, in that place, a part which is wide. It is narrow in the suburbs because a *distinct* part of it is narrow there. This is why there is no 'Problem of Spatial Variation', as there is no incompatibility between one part of a road's being wide and another part of its being narrow. (This is also why the temporal parts solution to the problem of change works.) In the change case, by contrast, the endurantist constraint ensures that the ultimate subject of the predication is identical, and hence that there is real incompatibility between what is the case in a situation before the change and in one afterwards. So, while it is indeterminate whether the road is wide in s^*, because the road is not the ultimate subject of predication this indeterminacy is not fundamental.[28] Thus, the situationalist maintains an important parallel between space and time yet offers a robust account of change on which there is real incompatibility in change but not in spatial variation.

I have argued that the situationalist account meets the constraints on explanation I have described and, in so doing, offers a novel account of the persistence of material objects. This account is, to be sure, contentious but it has the advantage that, in a clear way, it maintains incompatibility between the states of affairs described by a change. In the next section, I will try to address some of the contentious features of the situationalist account.[29]

---

[28] A slightly different example might give us pause: it is hot in New York but not hot in London. Here, there is no obvious entity with parts such that one part is hot (in New York) and another part is not (in London). Nevertheless, I take a statement like 'it is hot' to refer to the local environment in such a way that there is no numerical identity between the ultimate subject of 'it is hot' in the New York situation and the ultimate subject of the same statement in the London situation.

[29] It is worth noting that situationalism can be augmented to provide a solution to Lewis's connected problem of variation across possible worlds, the problem of accidental intrinsics (see Lewis 1986 sect. 4.2). Given that there are transworld situations (which depends on a choice in one's situation theory), a situationalist can maintain strict transworld identity for entities whose properties vary between worlds. On this view, an entity can have a property in one (possible)

8.4 Worries

(a) Monotonicity

It is key to the situationalist solution that when something changes, what is true in a situation before the change needn't be true in a larger situation which includes times after the change as well. This contravenes a principle which might seem attractive, namely that whenever something is true in a situation it is thereby true in any further situations which have the former as a part. In situation theory, this is known as the question of the *universal persistence* of propositions across situations. This is somewhat unhelpful terminology in the present context, so I will refer to this property as the *monotonicity* of situations. It can be formally expressed as follows:

Monotonicity

If a proposition $p \in P$ is true in a situation $s \in S$ then p is true in any s^* such that $s \le s^{*30}$

As I say, the monotonicity of situations might initially seem desirable. After all, if something is the case in a portion of the world, why wouldn't it be the case in extensions of that portion of the world? If a proposition is true in a situation how could it be that adding further content to that situation makes it false?

However, there isn't agreement in situation semantics on monotonicity. Kratzer, for instance, accepts it (1989 sect. 3.4), while Elbourne (2005 p75–78) denies it. As it is central to my proposal that situations are not always monotonic, I will give some indicative reasons to support the general denial of monotonicity. I will not, however, exhaustively defend this claim as that would be beyond the scope of the chapter.

The first point to make is that there are immediate cases which look like counterexamples to *universal* persistence (i.e. exceptionless monotonicity). Take, for instance, the proposition that all the students passed the exam. This proposition could be true in a particular situation, such as a situation in which all first-year students on a particular course passed an exam. But there

---

situation, lack it in another, and it will be indeterminate in transworld situations combining these. See Iaquinto (2020) for a rather different but parallel move from temporal to modal disunity.

[30] P is the set of all propositions, S the set of all situations, and $\le$ is parthood. For present purposes, Classical Extensional Mereology for situations can be assumed.

are extensions of this situation in which that proposition is false. Take, for instance, the situation including all students at the university taking exams that year. This latter situation has the former as a part, but the proposition is true in the first and false in the second. There will be many similar apparent counterexamples which involve universal quantification, negative existentials, quantification using phrases such as 'no more than seven' and propositions expressing proportions using phrases such as 'half of'. In case like these, it seems clear that adding content to a situation could make a proposition that was true in that smaller situation fail to be true in an extension of it.

There are ways of maintaining monotonicity even in the face of such examples. One option is to introduce implicit domain restriction (this is a familiar move from other areas). But notice that this takes away from something which is initially an advantage of the situation-theoretic approach. Using situations, we can say that exactly the same proposition is expressed in different situations with correspondingly different truth-values. The proposition that all the children are tired makes precisely the same claim about the world in different situations: it states that every child (in the situation) is tired. This will be true about some portions of the world and false about others, but the claim being made is the same. Austin's work on truth (Austin 1950) is a historical precedent here: he distinguished between *types* of utterance and *token* utterances, the former given by rules concerning what is said (descriptive conventions) and the latter by rules concerning what it is said about (demonstrative conventions). In these terms, denying monotonicity allows us to say that the type of utterance is the same in different situations, while the token utterance is distinct. Because the token utterance is distinct, the truth-value can vary. Implicit domain restriction and similar approaches, by contrast, require that a different type of utterance is made by the same linguistic string in different situations. This means that something different is meant by these words in different situations, and what is claimed then has the same truth-value in all situations. As Kratzer makes clear (1989 p617) using implicit domain restriction requires a *different* proposition to be expressed by different utterances of the same sentence. While consistent, this seems somewhat against the grain of a situation-theoretic approach.

Suppose we accept that situations are not always monotonic in such cases. Is the situationalist solution given a firm grounding? Not yet. For notice that the counterexamples considered so far all involve complex propositions (generally involving quantifiers). The situationalist requires that even *atomic* propositions can fail to be monotonic. Propositions such as '*o* is F' are not true in some larger situations despite being true in some of their proper parts. The motivation for monotonicity seems especially strong when considering atomic propositions because it isn't obvious how adding extra content could prevent the orange from being ripe in the way that adding extra exam-taking students can make 'all the students passed the exam' false.[31]

I will not suggest that denying monotonicity is easy in the change case. I believe it to be a cost of the situationalist view that monotonicity can fail even when there are no extra entities in the larger situation. But I am suggesting that it is worth seeing what denying monotonicity can do. The cost it incurs is derived from the core commitment of situationalism: in cases of change the extra content added by material concerning the entity before/after the change is relevant to the truth-value of the proposition. This is because the world itself is irreducibly conflicted about the properties of the entity, and so parts of the world containing members from both sides of the conflict are situations which are themselves unsettled about the state of the entity.[32] The failure of monotonicity for such propositions is therefore intimately connected to the incompatibility that is preserved in the situationalist's account of change.

Monotonicity fails where the parts of the world disagree about what is the case. In many cases, such as those involving quantifiers, the disagreement arises because different parts of the world contain different *things*. Bits of the world with failing exam students disagree with those containing only passing students on the question of whether everyone passed the exam. What is distinctive about cases which give rise to metaphysical indeterminacy is that the things involved stay the same, but the way those things are is different in different parts of the world. Change is the paradigmatic example of this robust form of a failure of monotonicity. Failures of monotonicity of this type, namely when the entities involved are fixed, also thereby limn the portions of the world into which reality fractures. In other words, the determinate pieces of reality are distinctive in that they contain no such failures of monotonicity.[33]

---

[31] The case mentioned earlier of a road which is wide in some places and narrow in others is of interest here. 'The road is wide' doesn't seem to involve quantification, but does violate monotonicity. Unlike the situation in the change case, though, there are extra relevant entities in the larger situation where it is indeterminate: additional portions of the road.

[32] Here, again, the comparison with a modal realist who accepts transworld identity gives a helpful parallel. See footnote 17.

[33] It is worth emphasising that, even for the situationalist, most propositions true in a part of a situation are thereby true in the whole situation. There is therefore an interesting semantic project to find a restricted version of monotonicity which does hold for the situationalist. I'll leave this avenue for further exploration.

THE SITUATIONALIST ACCOUNT OF CHANGE 267

I now wish to move on to discuss another connected concern one might have with situationalism, namely that it requires indeterminacy and the corresponding supporting metaphysics.

(b) Indeterminacy/reality in pieces

It is distinctive of situationalism that it posits metaphysical indeterminacy in some situations. This is contentious: metaphysical indeterminacy has been considered suspect in various quarters.[34] It is at least respectable enough to also be defended in several places.[35] I won't argue for the cogency of metaphysical indeterminacy here (though see Darby, Pickup and Robson (2017) and Darby and Pickup (2021) for some of my views on this). Instead I want to spell out in more detail the picture of reality that situationalism suggests so that the theory can be evaluated with full appreciation for the underlying account of the world it invokes.

According to situationalism, there are parts of the world which fundamentally disagree. This disagreement is deep and serious: different parts of the world make true propositions which are incompatible. In our world, reality is in pieces.[36] I take *this* to be the fundamental claim of situationalism, and I grant that it is hard to countenance. A natural aim in systematic metaphysics is to promote harmony, while this account contains irreducible disharmony. For metaphysicians of a certain mindset, it would be disappointing to discover that the parts of reality didn't neatly cohere. I therefore admit that situationalism is radical and, to some extent, costly.

However, it is important to recognise that by accepting that different parts of the world have incompatible propositions true in them we are not proposing a dialetheist view.[37] In other words, on the situationalist account there are no true contradictions. How so? Well, truth is evaluated with respect to situations, so for a contradiction to be true is for there to be a situation in which some proposition and its negation are both true. But there

---

[34] A representative sample of those who think all indeterminacy is representational (i.e. not metaphysical) include Russell, Dummett, Lewis and Sainsbury. See Keil (2013) for an introduction.

[35] See, e.g., Williams (2008), Barnes (2010), Bokulich (2014) and Wilson (2016).

[36] Perhaps in other worlds, which contained no change, reality wouldn't have to contain fundamental disagreement. One could still have a situationalist account of such a world. (Thanks to Stephen Williams for focusing my attention on this possibility.)

[37] A dialetheist can say some interesting things about change. As an example, see chs. 11, 12 and 15 of Priest (2006).

is no such situation. In a change case some proposition is true in a situation, the negation of this proposition is true in a distinct situation, but because monotonicity is denied any larger situation which has both of these as parts is not a situation which verifies both the proposition and its negation. In particular, if there is a situation corresponding to the whole actual world this situation will contain no true contradictions. It will, however, be gappy: it will lack truth-values for some propositions.

The fact that there are no true contradictions in situationalism distinguishes it from dialetheism. There is no risk, for instance, of explosion. Nevertheless, we might still be concerned that the intuitions driving the distaste for dialetheism are not merely that no *formal* contradiction should be endorsed (and the semantic consequences of doing so), but also what might be termed a metaphysical intuition that reality is unitary. Depending on exactly how this intuition is spelt out, situationalism may be in tension with it.

According to situationalism, metaphysical indeterminacy arises from the deeply conflicted parts of reality. Truth-value gaps appear when conflicting parts of reality are put together. Reality is therefore not unitary in the sense of containing only elements which can be combined in a straightforward additive way without giving rise to disagreement. The pieces of reality into which the situationalist carves the world are robustly independent of one another. Though they can be combined they cannot be integrated, if by integration we mean that how things are in these distinct portions of reality is incorporated *tout court* into a broader portion of reality. The denial of monotonicity informs us that some discrete chunks of the world are not able to be integrated in this way. These chunks are not homogenous, and by way not merely of exhibiting variety of *which* entities and properties there are but also of *how* those entities and properties are. To reiterate, this heterogeneity is not to be relativised away.

While this is indeed controversial, I think it can be motivated by reflection on change. If we ask of the changing orange whether it is ripe, a straightforward answer isn't forthcoming. We might reply, 'When?'. We are asking which portion of the world is under consideration.[38] Definitive answers can be given if a time before the change or a time after the change is specified.

---

[38] Those favouring a different account of change will take this question to be a request to disambiguate several different, temporally relativised things which could be asked by 'is the orange ripe?'. But it seems, at least to me, that we want to know what *part of the world* is relevant, not which (temporally relativised) object, property or instantiation relation is being referred to.

But what happen if we are to assess whether the orange is ripe across a timespan which includes the change? It seems plausible to say there is no answer to this question: it is unripe in some parts of that timespan and ripe for other parts of that timespan. In the timespan as a whole, it is neither unripe nor ripe.

If this way of thinking is on the right track, it provides some support for the situationalist account. For the situationalist takes statements like this at face value. While the temporal parts theorist chops objects into parts, the relational properties theorist chops properties into parts, and the instantiation-indexer chops instantiation into parts, the situationalist chops reality into parts. Importantly, these parts of reality are equally privileged (unlike on A-theory). The very same orange just is unripe in the earlier chunk of the world and ripe in the later chunk of the world. These chunks are metaphysically on a par. But when the chunks are put together, reality is unsettled about how the orange is.[39]

This, in brief, is the metaphysics of situationalism. As I have been at pains to make clear, it is controversial. However, I believe it offers a distinctive approach to accounting for change. In order to underline this, in the final section I will compare the view to a couple of recent alternatives to which it bears a resemblance. This will both serve to highlight the ways it is different, hence making the view clearer, and perhaps offer some indicative reasons to take situationalism as a serious contender.

8.5 Comparisons

(a) Fragmentalisms

Kit Fine's fragmentalism (in his 2005 and 2006, and explored in a small literature including Lipman (2015, 2016), Loss (2017, 2018) and Simon (2018)) is a view which bears significant similarities to the situationalism I'm presenting. Fragmentalism is a view which allows perspectival facts to be taken seriously without metaphysical privilege being given to one perspective. The most developed application is to tense, where fragmentalism offers

---

[39] As mentioned earlier, it would be natural to add to this picture the idea that the smaller situations are more fundamental than the larger ones they compose. Thus determinacy and fundamentality would be aligned. I think this is probably the right way to develop the view, but nothing I have said so far requires it.

a novel way to be a realist about tense. I'll very briefly recount Fine's view and its further specification by commentators and show some key differences between it and situationalism.

The standard way of being a realist about tense is to say that there is an ontological or metaphysical priority of some time (or times) over the others. Fragmentalism denies this and holds that all times are ontologically and metaphysically on a par; on this point it agrees with the B-theory of time. However, and unlike B-theory, it is a realist view about tense: it contends that reality really is perspectival with respect to time. No time is privileged, but tense is irreducible.

To be more precise, Fine introduces fragmentalism as the denial of the following thesis:

Coherence
Reality is not irreducibly incoherent, i.e. its composition by incompatible facts must be explained in terms of its composition by compatible facts.[40]

In effect, what the fragmentalist denies is that there is a holistic picture of reality which contains all the facts and is coherent. There are chunks of reality—fragments—which are coherent. But these fragments do not necessarily cohere with each other. That is, different but equally privileged parts of the sum total of reality are in disagreement. This has clear parallels with my situationalism. But there are differences.

Note first that situationalism and fragmentalism talk about different things: fragmentalism in this context is concerned with *tense*, while situationalism is a tenseless account.[41] Fragmentalism is realist about tense, by which Fine means that fragmentalism takes reality to be composed of tensed facts. What the fragments of fragmentalism disagree about is the attributions of past/present/future to the ways things are. One fragment, for instance, will have KF's sitting as being present and his standing as being future, while another will have his sitting as being past and his standing as present. Reality is irreducibly tensed, and the view is fragmentalist because the different

---

[40] Fine 2005 p273. It is important to note that the use of 'facts' here does not commit Fine, or his interpreters, to an ontology containing facts as fundamental constituents: the claims can be expressed using only sentential operators. This should be borne in mind throughout this section.

[41] Fine also applies fragmentalism to the first-person perspective and there may be other versions of fragmentalism applying the view to different domains. I'll focus on the temporal case for the contrast with situationalism.

fragments are incompatible with respect to *how* reality is tensed. Fragments agree about what is (tenselessly) the case, but disagree about attributions of tense to what is (tenselessly) the case.

By contrast, there is nothing in situationalism which requires or even suggests that tense be taken seriously or be irreducible. The propositions we have been considering are to be interpreted as tenseless.[42] As a straightforward B-theoretic view, situationalism rejects Fine's premise that reality is composed of tensed facts.[43] Situationalism, as applied to the problem of change, is about objects having properties, not about the past, present or future. The situations which fundamentally disagree in the situationalist account disagree about what is (tenselessly) the case: in one situation the orange is (tenselessly) ripe, in another is it not. But in neither is there an important fact about what is present. This is a major difference between the views.

A second significant distinction is connected. Fragmentalism is perspectival: the fragments are irreducibly from a certain point of view, and they are incoherent because the points of view attribute different tensed features to the world. This suggests that in each fragment we have a complete account of all facts, but from a particular (tensed) perspective. e.g. in any fragment KF's sitting and KF's standing will be accounted for, but from varying tensed views. Finean fragments are not times but particular temporal perspectives on the whole of history.

Situationalism is not perspectival: situations are not *perspectives* on reality but *parts* of reality. This is an important point. Situations do not encode, require, or bring with them an outlook on the world. They are rather elements of the world. It is because of this that situations involve what is *tenselessly* the case: there is no implicit or explicit appeal to a point of view on reality.[44] Temporally constrained situations say nothing about other

---

[42] Given that the situationalist is concerned with what is tenselessly the case, accounting for the behaviour of tensed sentences will be an additional project. Although, as I have said, my aims in this chapter are metaphysical rather than semantic, it is worth indicating the resources available to the situationalist here. As with other B-theories, situationalism will take tense to be a derivative (if not reducible) feature, dependent on the truth of tenseless propositions at certain times. Given that times can be associated with particular instantaneous situations, truth in such situations and their relative ordering can naturally generate a structure to give a foundation for B-theoretic accounts of tensed sentences. (Relativistic concerns can be assuaged by making the designation of situations as instantaneous a frame-relative matter.)

[43] To repeat footnote 40: Fine is not ontologically committed to facts. Nevertheless, reality is tensed in a way that can be represented through its composition by tensed facts (even if the tensed nature of reality can ultimately be captured using sentential operators rather than facts).

[44] This is discussed in more detail in part (c) of this section.

times, whether tensed or tenselessly. What they do is say *how things are*, in an unvarnished and unrelativised way. This is what gives rise to the disagreement between situations.

So in one sense, fragmentalism is more radical than situationalism, while in another sense situationalism is more radical than fragmentalism. Fragmentalism is more radical in that the perspectives encoded by the different fragments are global: each is like a view of the whole world. The incoherence between fragments is incoherence between different holistic accounts of how all of reality is. By contrast, situationalism only posits a disagreement between *parts* of reality: the incompatible situations which are the equivalent of the fragments of the fragmentalist are not holistic, nor do they attempt to capture everything which is the case.

But situationalism is more radical than fragmentalism in that the disagreements between the chunks of reality are disagreements about what is (tenselessly) the case: they are disagreements about the attributions of properties to objects. The disagreements in the fragmentalist's case, by contrast, are disagreements about the tensed features of reality or, in other words, the temporal relationship between subject and what is (tenselessly) the case.

To illustrate this, consider what a fragmentalist and a situationalist will say about the changing orange. The fragments of a fragmentalist will each include the whole career of the orange, from its unripe to ripe states. But different fragments will have different tense perspectives on the orange's ripeness. For instance, one fragment will include the facts that the orange is (presently) unripe and that it will be ripe. Another fragment will include the facts that the orange was unripe and that it is (presently) ripe. The facts of the different fragments are incompatible, hence the fragmentation. By contrast, as we have seen, the situationalist has distinct situations, which need not contain the whole career of the orange. Some situations will disagree about the orange, but they disagree about whether the orange is (tenselessly) ripe. In one situation, the orange is (tenselessly) unripe, and hence it's not the case that it is (tenselessly) ripe. In another, later situation the orange is (tenselessly) ripe. The cross-change situations containing both are indeterminate.

Situationalism and fragmentalism concern different things, namely what's tenselessly the case and what the time is. They also have different mechanisms: partiality for situationalism and perspective for fragmentalism. They thereby are different in scope, for fragments are accounts of everything that happens, but each from a particular point of view, while disagreeing situations are accounts of less than everything, but not from a point of view. Situationalism is a B-theoretic way to capture change, whereas fragmentalism attempts to combine A-theory with the denial that any perspective is to be prioritised.

I will highlight a final key difference. This is the role indeterminacy plays in the situationalist picture. Fine doesn't expand in detail on how the fragmentalist should conceive of the 'über-reality' which contains disagreeing fragments. He notes that fragmentalism doesn't lead to accepting contradictions, because, while reality is in a sense contradictory, no contradiction will ever be assertible (Fine 2005 p282). However, he doesn't say what happens when disagreeing fragments are put together (if this is even possible). On the view I have presented, disagreeing parts of reality can be put together, and this is where metaphysical indeterminacy enters in: it is in combining incompatible parts of reality that we generate gaps. Indeterminacy doesn't feature in fragmentalism but is essential to situationalism.

The interpretations of fragmentalism in the literature take up, in different ways, the challenge of filling in Fine's sketch of the view. I wish to quickly flag that the way I develop situationalism is importantly distinct from each of them.

Lipman (2015, 2016) uses a primitive co-obtainment relation to formalise the fragmentalist claims (see esp. (2016) sect. 4). On this view, obtaining and co-obtaining are distinct. Co-obtaining is a relation which holds between facts when they obtain *together*. Pairs of facts can both obtain without co-obtaining, and can co-obtain without both obtaining. The distinction between obtaining and co-obtaining gives Lipman two different ways facts can conflict; firstly, by being unable to both obtain (being *contrary*) and secondly, by being unable to co-obtain (being *incompatible*). A semantics is provided that shows how incompatibility (in Lipman's sense) doesn't lead to contradiction.

Lipman's interpretation of fragmentalism is novel and promising. Co-obtainment might be the best way to render Fine's views. But it will not be the best way to grasp the parallel claim in the change case. This is because a central motivation for situationalism is the desire to capture *real* incompatibility. This is a supposed advantage of the view. Incompatibility as defined by Lipman, however, is not incompatibility in the straightforward sense. In fact, as it is definitional that two facts can be incompatible but both obtain, facts which are incompatible in Lipman's sense can both be true. Thus, for instance, in the change case the orange's being unripe obtains and the orange's being ripe obtains. What isn't the case is that the orange's being unripe *co-obtains* with the orange's being ripe. Rather, the orange's being unripe co-obtains with it not being the case that the orange is ripe, though this latter proposition does not obtain.

Our ordinary notion of incompatibility doesn't use co-obtainment but rather obtainment: two states are incompatible when they cannot both obtain. Given this, Lipman's interpretation doesn't give us what we want in the change case, because no pairs of facts both obtain which are incompatible in this sense (in Lipman's terminology: *contrary*). Situationalism, however, allows that contrary facts can be true in different actual situations. A proposition and its negation can be true (i.e. obtain) in distinct situations. There is therefore no distinction between facts being contrary and incompatible in situationalism. This makes the incompatibility in change cases more robust.[45]

Simon (2018) applies fragmentalism to B-theory endurance (as well as interpretation of quantum theory) and so the issues that he addresses are closer to those I discuss than the tense-related concerns of Fine, Lipman and Loss. Simon's own proposal is 'smooth' fragmentalism, a view which softens fragmentalism so that there is no real (logical) incompatibility even between different fragments. The facts in different fragments are logically compatible: nothing co-obtains with anything contrary to anything else which obtains. They are, however, incompatible in a different sense: they are incompatible just in virtue of being unable to co-obtain. Again, the view is interesting and novel, but distinct from my suggestion here. Smooth fragmentalism has even less incompatibility than Lipman's 'jagged' fragmentalism, as Simon himself points out. It is a virtue for him that this is so. From my point of view, however, we want a more jagged version, albeit one which doesn't tip into what he terms dialethic fragmentalism. That is what I hope to have offered.

Mention of dialethic fragmentalism brings us to Loss (2017) (see also his (2018)). Loss's version of fragmentalism denies the principle of adjunction, that the truth of p and of q entails the truth of 'p and q'. Reality is fragmented because true propositions cannot always be conjoined. This allows him to adopt a subvaluation view according to which something is true iff it is true in some fragment. As a consequence, some proposition and its negation can both be true (*simpliciter*) by being true in different fragments while their conjunction is not true. Thus the law of

---

[45] Though this comes at a cost: see the previous section.

non-contradiction, stating that no conjunction of proposition and its negation is true, is upheld despite contradictory propositions being true.

Although Loss avoids introducing a new primitive co-obtainment relation, to which Lipman and Simon are committed, his resulting theory goes further than the situationalist, as can be seen by way of a couple of observations. Firstly, on Loss's view it could be the case even within a fragment that a proposition and its negation are assertible: all that is debarred is their conjunction being assertible (see his fn 19). This suggests that, for Loss, propositions and their negations can both be *true* in a fragment, although their conjunction will not be. Secondly, while for the situationalist truth is always relative to a situation, Loss has a subvaluation approach to truth. This gives reality as a whole (i.e. Fine's über-reality) a contradictory character, while the situationalist's denial of monotonicity allows for gappiness instead. I doubt situationalism will be seen as a bastion of classical logic, but it seems as least less revisionary than this proposal.

So, to conclude, there are interesting and noteworthy overlaps between the fragmentalisms discussed here and situationalism. Space has constrained a detailed comparison, but I hope to have shown that the position I have carved out has something distinct to say here on the issue of persistence through change. In particular, I hope it warrants the claim that situationalism steers a unique course between compatibility and contradiction which is profitable in the case of change.

(b) Bottani's indeterminacy

Andrea Bottani (2020) offers a response to Lewis's temporary intrinsics argument which invokes indeterminacy in an attempt to maintain that things have properties *simpliciter*. His intentions are somewhat aligned with mine, as Bottani recognises the need to uphold a straightforward relationship between objects and properties as well as proposing radical indeterminacy as a way of retaining this.[46]

However, there are significant differences between the two views. Bottani interprets having *simpliciter* as having eternally and essentially, i.e. having regardless of the time. So, for him, no temporary (or even contingent but permanent) properties are had *simpliciter* by their bearers. Rather, if

---

[46] He also makes what I consider to be plausible criticisms of adverbialism and SOFism, other views in the vicinity. The positive proposal appears in sect. 7.

an object doesn't have a property eternally and essentially it is radically indeterminate whether it has it. (Radical indeterminacy here means it is indeterminate whether the sentence expressing that the entity has the property is true, and indeterminate whether it is false.)

By contrast, situationalism allows that temporary properties can be had *simpliciter*, but this is the case within a particular situation. Having *simpliciter* is not having in all situations: having *simpliciter* is rather having in an unmediated way. It is a matter of the instantiation of a property by an object being univocal. Thus it needn't follow from the essence of an individual that it has a property in order for it to have that property *simpliciter*. No appeal to essences is required. What is the case, however, depends on the situation under consideration. (Notice, too, that the indeterminacy in situationalism is not of the radical kind Bottani envisages; it is just that the relevant propositions are neither true nor false.)

There are a couple of advantages I see to the situationalist approach. Firstly, of course, it is better not to be committed to an ontology of essences if one needn't be: it's contentious whether there are such things. Secondly, as it stands Bottani's view seems to lose expressive power. If all claims of the form '*o* is F' are (radically) indeterminate when F-ness isn't part of *o*'s essence, how can we capture the obvious truth that the orange is ripe at the later time? For surely the orange is indeed ripe at the later time. But the orange is not essentially ripe so, for Bottani, not ripe *simpliciter*. In what sense is it ripe? Nothing has been said about how to keep hold of the true statements we make about changing particulars. It might be that Bottani's account can be supplemented here, but as it stands there is no contextual constraint to the indeterminacy of the orange's ripeness.

So, despite the fact that Bottani's critical arguments are useful for providing motivation for an indeterministic account of persistence, the positive account is wanting. This provides a form of support for the situationalist alternative.

(c) Moore's disunified world(s)

In several places, Adrian Moore develops, though does not defend, views which have parallels to the situationalist picture of reality (see his 1997, and several essays collected in his 2019). The issue motivating his discussion is the question of whether reality, understood as the totality of what is actual, is unified or not. This connects to the question of whether there is an absolute perspective, i.e. a possible representation of reality which is not from any point of view.[47] Moore's own position is that absolute representations are possible and that reality is unified, though he is careful to note that he doesn't take himself to have conclusively demonstrated this.

I do not have space to elaborate on or deeply engage with Moore's rich reflections on this topic. But I will briefly highlight some features of the alternatives he considers, in order to make clear some important differences between them and the situationalist theory I am presenting.

Reality being disunified is a matter of multiple different worlds being real. 'Worlds' here is not meant in the modal sense: the disunity of reality is not modal realism. Rather, these multiple worlds are multiple *actualities*. Strikingly, Moore several times turns to tense as an example candidate for how a theorist could maintain multiple actualities, anticipating a fragmentalist-style account. He says:

> Given some tensed item of knowledge, there is no indicating what makes it true except from the same temporal point of view ... Reality fractures into different temporal worlds, then. Each temporal point of view carries its own world with it. The facts that peculiarly constitute one of *these* worlds can be indicated only from the corresponding temporal point of view. It immediately follows that there are some items of knowledge, namely items of knowledge from different temporal points of view, for which there is no single way of indicating how reality is thereby known to be.[48] (2019 p178)

It being humid today is a fact which is not able to be represented from any other temporal perspective: is not identical to the fact that it was humid yesterday, from the perspective of tomorrow (though there may be some other connection between these facts). Each temporal standpoint, therefore, provides a universe of facts which are not able to be united into a single point of view.

As I have said, Moore does not accept these claims. He believes that tense and all other perspectival markers do not undermine the possibility of

---

[47] The exact connection between these questions is a matter of some delicacy. For Moore, the unity of reality is an assumption in an argument for the possibility of absolute representations (see his 1997 ch. 4).

[48] Chapters 11, 12, 13 and 14 of Moore's 2019 engage with versions of this view. These chapters are drawn from papers dating from 2001 to 2016. The Moorean theory is attested in the earliest paper: "The picture ... is that reality fractures into different worlds, where a world is constituted by a set of facts. Each temporal point of view carries its own world with it." (2019 p151)

an absolute perspective. Indeed, he thinks an absolute perspective may be constitutive of what it is for something to answer to the title of 'reality'. Nevertheless, we have here a noteworthy precursor to the situationalist account.

The situationalist will agree that reality is disunified, because for the situationalist there are portions of reality which disagree. Reality is, indeed, in pieces, just as Moore's interlocutor proposes. Depending on exactly how the meaning of 'world' is specified, the situationalist can also therefore accept that there are multiple 'worlds'. These 'worlds', however, are not intuitively world-sized: they do not claim to cover everything. Rather, they are portions of the whole of reality which contain no disagreements (and hence within which monotonicity is preserved). They are neither the worlds of modal realism, nor the fragments of Fine. This is why I am wary of using the term 'worlds' to speak of such situations. Nevertheless, the monotonic situations which are parts into which reality fractures, on the situationalist's account, can be conceived as a multiplicity or plurality that cuts against the claim that reality is unified, in Moore's sense.

There are, however, several ways in which situationalism fails to exactly correspond to the views Moore considers. First, as mentioned in the previous paragraph, the elements of the situationalist's disunified reality do not even purport to be maximal, world-sized entities: they are explicitly partial. Secondly, situationalism as presented is concerned with reality itself, without involving representations of or perspectives on reality.[49] It is an attempted description of the way things are, separate from the issue of how we engage with what there is. Situationalism, therefore, does not involve the claim that reality is perspectival. This is because, thirdly, competing situations are not competing accounts of one and the same phenomenon but of distinct parts of reality. It is not that equally robust facts have competing, irremovable inflections, but that there are equally robust, competing inflectionless facts. Finally, situationalism essentially involves metaphysical indeterminacy whereas that is absent from the views Moore is concerned with. Depending

---

[49] Moore, I suspect, would be interested in interrogating the distinction between a concern with reality itself and a concern with representations of reality. There are many interesting issues which arise here.

The view he considers is supposed to be an account of *reality*, not just of our representations of reality, which might seem to undercut the difference I am trying to indicate. But, nevertheless, on this view the phenomena of disunity is ultimately derived from the inescapably perspectival nature of reality. So while the Moorean multiplicity of worlds does not require *actual* representation or an inhabited perspective, it plausibly *does* require that reality is structured representationally. This is not the case for situationalism.

on exactly what is meant by 'world' and 'unity', the situationalist can say that there *is* a single, unified world; it is just unavoidably indeterminate.[50]

There is an interesting feature of these four points of difference between situationalism and Moore's multiplicity of worlds: each of them is also a distinction between situationalism and fragmentalism (see (a)). This lends weight to the idea that Moore and Fine are articulating accounts which are sympathetic to one another. Situationalism's distinctive position certainly bears a resemblance to these earlier theories, but it makes a set of different, and differently challenging, claims.

8.6 Conclusion

Situationalism offers a novel account of the persistence of changing objects. It suggests that reality is in pieces, and that these pieces fundamentally disagree about how changing things are. Persistence through change, then, is a matter of existing across situations which disagree in this way. Situationalists can allow that one and the same object has and lacks one and the same property in one and the same way in different portions of the world. Given the metaphysical equality between these portions of the world, reality is fragmented. Reality as a whole, however, is not contradictory because what is true in disagreeing parts of the world does not straightforwardly compose what is true in the whole. Where reality disagrees, the whole world is indeterminate. Though this picture is radical, it does have the virtue of maintaining serious incompatibility in instances of change: what is the case before the change is simply not consistent with what is the case afterwards. Insofar as change involves serious incompatibility, situationalism has an advantage. While there are costs to situationalism, some of which I've highlighted, it is an instructive theory for showing how things could exist through change even when change is interpreted in this strong sense. For that reason, I suggest it is added to the menu of options. A full evaluation of its worth will require a broader investigation of the value of situationalism in a number of other contexts, to assess whether the costs are worth the advantages.[51]

---

[50] Of course, if being unified and being a world are understood in terms of determinacy (and thereby, in the situationalist set-up, non-conflict) there would be no such single, unified world. But there will be other ways to understand these terms too.

[51] This chapter has been through various forms, and I have received much helpful feedback on it. I would especially like to thank Gonzalo Rodriguez-Pereyra, Nick Jones, Stephen Williams, Adrian Moore, Dominic Duguid-Alford, the reviewers for the Sanders Prize, and audiences in Birmingham, Stockholm, Milan, Oxford, St Andrews and Dublin.

References

Austin, John L. 1950. "Truth." *Aristotelian Society Supplement*, 24: 111–129.

Barnes, Elizabeth. 2010. "Ontic Vagueness: A Guide for the Perplexed." *Nôus*, 44(4): 601–627.

Barwise, Jon. 1988. "Notes on branch points in a situation theory." In his *The Situation in Logic* 255–276. Stanford: CSLI.

Barwise, Jon and John Perry. 1999. *Situations and Attitudes*. Stanford, CA: CSLI.

Bokulich, Alisa. 2014. "Metaphysical Indeterminacy, Properties, and Quantum Theory." *Res Philosophica*, 91(3): 449–475.

Bottani, Andrea C. 2020. "Bringing back Intrinsics to Enduring Things." *Synthese*. 197(11): 4813–4834. https://doi.org/10.1007/s11229-016-1157-2.

Darby, George and Pickup, Martin. 2021. "Modelling Deep Indeterminacy." *Synthese*, 198 (2): 1685–1710.

Darby, George, Pickup, Martin, and Robson, Jon. 2017. "Deep Indeterminacy in Physics and Fiction." In O. Bueno, G. Darby, S. French and D. Rickles (eds.), *Thinking about Science, Reflecting on Art*, 99-118. London: Routledge.

Einhouser, Iris. 2012. "Is There a (Meta)Problem of Change?" *Analytic Philosophy*, 53 (4): 344–351.

Elbourne, Paul. 2005. *Situations and Individuals*. Cambridge, MA: MIT Press.

Elbourne, Paul. 2013. *Definite Descriptions*. Oxford: Oxford University Press.

Fine, Kit. 2005. "Tense and Reality." In his *Modality and Tense: Philosophical Papers*. Oxford: Oxford University Press, 261–320.

Fine, Kit. 2006. "The Reality of Tense." *Synthese*, 150 (3): 399–414.

Fine, Kit. 2014. "Truth-Maker Semantics for Intuitionistic Logic." *Journal of Philosophical Logic*, 43: 549–577.

Fine, Kit. 2020. "Yablo on Subject-Matter." *Philosophical Studies*, 177: 129–171.

Gallois, André. 1998. *Occasions of Identity: A Study in the Metaphysics of Persistence, Change and Sameness*. Oxford: Clarendon Press.

Geach, P. T. 1967. "Identity." *Review of Metaphysics*, 21: 3–12.

Giberman, Daniel. 2017. "Bent, Not Broken: Why Exemplification Simpliciter Remains a Problem for Eternalist Endurantism." *Erkenntnis*, 82: 947–966.

Goodman, Nelson. 1978. *Ways of Worldmaking*. Indianapolis, IN: Hackett.

Goodman, Nelson. 1984. *Of Mind and Other Matters*. Cambridge, MA: Harvard University Press.

Hansson, Tobias. 2007. "The Problem(s) of Change Revisited." *Dialectica*, 61: 265–274.

Heim, Irene. 1990. "E-Type Pronouns and Donkey Anaphora." *Linguistics and Philosophy*, 13: 137–178.

Hofweber, Thomas. 2009. "The Meta-problem of Change." *Nous*, 43: 286–314.

Iaquinto, Samuele. 2020. "Modal Fragmentalism." *The Philosophical Quarterly*, 70 (280): 570–587.

Keil, Geert. 2013. "Introduction: Vagueness and Ontology." *Metaphysica*, 14: 149–164.

Kratzer, Angelika. 1989. "An Investigation of the Lumps of Thought." *Linguistics and Philosophy*, 12 (2): 607–653.

Kratzer, Angelika. 2019. "Situations in Natural Language Semantics." *The Stanford Encyclopedia of Philosophy* (Summer 2019 Edition), Edward N. Zalta (ed.), available at https://plato.stanford.edu/archives/sum2019/entries/situations-semantics/. Accessed 10/02/2022.

Lewis, David. 1986. *On the Plurality of Worlds*. Oxford: Blackwell.

Lewis, David. 2002. "Tensing the Copula." *Mind*, 111: 1–14.

Lipman, Martin. 2015. "On Fine's Fragmentalism." *Philosophical Studies*, 172 (12): 3119–3133.

Lipman, Martin. 2016. "Perspectival Variance and Worldly Fragmentation." *Australasian Journal of Philosophy*, 94 (1): 42–57.

Loss, Roberto. 2017. "Fine's McTaggart: Reloaded." *Manuscrito—Rec. Int. Fil. Campinas*, 40: 209–239.

Loss, Roberto. 2018. "Fine's Trilemma and the Reality of Tensed Facts." *Thought*, 7: 209–217.

Markosian, Ned. 2016. "Time." *The Stanford Encyclopedia of Philosophy* (Fall 2016 Edition), Edward N. Zalta (ed.), available at https://plato.stanford.edu/archives/fall2016/entries/time/. Accessed 10/02/2022.

Mellor, D. H. 1998. *Real Time II*. London: Routledge.

Moore, A. W. 1997. *Points of View*. Oxford: Oxford University Press.

Moore, A. W. 2019. *Language, World, and Limits*. Oxford: Oxford University Press.

Mortensen, Chris. 2016. "Change and Inconsistency." *The Stanford Encyclopedia of Philosophy* (Winter 2016 Edition), Edward N. Zalta (ed.), available at https://plato.stanford.edu/archives/win2016/entries/change/. Accessed 10/02/2022.

Ney, Alyssa. 2014. *Metaphysics: An Introduction*. London: Routledge.

Oderberg, David. 2004. "Temporal Parts and the Possibility of Change." *Philosophy and Phenomenological Research*, 69 (3): 686–703.

Pickup, Martin. 2016. "A Situationalist Solution to the Ship of Theseus Puzzle." *Erkenntnis*, 81 (5): 973–992.

Pickup, Martin. 2021. "The Problem of Change Restored." In B. Göcke and R. Weir (eds.), *From Existentialism to Metaphysics: The Philosophy of Stephen Priest*, 203–222. Berlin: Peter Lang.

Priest, Graham. 2006. *In Contradiction: A Study of the Transconsistent*. 2nd Edition. Oxford: Oxford University Press.

Raven, Michael. 2011. "There is a Problem of Change." *Philosophical Studies*, 149: 77–96.

Rodriguez-Pereyra, Gonzalo. 2003. "What is wrong with the Relational Theory of Change?" In H. Lillehammer and G. Rodriguez-Pereyra (eds.), *Real Metaphysics*, 184–195. London: Routledge.

Rychter, Pablo. 2009. "There is No Problem of Change." *Dialectica*, 63: 7–22.

Sider, Ted, John Hawthorne, and Dean Zimmerman. 2008. *Contemporary Debates in Metaphysics*. Oxford: Blackwell.

Simon, Jonathan. 2018. "Fragmenting the Wave Function." In K. Bennett and D. Zimmerman (eds.), *Oxford Studies in Metaphysics* 11, 123–148. Oxford: Oxford University Press.

Williams, J. R. G. 2008. "Ontic Vagueness and Metaphysical Indeterminacy." *Philosophy Compass*, 3(4): 763–788.

Williams, S. G. Forthcoming "Focality, Analogy, and the Articulation of Concepts." In a Festschrift for David Charles (title pending).

Wilson, Jessica. 2016. "Are there Indeterminate States of Affairs? Yes." In E. Barnes (ed.), *Current Controversies in Metaphysics*, 105–119. London: Taylor and Francis.

Yablo, Stephen. 2014. *Aboutness*. Princeton, NJ: Princeton University Press.

Yablo, Stephen. 2017. "Reply to Fine on Aboutness." *Philosophical Studies*, 175: 1495–1512.

9

The Logic of Past-Alteration

Alex Kaiserman

9.1 Introduction

There are many reasons to want to travel to the past—see the dinosaurs, talk to a prophet, find out what the Voynich manuscript was really all about. But ask most people what they'd do with a time machine and they'll tell you not just of their hopes of *seeing* the past, but also of *changing* it—of killing baby Hitler to prevent the Holocaust, warning previous generations of impending environmental disasters, maybe thinking twice before sending that passive-aggressive email to Kevin in marketing yesterday. Are such hopes really coherent? Is it possible to change the past?

Many philosophers believe that the answer to this question is *no*. After all, they point out, these events (Hitler's atrocities, the email to Kevin, and so on) have, by hypothesis, *already happened*; the idea that there is anything we could do now to make these things *not* have happened is "logically incoherent" (Fulmer 1983: 33), "senseless" (Brown 1985: 85), "radically absurd" (Flew 1954: 57), "a logical impossibility" (Hospers 1967: 177). The past is unshake-able; it cannot be altered.

Against this prevailing sentiment, some philosophers have recently suggested that we can make sense of past-alteration if we are willing to postulate an extra dimension of time.[1] But for all the talk of past-alteration's 'logical impossibility', there have been few attempts to actually apply logical resources to the question of whether past-alteration is possible.[2] This is

---

[1] See, e.g., Meiland (1974), Goddu (2003, 2011), van Inwagen (2010), Hudson and Wasserman (2010), Bernstein (2017).

[2] A notable exception is Wasserman (2017: 102–6), who in a suggestive passage correctly identifies that any logic of past-alteration would have to permit violations of the (GP) axiom of standard tense logic. Wasserman doesn't actually provide such a logic, however. Moreover, he appears to presuppose that the option of constructing a tense logic that permits violations of (GP) to make sense of past-alteration is one which is only available to A-theorists, though as

Alex Kaiserman, *The Logic of Past-Alteration* In: *Oxford Studies in Metaphysics Volume 13*.
Edited by: Karen Bennett and Dean W. Zimmerman, Oxford University Press. © Alex Kaiserman 2023.
DOI: 10.1093/oso/9780192886033.003.0009

what I propose to do in this chapter. I start by showing that past-alteration scenarios violate two important tense-logical principles: (LIN-P) (roughly, the claim that *whatever will have been the case is at some time the case*) and (GP) (roughly, the claim that *whatever is the case will always have been the case*). I'll then construct a tense logic which allows for violations of (LIN-P) and (GP), and use it to argue that past-alteration is possible—with just a *single* dimension of time—if, but only if, it's possible for time to be 'backwards-branching' in structure and for the relation of precedence to 'come apart' from the relation of succession (in a sense that will be made more precise shortly). The rest of the chapter will explore some of the metaphysical implications of this novel account of what it is to change the past.

9.2 Clarifying the target

Before we begin, we should distinguish three quite different things that might be meant by 'changing the past'. On the first interpretation, to change the past is to have a *causal effect* on the past; to cause something which did in fact happen to have happened. If JFK was killed, not by Oswald, but by a time-traveller from the future, then the time-traveller will 'change the past' in this sense—the past is the way it is in part because of the time-traveller's future decision to travel back in time. I accept, along with many others,[3] that it's possible to change the past in this sense. But this is not the kind of past-alteration I am interested in. The kind of past-alteration I am interested in involves more than simply causing the past to be the way it is; it involves making the past *different* from how it (now) is.

As Vranas (2005) points out, though, even this definition of past-alteration is ambiguous between two different readings. On the first reading, changing the past involves making the past different to how it *actually* is. I also accept—again, along with many others[4]—that it's possible to change the past in this sense. Suppose that a time-traveller from the future appeared

---

I argue in §9.5, the strategy is in fact perfectly neutral with respect to the debate between A-theorists and B-theorists. Nevertheless, this chapter can be seen as a development of ideas already nascent in Wasserman's discussion.

[3] See, e.g., Brier (1973: 363), Dwyer (1977) and Horwich (1975: 435–7). For a discussion of common objections to the claim that time-travellers could causally affect the past, see Wasserman (2017: ch.5).

[4] See especially Lewis (1976: 149–50).

in her time machine in late 19th-century Austria, with the sole intention of killing Hitler before his rise to power. There's a sense in which she *could* have killed Hitler—she had the motive and the means, her weapon was loaded, the line of sight was good, and so on. Of course we know that she *didn't*, in fact, kill Hitler, since Hitler actually died in 1945 by his own hand. But there is still a possible world, relevantly similar to the actual world, in which this time-traveller kills Hitler, thereby making the past different from how it actually is.[5] Again, though, this is not the kind of past-alteration I am interested in. What I am interested in is not whether there is a possible world in which someone makes the past different from how it actually is; what I am interested in is whether there is a possible world in which someone makes the past different from how it used to be *in that world*.

To illustrate, consider the following case:

Back to the Future

It's 1.22am on the 26th October 1985. Local eccentric Doc Brown has per-suaded his friend Marty to help him test out his latest invention—a time-machine made from a DeLorean car. The necessary 1.21 gigawatts of energy is supplied by a plutonium nuclear reactor, the fuel for which Doc has stolen from a group of Libyan terrorists. Unfortunately the Libyans have tracked Doc down and, seconds earlier, they shot him dead. Marty escaped into the DeLorean and is now accelerating away from the scene. Very soon, he will hit 88mph, the flux capacitor will activate, and Marty will travel back to the last time entered into the computer: 06.38 on the 5th November 1955. After that happens, the past will be very different to how it is now—Marty will have played Johnny B. Goode at a high school prom, met his mother as a teenager, and warned Doc about the terrorists, thereby saving his life.[6]

Notice that, in *Back to the Future*, the past is not the way it *is* because of anything that Marty will do in the future. Nor is *Back to the Future* merely a

---

[5] According to Vihvelin (1996), it's not sufficient for one to be *able* to φ, in the ordinary sense, that there is some relevantly similar possible world in which one φs; it must also be the case that *were one to try* to φ, one would (or at least might) succeed. Vihvelin argues on these grounds that although time-travellers might be able to, say, kill baby Hitler, they wouldn't be able to kill their grandfathers, or their past selves, because (roughly speaking) the worlds where they try to kill their past selves and succeed are all further away from actuality than the worlds where they try to kill their past selves and fail; c.f. Sider (2002) and Vranas (2010) on this point.

[6] Note that *Back to the Future* is set at a particular time. Here and throughout, when I say that a sentence is true in a case like *Back to the Future*, I will mean that it is true *at the time at which the case is set*, in this case, 1.22am on 26th October 1985.

situation in which Marty could have acted differently in the past from how he actually acted. Instead, what *Back to the Future* represents, or purports to represent, is a situation in which the past (including the distant past[7]) will soon be *different*, because of what Marty is about to do, from how it *is* now. The question I am interested in is whether such situations are metaphysically possible.

As I noted at the outset, the received wisdom among philosophers is that cases like *Back to the Future* are not metaphysically possible. Even the very first explicit written discussion of past-alteration, in Enrique Gaspar's *El Anacronópete*, makes clear that although "[w]e may be present to witness facts consummated in preceding centuries... we may never undo their existence" (Gaspar 1887: 59).[8] Indeed, time-travel fiction is replete with cautionary tales of time-travellers who, in trying to prevent past events from happening, end up causing those very events to occur.[9] The message to those foolish enough to think they can change the past seems clear: don't bother. At *best* you'll fail; and at worst, you'll end up causing the very events you're trying to prevent!

This assessment strikes me as premature, however. *Back to the Future* is not *obviously* contradictory; it doesn't say of any fact that it both does and doesn't obtain, for example. Before we can determine whether the situation it describes is metaphysically possible, then, we need to know more about what would have to be true about the temporal structure of the universe for such a situation to obtain. This is my goal in what follows. My strategy, outlined in the next section, will be to use the resources of tense logic to characterise, in precise terms, the metaphysical principles I take to be at stake in the debate over whether past-alteration is possible. I start with a brief introduction to tense logic, before applying the framework to cases like *Back to the Future*.

9.3 Past-alteration in tense logic

Standard tense logic (TL), originally developed over a series of papers in the 1950s and 60s by Arthur Prior,[10] extends classical propositional logic with

---

[7] Of course, there's a trivial sense in which every action makes the past different from how it was—the past used to not contain that action, and now it does. Clearly, though, *Back to the Future* involves more than just this trivial kind of past-alteration.

[8] Thanks to Michael Main and his 'Big List of Time Travel Adventures', available at www.storypilot.com/, for this historical detail.

[9] See, e.g., *One Life, Furnished in Early Poverty* from the Twilight Zone series.

[10] Prior (1957, 1967, 1969). My presentation is based on Goranko and Galton (2015).

two operators, **P** and **F**, intuitively paraphrased as 'It has at some time been the case that' and 'It will at some time be the case that', respectively. Other operators can then be defined in terms of **P** and **F**, including:

$H\varphi =_{df} \neg P \neg \varphi$ ("It has always been the case that")

$G\varphi =_{df} \neg F \neg \varphi$ ("It will always be the case that")

$S\varphi =_{df} (\varphi \lor P\varphi \lor F\varphi)$ ("It's sometimes the case that")

$A\varphi =_{df} (\varphi \land H\varphi \land G\varphi)$ ("It's always the case that")

The semantics of TL are modelled on the Kripke semantics for modal logic. Let a *temporal frame* be an ordered pair $\langle T, \prec \rangle$, where T is a non-empty set and $\prec$ is a relation over T (that is, a set of ordered pairs of elements of T). Informally, one can think of T as the set of 'times' and $\prec$ as the relation of 'temporal precedence', though these informal characterisations should not be understood as constraints on what counts as a temporal frame. A *temporal model* is an ordered triple $M = \langle T, \prec, V \rangle$, where V is a function that assigns a subset of T to every atomic formula of TL (informally, one can think of $V \in M$ as the function which assigns to every atomic formula the set of times at which, according to M, that formula is true). The truth of a formula φ in a model M at a time t is defined as follows (where '$M, t \vDash \varphi$' abbreviates 'φ is true in M at t'):

- If φ is an atomic formula of TL, $M, t \vDash \varphi$ iff $t \in V(\varphi)$.
- $M, t \vDash P\varphi$ iff $M, t` \vDash \varphi$ for some $t`$ such that $t` \prec t$.
- $M, t \vDash F\varphi$ iff $M, t` \vDash \varphi$ for some $t`$ such that $t \prec t`$.

To the above we should also add, of course, the usual semantic clauses for the propositional connectives. A formula φ is a *theorem* of TL iff $M, t \vDash \varphi$ for all M and t.

It's important to emphasise that TL is, in-and-of-itself, metaphysically neutral. Merely by using the resources of tense logic to regiment one's claims about what was and will be the case, one doesn't commit oneself to any particular metaphysics of time, just as by using the resources of modal logic to regiment one's claims about what is necessary or possible one doesn't commit oneself to any particular metaphysics of modality. Nevertheless, TL is a powerful formal framework within which competing metaphysical hypotheses can be precisely stated and their relative merits systematically assessed.

To see this, let's go back to *Back to the Future*. Two distinctive features of *Back to the Future* are worth highlighting. First, there are things which *will have* been true in *Back to the Future* which are *never* true now. For example, the following is true in *Back to the Future*:

(1)   Marty has never played and will never play Johnny B. Goode at a high school prom, but it will soon be the case that he did.

Here's the same claim formalised in TL (where '*p*' stands for the sentence 'Marty is playing Johnny B. Goode at a high school prom'):

(1*) $\neg Sp \land FPp$

(1*) is a violation of the following schema:

(LIN-P): $FP\varphi \rightarrow S\varphi$ ("Whatever will have been the case is at some time the case")

In TL, (LIN-P) corresponds to the claim that $\prec$ is *linear in the past*, i.e. that for all $t, t`, t^* \in T$, if $t \prec t^*$ and $t` \prec t^*$, then either $t \prec t`$ or $t` \prec t$ or $t = t`$ (or in other words, if two distinct times have a successor in common, one must precede the other). This means that any model of TL in which (1) comes out true would have to be 'backwards-branching' in structure. Consider the model in figure 9.1, for example:

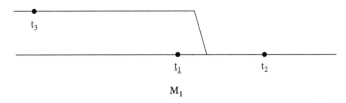

Figure 9.1

Each point in this diagram represents a time, and the order of precedence runs from left to right (so for example $t_1 \prec t_2$ and $t_3 \prec t_2$, but $t_3 \nprec t_1$, $t_1 \nprec t_3$, $t_3 \neq t_1$). t_1 represents the time at which *Back to the Future* is set (1.22am on the 26th October 1985), t_2 a time after Marty hits 88mph, and t_3 a time in the 'altered' past. Suppose that p (the sentence 'Marty is playing Johnny B. Goode at a high school prom') is true at t_3 but not true at t_1 or at any time preceding or preceded by t_1. Then it's easy to show that (1) is true at t_1: $\neg Sp$ is true at t_1, since there is no time t such that either $t \prec t_1$ or $t_1 \prec t$ or $t = t_1$ at which p is true (i.e. p is false everywhere along the right and lower-left branches); and $\mathbf{FP}p$ is true at t_1, since p is true at t_3, and there is a time—e.g. t_2—such that $t_1 \prec t_2$ and $t_3 \prec t_2$. More informally, (1) turns out true at t_1 because although there is no time in t_1's future or past at which Marty is playing Johnny B. Goode at a high school prom, there is a time in t_1's future which includes as part of *its* past a time at which Marty is playing Johnny B. Goode at a high school prom.

Unfortunately, though, we don't yet have a model on which *Back to the Future* is true. This is because there are also things which *are* true in *Back to the Future* which *will always* have been false. For example, the following is true in *Back to the Future*:

(2)   Doc Brown's body is ridden with bullets, but it will be the case that Doc's body has never been ridden with bullets.

Formalised in TL (where 'q' stands for 'Doc Brown's body is ridden with bullets'):

(2*) $q \wedge \mathbf{FH}\neg q$

(2*) is a violation of the following schema:

(GP): $\varphi \rightarrow \mathbf{GP}\varphi$ ("Whatever is the case will always have been the case")

And the problem is that (GP) is simply a *theorem* of TL—every one of its instances is true at every time in every model, regardless of the formal properties of $\prec$.[11] It follows, therefore, that (2) is a TL-contradiction, and hence that *Back to the Future* is a TL-contradiction too.

Some people might be tempted to point to this as conclusive evidence that past-alteration is impossible. But this would be too hasty. TL, remember, is merely a formal tool—it is not in-and-of-itself an arbiter of what is necessary or possible. As Wasserman notes, standard tense logic arguably "begins with

---

[11] *Proof*: Suppose for *reductio* that there is some φ, t and M such that M, $t \vDash \varphi$ but M, $t \nvDash \mathbf{GP}\varphi$. Then, by the semantic clause for $\mathbf{F}$, there is some t' such that $t \prec t'$ and M, $t' \nvDash \mathbf{P}\varphi$; and so, by the semantic clause for $\mathbf{P}$, there is no t^* such that $t^* \prec t'$ and M, $t^* \vDash \varphi$. But there is such a t^*—namely, t! Contradiction. So there is no φ, t and M such that M, $t \vDash \varphi$ but M, $t \nvDash \mathbf{GP}\varphi$. Hence M, $t \vDash \varphi \rightarrow \mathbf{GP}\varphi$, for all φ, t and M.

the assumption that the past cannot change," and so "cannot provide an *independent* reason to give up that possibility" (Wasserman 2017: 104). To quote Prior himself:

> The logician must be rather like a lawyer... in the sense that he is there to give the metaphysician, perhaps even the physicist, the tense-logic that he wants, provided that it be consistent. He must tell his client what the consequences of a given choice will be... and what alternatives are open to him; but I doubt whether he can, *qua* logician, do more. We must develop, in fact, alternative tense-logics, rather like alternative geometries; though this is not to deny that the question of what sort of time we actually live in, like the question of what sort of space we actually live in, is a real one, or that the logician's exploration of the alternatives can help one to decide it.   (Prior 1967: 59)

I propose to follow Prior's advice. If we're to have any chance of understanding what a world in which past-alteration occurs would actually be like, we need a tense logic that is weaker than TL, one on which (GP) is not automatically a theorem. In fact there's a fairly straightforward way of achieving this. The reason why (GP) turns out to be a theorem of TL is that the semantics of **P** and **F** in TL are both defined in terms of the same relation, $<$. What we need instead is *two* relations: a relation of temporal *precedence* and a relation of temporal *succession*. Let $TL^{(-)}$ be a tense logic whose models are ordered quadruples, $\langle T, <, >, V \rangle$, where T is a set, $<$ and $>$ are relations over T, and V is a function that assigns a subset of T to every atomic formula of $TL^{(-)}$. The truth of a formula φ of $TL^{(-)}$ in model M is then defined as follows:

- If φ is an atomic formula of $TL^{(-)}$, M, $t \vDash \varphi$ iff $t \in V(\varphi)$.
- M, $t \vDash \mathbf{P}\varphi$ iff M, $t` \vDash \varphi$ for some $t`$ such that $t` < t$.
- M, $t \vDash \mathbf{F}\varphi$ iff M, $t` \vDash \varphi$ for some $t`$ such that $t` > t$.

Notice that while the first two clauses are the same as those for TL, the third clause for **F** is defined in terms of $>$, not, as it is in TL, in terms of $<$.[12]

---

[12] Although $<$ and $>$ are distinct accessibility relations, our preferred logic can still impose constraints on how they are able to interact. For example, although the minimal logic of $TL^{(-)}$ allows for models where $t < t`$ and $t > t`$, as well as models with larger 'loops' (e.g. models where

In $TL^{(-)}$, (GP) corresponds to the claim that precedence is the *inverse* of succession, i.e. that for all t and t', if $t' > t$, then $t < t'$. This fits with our ordinary understanding of precedence and succession, of course—usually, a time precedes every time which succeeds it. Crucially, however, $TL^{(-)}$ allows for models in which this is not the case. Consider the model in figure 9.2, for example:

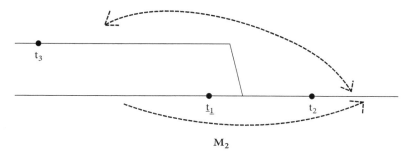

M_2

Figure 9.2

The dotted lines here indicate relations of precedence and succession—so, all the times in the right branch precede and are succeeded by all the times in the upper-left branch (and in particular, $t_3 < t_2$ and $t_2 > t_3$), but while every time in the right branch succeeds every time in the lower-left branch, no time in the lower-left branch precedes any time in the right branch (and in particular, $t_2 > t_1$, but $t_1 \nless t_2$). It's easy to show then that both (1) and (2) are true in M_2 at t_1. (1) is true in M_2 for much the same reason as it was in M_1; namely, that p is false at all times t such that $t < t_1$, $t > t_1$ or $t = t_1$, but there *is* a time $t > t_1$ and a time $t' < t$ such that p is true at t' (in particular, p is true at t_3, and $t_3 < t_2 > t_1$). (2), meanwhile, is true in M_2 at t_1 because q is true at t_1, and there is a time $t > t_1$ such that q is false at all times t' such that $t' < t$ (in particular, $t_2 > t_1$, and q is false at all times preceding t_2). More informally, (2) turns out true in M_2 at t_1 because there is a time in t_1's future which *doesn't* include t_1, or any other time at which Doc Brown's body is ridden with bullets, as part of its past.

Let me summarise where we've got to so far. Past-alteration scenarios like *Back to the Future* can be characterised by their failure to conform to two important principles—(LIN-P), the principle that *whatever will have been*

$t_1 < t_2, t_3 > t_2$, and yet $t_3 < t_1$), there might be good reasons to add additional axioms to our logic that specifically rule out such models (which would still allow for violations of (GP), i.e. models on which $t < t'$ but not $t' > t$). Thanks to Bernhard Salow here.

the case is at some time the case, and (GP), the principle that *whatever is the case will always have been the case.* Although there are models of TL which violate (LIN-P), (GP) is simply a theorem of standard tense logic. But there is a weaker logic we can construct, $TL^{(-)}$, on which (GP) is not a theorem. In this logic, cases like *Back to the Future* are not contradictory—there are models, like M_2, on which they come out true, ones which are 'backwards-branching' in structure (i.e. where two distinct times can have a successor in common without either preceding or succeeding the other), and on which precedence 'comes apart' from succession (i.e. where one time can succeed another without the second preceding the first). I conclude, therefore, that past-alteration is metaphysically possible if, but only if, it is metaphysically possible for time to be backwards-branching and for succession to come apart from precedence, in the senses just described. This is, as we'll see, an entirely novel characterisation of what is at stake in the debate over whether past-alteration is possible. Yet it falls out naturally from formalisations of past-alteration scenarios in tense logic.[13]

Perhaps it just seems obvious to you that succession couldn't come apart from precedence in this way. *Surely,* you might be thinking, one time cannot precede another without the second succeeding the first, just as one person can't be taller than another without the second being shorter than the first. But it's important to remember that 'precedence' and 'succession' in this context are mere labels for the accessibility relations governing the semantics of the tense operators. Consider the analogy with modal logic again. Clearly it wouldn't be acceptable to argue for the (S4) axiom for metaphysical possibility on the grounds that the corresponding accessibility relation between possible worlds is 'intuitively' transitive—our only grip on the modal accessibility relation is via the modal truths it is used to regiment (if pushed to explain what makes one possible world accessible from another, it's not clear that we could say any more than that v is accessible from w iff everything that is the case at v might have been the case at w). I think the same is true of precedence and succession. Since our only grip on these relations is via the tensed truths they are used to regiment, we cannot simply rely on our intuitions about how they ought to interact. The real

---

[13] Since I submitted this paper in 2019, two other articles have appeared (Effingham 2021, Meyer forthcoming) which, notwithstanding some important differences in presentation, also defend the same core idea that accommodating past- (and future-)alteration requires giving up the view that precedence and succession are converses.

substantive question here is whether violations of (GP) and (LIN-P) are metaphysically possible. And this, it seems to me, is a genuinely open metaphysical question, to be resolved in the usual ways such questions are resolved—by teasing out the consequences of different answers and examining how they interact with our background metaphysical commitments.[14] I will attempt to do some of this work in later sections. But first, it will be worth examining how the approach developed above applies to the equally interesting—though comparatively neglected[15]—phenomenon of *future*-alteration.

9.4 Future-alteration in tense logic

It's often alleged that unlike travel to the past, "[t]ravel to the future raises no conceptual problems" (van Inwagen 2010: 3). This is a mistake, however; in fact, exactly the same considerations apply to travel to the future as do to travel to the past. Presumably no-one would deny that a time-traveller could *cause* something which will in fact happen far in the future to happen; the more interesting question is whether anyone could *alter* the future, i.e. prevent something which *will* in fact happen from happening (or cause something which *won't* happen to happen). Consider the following story, for example:

Back to the Future II
It's the 21st October 2015. Doc Brown and Marty have recently arrived in the DeLorean from the 26th October 1985. Under Doc's instructions, Marty has donned an iridescent baseball cap to disguise himself as his son, Marty Jr. Soon Marty will head to Café 80s (one of those "not-well-executed nostalgic-themed restaurants") to prevent Griff (grandson of Marty's father's tormenter Biff) from meeting Marty Jr.; Marty Jr. will then go on to live a full and happy life. Before 1985, however, the future was very different to how it is now—back then, it was going to be the case that, in 2015, Marty Jr. will be coaxed by Griff into committing robbery, caught by the police, and convicted to 15 years in jail.

---

[14] My thanks to an anonymous referee for helping me to articulate this point.
[15] An exception is Hudson and Wasserman (2010); see also Wasserman (2017).

As with *Back to the Future*, two distinctive features of *Back to the Future II* are worth highlighting for our purposes. First, there are things which *were going to be* the case in *Back to the Future II* which are *never* true now. For example, the following seems true in *Back to the Future II*:

(3)   Marty Jr. was going to be convicted of robbery, though he has never and will never be convicted of robbery.

Here is (3) formalised in tense logic (where 'r' stands for the sentence 'Marty Jr. is convicted of robbery'):

(3*) $\mathbf{PF}r \wedge \neg \mathbf{S}r$

(3*) is a violation of the following schema:

(LIN-F): $\mathbf{PF}\varphi \rightarrow \mathbf{S}\varphi$ ("Whatever was going to be the case is at some time the case")

In TL, (LIN-F) corresponds to the claim that $\prec$ is *linear in the future*, i.e. that for all $t, t`, t^* \in$ T, if $t^* \prec t$ and $t^* \prec t`$, then either $t \prec t`$ or $t` \prec t$ or $t = t`$ (or in other words, if two distinct times have a predecessor in common, one must precede the other). This means that any model of TL in which (3) comes out true would have to be *forwards*-branching in structure.

As with past-alteration, however, there are also things which *are* true in *Back to the Future II* which *were never going to be* true before 1985. For example, the following is true in *Back to the Future II*:

(4)   Marty is wearing an iridescent cap, though it used to be the case that he will never wear an iridescent cap.

Formalised in tense logic (with 's' standing for 'Marty is wearing an iridescent cap'):

(4*) $s \wedge \mathbf{PG}\neg s$

(4*) is a violation of the following schema:

(HF): $\varphi \rightarrow \mathbf{HF}\varphi$ ("Whatever is the case was always going to be the case")

And (HF) is a theorem of TL—all its instances are true in every model at every time, regardless of the formal properties of $\prec$. It follows that (4), and by extension *Back to the Future II*, are TL-contradictions; there are no TL-models on which they're true. But there *is* a $TL^{(-)}$-model on which (4) is true. Consider the model in figure 9.3, for example:

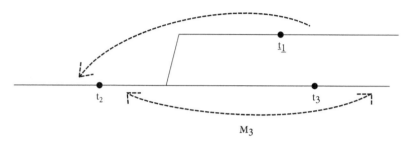

M_3

Figure 9.3

   As before, the dotted lines indicate relations of precedence and succession, so all the times in the left branch precede and are succeeded by all the times in the lower-right branch (and in particular, $t_2 \prec t_3$ and $t_3 \succ t_2$), but while every time in the left branch precedes every time in the upper-right branch, no time in the upper-right branch succeeds any time in the left branch (in particular, $t_2 \prec t_1$, but $t_1 \not\succ t_2$). Suppose r is true at t_3 but not at any time in the left or upper-right branches, and suppose s is true at t_1 but not at any time in the left or lower-right branches. It's easy then to show that both (3) and (4) are true in M_3 at t_1. (3) is true at t_1 because there is a time $t \prec t_1$ and a time $t` \succ t$ such that $r$ is true at $t`$, but r is false at all times t such that $t \prec t_1$, $t \succ t_1$ or $t = t_1$ (in other words, although there is no time in t_1's future or past at which Marty Jr. is convicted of robbery, there is a time in t_1's past which includes as part of *its* future a time at which Marty Jr. is convicted of robbery). (4), meanwhile, is true at t_1 because s is true at t_1, and there is a time $t \prec t_1$ such that s is false at all times $t`$ such that $t` \succ t$ (in other words, although Marty is wearing an iridescent cap at t_1, there is a time in t_1's past which doesn't include t_1, or any other time at which Marty is wearing an iridescent cap, as part of its future). We can conclude, therefore, that future-alteration is metaphysically possible if, but *only* if, it is metaphysically possible for time to be 'forwards-branching' in structure (i.e. for two distinct times to have a predecessor in common without either preceding or succeeding the other) and for precedence to 'come apart' from succession (i.e. for one time to precede a second without the second succeeding the first).

For the most part, I will continue to focus on past-alteration rather than future-alteration in what follows. As we've seen in this section, however, there are important parallels between travelling to the past and travelling to the future, and much of what I will have to say about past-alteration will apply, *mutatis mutandis*, to future-alteration too.

9.5 Interpreting the models

So far, I have presented tense logical models on which past-alteration scenarios, like *Back to the Future* (and future-alteration scenarios, like *Back to the Future II*), come out true. But how should we, *qua* metaphysicians, interpret these models? What would a world accurately represented by such models actually be like?

The answer to this question will depend, to some extent, on one's background metaphysics of time. Let's start by thinking about how a *B-theorist* would interpret models like M_2. According to the B-theory, all times are metaphysically on a par. In particular, there is no objectively present moment—the best we can say is that every time is present relative to itself. Reality as a whole is a vast, four-dimensional manifold, with concrete objects spread throughout that manifold. Speaking unrestrictedly, the B-theorist insists, there are dinosaurs and dodos and (presumably) female US presidents—it's just that most of our utterances have their quantifiers restricted to the set of things located at the time the utterance is made. There's a sense, then, in which the state of reality *as a whole* is fixed for all time, on the B-theory;[16] to say that things 'change over time' is really just to say that there's a qualitative difference between different parts of

---

[16] There's an interesting debate I'm sidestepping here about how the B-theorist should think about the interaction between tense operators and quantifiers. On what might be called the 'standard' view (see, e.g., Sider 2001, 2006), tense operators restrict the domains of quantifiers within their scope to the set of things located at the relevant time—for example, 'P(There are dodos)' is true at t iff there is a time preceding t at which dodos are located. But as Deasy (2021) convincingly argues, there are serious problems with this view. Instead, Deasy suggests, B-theorists should think of the tense operators as *logically redundant* when the sentences in their scope are purely qualitative—for example, 'P(There are dodos)' is logically equivalent to 'There are dodos', on the B-theory (so long as they are both evaluated in the same context). This debate needn't concern us, however, since the tensed sentences at issue for us (namely, (1)–(4)) are *not* purely qualitative. Even if it follows from the B-theory that 'There are dodos' is true at every time if it is true at some time, it doesn't follow from the B-theory that 'Marty is playing Johnny B. Goode' is true at every time if it is true at some time (though B-theorists will disagree, of course, about whether such sentences should be analysed in terms of temporal parts, temporal counterparts, in some other way, or not at all).

reality along the temporal dimension, "just as a 'change' in scenery from east to west is a qualitative difference between the eastern and western spatial parts of the landscape" (Lewis 1976: 145).

Suppose the B-theorist is correct. Then what models like M_2 represent is a four-dimensional concrete universe, albeit one with a non-standard spatio-temporal structure. In 'standard' universes, for example, every time-slice either precedes or succeeds every other. But in the universe represented by M_2, the time-slice at t_1 neither precedes nor succeeds the time-slice at t_3. This means that although it's true at t_1 that an event of Marty playing Johnny B. Goode at a high school prom *exists* (speaking unrestrictedly, in some bit of the universe), it's also true at t_1 that this event never has occurred and will never occur, since the bit of the universe in which Marty is playing Johnny B. Goode at a high school prom is temporally inaccessible from the bit of the universe located at t_1.

Some might worry that M_2 on the B-theoretic interpretation seems more like a case of *swapping one past for another* than it does a case of genuine past-*alteration*. "Marty doesn't actually *change* the lower-left branch," it might be objected; "nor, indeed, does he change the upper-left branch. He just moves from a bit of reality where the lower-left branch is in his past to a bit of reality where the upper-left branch is in his past."[17] It's important to remember, though, that change for the B-theorist *just is* variation along the temporal dimension. For the past to change between t_1 and t_2, for the B-theorist, is just for there to be a difference between the parts of the universe which are precedence-related to t_1 and those which are precedence-related to t_2; and this is exactly what the B-theorist thinks is represented by M_2. You might well continue to feel like something fishy is going on here—that notwithstanding the fact that there is a difference between which bits of the universe are precedence-related to t_1 and which bits are precedence-related to t_2, there's still an important sense in which the past doesn't *really* change on the B-theoretic interpretation of M_2. But if so, your complaint is with the B-theorist's conception of change *simpliciter*, not with their conception of past-alteration *per se*.

Consider next, therefore, how models like M_2 would be interpreted by an *A-theorist* about time. The A-theorist objects to the B-theory on the grounds that it cannot account for *genuine* change, since how things are, unrestrict-edly speaking, is fixed for all time on the B-theory. When an A-theorist

---

[17] See Smith (1997: 365–6) for a version of this objection.

considers the vast, four-dimensional concrete reality postulated by the B-theorist, they only see more of what there *is*, not what there was or will be. According to the A-theory, tensed claims are true when uttered at some times and false when uttered at others, not because those utterances express different things about different bits of an unchanging four-dimensional universe, but because how things are—unrestrictedly speaking, with our quantifiers ranging over everything—*changes over time*. What's interesting about past-alteration scenarios like *Back to the Future* is that they involve genuine change, not just in how things *are*, but also in how things *were*. We can model such scenarios by means of mathematical objects like M_2 with 'branching' structures; but as the A-theorist thinks of them, these models shouldn't be interpreted as carrying any commitment to the concrete existence of the 'branches' themselves. All such models imply is that there are times at which things will have been different from how they were—and it's not the case, according to the A-theory at least, that every way concrete reality *used to* or *will* be is a way a part of concrete reality, unrestrictedly speaking, *is*.

It's important to note, however, that the A-theory is compatible with many different views about the persistence of objects over time. Some A-theorists, of course, think that only *present* things exist. According to them, for example, although Socrates used to exist, he exists no longer. But the A-theory is also compatible with the following view:

Permanentism: $A\forall xA\exists y\ x=y$ ("Always, everything is always something")

According to Permanentism, Socrates still exists, given that he used to exist—there is still something that is Socrates. But this thing isn't a person, or a philosopher, or even concrete, though of course it *used* to be all these things. According to the A-theory, there are no dinosaurs, even speaking unrestrictedly—there is no bit of the universe in which dinosaurs (still) exist. But there *used* to be dinosaurs, of course—the universe *used* to be such that it contained dinosaurs. If Permanentism is true, therefore, it follows that there are *things which used to be* dinosaurs—'former-dinosaurs', as we might call them. Mere former-dinosaurs aren't dinosaurs, any more than mere alleged crimes are crimes. Indeed former-dinosaurs aren't even concrete, insofar as they are not (any longer) located anywhere in space. But they still exist, according to Permanentism—there is still something they are identical to.

Interestingly, however, even Permanentism leaves open some important questions about past-alteration cases like *Back to the Future*. Consider the thing which, at t_3, is the event of Marty's playing Johnny B. Goode—call this thing *Guitar Solo*. Consider also the thing which, at a time shortly before t_1, is the event of Doc Brown being shot by terrorists—call this thing *Terrorist Attack*. Does *Guitar Solo* exist at t_1, i.e. even before the past is altered? And does *Terrorist Attack* still exist at t_2, i.e. even after the past has been altered? It doesn't follow from Permanentism either that *Guitar Solo* exists at t_1 or that *Terrorist Attack* exists at t_2, since at t_1, *Guitar Solo* never has occurred and never will occur, and similarly for *Terrorist Attack* at t_2.

We can therefore distinguish two different views about past-alteration, both of which are consistent with the conjunction of Permanentism and the A-theory. According to the first view, something exists at every time if and only if it exists at some time, *regardless* of how those times are related. On this view, past-alteration, like all change, makes no difference to *what there is*, only to *what those things are like*. In particular, it involves turning a bunch of former-events (like *Terrorist Attack*) into non-former-events, and a bunch of non-former-events (like *Guitar Solo*) into former-events. According to the second view, things like *Guitar Solo* exist only at times where they either have occurred, will occur, or are occurring. On this view, past-alteration, *unlike* other sorts of change, *does* make a difference to what there is. In particular, it involves *taking out of* existence a bunch of former-events (such as *Terrorist Attack*) and *bringing into* existence a different bunch of former-events (such as *Guitar Solo*).

We've seen in this section that how one interprets models like M_2 will depend on one's background metaphysics of time and change. Nevertheless, I won't take a stand here on which metaphysics of time is correct. Indeed, the main point I want to emphasise is that *whatever* one's background metaphysical theory, models like M_2 represent genuine change in what is past, as that background metaphysical theory conceives of it. Unlike some other approaches, then, my approach to understanding past-alteration does not presuppose either the A-theory, or the B-theory, or particular versions of these views.[18] As long as one is willing to contemplate the possibility of time being branching in structure and succession coming apart from precedence, then one has the resources to make sense of past-alteration, regardless of

[18] Wasserman's account, for example, "*presupposes the A-theory of time*" (Wasserman 2017: 106); van Inwagen's account "presupposes the 'growing block' theory of time" (van Inwagen 2010: 6); Loss's account "assume[s] exdurantism as the correct theory of persistence" (Loss 2015: 6); and Goddu's (2003, 2011) account is "seeking to understand time travel within a B-theoretic framework," albeit a two-dimensionalist one (at least according to Baron (2017: 132)).

one's views about what times are, how objects persist, and what it is for things to change.

9.6 Hypertemporal accounts

I am not the first in the literature to suggest that it might, after all, be metaphysically possible to change the past. In particular, several authors (Meiland 1974; Goddu 2003, 2011; van Inwagen 2010; Hudson and Wasserman 2010; Bernstein 2017) have argued that we could make sense of past-alteration if there was an extra dimension of time relative to which we could sensibly talk of *change in what is true at a time*.

To illustrate, consider the following (lightly butchered) analogy due to Goddu (2003). Imagine I insert a DVD of *The Lion King* into a (rewritable) DVD player. There is a display on the machine indicating how much time has elapsed on the DVD being viewed—call this 'disk-time'. There is also a digital clock on the wall measuring ordinary external time. I press play on the DVD player at midnight, so that disk-time starts out synchronised with external time. At half past midnight, however, I rewind the DVD to the beginning and, five minutes later, start recording the latest episode of *Love Island: The Unseen Bits*. After ten minutes of this, at 00:45 external time, I stop recording. The data on the disk during the first ten minutes of disk-time is now different from what it was 15 minutes ago—there used to be an uplifting Elton John song at 00:05 disk-time, and now there's footage of reality TV contestants making pancakes. But there's no contradiction here—what data the disk contains at a given disk-time can be different at different external times.

According to proponents of the hypertime account, something similar is going on in cases of past-alteration. To make sense of these cases, they argue, we need to imagine that there are not one but *two* temporal dimensions— time and *hyper*time—such that what is the case at a time can be different at different hypertimes. Proponents of this approach don't usually provide alternative tense logics to accompany their view, but here is a sketch of what such a logic might look like. First, we extend TL by adding two hyper-tense operators, $\mathscr{P}$ and $\mathscr{F}$—call the resulting language $\text{TL}^{(+)}$. As before, several other operators can be defined in terms of $\mathscr{P}$ and $\mathscr{F}$; so, for example, $\mathscr{G}\varphi =_{\text{df}} \neg\mathscr{F}\neg\varphi$. A model of $\text{TL}^{(+)}$ is an ordered *sextuple*, $\text{M} = \langle \text{T, H}, \prec, \lhd, \text{V}, now \rangle$, where T and H are non-empty sets (which can informally be thought of as the set of times and the set of *hyper*times, respectively), $\prec$ and $\lhd$ are binary relations over T and H, respectively (these can informally be thought of as the relations of precedence and *hyper*-precedence), V is a function which assigns a subset of $\{<t, h>: t \in T, h \in H\}$ to every atomic formula of $TL^{(+)}$ (informally, the set of pairs $<t, h>$ at which that atomic formula is true), and *now* is a function which assigns to every element of H an element of T (informally, the time that is *present* at that hypertime). The truth of a formula φ of $TL^{(+)}$ in model M at time t and hypertime h is then defined as follows:

- If φ is an atomic formula of $TL^{(+)}$, M, $t, h \vDash \varphi$ iff $<t, h> \in V(\varphi)$.
- M, $t, h \vDash \mathbf{P}\varphi$ iff M, $t`, h \vDash \varphi$ for some $t`$ such that $t` \prec t$.
- M, $t, h \vDash \mathbf{F}\varphi$ iff M, $t`, h \vDash \varphi$ for some $t`$ such that $t \prec t`$.
- M, $t, h \vDash \mathscr{P}\varphi$ iff M, $now(h`), h` \vDash \varphi$ for some $h`$ such that $h` \lhd h$.
- M, $t, h \vDash \mathscr{F}\varphi$ iff M, $now(h`), h` \vDash \varphi$ for some $h`$ such that $h \lhd h`$.

To see how $TL^{(+)}$ might apply to *Back to the Future*, consider first the following visualisation (figure 9.4) of an 'ordinary' $TL^{(+)}$ model (i.e. one in which no time-travel occurs):

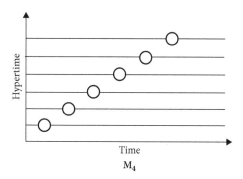

M_4

Figure 9.4

As we move up the hypertime dimension in M_4, successive times acquire the property of *being present*, as represented by the circles. But other than that, what is true at a particular time is the same at every hypertime. In models like M_4, so long as φ doesn't make reference to the property of being present, $\mathbf{P}\varphi$ iff $\mathscr{P}\varphi$, and $\mathbf{F}\varphi$ iff $\mathscr{F}\varphi$. (Roughly, this is because any time which can be reached by moving right/left along the time dimension can also be reached by moving up/down along the hypertime dimension and across to the circle.)

Things get more complicated in cases of time-travel, however. There are actually two rival hypertemporal accounts of past-alteration in the literature. According to the first view,[19] *Back to the Future* is best represented by the model in figure 9.5:

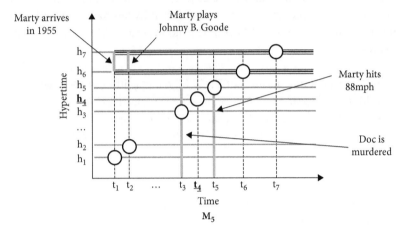

Figure 9.5

Here t_1 is 06.38 on 5th November 1955 (the time Marty travels back to), and t_2 is later that same day. t_5 is the time Marty travels back from. The current time and hypertime are t_4 and h_4, respectively. The temporal co-ordinates of important events mentioned in *Back to the Future* are labelled. At hypertimes h_1–h_5, Marty doesn't exist at t_1 and t_2, Doc is murdered at t_3, and Marty disappears after hitting 88mph at t_5. At hypertimes h_6 onwards, however, Marty pops into existence at t_1, plays Johnny B. Goode at t_2, and Doc isn't murdered at t_3 (having been warned by Marty about the Libyans).

It might not be clear, on the face of it, how this model could get us the results we want in *Back to the Future*. After all, (GP) and (LIN-P), the principles apparently violated in *Back to the Future*, are *both true at all times and hypertimes* in M_5, as indeed are their hypertemporal counterparts. But the hypertime view has a trick up its sleeve here. Once we introduce hypertime, there are two different things one might mean by English sentences of the form 'It was the case that φ'—either $\mathbf{P}\varphi$ or $\mathscr{P}\varphi$. In normal

[19] This is the view described in Hudson and Wasserman (2010).

cases we don't need to be sensitive to this distinction, since $\mathbf{P}\varphi$ iff $\mathscr{P}\varphi$ (for all φ except those that mention the property of presentness). In models like $\mathbf{M_5}$, however, this is no longer the case. If d is the sentence 'Doc is murdered by terrorists', for example, then at the temporal co-ordinate $<t_6, h_6>$, $\mathbf{P}d$ is false in $\mathbf{M_5}$ (because there is no time $t < t_6$ along the h_6 axis at which Doc is murdered) but $\mathscr{P}d$ is true (because there is a hypertime $h \lhd h_6$ such that Doc is murdered at $<now(h), h>$, namely h_3).

Now consider again the sentences that are seemingly entailed by *Back to the Future*, starting with (1):

(1)   Marty has never played and will never play Johnny B. Goode at a high school prom, but it will be the case that he did.

(1) has several interpretations in $\mathrm{TL}^{(+)}$, depending on whether the English tense operators are interpreted as expressing the ordinary Priorian tense operators or the hypertense operators. As before, let p stand for the sentence 'Marty is playing Johnny B. Goode at a high school prom'. The first conjunct has two interpretations: $\neg Sp$ and $\neg\mathscr{S}p$. As it happens, both of these are true in $\mathbf{M_5}$ at $<t_4, h_4>$ (the time and hypertime at which *Back to the Future* is set)—the former is true because p is false at all times on the h_4 axis, and the latter is true because p is false at $<now(h), h>$ for all h (i.e. at all the circles). The more interesting conjunct is the second, namely 'It will soon be the case that Marty played Johnny B. Goode at a high school prom'. This has four interpretations: (a) $\mathbf{FP}p$, (b) $\mathscr{F}\mathscr{P}p$, (c) $\mathbf{F}\mathscr{P}p$, and (d) $\mathscr{F}\mathbf{P}p$. (a) is false in $\mathbf{M_5}$ at $<t_4, h_4>$ because there is no time on the h_4 axis at which p is true. (b) is false because p is false at $<now(h), h>$ for all h (i.e. at all the circles), and (c) is false for the same reason. But (d) is true in $\mathbf{M_5}$ at $<t_4, h_4>$. This is because there is a hypertime h such that $h_4 \lhd h$, and a time $t < now(h)$, such that p is true at $<t, h>$ (for example, p is true at $<t_2, h_6>$). By postulating an additional temporal dimension, then, the proponent of the hypertime view can coherently maintain that there is a true interpretation of claims like (1) in *Back to the Future*, even though all instances of (LIN-P) and its hypertemporal analogue are true in $\mathbf{M_5}$.

The same is true of (2):

(2)   Doc Brown's body is ridden with bullets, but it will be the case that Doc's body has never been ridden with bullets.

As before, let q stand for the sentence 'Doc's body is ridden with bullets'. The first conjunct of (2) is straightforwardly true at $<t_4, h_4>$. The second again has several interpretations, namely $\mathbf{FH}\neg q$, $\mathcal{F}\mathcal{H}\neg q$, $\mathbf{F}\mathcal{H}\neg q$, and $\mathcal{F}\mathbf{H}\neg q$. The first three are false in $\mathbf{M_5}$ at $<t_4, h_4>$, but the fourth is true, since there is a hypertime h such that $h_4 \lhd h$ (for example, h_6) such that at no time along h's axis is Doc's body ridden with bullets. So the proponent of the hypertime view can again coherently maintain that there is a true interpretation of claims like (2) in *Back to the Future*, even though all instances of (GP) and its hypertemporal analogue are true in $\mathbf{M_5}$.

On the second version of the hypertime view—the 'moveable present' view[20]—*Back to the Future* is better represented by means of the model in figure 9.6:

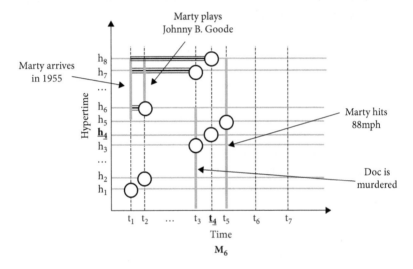

Figure 9.6

In $\mathbf{M_6}$, the present moment travels back *with* Marty from 1985 to 1955, and the changes to what is the case from t_1 onwards happen, not all at once, but gradually as hypertime evolves. For example, at h_6 Marty exists at t_1 but goes out of existence at t_2; by h_7, Marty is playing Johnny B. Goode at t_2, but Doc is still murdered at t_3; by h_8, Doc is alive at t_3. (I'm assuming here that the present moment travels instantaneously back to t_1 as soon as Marty hits 88mph, but this isn't required—TL$^{(+)}$ allows for models where the present takes a certain interval of hypertime to travel back, just like the DVD takes a certain interval of external time to rewind.)

M_6, just like M_5, allows for true interpretations of (1) and (2). But there are also some interesting differences between the two models. Recall that, in M_5, both interpretations of 'Marty has never and will never play Johnny B. Goode at a high school prom'—namely $\neg Sp$ and $\neg \widetilde{\mathcal{S}} p$—are true at $<t_4, h_4>$. In M_6, however, the former interpretation is true but the latter is false—there *is* a hypertime h such that Marty is playing Johnny B. Goode at $<now(h), h>$, namely h_6. According to M_6, then, there is a sense in which Marty will be playing Johnny B. Goode at a high school prom in *Back to the Future*, as well as a (different) sense in which he will never do so.

I mention these differences between the two models only to illustrate how their predictions come apart; I'll leave it up to proponents of the hypertime account to debate their relative benefits. I also won't get into the difficult question of whether the situations represented by models like M_5 and M_6 are metaphysically possible, and in particular, whether it's metaphysically possible for there to be more than one dimension of time. Instead I want to focus on what I think is a more fundamental issue with the hypertime accounts of past-alteration. Recall that what we wanted was a way of making sense of change (in the ordinary sense) in what is past (in the ordinary sense). But this is not, in fact, what the hypertime accounts give us. Instead what they give us is models in which there is *hyper*-change in what is past, where hyper-change stands to ordinary change as hypertime stands to ordinary time. The question of whether there could be hyper-change in what is past might, of course, be an independently interesting metaphysical question. But it is not, I think, the question we started out with. The question we started out with was *not* whether there could have been an additional dimension along which there is variation in what is true at a time; it was whether there could be *change* in what is *past*, with 'change' and 'past' interpreted as they are standardly interpreted, relative to the same dimension (namely, *time*).

Now, proponents of the hypertime account may well protest that if 'change' and 'past' are interpreted relative to the same dimension, then change in what is past would necessarily require there to be a difference in what is true at a time *at different times*, and this is straightforwardly incoherent. But in fact, as I have showed, past-alteration does *not* require change, in *any* sense, in what is true at particular times. Consider models like M_2 (see figure 9.7) again:

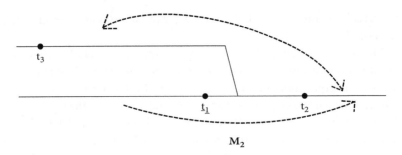

Figure 9.7

In M_2, there is no 'change' in what is true at t_1, or t_3, or any other time; what changes is rather *which of those times are in the past*. Before Marty hits 88mph in *Back to the Future*, the times 30 years in his past are ones in which he isn't alive; after Marty hits 88mph, the times 30 years in his past are ones in which he's playing Johnny B. Goode at a high school prom. There is no contradiction here, because the times precedence-related to t_1 are different to those precedence-related to t_2. And to repeat, this is not some *ad hoc* stipulation—it falls very naturally out of attempts to construct temporal models on which past-alteration scenarios come out true, models in which the principles apparently violated in past-alteration scenarios, namely (LIN-P) and (GP), are falsified, not just on *some* interpretations, but *simpliciter*.

In summary, the received wisdom is mistaken in thinking that past-alteration requires hypertime. What matters for whether past-alteration is possible is not whether there could have been an additional dimension of time, but rather whether the single dimension of time that actually exists could have had a particular kind of *structure*, the kind of structure represented by models like M_2.

9.7 Past-alteration and explanatory gaps

So far, my focus has been on explaining how there could be change in what is past. But there is another important feature of cases like *Back to the Future* that needs to be considered. Marty wasn't alive 30 years ago in *Back to the Future*; after he hits 88mph in the DeLorean, it will be the case that he was. But there is also a *causal* connection between these facts. It is no mere coincidence that the past will be different from how it is now after Marty hits

88mph; it's *because* Marty is about to hit 88mph that the past is about to change. In particular, the following seems true in *Back to the Future*:

(5)   It is because Marty is about to hit 88mph in the DeLorean that he will soon have been playing Johnny B. Goode at a high school prom.

The question is whether we can adequately capture (5) on the model of past-alteration I have been advocating.[21]

Here's one reason for doubting that (5) can be adequately captured. Causation, according to many philosophers, is a *relation* between two events or states of affairs. But at t_1, the time when *Back to the Future* is set, there is no past (or future) event of Marty's playing Johnny B. Goode at a high school prom—the past, after all, has not yet been altered. How, then, could (5) possibly be grounded in a relation holding between two things, if one of them never has occurred and will never occur?

Now, as discussed in §9.5, it doesn't necessarily follow from the fact that *Guitar Solo* (the thing which at t_3 is the event of Marty's playing Johnny B. Goode) has never occurred and will never occur at t_1 that it doesn't *exist* at t_1. Assuming it does exist at t_1, it is not a former-event at t_1, since it never has been an event; nor is it a future-event, since it never will be an event. But it is a *future-former-event*—something which *will have been* an event. It would therefore be open to a proponent of this view to ground the truth of (5) at t_1 in a relation that holds between two, existing things: a future-event (the thing which will be Marty's hitting 88mph) and a future-former-event (*Guitar Solo*). But the idea that the causal relation could hold between two things neither one of which precedes the other is, to say the least, very strange indeed. Philosophers disagree, of course, about whether causes must precede their effects. But as far as I know, no-one has taken seriously the idea that a cause could occur neither before, nor after, nor at the same time as its effect!

Perhaps a better strategy, then, might be to simply deny that facts like (5) need be grounded in a relation between two events. It's long been recognised that presentists face a problem accounting for even simple causal claims like 'The short circuit caused the fire' in terms of a relation between two things, since on their view there is no time at which the short circuit and the fire

---

[21] Wasserman (2017: 104–5) briefly raises what I think is a similar challenge, although his objection is directed much more narrowly at attempts to make sense of past-alteration that combine the A-theory with eternalism.

both exist. In response, these philosophers have mostly argued that causation shouldn't be thought of as a relation between events after all.[22] Instead, basic causal claims are simply claims of the form 'φ BECAUSE ψ', where 'BECAUSE' is a special kind of sentential connective.[23] Claims that seem to predicate a causal relation between events, like 'The short circuit caused the fire', should really be understood as paraphrases of claims of the form 'A fire broke out BECAUSE a short circuit occurred', which aren't committed to the existence of non-present events. Similarly, on this view, we can truly say that Marty will have been playing Johnny B. Goode at a high school prom *because* he is about to hit 88mph in the DeLorean, without committing ourselves to the present existence of something which will have been Marty's playing Johnny B. Goode.

Applying this strategy to *Back to the Future* reveals an interesting difference between everyday causal claims and the sorts of causal claims that arise in past-alteration scenarios. In most everyday cases, *iterated* tensed claims like FPp plausibly don't admit of direct causal explanations; rather, their truth is simply *grounded* in the truth of non-iterated tensed claims like Pp (which may themselves, of course, have causal explanations). The fact that it will be the case tomorrow that France won the 1998 FIFA World Cup, for example, is true simply in virtue of the fact that France won the 1998 FIFA World Cup in 1998. Interestingly, however, this is not the case in *Back to the Future*. That Marty will soon have been alive 30 years ago is *not* true in virtue of the fact that Marty was alive 30 years ago, since he wasn't; rather, the fact that Marty will soon have been alive 30 years ago is *directly* causally explained by the fact that he will soon hit 88mph in the DeLorean. This is precisely what is distinctive about past-alteration: genuinely altering the past involves more than just doing something that causally explains why the past is as it is; it involves doing something that causally explains why the past *will* soon be *different* from how it now is.

Unfortunately, though, things get more complicated when we consider what *will* be true in *Back to the Future*, after Marty hits 88mph. Here again (see figure 9.8) is my TL$^{(-)}$ model of the case:

---

[22] See Sider (1999); cf. Markosian (2004).
[23] It's possible to think of 'BECAUSE' as expressing a relation between *facts*, but one needn't reify things in this way, and indeed many proponents of this view explicitly deny that causation is any kind of relation at all.

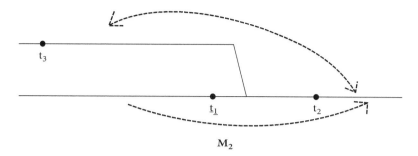

Figure 9.8

Consider what is true at t_2 in $\mathbf{M_2}$:

Back to the Future (Future)

It's 1.30am on the 26th October 1985. Thirty years ago, something strange happened: a teenage boy appeared out of nowhere in a DeLorean car, claiming to have memories of all kinds of things—the death of his friend Doc Brown at the hands of Libyan terrorists, for example—that have never happened nor will ever happen.

Here's the problem. In *Back to the Future (Future)*, it's the case that Marty appeared out of nowhere 30 years ago (i.e. at t_3) with a bunch of memories of things that, from the perspective of t_2, never happened and will never happen. But what, if anything, causally explains this fact? The description of *Back to the Future* leaves open what exactly happens after t_3 on the upper-left branch; in particular, it leaves open whether Marty hits 88mph in a DeLorean at any point.[24] But even if he did, it's not at all clear that this would explain why he turned up 30 years ago with a bunch of apparent memories of things which never happened. So even though, from the perspective of t_1, we can truly say that Marty will have appeared 30 years ago because he is about to hit 88mph in the DeLorean and travel back in time, it nevertheless seems that from the perspective of t_2, it is *inexplicable* why Marty appeared 30 years ago, because the fact which at t_1 explains why he will have appeared 30 years ago is no longer the case after he hits 88mph. In other words, past-alteration creates *explanatory gaps*: by changing the

---

[24] As it happens, in the *Back to the Future* movie Marty does indeed hit 88mph in the DeLorean at the last instant of the 'altered' past, watched by himself; but this certainly isn't required to make the story consistent.

past, we often also change that which now explains why the past will soon be different.

The problem here is in some ways even more vivid in cases of future-alteration, like *Back to the Future II*. Recall that in *Back to the Future II*, Marty Jr. was *going* to be convicted of robbery, but ever since Marty and Doc hit 88mph in the DeLorean in 1985 he has never and will never be convicted of robbery. Here again (figure 9.9) is my $TL^{(-)}$ model of this case:

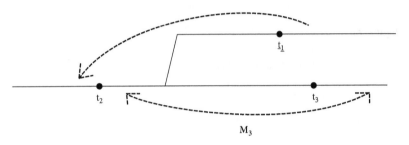

Figure 9.9

As with *Back to the Future*, there seems to be some important explanatory connection between the fact that Marty Jr. won't be convicted of robbery and the fact that Marty and Doc hit 88mph in 1985—it's *because* Marty and Doc did what they did 30 years ago that Marty Jr. now won't go to prison. But now consider the same case from the point of view of t_2, before the future was altered:

Back to the Future II (Past)

It's the 26th of October 1985. Doc and Marty are about to hit 88mph in the DeLorean. They intend to travel to 2015 to prevent Griff from meeting Marty Jr. and ruining his life. But they will fail—Marty Jr. will be coaxed by Griff into committing a robbery, caught by the police, and sentenced to 15 years in prison.

It's part of the set-up of *Back to the Future II* that at t_2, it's the case that Marty Jr. will be convicted of robbery; *a fortiori* it's part of the set-up of *Back to the Future II* that, at t_2, any attempts to prevent this will fail. Moreover, Doc presumably knows this (it's only because of his knowledge of the future that he intends to change it). From the perspective of t_2, then, it seems hard to explain why Doc is going to so much trouble to try to prevent something he already knows will happen. Even though, from the perspective of t_1 (the time *Back to the Future II* is set), we can truly say that Doc's attempt to change the future was successful—the future is indeed different now from how it was going to be—nevertheless from the perspective of t_2, Doc's future actions seem inexplicable, since he knows (or at least should know) that Marty Jr. will be convicted of robbery despite his actions. So future-alteration also seems to involve explanatory gaps: any evidence which could motivate an attempt to change the future is necessarily evidence that it will fail, and so any such attempts must seemingly be irrational, even if with the benefit of hindsight we can truly say that past such attempts were successful.

What we've revealed in this section is yet another way in which past- and future-alteration scenarios confound our usual expectations about what can change over time. Usually, if it's explicable *now* why p will be true at some future time, it will still be explicable, at that future time, why p is true at that time; *not so* in past-alteration cases, where by altering the past we can also alter what now explains why the past will soon be different. Usually, if an action at a past time is rationalisable now, then it was also rationalisable at that past time; *not so* in future-alteration cases, where the reasons which now make an action rational came into existence only after, and indeed *because*, that very action was performed. One might well wish to leverage these results into an argument that past- and future-alteration scenarios, no matter how coherent they might appear at first, are indeed impossible, on the grounds that the theoretical costs of admitting their possibility are simply not worth the benefits. But I will not come down on either side of this debate. My goal in this chapter has merely been to arrive at a richer understanding of what the world would have to be like for past- and future-alteration to occur; I will leave it to others to judge whether the world could, in fact, have been that way.

9.8 Conclusion

In this chapter, I have sought to tackle head-on the commonly expressed, but rarely defended, accusation that past-alteration is 'logically impossible'. I started by showing that past-alteration cases violate two important tense-logical principles: (LIN-P) and (GP). I then sketched a novel tense logic whose models allow for false instances of these principles, before discussing in detail what a world accurately described by such models would actually be like. Against the received philosophical wisdom, I argued that such a world would *not* be one in which there are two dimensions of time, but rather one in which time has a certain kind of *structure*: one which is 'backwards-branching', and where the relation of succession 'comes apart' from the relation of precedence. Whether time could indeed have had that structure is a metaphysical question, not a logical one. Nevertheless, I hope to have demonstrated how tense logic can play an important role in helping us to get clear on what is at stake in the debate over whether past-alteration is possible.

Acknowledgements

My thanks to Daniel Deasy, Kevin Dorst, Bernhard Salow, Jonny McIntosh, Martin Pickup, Ofra Magidor, Dean Zimmerman, and three anonymous referees for valuable comments and discussion. The central idea for this chapter emerged during an undergraduate tutorial with Tim Hunt and Ilya Shemmer in 2019—thanks especially to them.

References

Baron, S. (2017). Back to the Unchanging Past. *Pacific Philosophical Quarterly* 98(1), 129–147.

Bernstein, S. (2017). Time Travel and the Movable Present. In J. Keller (ed.), *Being, Freedom, and Method: Themes from the Philosophy of Peter van Inwagen*, 80–94 Oxford: Oxford University Press.

Brier, B. (1973). Magicians, Alarm Clocks, and Backward Causation. *Southern Journal of Philosophy* 11(4), 359–364.

Brown, G. (1985). Praying about the Past. *Philosophical Quarterly 35*, 83–86.

Deasy, D. (2021). *Advanced Temporalising.* Oxford Studies in Metaphysics, Volume 12. Oxford: Oxford University Press.

Dwyer, L. (1977). How to Affect, but not Change, the Past. *Southern Journal of Philosophy 15*(3), 383–385.

Effingham, N. (2021). Vacillating Time: A Metaphysics for Time Travel and Geachianism. *Synthese 199*(3–4), 7159–7180.

Flew, A. (1954). Can an Effect Precede its Cause? *Proceedings of the Aristotelian Society 28*, 45–62.

Fulmer, G. (1983). Cosmological Implications of Time Travel. In R. E. Myers (ed.), *The Intersection of Science Fiction and Philosophy*, Westport, CT: Greenwood.

Gaspar, E. (1887 [2012]). *The Time Ship: A Chrononautical Journey* (trans. Yolanda Molina-Gavilán and Andrea Bell). Middletown, CT: Wesleyan University Press.

Goddu, G. C. (2003). Time Travel and Changing the Past: (Or How to Kill Yourself and Live to Tell the Tale). *Ratio 16*(1), 16–32.

Goddu, G. C. (2011). Avoiding or Changing the Past? *Pacific Philosophical Quarterly 92(1)*, 11–17.

Goranko, V. and Galton, A. (2015). Temporal Logic. In E. N. Zalta (ed.), *The Stanford Encyclopedia of Philosophy (Winter 2015 Edition)*, available at <https://plato.stanford.edu/archives/win2015/entries/logic-temporal/.

Horwich, P. (1975). On Some Alleged Paradoxes of Time Travel. *The Journal of Philosophy 72*(14), 432–444.

Hospers, J. (1967). *An Introduction to Philosophical Analysis*. London: Routledge & Kegan Paul.

Hudson, H. and Wasserman, R. (2010). Van Inwagen on Time Travel and Changing the Past. In D. Zimmerman (ed.), *Oxford Studies in Metaphysics, Volume 5*, 41–52 Oxford: Oxford University Press.

Lewis, D. (1976). The Paradoxes of Time Travel. *American Philosophical Quarterly 13*(2), 145–152.

Loss, R. (2015). How to Change the Past in One-Dimensional Time. *Pacific Philosophical Quarterly 96*(1), 1–11.

Markosian, N. (2004). A Defense of Presentism. In D. Zimmerman and K. Bennet (eds.), *Oxford Studies in Metaphysics, Volume 1*, 47–82 Oxford: Oxford University Press.

Meiland, J. W. (1974). A Two-Dimensional Passage Model of Time for Time Travel. *Philosophical Studies 26*(3–4), 153–173.

Meyer, U. (forthcoming). The Future of the Present. *Erkenntnis.*

Prior, A. N. (1957). *Time and Modality*. Oxford: Clarendon Press.

Prior, A. N. (1967). *Past, Present and Future*. Oxford: Clarendon Press.

Prior, A. N. (1969). *Papers on Time and Tense*. Oxford: Clarendon Press.

Sider, T. (1999). Presentism and Ontological Commitment. *The Journal of Philosophy 96*(7), 325–347.

Sider, T. (2001). *Four-Dimensionalism: An Ontology of Persistence and Time.* Oxford: Oxford University Press.

Sider, T. (2002). Time Travel, Coincidences and Counterfactuals. *Philosophical Studies 110*(2), 115–138.

Sider, T. (2006). Quantifiers and Temporal Ontology. *Mind 115*(457), 75–97.

Smith, N. J. J. (1997). Bananas Enough for Time Travel? *British Journal for the Philosophy of Science 48*, 363–389.

van Inwagen, P. (2010). Changing the Past. In D. Zimmerman (ed.), *Oxford Studies in Metaphysics, Volume 5*, 3–28 Oxford: Oxford University Press.

Vihvelin, K. (1996). What Time Travelers Cannot Do. *Philosophical Studies 81*(2–3), 315–330.

Vranas, P. B. (2005). Do Cry Over Spilt Milk: Possibly You can Change the Past. *The Monist 88*(3), 370–387.

Vranas, P. B. (2010). What Time Travelers May be Able to Do. *Philosophical Studies 150*(1), 115–121.

Wasserman, R. (2017). *Paradoxes of Time Travel*. Oxford: Oxford University Press.

Index